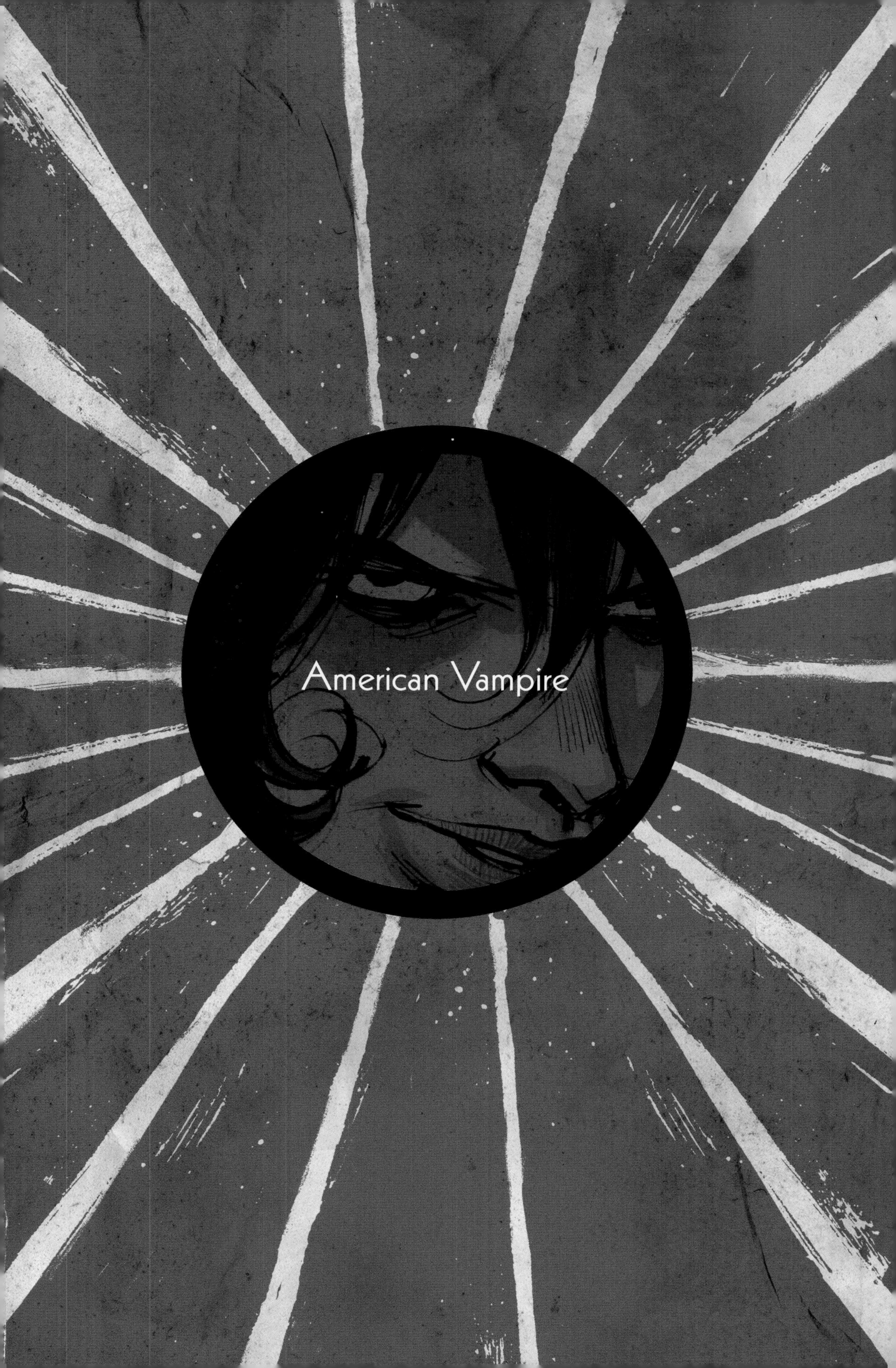
American Vampire

AMERICAN

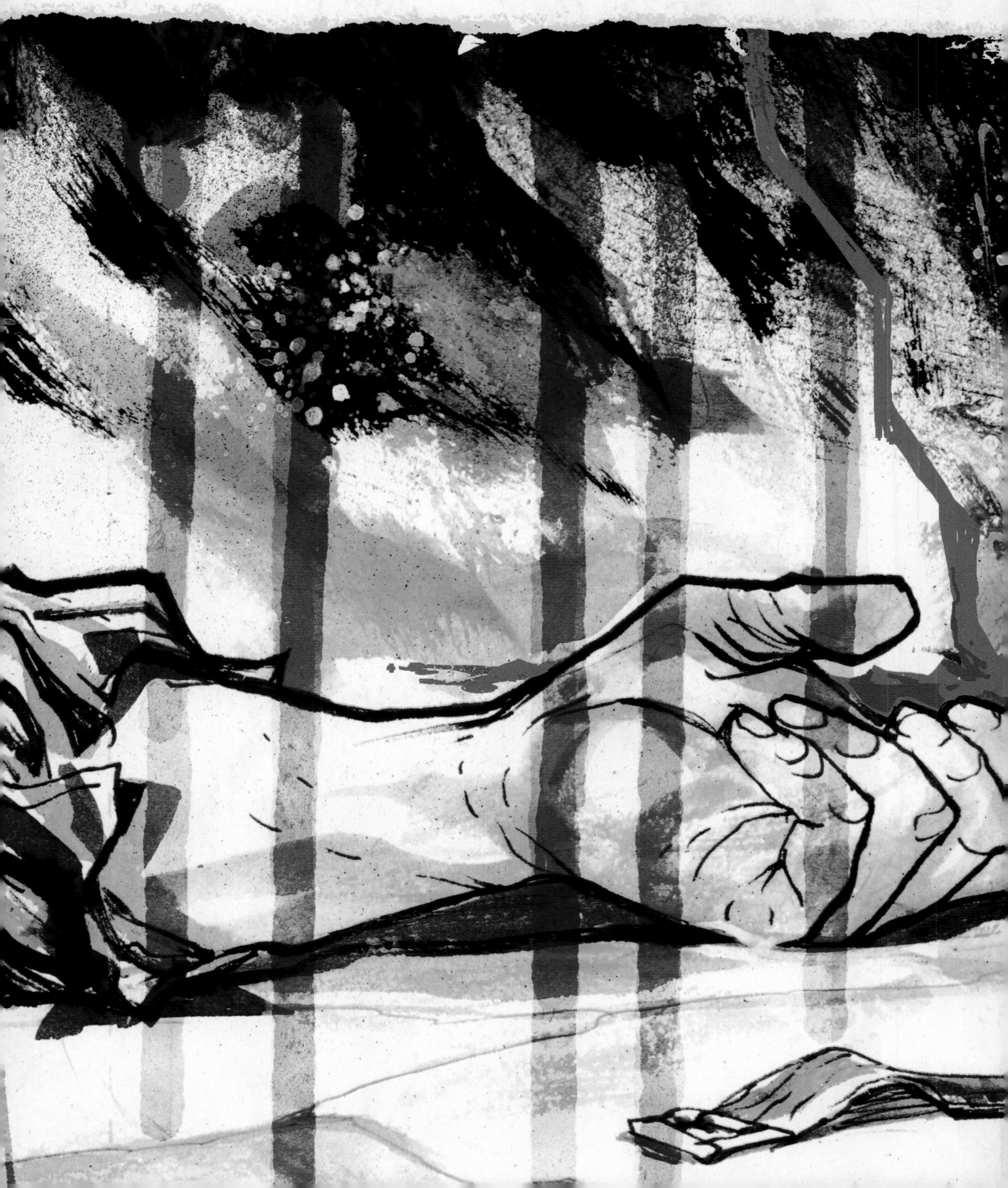

VAMPIRE

VOLUME THREE

Scott Snyder Writer

Rafael Albuquerque Sean Murphy Danijel Zezelj Artists

Dave McCaig Dave Stewart Colorists

Steve Wands Pat Brosseau Letterers

Rafael Albuquerque Cover Artist

American Vampire created by Scott Snyder and Rafael Albuquerque

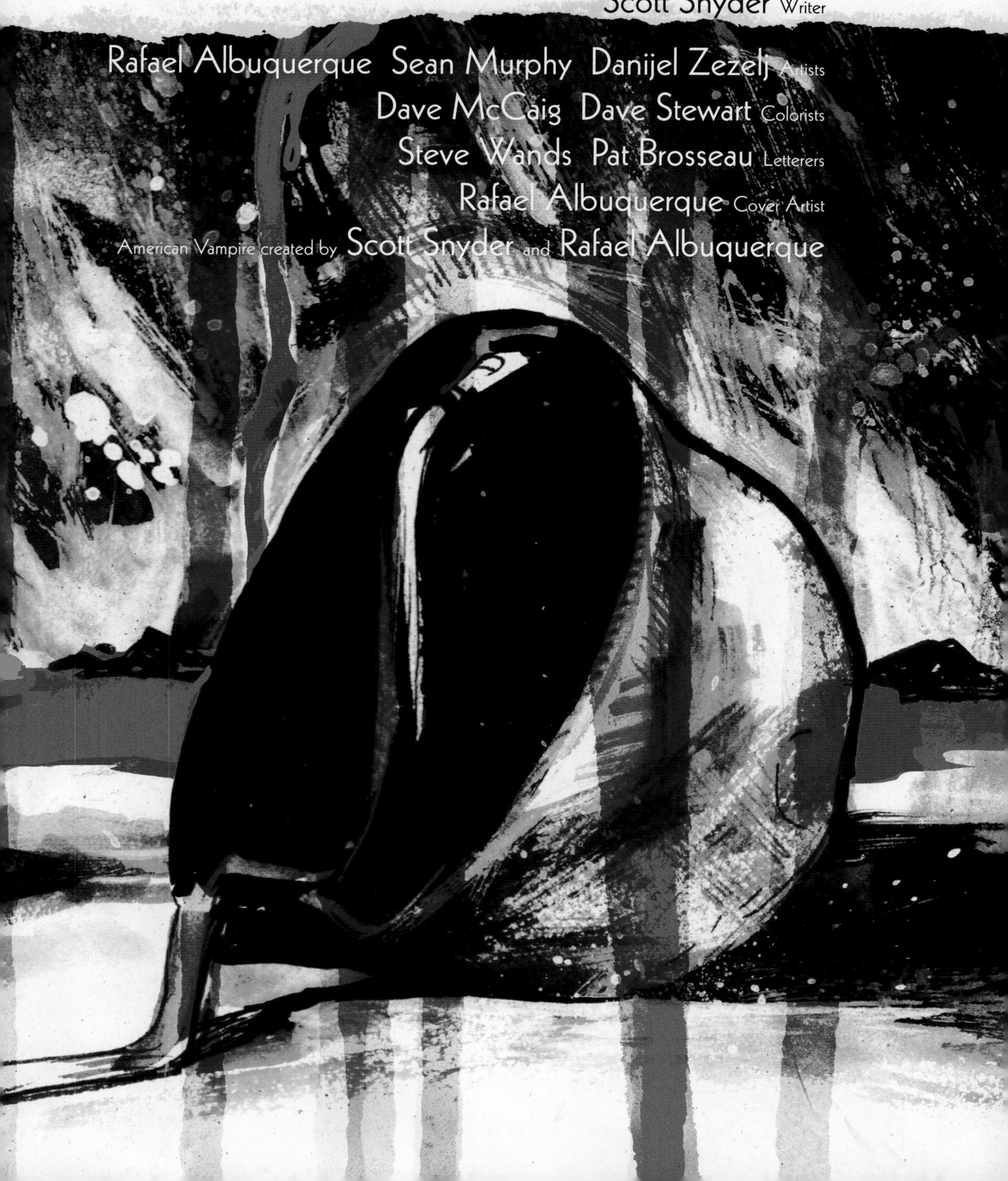

Mark Doyle Editor – Original Series
Joe Hughes Assistant Editor – Original Series
Ian Sattler Director-Editorial, Special Projects and Archival Editions
Peter Hamboussi Editor
Robbin Brosterman Design Director – Books
Louis Prandi Publication Design

Karen Berger Senior VP — Executive Editor, VERTIGO
Bob Harras VP – Editor-In-Chief

Diane Nelson President
Dan DiDio and Jim Lee Co-Publishers
Geoff Johns Chief Creative Officer
John Rood Executive VP – Sales, Marketing and Business Development
Amy Genkins Senior VP – Business and Legal Affairs
Nairi Gardiner Senior VP – Finance
Jeff Boison VP – Publishing Operations
Mark Chiarello VP – Art Direction and Design
John Cunningham VP – Marketing
Terri Cunningham VP – Talent Relations and Services
Alison Gill Senior VP – Manufacturing and Operations
David Hyde VP – Publicity
Hank Kanalz Senior VP – Digital
Jay Kogan VP – Business and Legal Affairs, Publishing
Jack Mahan VP – Business Affairs, Talent
Nick Napolitano VP – Manufacturing Administration
Sue Pohja VP – Book Sales
Courtney Simmons Senior VP – Publicity
Bob Wayne Senior VP – Sales

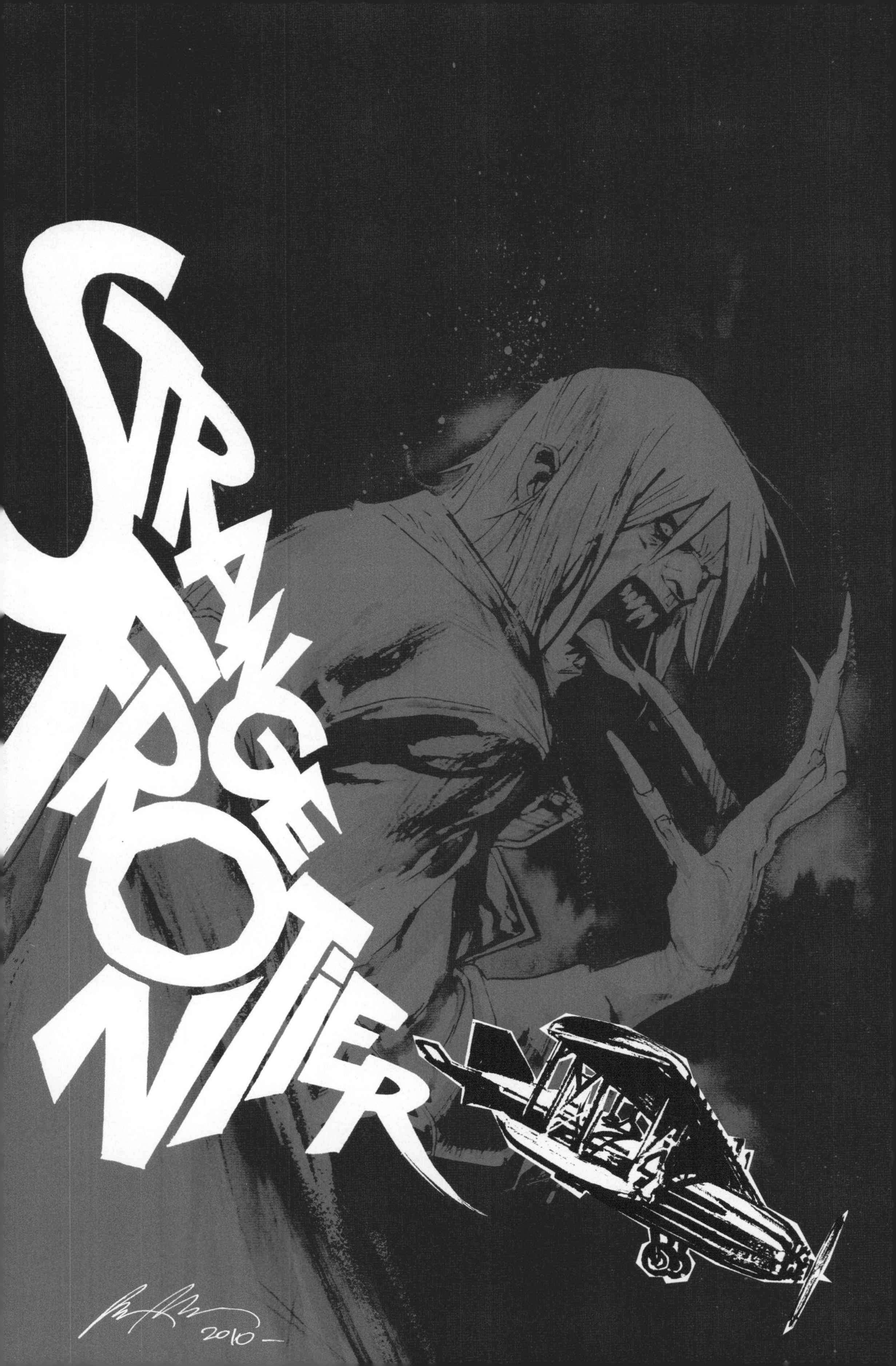
STRANGE FRONTIER
2010

Strange Frontier

Danijel Zezelj
Artist

Rafael Albuquerque
Cover

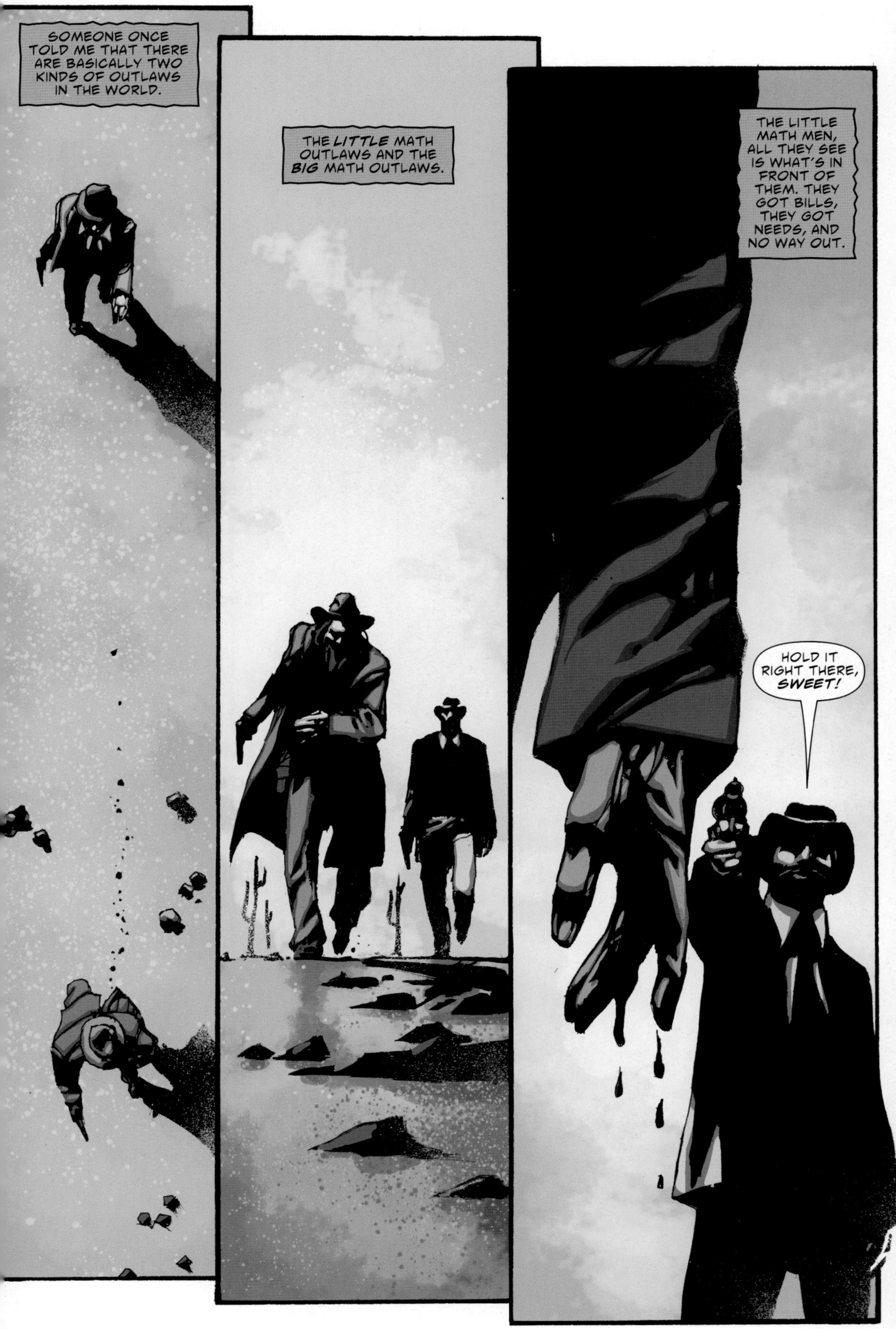
SOMEONE ONCE TOLD ME THAT THERE ARE BASICALLY TWO KINDS OF OUTLAWS IN THE WORLD.
THE *LITTLE* MATH OUTLAWS AND THE *BIG* MATH OUTLAWS.
THE LITTLE MATH MEN, ALL THEY SEE IS WHAT'S IN FRONT OF THEM. THEY GOT BILLS, THEY GOT NEEDS, AND NO WAY OUT.
HOLD IT RIGHT THERE, **SWEET!**

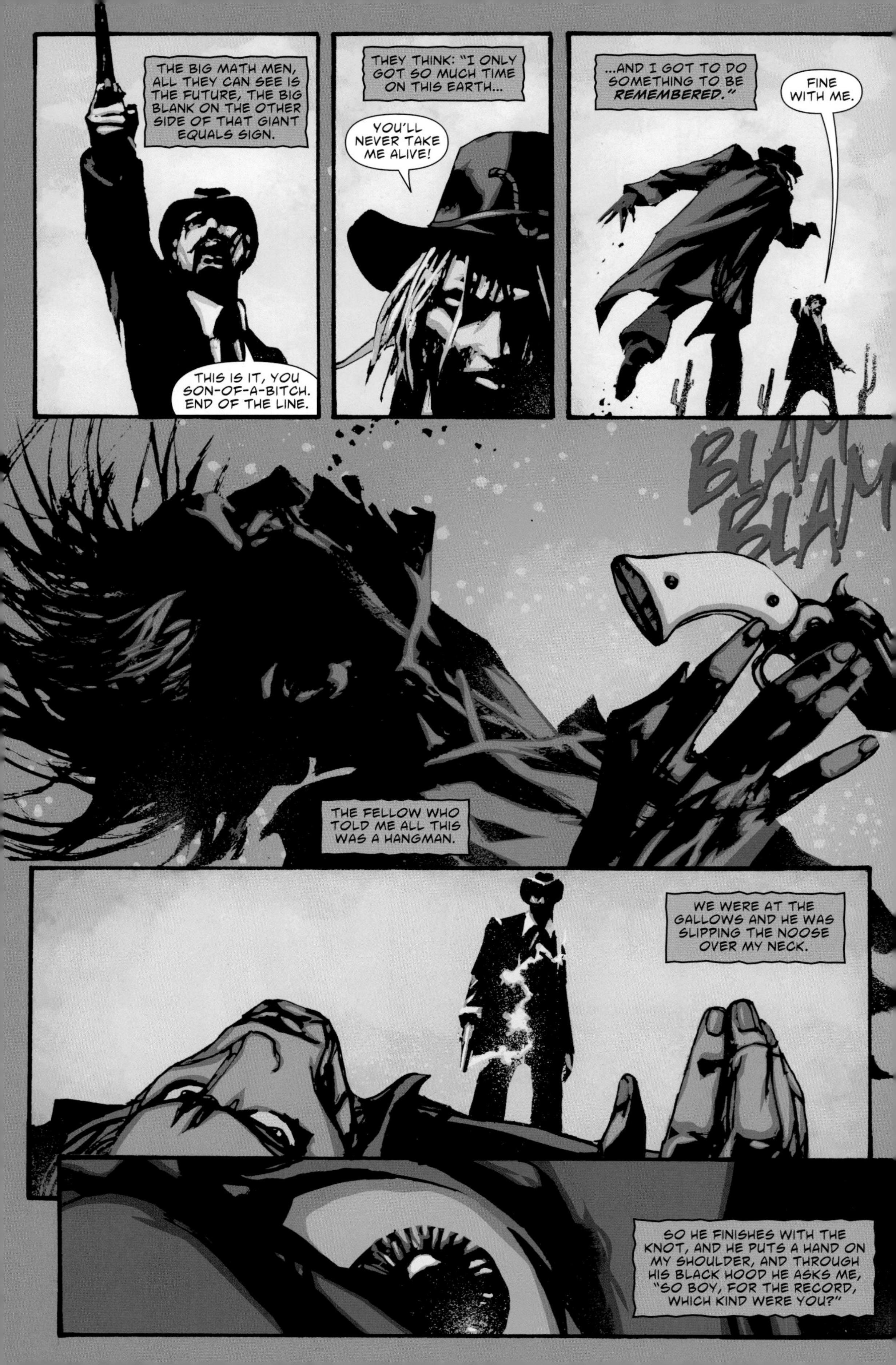
THE BIG MATH MEN, ALL THEY CAN SEE IS THE FUTURE, THE BIG BLANK ON THE OTHER SIDE OF THAT GIANT EQUALS SIGN.
THIS IS IT, YOU SON-OF-A-BITCH. END OF THE LINE.
THEY THINK: "I ONLY GOT SO MUCH TIME ON THIS EARTH...
YOU'LL NEVER TAKE ME ALIVE!
...AND I GOT TO DO SOMETHING TO BE *REMEMBERED.*"
FINE WITH ME.
BLAM BLAM
THE FELLOW WHO TOLD ME ALL THIS WAS A HANGMAN.
WE WERE AT THE GALLOWS AND HE WAS SLIPPING THE NOOSE OVER MY NECK.
SO HE FINISHES WITH THE KNOT, AND HE PUTS A HAND ON MY SHOULDER, AND THROUGH HIS BLACK HOOD HE ASKS ME, "SO BOY, FOR THE RECORD, WHICH KIND WERE YOU?"

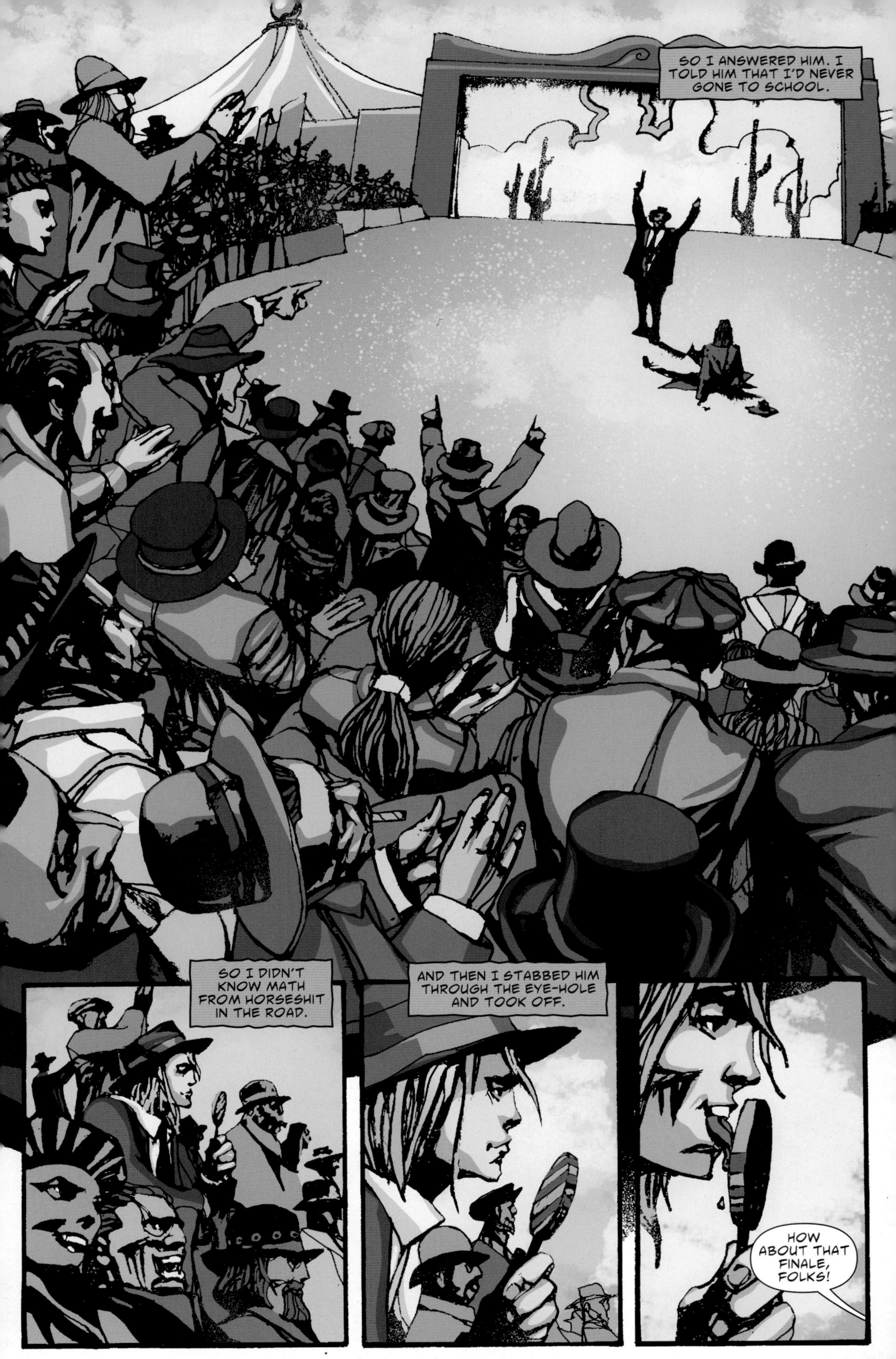
SO I ANSWERED HIM. I TOLD HIM THAT I'D NEVER GONE TO SCHOOL.
SO I DIDN'T KNOW MATH FROM HORSESHIT IN THE ROAD.
AND THEN I STABBED HIM THROUGH THE EYE-HOLE AND TOOK OFF.
HOW ABOUT THAT FINALE, FOLKS!

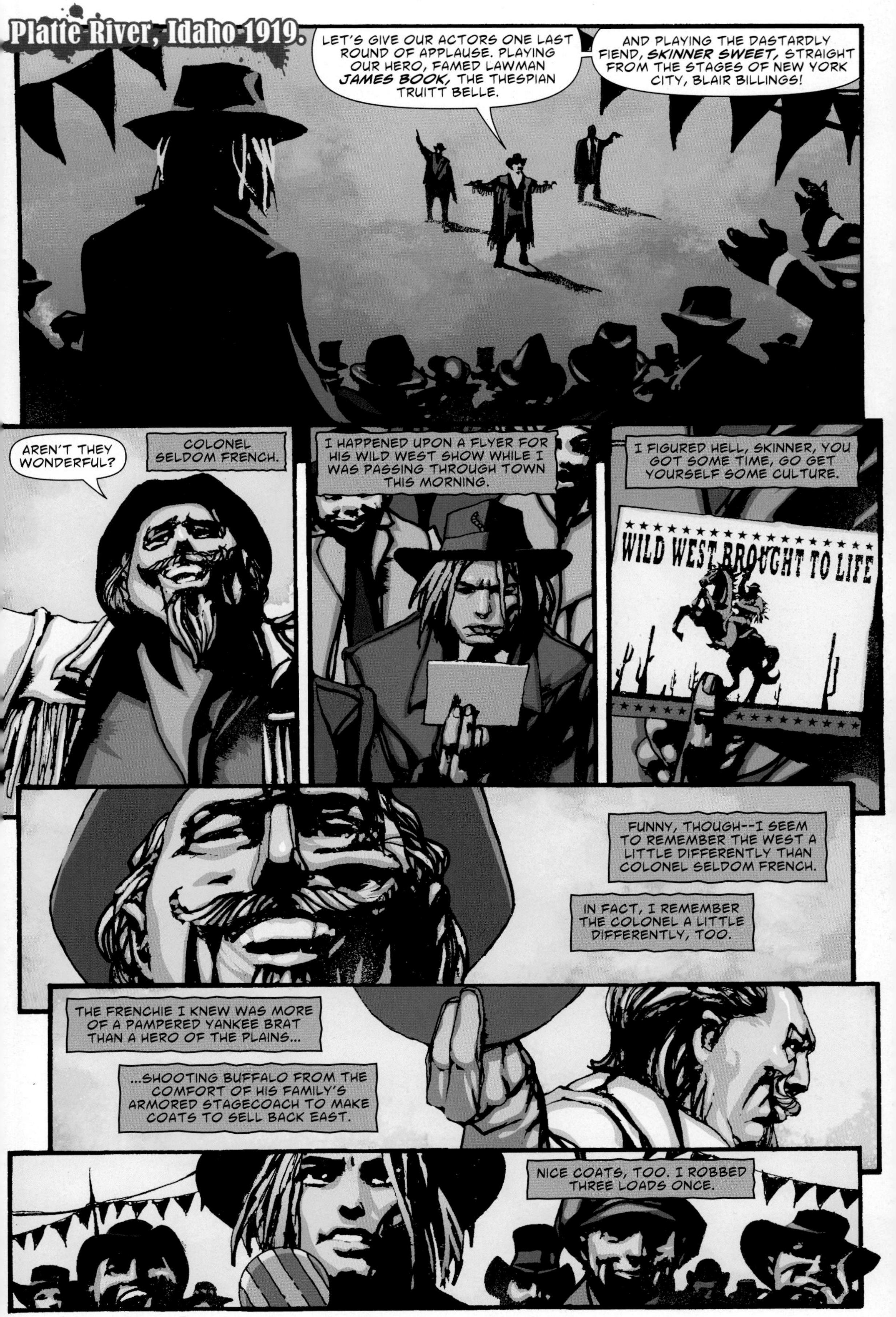
Platte River, Idaho 1919.
LET'S GIVE OUR ACTORS ONE LAST ROUND OF APPLAUSE. PLAYING OUR HERO, FAMED LAWMAN JAMES BOOK, THE THESPIAN TRUITT BELLE.
AND PLAYING THE DASTARDLY FIEND, SKINNER SWEET, STRAIGHT FROM THE STAGES OF NEW YORK CITY, BLAIR BILLINGS!
AREN'T THEY WONDERFUL?
COLONEL SELDOM FRENCH.
I HAPPENED UPON A FLYER FOR HIS WILD WEST SHOW WHILE I WAS PASSING THROUGH TOWN THIS MORNING.
I FIGURED HELL, SKINNER, YOU GOT SOME TIME, GO GET YOURSELF SOME CULTURE.
WILD WEST BROUGHT TO LIFE
FUNNY, THOUGH--I SEEM TO REMEMBER THE WEST A LITTLE DIFFERENTLY THAN COLONEL SELDOM FRENCH.
IN FACT, I REMEMBER THE COLONEL A LITTLE DIFFERENTLY, TOO.
THE FRENCHIE I KNEW WAS MORE OF A PAMPERED YANKEE BRAT THAN A HERO OF THE PLAINS...
...SHOOTING BUFFALO FROM THE COMFORT OF HIS FAMILY'S ARMORED STAGECOACH TO MAKE COATS TO SELL BACK EAST.
NICE COATS, TOO. I ROBBED THREE LOADS ONCE.

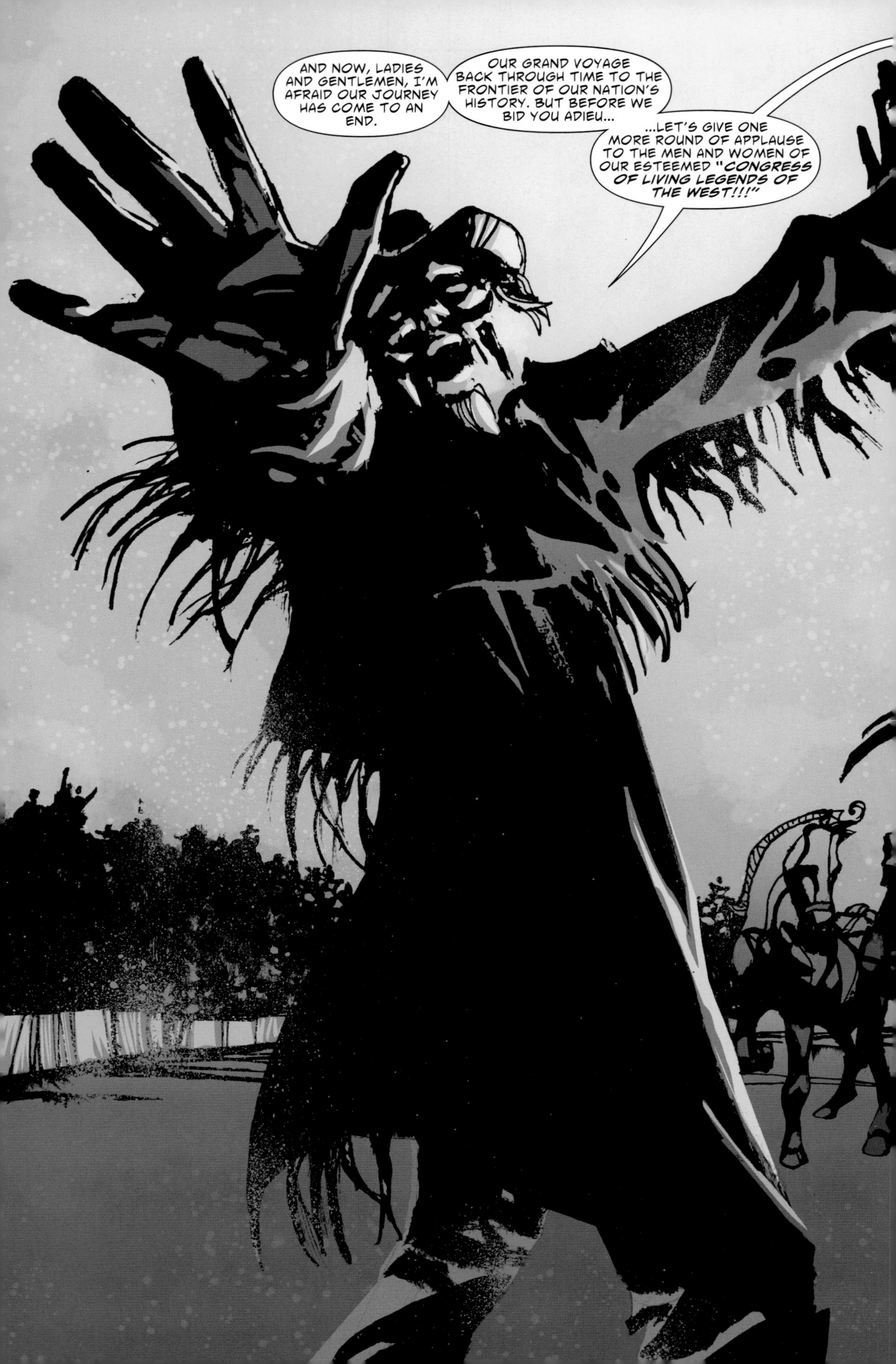
AND NOW, LADIES AND GENTLEMEN, I'M AFRAID OUR JOURNEY HAS COME TO AN END.
OUR GRAND VOYAGE BACK THROUGH TIME TO THE FRONTIER OF OUR NATION'S HISTORY. BUT BEFORE WE BID YOU ADIEU...
...LET'S GIVE ONE MORE ROUND OF APPLAUSE TO THE MEN AND WOMEN OF OUR ESTEEMED "CONGRESS OF LIVING LEGENDS OF THE WEST!!!"

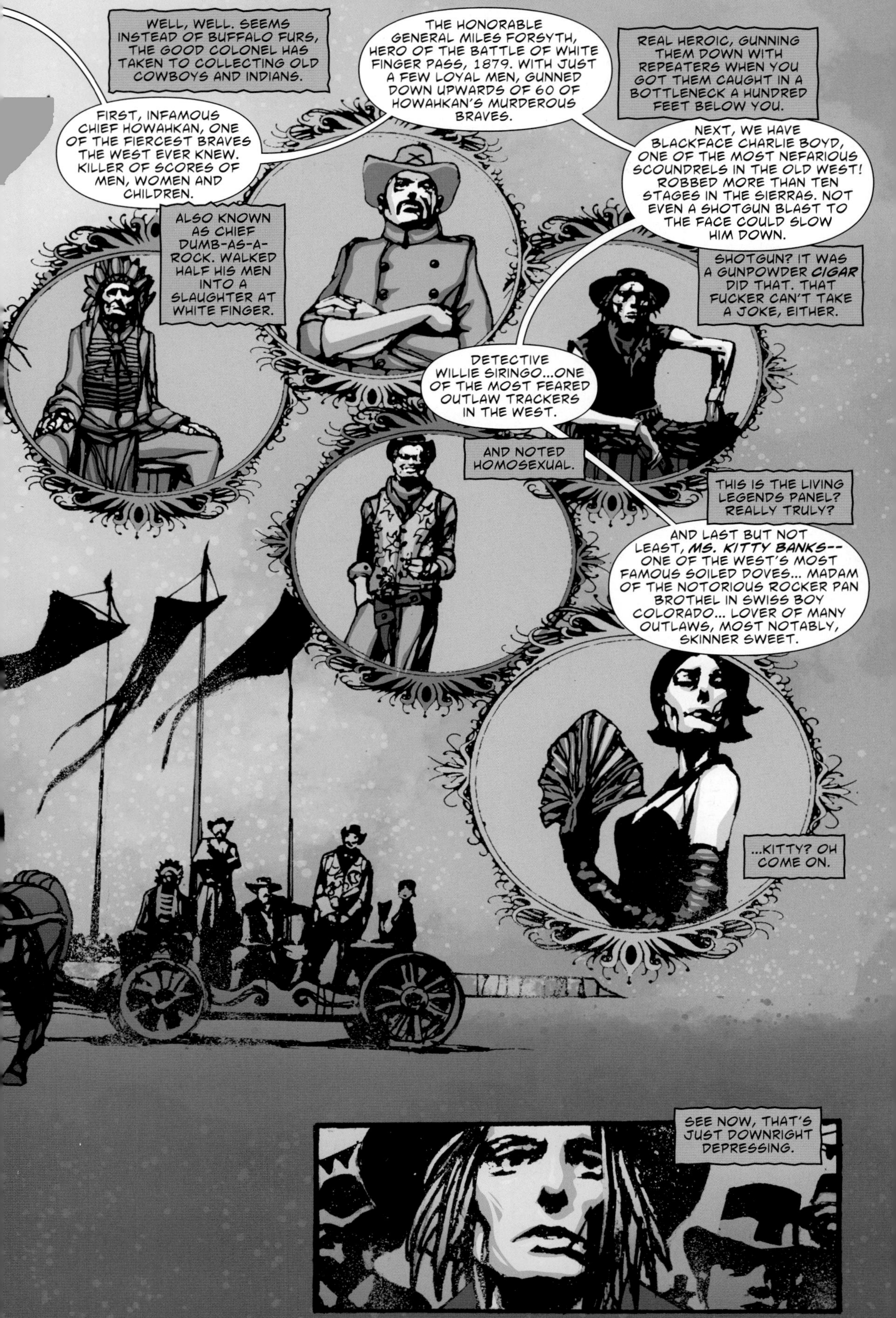
WELL, WELL. SEEMS INSTEAD OF BUFFALO FURS, THE GOOD COLONEL HAS TAKEN TO COLLECTING OLD COWBOYS AND INDIANS.
FIRST, INFAMOUS CHIEF HOWAHKAN, ONE OF THE FIERCEST BRAVES THE WEST EVER KNEW. KILLER OF SCORES OF MEN, WOMEN AND CHILDREN.
ALSO KNOWN AS CHIEF DUMB-AS-A-ROCK. WALKED HALF HIS MEN INTO A SLAUGHTER AT WHITE FINGER.
THE HONORABLE GENERAL MILES FORSYTH, HERO OF THE BATTLE OF WHITE FINGER PASS, 1879. WITH JUST A FEW LOYAL MEN, GUNNED DOWN UPWARDS OF 60 OF HOWAHKAN'S MURDEROUS BRAVES.
REAL HEROIC, GUNNING THEM DOWN WITH REPEATERS WHEN YOU GOT THEM CAUGHT IN A BOTTLENECK A HUNDRED FEET BELOW YOU.
NEXT, WE HAVE BLACKFACE CHARLIE BOYD, ONE OF THE MOST NEFARIOUS SCOUNDRELS IN THE OLD WEST! ROBBED MORE THAN TEN STAGES IN THE SIERRAS. NOT EVEN A SHOTGUN BLAST TO THE FACE COULD SLOW HIM DOWN.
SHOTGUN? IT WAS A GUNPOWDER *CIGAR* DID THAT. THAT FUCKER CAN'T TAKE A JOKE, EITHER.
DETECTIVE WILLIE SIRINGO...ONE OF THE MOST FEARED OUTLAW TRACKERS IN THE WEST.
AND NOTED HOMOSEXUAL.
THIS IS THE LIVING LEGENDS PANEL? REALLY TRULY?
AND LAST BUT NOT LEAST, ***MS. KITTY BANKS***-- ONE OF THE WEST'S MOST FAMOUS SOILED DOVES... MADAM OF THE NOTORIOUS ROCKER PAN BROTHEL IN SWISS BOY COLORADO... LOVER OF MANY OUTLAWS, MOST NOTABLY, SKINNER SWEET.
...KITTY? OH COME ON.
SEE NOW, THAT'S JUST DOWNRIGHT DEPRESSING.

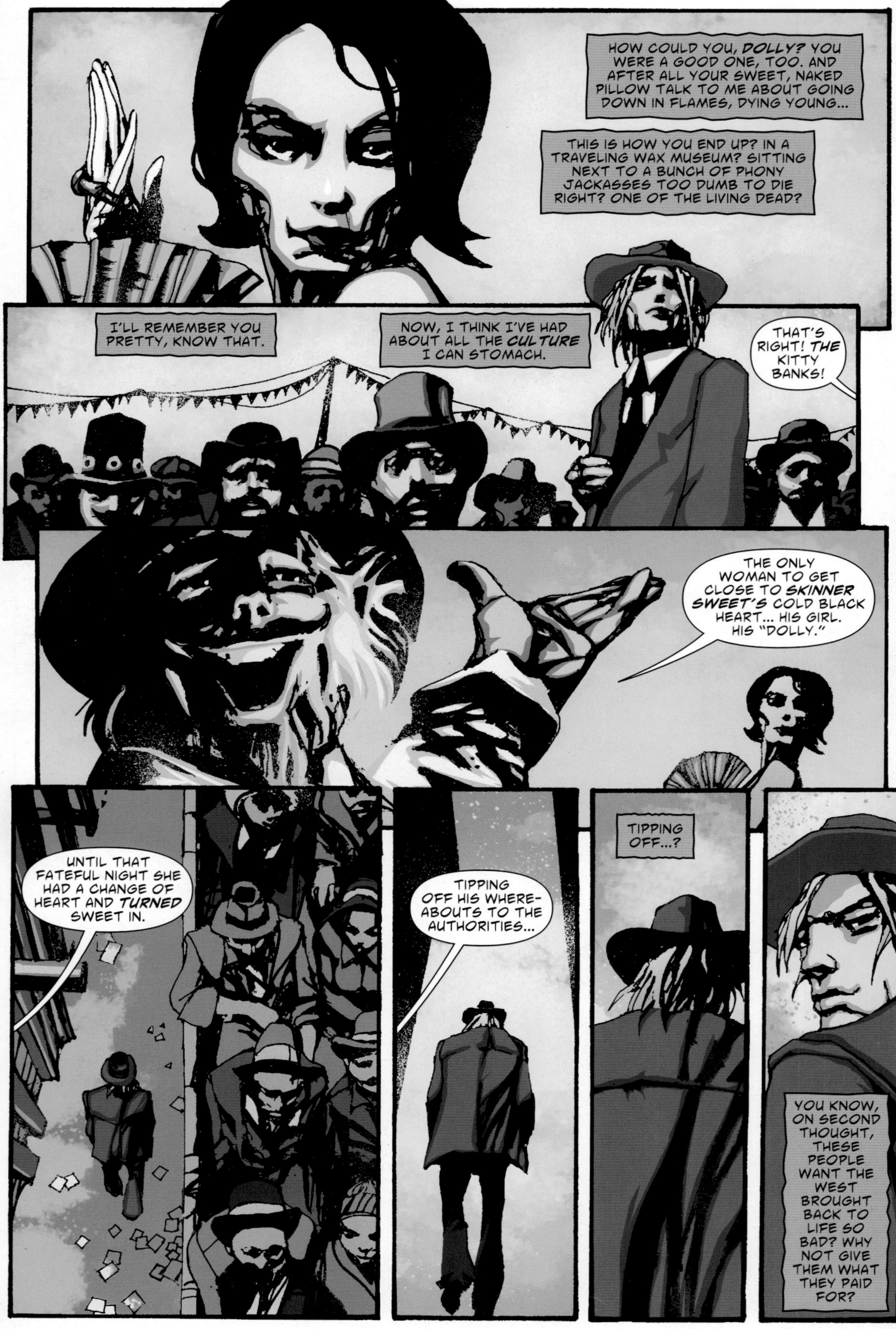
HOW COULD YOU, DOLLY? YOU WERE A GOOD ONE, TOO. AND AFTER ALL YOUR SWEET, NAKED PILLOW TALK TO ME ABOUT GOING DOWN IN FLAMES, DYING YOUNG...
THIS IS HOW YOU END UP? IN A TRAVELING WAX MUSEUM? SITTING NEXT TO A BUNCH OF PHONY JACKASSES TOO DUMB TO DIE RIGHT? ONE OF THE LIVING DEAD?
I'LL REMEMBER YOU PRETTY, KNOW THAT.
NOW, I THINK I'VE HAD ABOUT ALL THE CULTURE I CAN STOMACH.
THAT'S RIGHT! THE KITTY BANKS!
THE ONLY WOMAN TO GET CLOSE TO SKINNER SWEET'S COLD BLACK HEART... HIS GIRL. HIS "DOLLY."
UNTIL THAT FATEFUL NIGHT SHE HAD A CHANGE OF HEART AND TURNED SWEET IN.
TIPPING OFF HIS WHERE-ABOUTS TO THE AUTHORITIES...
TIPPING OFF...?
YOU KNOW, ON SECOND THOUGHT, THESE PEOPLE WANT THE WEST BROUGHT BACK TO LIFE SO BAD? WHY NOT GIVE THEM WHAT THEY PAID FOR?

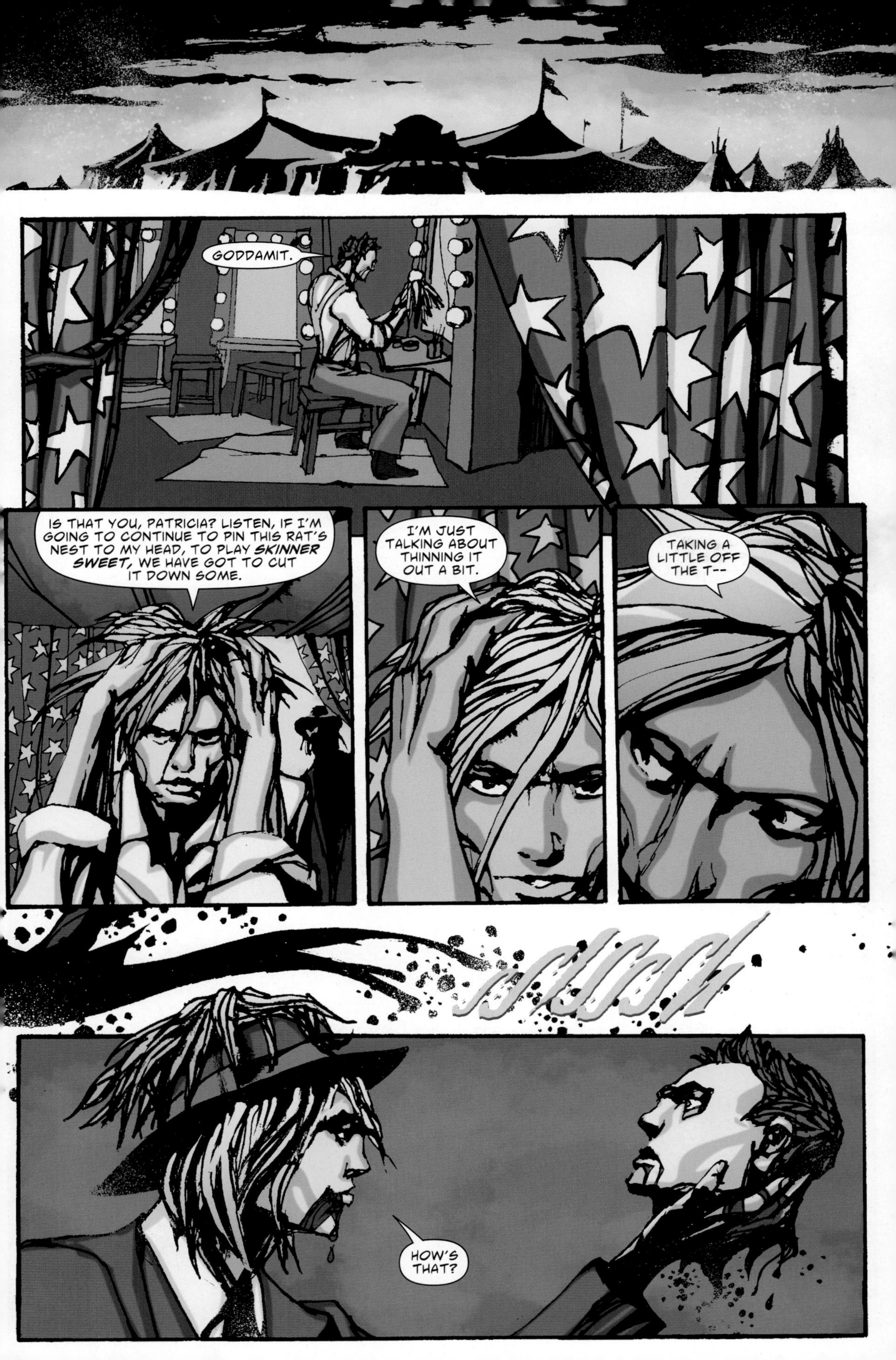
GODDAMIT.
IS THAT YOU, PATRICIA? LISTEN, IF I'M GOING TO CONTINUE TO PIN THIS RAT'S NEST TO MY HEAD, TO PLAY *SKINNER SWEET*, WE HAVE GOT TO CUT IT DOWN SOME.
I'M JUST TALKING ABOUT THINNING IT OUT A BIT.
TAKING A LITTLE OFF THE T--
SSSCCCH
HOW'S THAT?

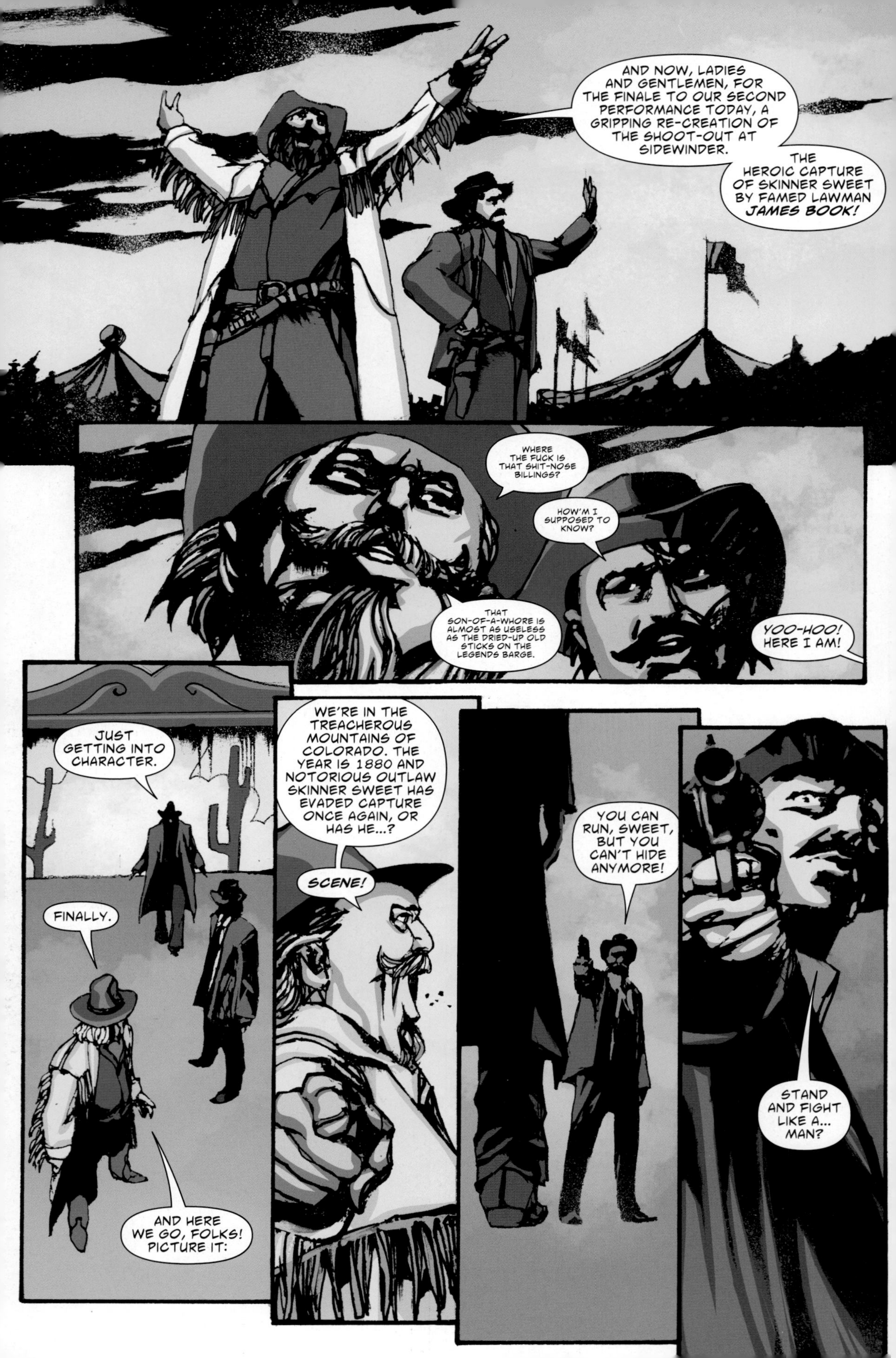
AND NOW, LADIES AND GENTLEMEN, FOR THE FINALE TO OUR SECOND PERFORMANCE TODAY, A GRIPPING RE-CREATION OF THE SHOOT-OUT AT SIDEWINDER.
THE HEROIC CAPTURE OF SKINNER SWEET BY FAMED LAWMAN JAMES BOOK!
WHERE THE FUCK IS THAT SHIT-NOSE BILLINGS?
HOW'M I SUPPOSED TO KNOW?
THAT SON-OF-A-WHORE IS ALMOST AS USELESS AS THE DRIED-UP OLD STICKS ON THE LEGENDS BARGE.
YOO-HOO! HERE I AM!
JUST GETTING INTO CHARACTER.
FINALLY.
AND HERE WE GO, FOLKS! PICTURE IT:
WE'RE IN THE TREACHEROUS MOUNTAINS OF COLORADO. THE YEAR IS 1880 AND NOTORIOUS OUTLAW SKINNER SWEET HAS EVADED CAPTURE ONCE AGAIN, OR HAS HE...?
SCENE!
YOU CAN RUN, SWEET, BUT YOU CAN'T HIDE ANYMORE!
STAND AND FIGHT LIKE A... MAN?

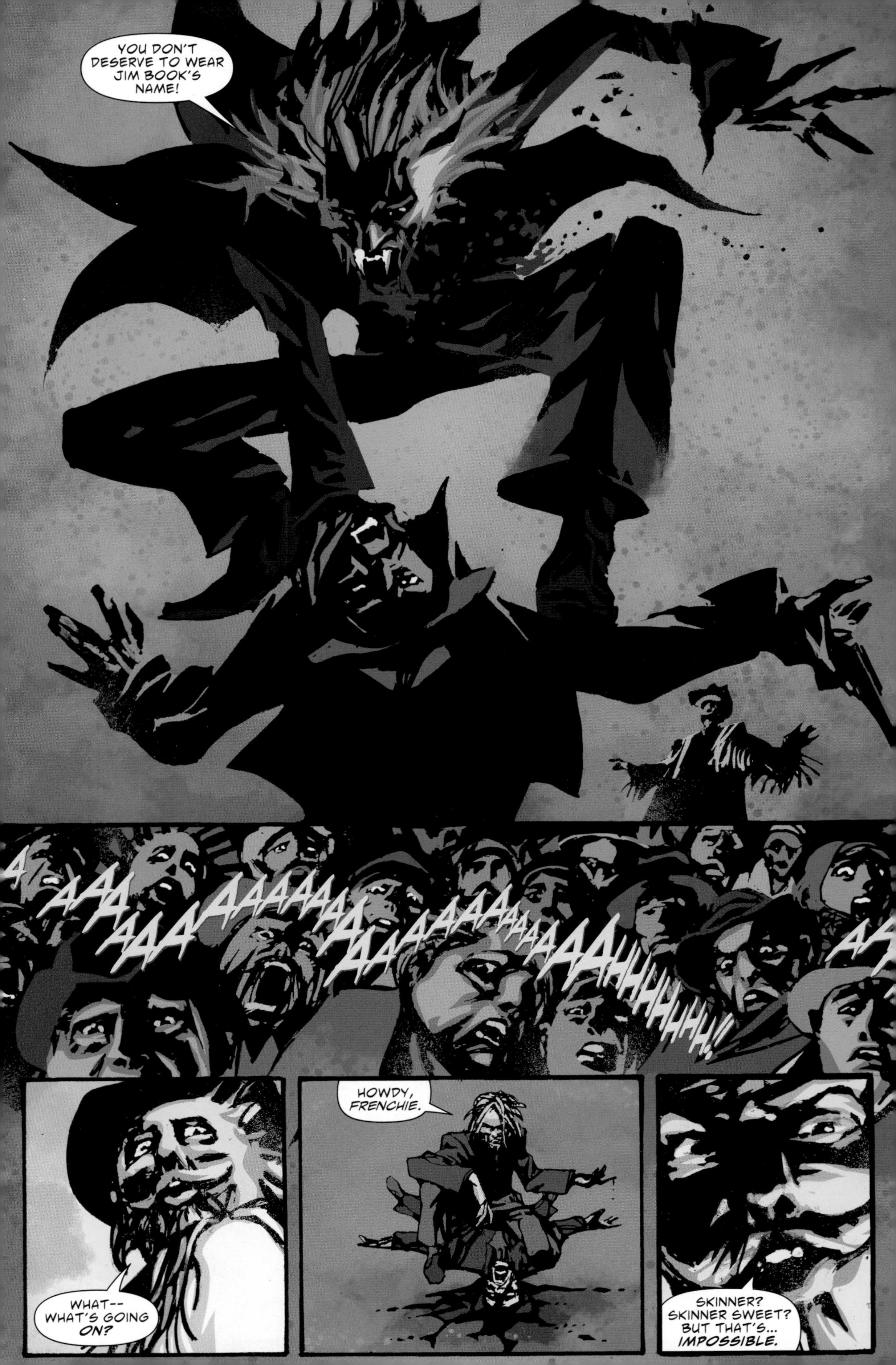
YOU DON'T DESERVE TO WEAR JIM BOOK'S NAME!
AAAAAAAAAAAAAAAAAAAAAAAAAAAAAHHHHHHH!!
HOWDY, FRENCHIE.
WHAT-- WHAT'S GOING ON?
SKINNER? SKINNER SWEET? BUT THAT'S... IMPOSSIBLE.

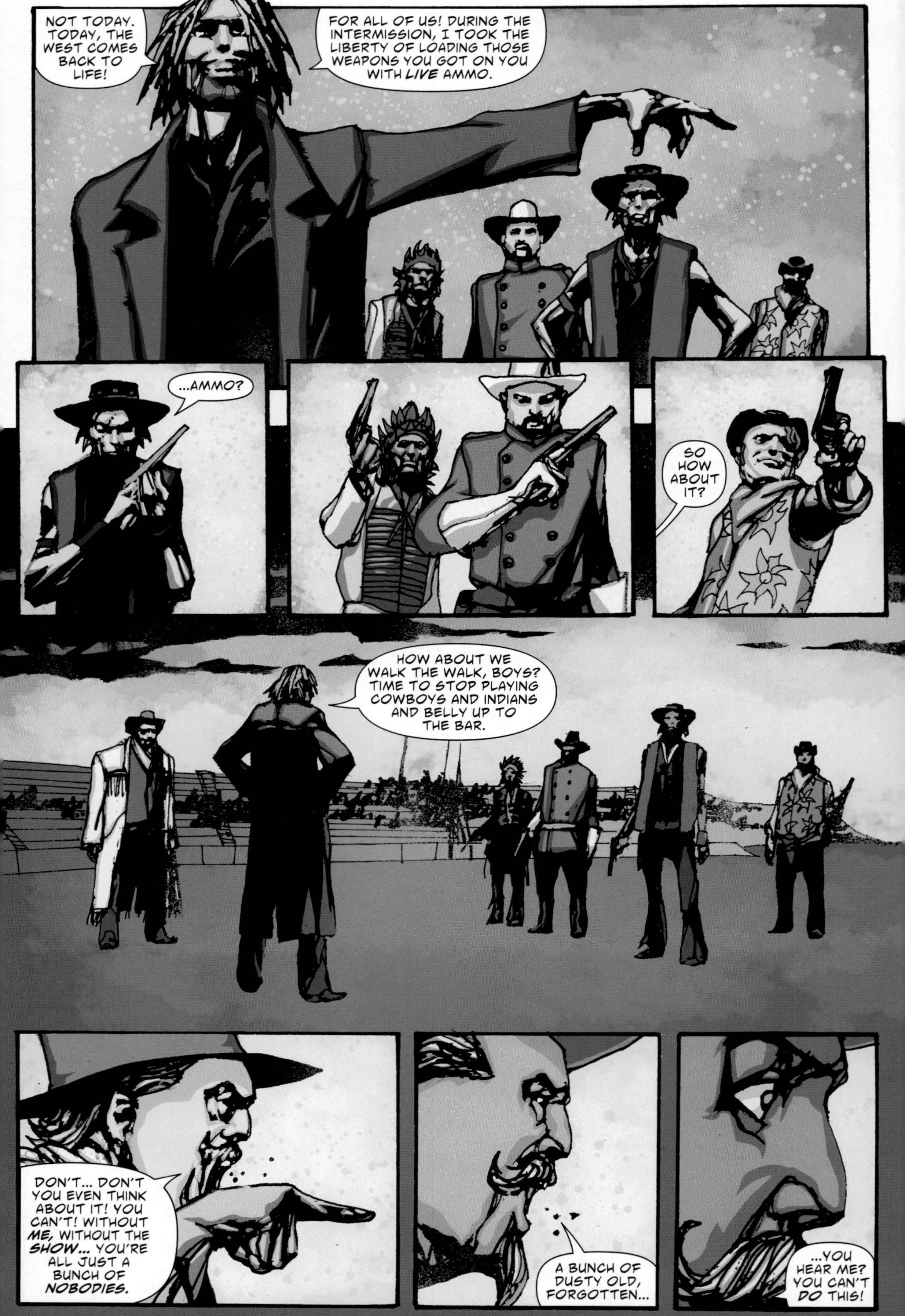
NOT TODAY. TODAY, THE WEST COMES BACK TO LIFE!
FOR ALL OF US! DURING THE INTERMISSION, I TOOK THE LIBERTY OF LOADING THOSE WEAPONS YOU GOT ON YOU WITH LIVE AMMO.
...AMMO?
SO HOW ABOUT IT?
HOW ABOUT WE WALK THE WALK, BOYS? TIME TO STOP PLAYING COWBOYS AND INDIANS AND BELLY UP TO THE BAR.
DON'T... DON'T YOU EVEN THINK ABOUT IT! YOU CAN'T! WITHOUT ME, WITHOUT THE SHOW... YOU'RE ALL JUST A BUNCH OF NOBODIES.
A BUNCH OF DUSTY OLD, FORGOTTEN...
...YOU HEAR ME? YOU CAN'T DO THIS!

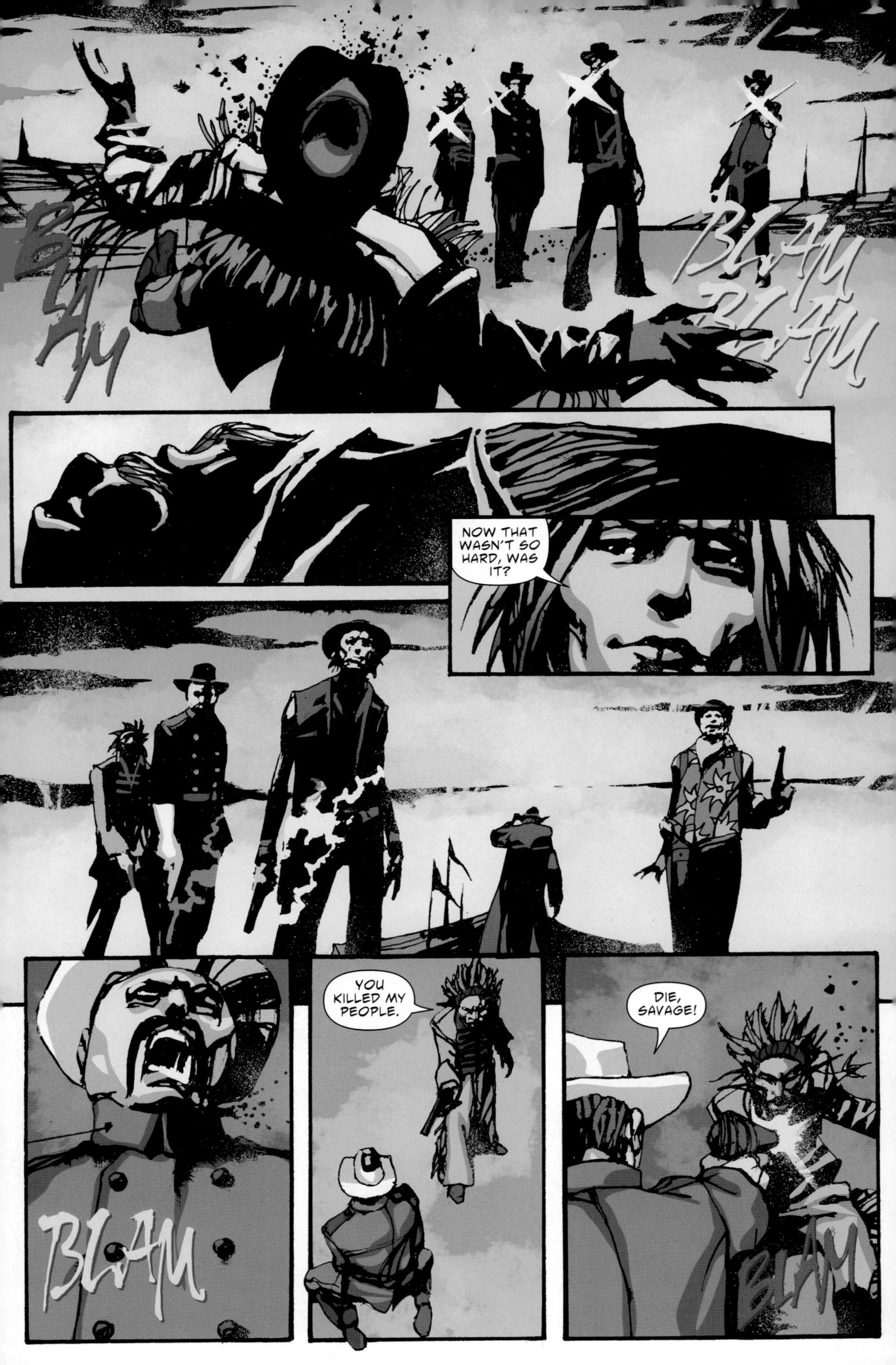
BLAM
BLAM
BLAM
NOW THAT WASN'T SO HARD, WAS IT?
BLAM
YOU KILLED MY PEOPLE.
DIE, SAVAGE!
BLAM

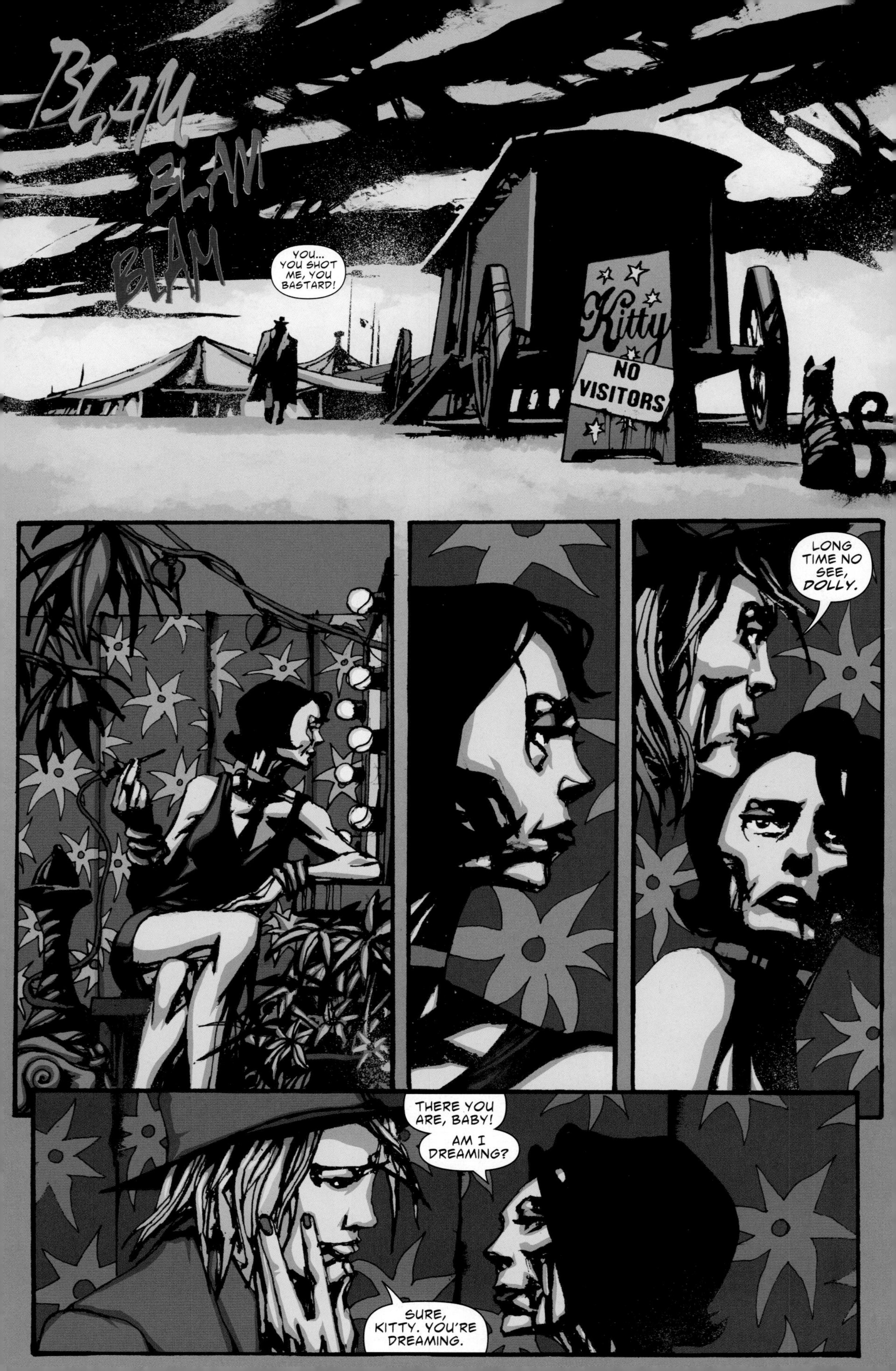
BLAM
BLAM
BLAM
YOU... YOU SHOT ME, YOU BASTARD!
Kitty
NO VISITORS
LONG TIME NO SEE, DOLLY.
THERE YOU ARE, BABY!
AM I DREAMING?
SURE, KITTY. YOU'RE DREAMING.

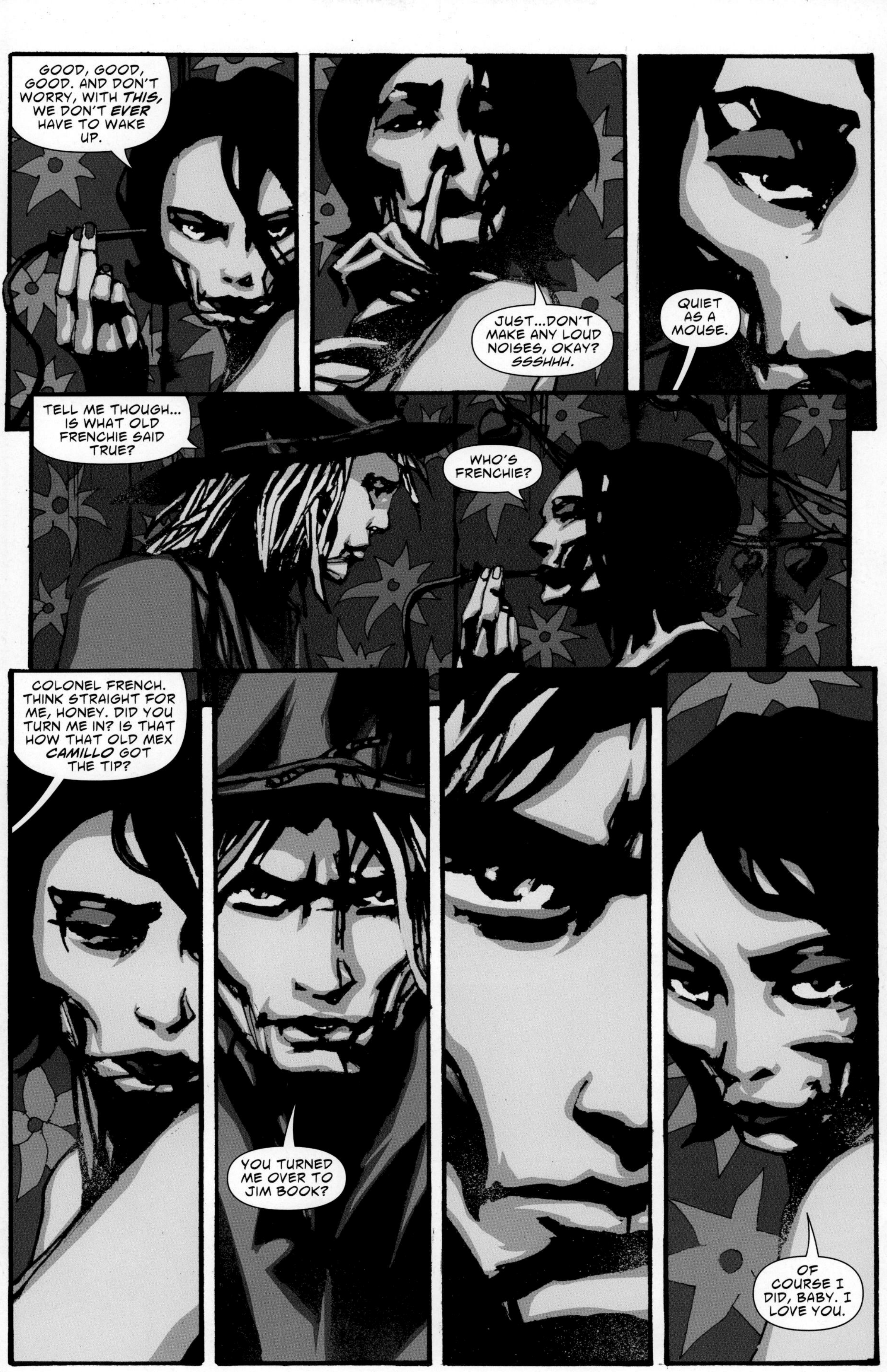
GOOD, GOOD, GOOD. AND DON'T WORRY, WITH *THIS,* WE DON'T *EVER* HAVE TO WAKE UP.
JUST...DON'T MAKE ANY LOUD NOISES, OKAY? *SSSHHH.*
QUIET AS A MOUSE.
TELL ME THOUGH... IS WHAT OLD FRENCHIE SAID TRUE?
WHO'S FRENCHIE?
COLONEL FRENCH. THINK STRAIGHT FOR ME, HONEY. DID YOU TURN ME IN? IS THAT HOW THAT OLD MEX *CAMILLO* GOT THE TIP?
YOU TURNED ME OVER TO JIM BOOK?
OF COURSE I DID, BABY. I LOVE YOU.

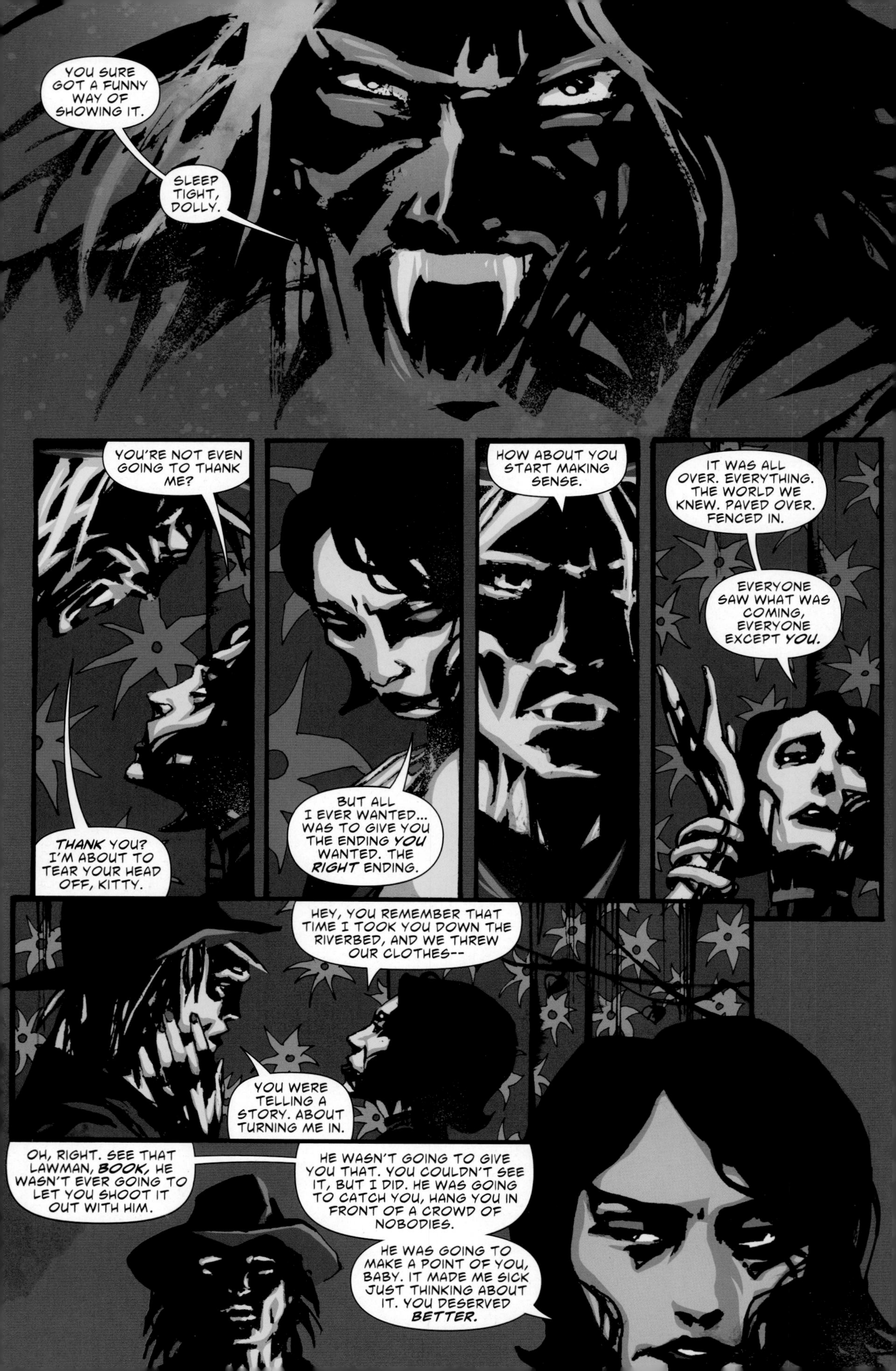
YOU SURE GOT A FUNNY WAY OF SHOWING IT.
SLEEP TIGHT, DOLLY.
YOU'RE NOT EVEN GOING TO THANK ME?
THANK YOU? I'M ABOUT TO TEAR YOUR HEAD OFF, KITTY.
BUT ALL I EVER WANTED... WAS TO GIVE YOU THE ENDING YOU WANTED. THE RIGHT ENDING.
HOW ABOUT YOU START MAKING SENSE.
IT WAS ALL OVER. EVERYTHING. THE WORLD WE KNEW. PAVED OVER. FENCED IN.
EVERYONE SAW WHAT WAS COMING, EVERYONE EXCEPT YOU.
HEY, YOU REMEMBER THAT TIME I TOOK YOU DOWN THE RIVERBED, AND WE THREW OUR CLOTHES--
YOU WERE TELLING A STORY. ABOUT TURNING ME IN.
OH, RIGHT. SEE THAT LAWMAN, BOOK, HE WASN'T EVER GOING TO LET YOU SHOOT IT OUT WITH HIM.
HE WASN'T GOING TO GIVE YOU THAT. YOU COULDN'T SEE IT, BUT I DID. HE WAS GOING TO CATCH YOU, HANG YOU IN FRONT OF A CROWD OF NOBODIES.
HE WAS GOING TO MAKE A POINT OF YOU, BABY. IT MADE ME SICK JUST THINKING ABOUT IT. YOU DESERVED BETTER.

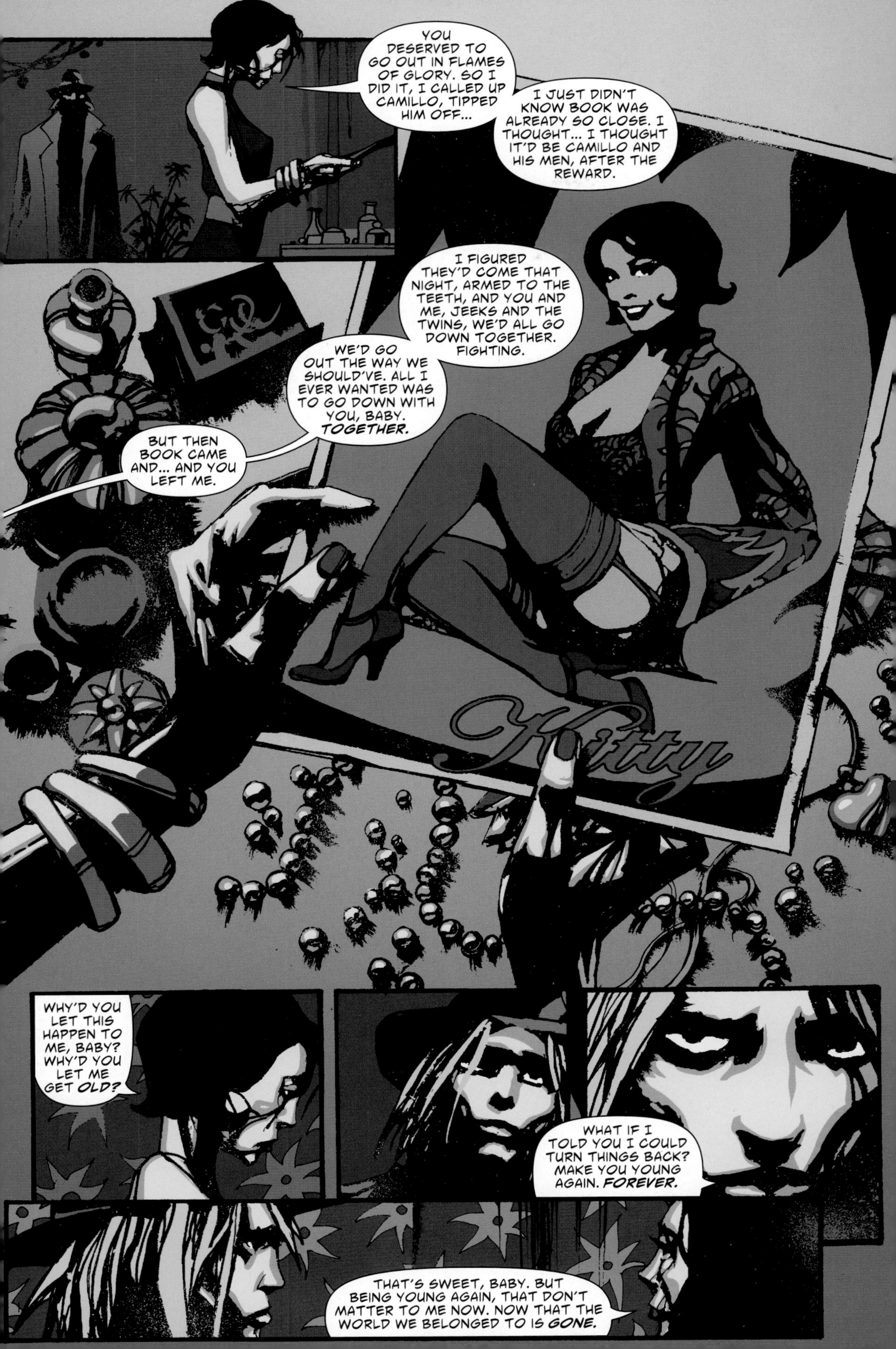
YOU DESERVED TO GO OUT IN FLAMES OF GLORY. SO I DID IT, I CALLED UP CAMILLO, TIPPED HIM OFF...
I JUST DIDN'T KNOW BOOK WAS ALREADY SO CLOSE. I THOUGHT... I THOUGHT IT'D BE CAMILLO AND HIS MEN, AFTER THE REWARD.
I FIGURED THEY'D COME THAT NIGHT, ARMED TO THE TEETH, AND YOU AND ME, JEEKS AND THE TWINS, WE'D ALL GO DOWN TOGETHER. FIGHTING.
WE'D GO OUT THE WAY WE SHOULD'VE. ALL I EVER WANTED WAS TO GO DOWN WITH YOU, BABY. ***TOGETHER.***
BUT THEN BOOK CAME AND... AND YOU LEFT ME.
Kitty
WHY'D YOU LET THIS HAPPEN TO ME, BABY? WHY'D YOU LET ME GET ***OLD?***
WHAT IF I TOLD YOU I COULD TURN THINGS BACK? MAKE YOU YOUNG AGAIN. ***FOREVER.***
THAT'S SWEET, BABY. BUT BEING YOUNG AGAIN, THAT DON'T MATTER TO ME NOW. NOW THAT THE WORLD WE BELONGED TO IS ***GONE.***

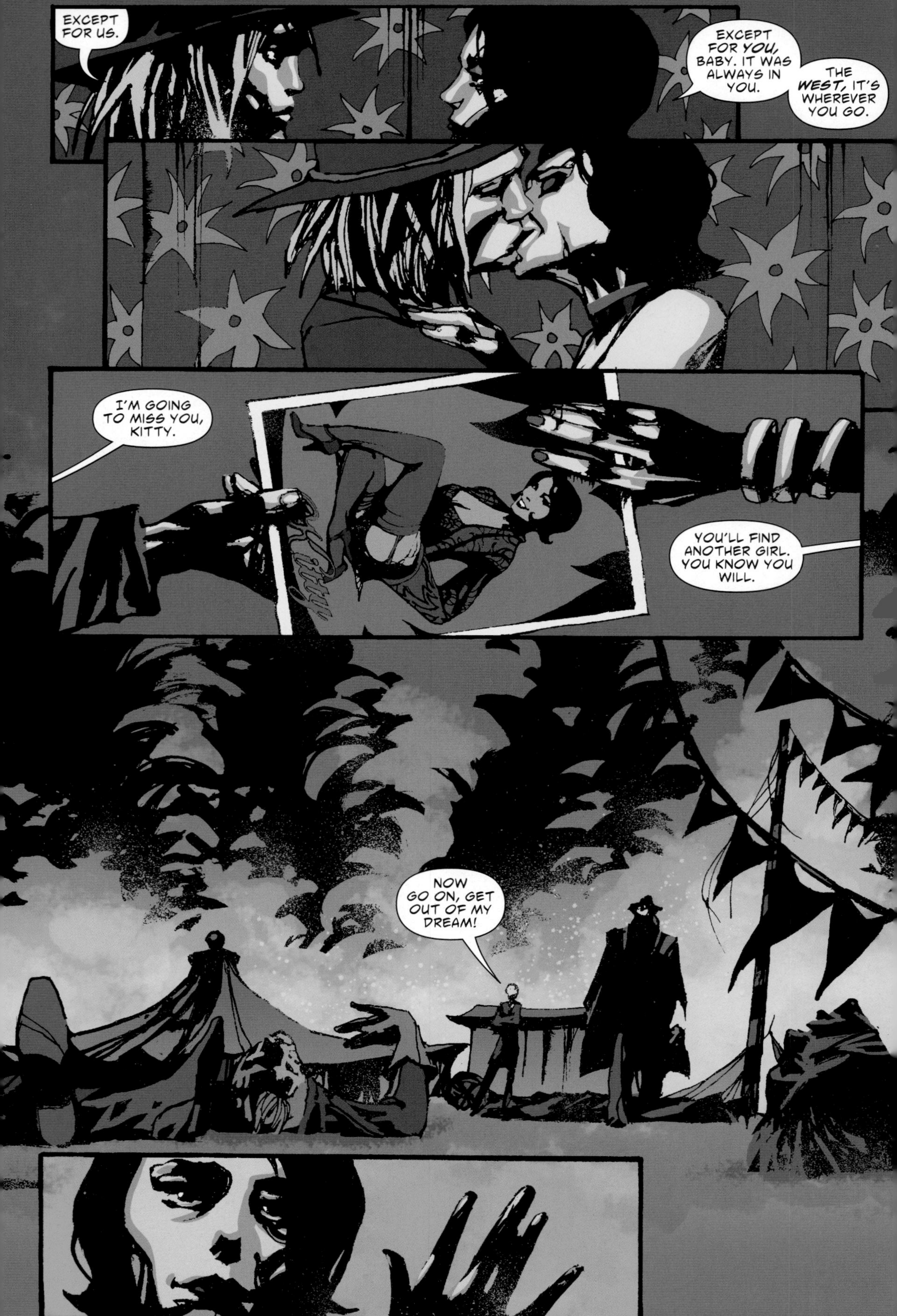
EXCEPT FOR US.
EXCEPT FOR YOU, BABY. IT WAS ALWAYS IN YOU.
THE WEST, IT'S WHEREVER YOU GO.
I'M GOING TO MISS YOU, KITTY.
Kitty
YOU'LL FIND ANOTHER GIRL. YOU KNOW YOU WILL.
NOW GO ON, GET OUT OF MY DREAM!

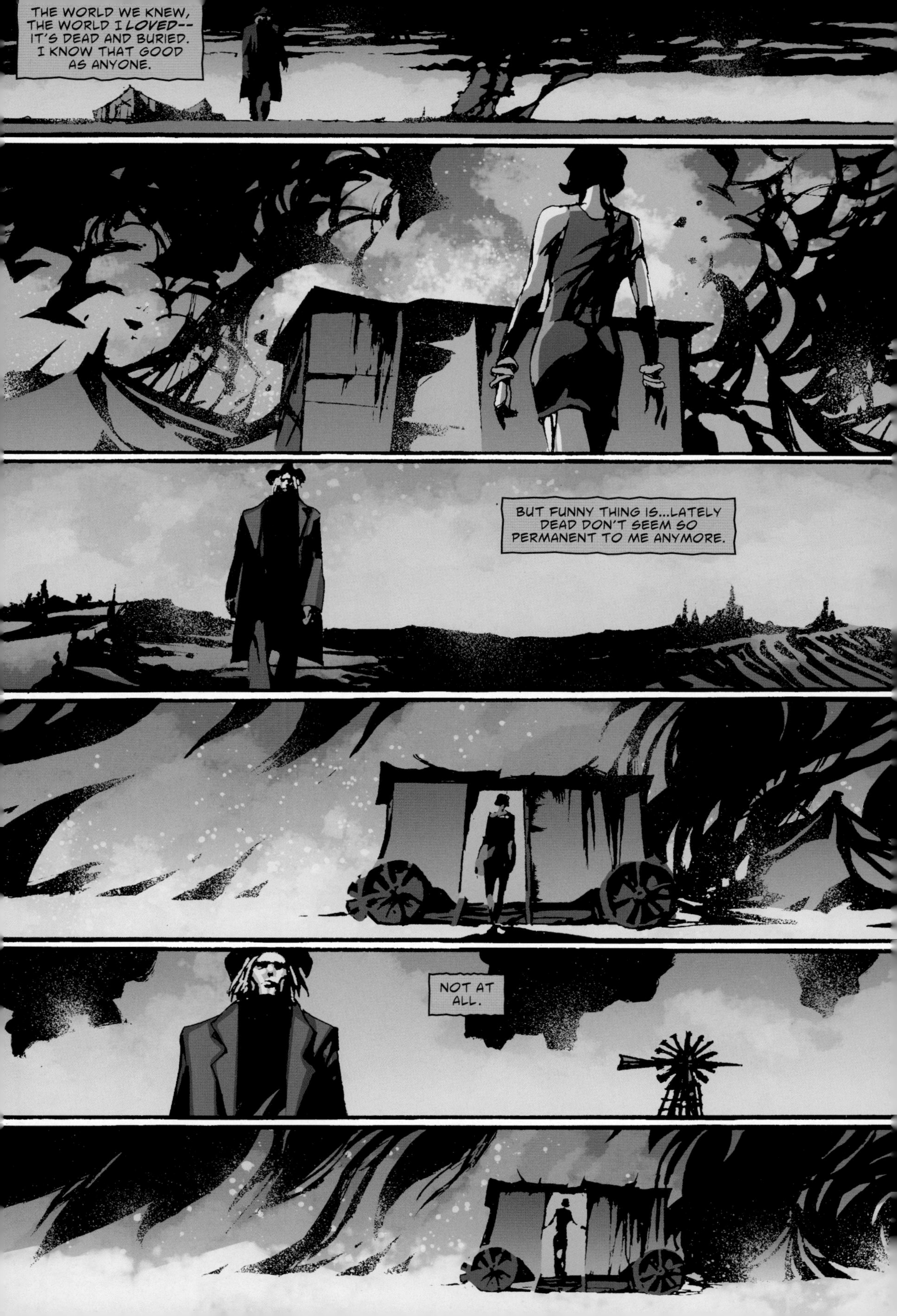
THE WORLD WE KNEW, THE WORLD I LOVED-- IT'S DEAD AND BURIED. I KNOW THAT GOOD AS ANYONE.
BUT FUNNY THING IS...LATELY DEAD DON'T SEEM SO PERMANENT TO ME ANYMORE.
NOT AT ALL.

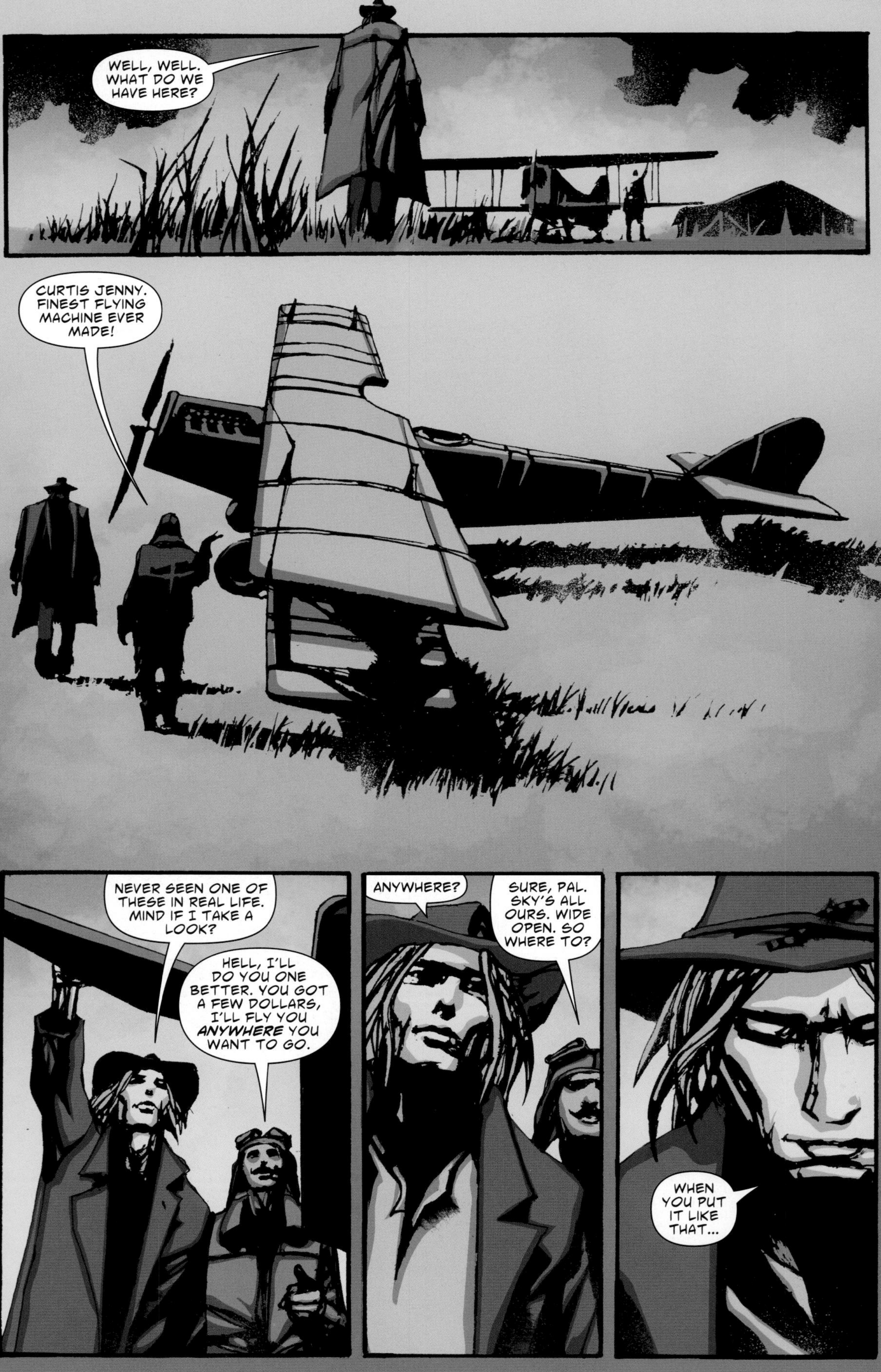
WELL, WELL. WHAT DO WE HAVE HERE?
CURTIS JENNY. FINEST FLYING MACHINE EVER MADE!
NEVER SEEN ONE OF THESE IN REAL LIFE. MIND IF I TAKE A LOOK?
HELL, I'LL DO YOU ONE BETTER. YOU GOT A FEW DOLLARS, I'LL FLY YOU *ANYWHERE* YOU WANT TO GO.
ANYWHERE?
SURE, PAL. SKY'S ALL OURS. WIDE OPEN. SO WHERE TO?
WHEN YOU PUT IT LIKE THAT...

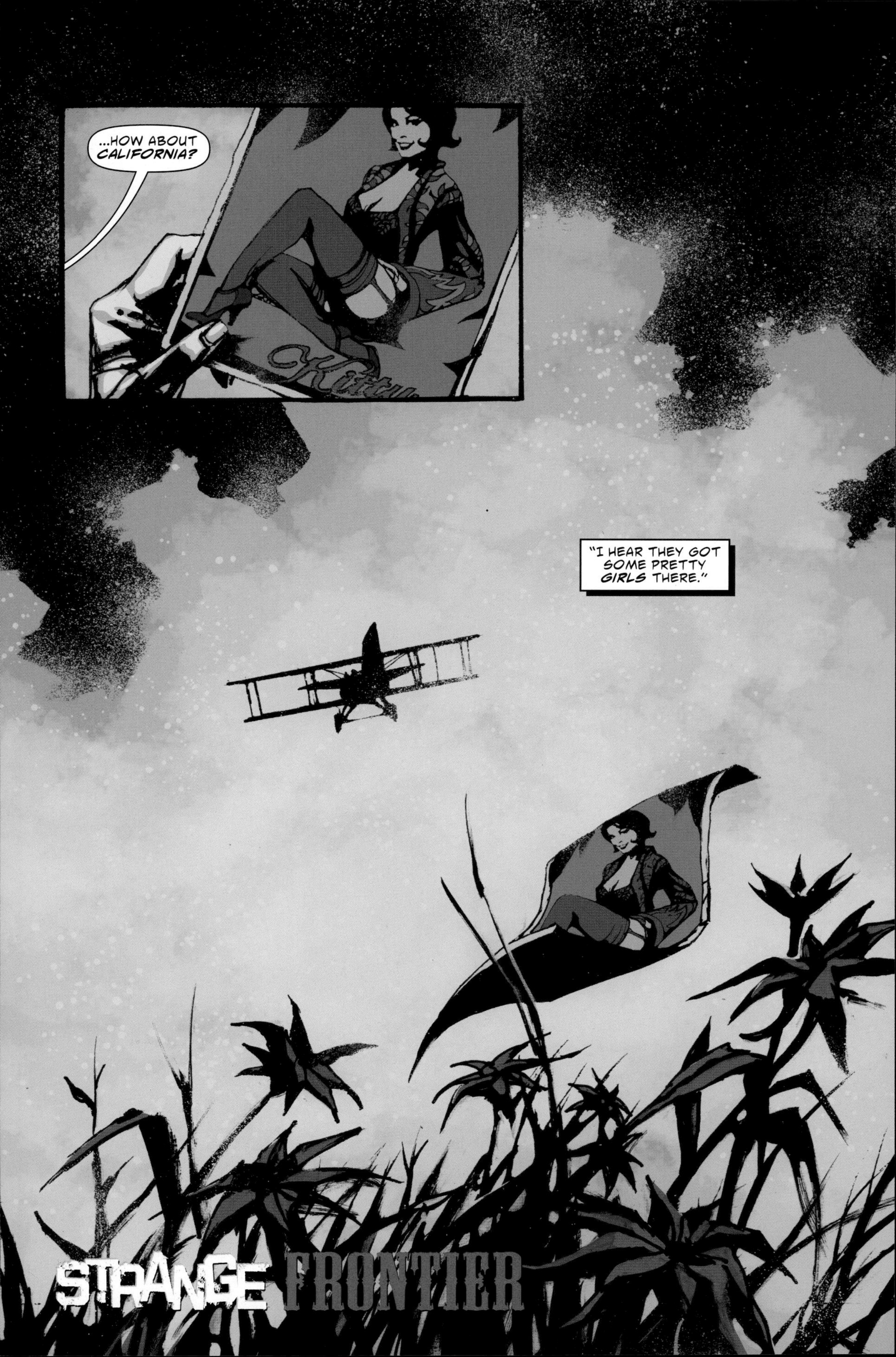
...HOW ABOUT CALIFORNIA?
"I HEAR THEY GOT SOME PRETTY GIRLS THERE."
STRANGE FRONTIER

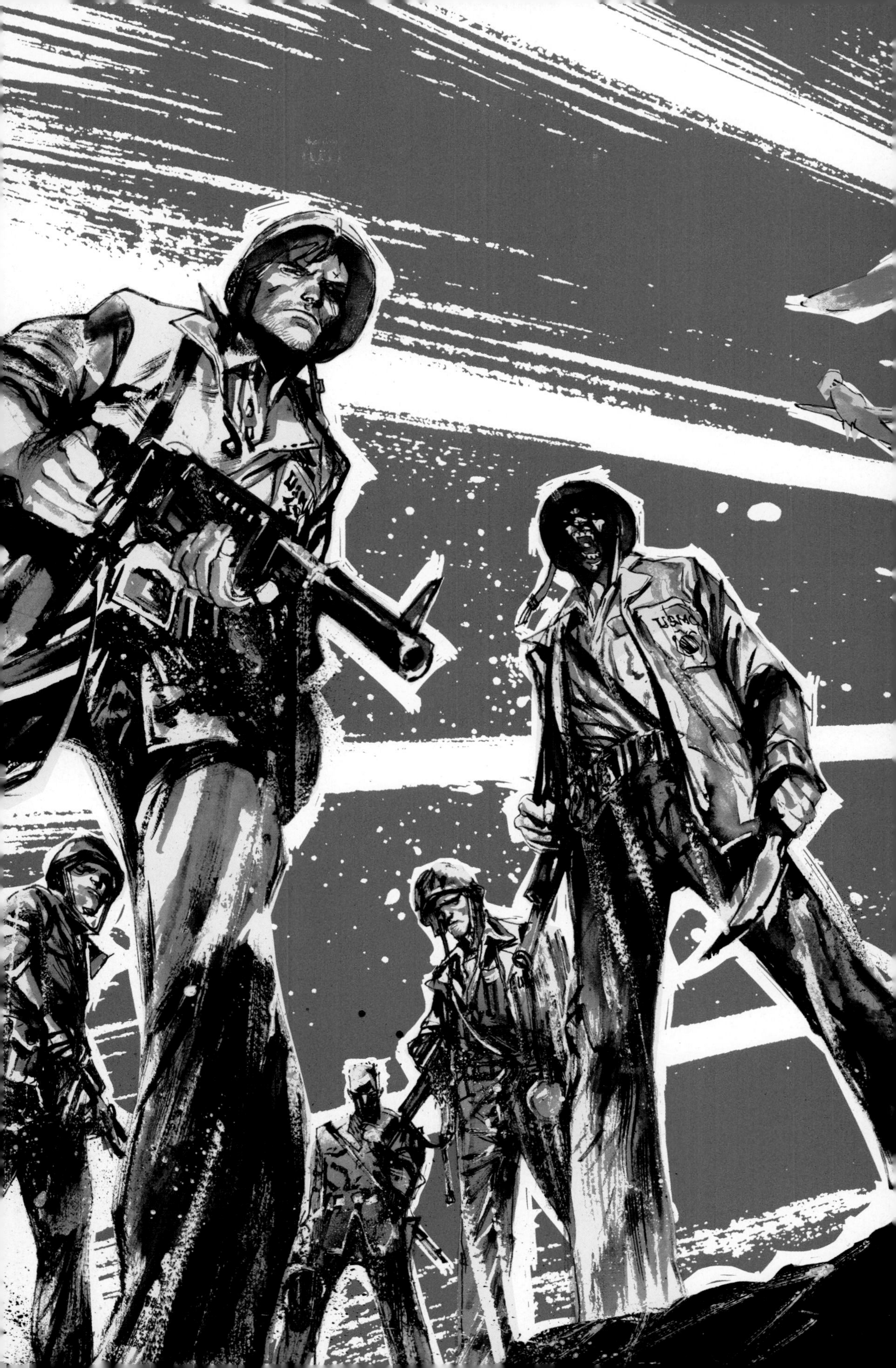
USMC

Ghost War

Part One

Rafael Albuquerque
Artist and cover

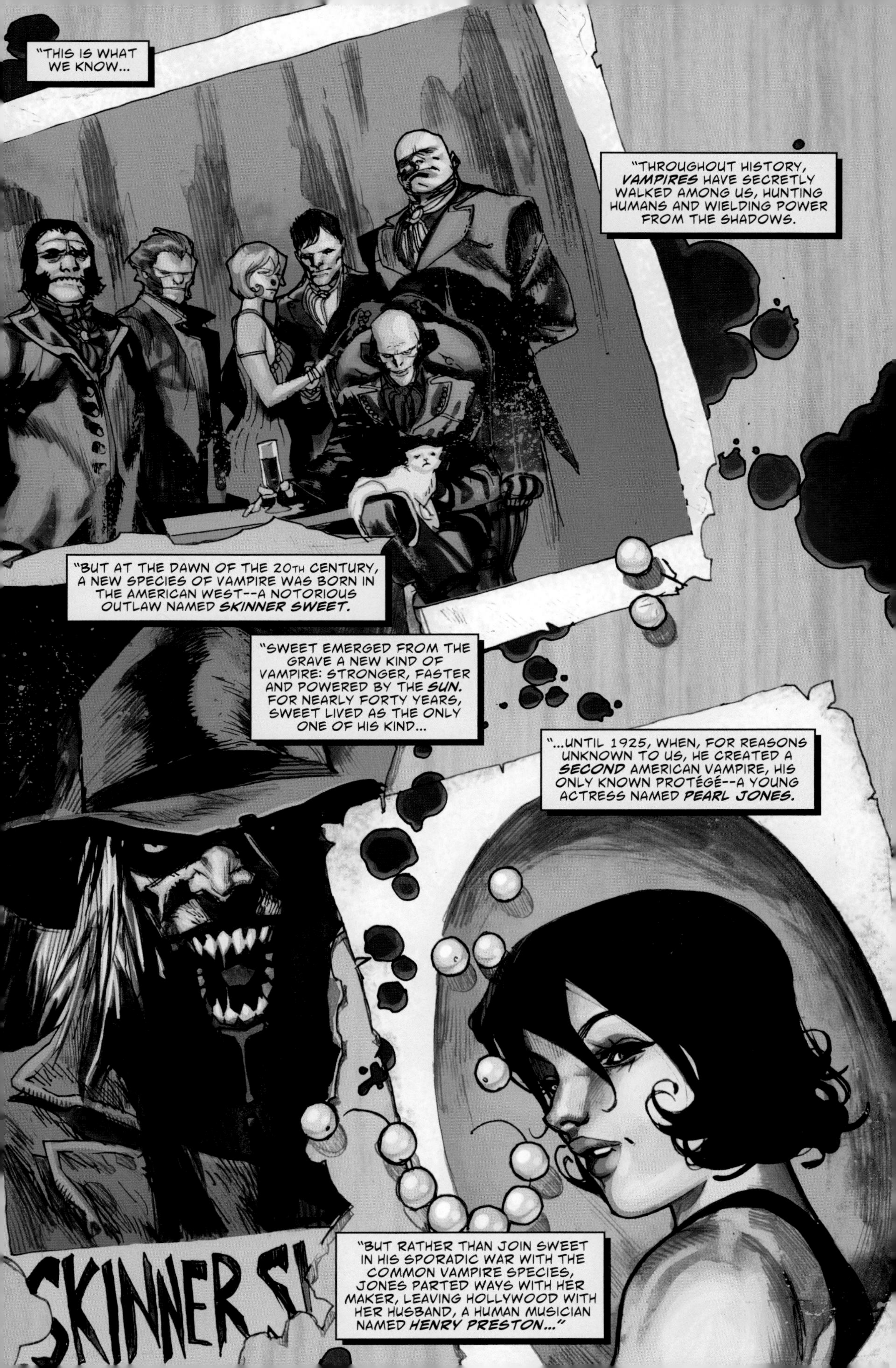
"THIS IS WHAT WE KNOW...
"THROUGHOUT HISTORY, VAMPIRES HAVE SECRETLY WALKED AMONG US, HUNTING HUMANS AND WIELDING POWER FROM THE SHADOWS.
"BUT AT THE DAWN OF THE 20TH CENTURY, A NEW SPECIES OF VAMPIRE WAS BORN IN THE AMERICAN WEST--A NOTORIOUS OUTLAW NAMED SKINNER SWEET.
"SWEET EMERGED FROM THE GRAVE A NEW KIND OF VAMPIRE: STRONGER, FASTER AND POWERED BY THE SUN. FOR NEARLY FORTY YEARS, SWEET LIVED AS THE ONLY ONE OF HIS KIND...
"...UNTIL 1925, WHEN, FOR REASONS UNKNOWN TO US, HE CREATED A SECOND AMERICAN VAMPIRE, HIS ONLY KNOWN PROTÉGÉ--A YOUNG ACTRESS NAMED PEARL JONES.
SKINNER S
"BUT RATHER THAN JOIN SWEET IN HIS SPORADIC WAR WITH THE COMMON VAMPIRE SPECIES, JONES PARTED WAYS WITH HER MAKER, LEAVING HOLLYWOOD WITH HER HUSBAND, A HUMAN MUSICIAN NAMED HENRY PRESTON..."

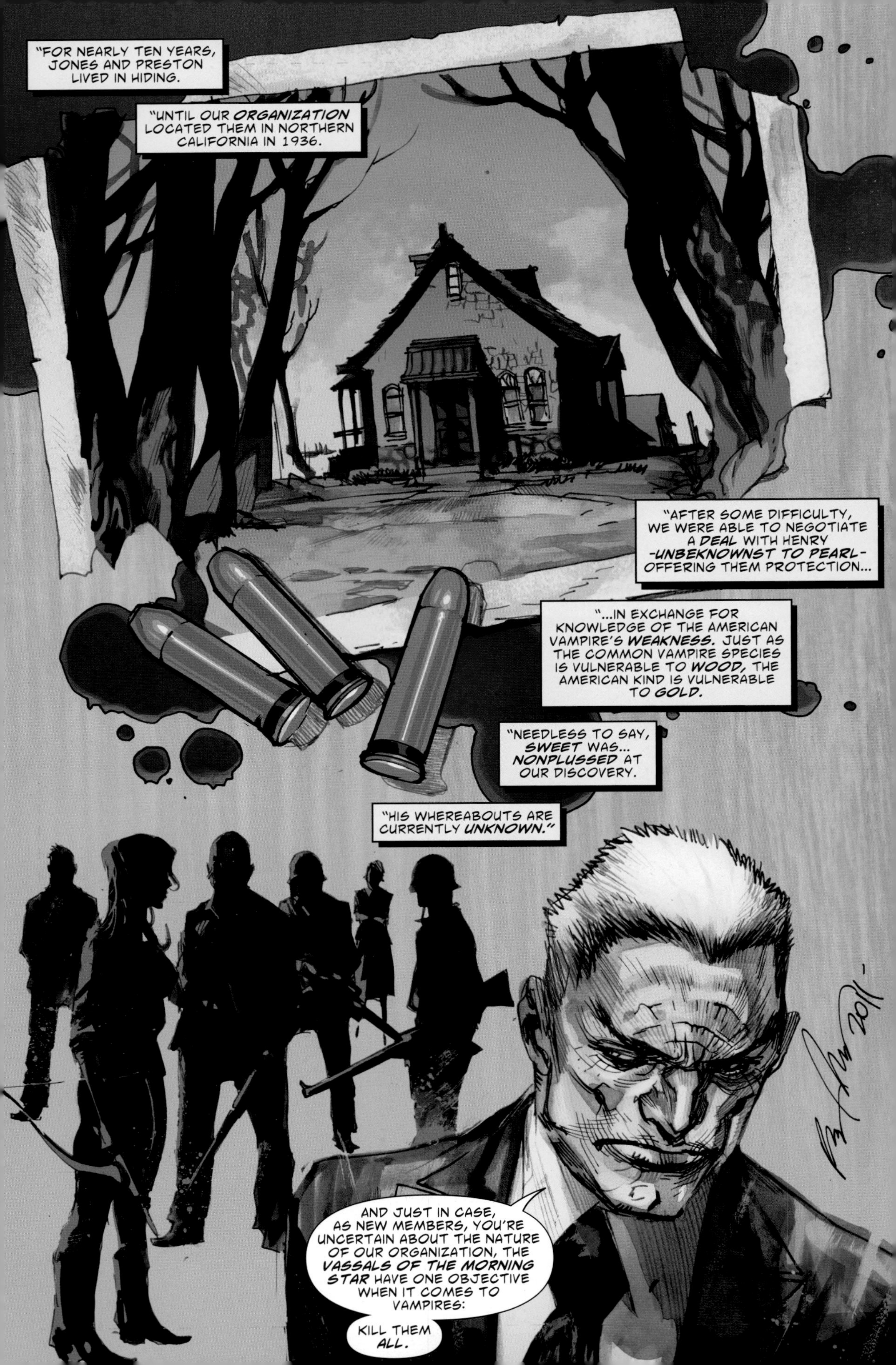
"FOR NEARLY TEN YEARS, JONES AND PRESTON LIVED IN HIDING.
"UNTIL OUR ORGANIZATION LOCATED THEM IN NORTHERN CALIFORNIA IN 1936.
"AFTER SOME DIFFICULTY, WE WERE ABLE TO NEGOTIATE A DEAL WITH HENRY -UNBEKNOWNST TO PEARL- OFFERING THEM PROTECTION...
"...IN EXCHANGE FOR KNOWLEDGE OF THE AMERICAN VAMPIRE'S WEAKNESS. JUST AS THE COMMON VAMPIRE SPECIES IS VULNERABLE TO WOOD, THE AMERICAN KIND IS VULNERABLE TO GOLD.
"NEEDLESS TO SAY, SWEET WAS... NONPLUSSED AT OUR DISCOVERY.
"HIS WHEREABOUTS ARE CURRENTLY UNKNOWN."
AND JUST IN CASE, AS NEW MEMBERS, YOU'RE UNCERTAIN ABOUT THE NATURE OF OUR ORGANIZATION, THE VASSALS OF THE MORNING STAR HAVE ONE OBJECTIVE WHEN IT COMES TO VAMPIRES:
KILL THEM ALL.

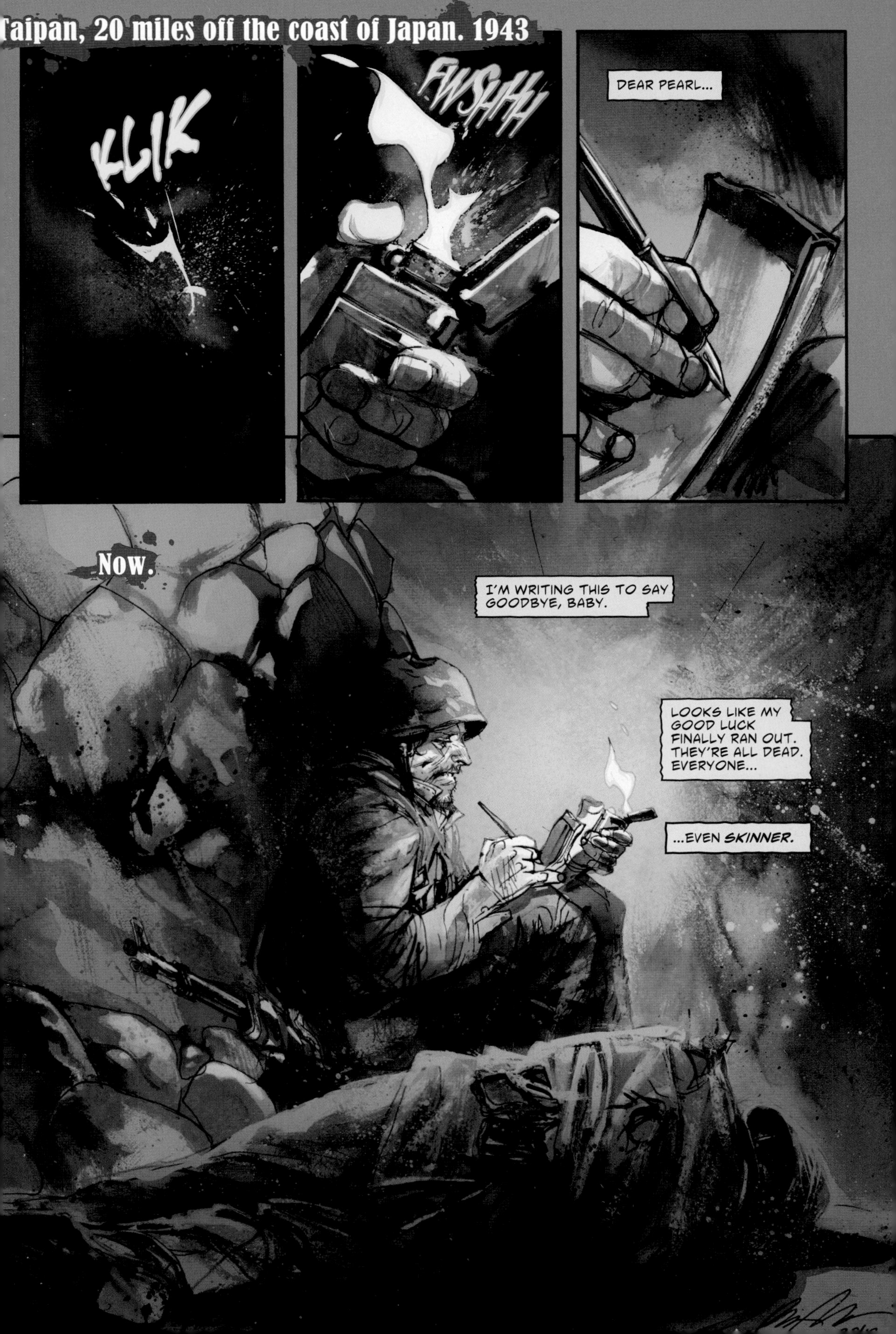
Taipan, 20 miles off the coast of Japan. 1943
KLIK
FWSHHH
DEAR PEARL...
Now.
I'M WRITING THIS TO SAY GOODBYE, BABY.
LOOKS LIKE MY GOOD LUCK FINALLY RAN OUT. THEY'RE ALL DEAD. EVERYONE...
...EVEN SKINNER.

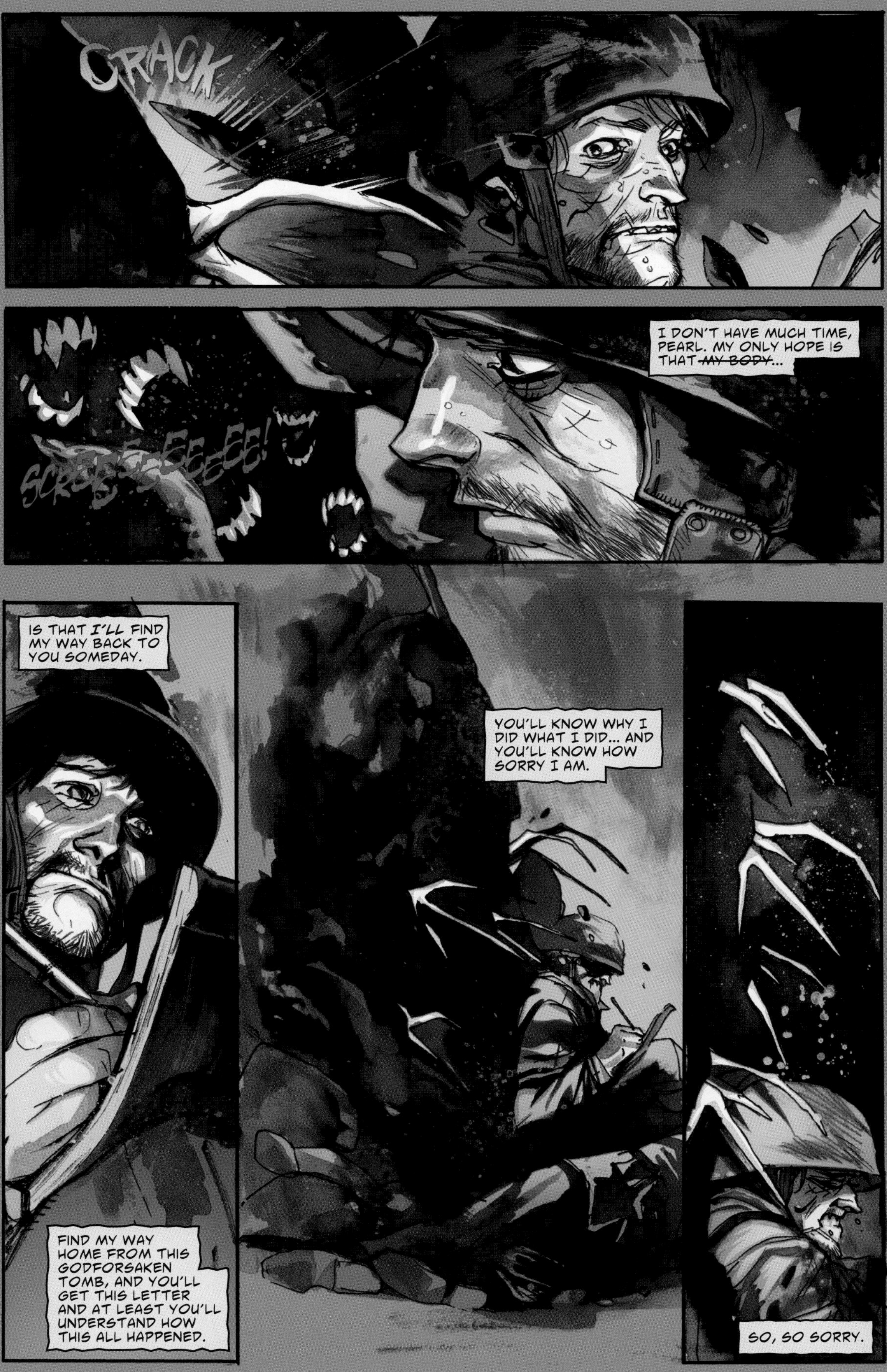
CRACK
I DON'T HAVE MUCH TIME, PEARL. MY ONLY HOPE IS THAT ~~MY BODY~~...
IS THAT I'LL FIND MY WAY BACK TO YOU SOMEDAY.
YOU'LL KNOW WHY I DID WHAT I DID... AND YOU'LL KNOW HOW SORRY I AM.
FIND MY WAY HOME FROM THIS GODFORSAKEN TOMB, AND YOU'LL GET THIS LETTER AND AT LEAST YOU'LL UNDERSTAND HOW THIS ALL HAPPENED.
SO, SO SORRY.

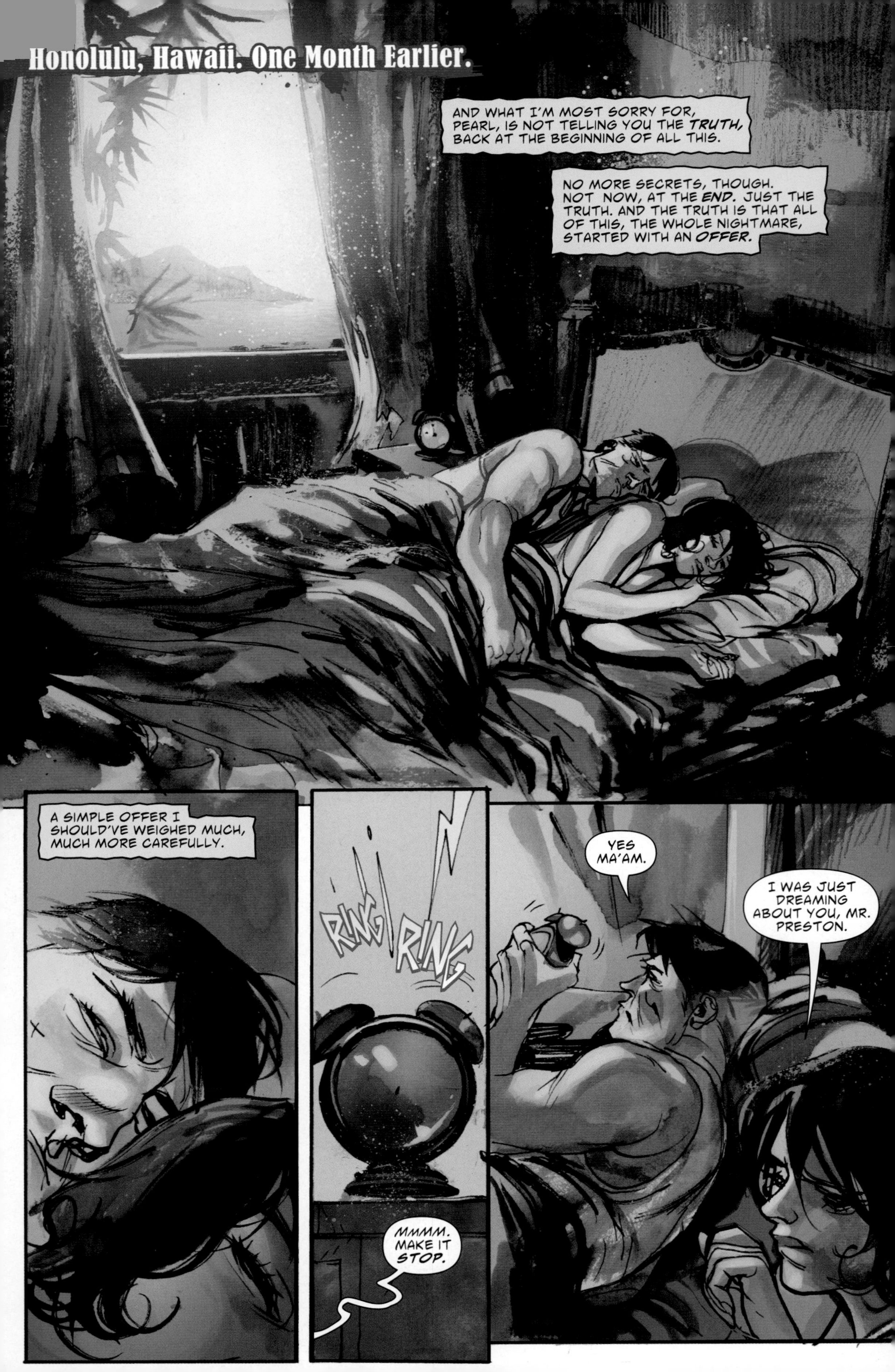
Honolulu, Hawaii. One Month Earlier.
AND WHAT I'M MOST SORRY FOR, PEARL, IS NOT TELLING YOU THE TRUTH, BACK AT THE BEGINNING OF ALL THIS.
NO MORE SECRETS, THOUGH. NOT NOW, AT THE END. JUST THE TRUTH. AND THE TRUTH IS THAT ALL OF THIS, THE WHOLE NIGHTMARE, STARTED WITH AN OFFER.
A SIMPLE OFFER I SHOULD'VE WEIGHED MUCH, MUCH MORE CAREFULLY.
RING RING
MMMM. MAKE IT STOP.
YES MA'AM.
I WAS JUST DREAMING ABOUT YOU, MR. PRESTON.

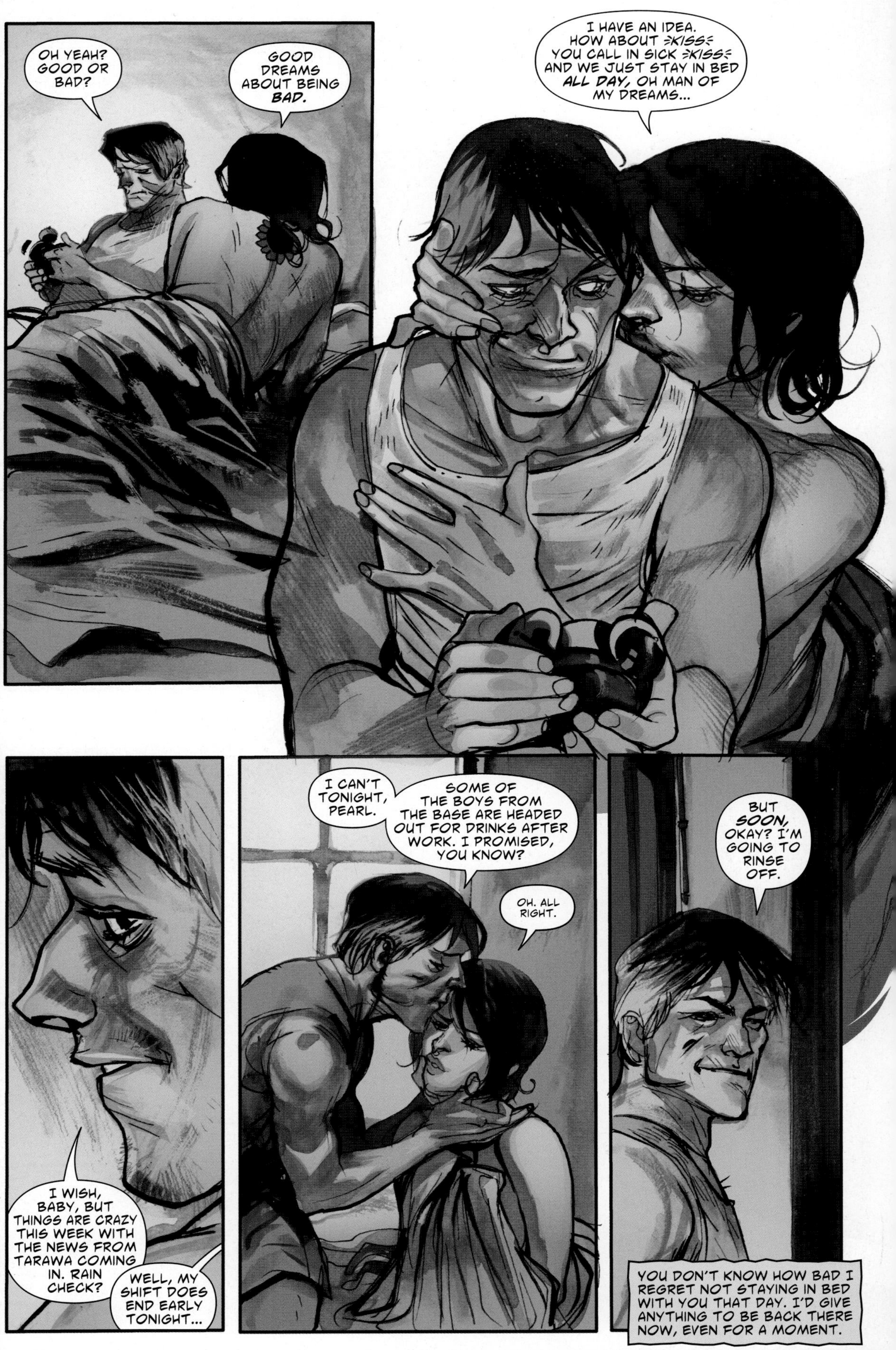
OH YEAH? GOOD OR BAD?
GOOD DREAMS ABOUT BEING BAD.
I HAVE AN IDEA. HOW ABOUT =KISS= YOU CALL IN SICK =KISS= AND WE JUST STAY IN BED ALL DAY, OH MAN OF MY DREAMS...
I WISH, BABY, BUT THINGS ARE CRAZY THIS WEEK WITH THE NEWS FROM TARAWA COMING IN. RAIN CHECK?
WELL, MY SHIFT DOES END EARLY TONIGHT...
I CAN'T TONIGHT, PEARL.
SOME OF THE BOYS FROM THE BASE ARE HEADED OUT FOR DRINKS AFTER WORK. I PROMISED, YOU KNOW?
OH. ALL RIGHT.
BUT SOON, OKAY? I'M GOING TO RINSE OFF.
YOU DON'T KNOW HOW BAD I REGRET NOT STAYING IN BED WITH YOU THAT DAY. I'D GIVE ANYTHING TO BE BACK THERE NOW, EVEN FOR A MOMENT.

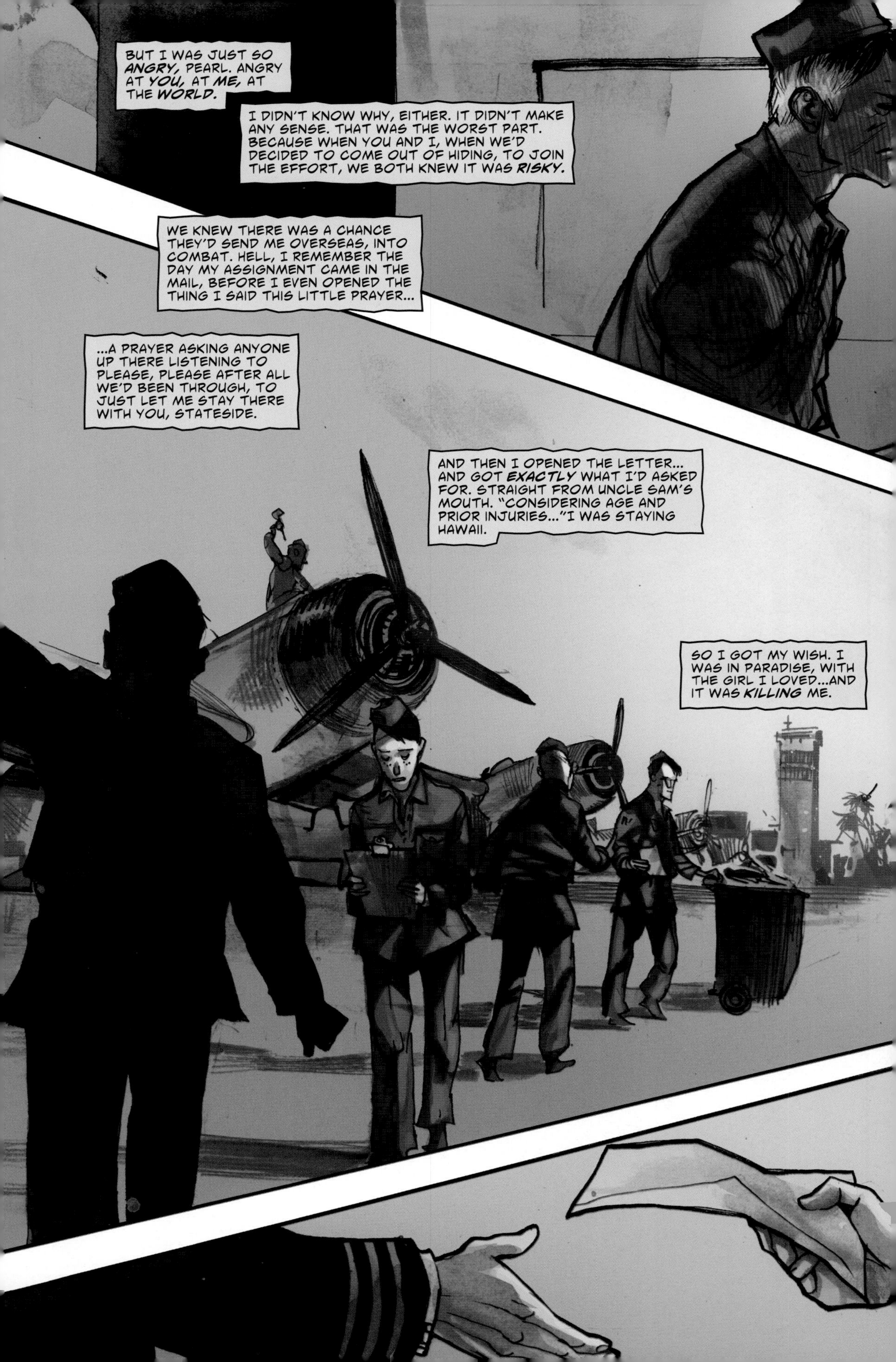
BUT I WAS JUST SO ANGRY, PEARL. ANGRY AT YOU, AT ME, AT THE WORLD.
I DIDN'T KNOW WHY, EITHER. IT DIDN'T MAKE ANY SENSE. THAT WAS THE WORST PART. BECAUSE WHEN YOU AND I, WHEN WE'D DECIDED TO COME OUT OF HIDING, TO JOIN THE EFFORT, WE BOTH KNEW IT WAS RISKY.
WE KNEW THERE WAS A CHANCE THEY'D SEND ME OVERSEAS, INTO COMBAT. HELL, I REMEMBER THE DAY MY ASSIGNMENT CAME IN THE MAIL, BEFORE I EVEN OPENED THE THING I SAID THIS LITTLE PRAYER...
...A PRAYER ASKING ANYONE UP THERE LISTENING TO PLEASE, PLEASE AFTER ALL WE'D BEEN THROUGH, TO JUST LET ME STAY THERE WITH YOU, STATESIDE.
AND THEN I OPENED THE LETTER... AND GOT EXACTLY WHAT I'D ASKED FOR. STRAIGHT FROM UNCLE SAM'S MOUTH. "CONSIDERING AGE AND PRIOR INJURIES..."I WAS STAYING HAWAII.
SO I GOT MY WISH. I WAS IN PARADISE, WITH THE GIRL I LOVED...AND IT WAS KILLING ME.

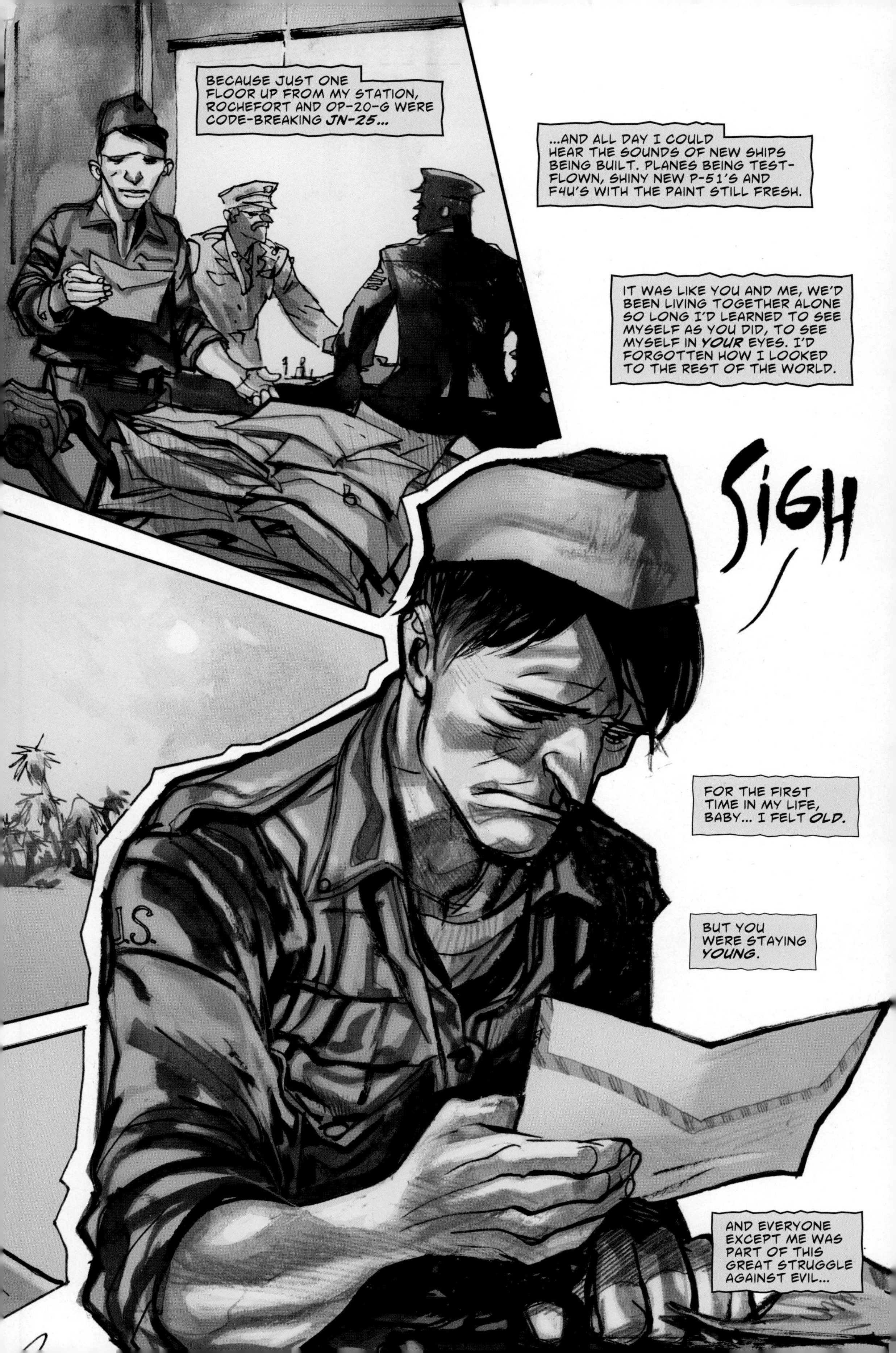
BECAUSE JUST ONE FLOOR UP FROM MY STATION, ROCHEFORT AND OP-20-G WERE CODE-BREAKING JN-25...
...AND ALL DAY I COULD HEAR THE SOUNDS OF NEW SHIPS BEING BUILT. PLANES BEING TEST-FLOWN, SHINY NEW P-51'S AND F4U'S WITH THE PAINT STILL FRESH.
IT WAS LIKE YOU AND ME, WE'D BEEN LIVING TOGETHER ALONE SO LONG I'D LEARNED TO SEE MYSELF AS YOU DID, TO SEE MYSELF IN YOUR EYES. I'D FORGOTTEN HOW I LOOKED TO THE REST OF THE WORLD.
SIGH
FOR THE FIRST TIME IN MY LIFE, BABY... I FELT OLD.
BUT YOU WERE STAYING YOUNG.
AND EVERYONE EXCEPT ME WAS PART OF THIS GREAT STRUGGLE AGAINST EVIL...
U.S.

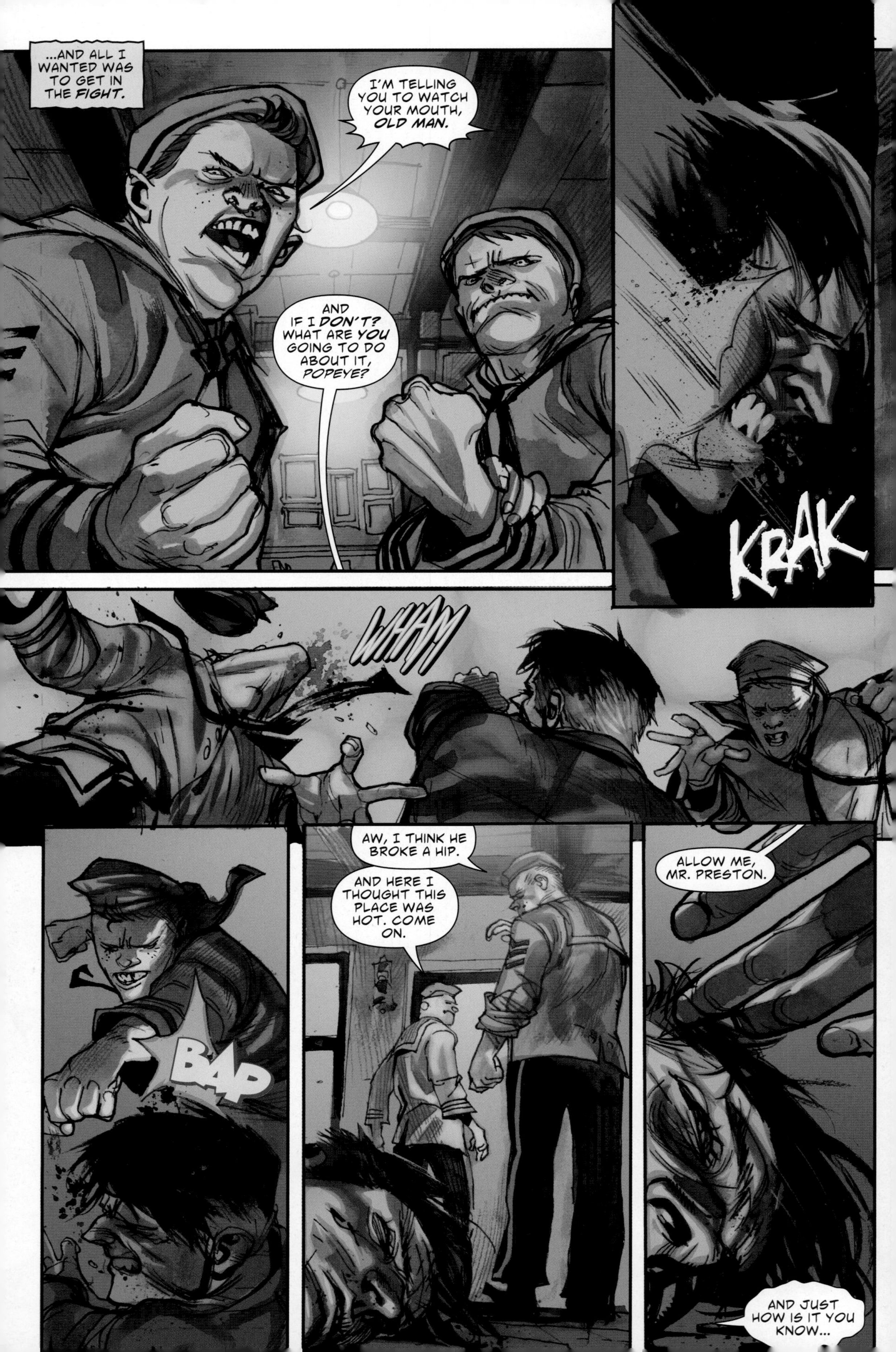
...AND ALL I WANTED WAS TO GET IN THE FIGHT.
I'M TELLING YOU TO WATCH YOUR MOUTH, OLD MAN.
AND IF I DON'T? WHAT ARE YOU GOING TO DO ABOUT IT, POPEYE?
KRAK
WHAM
BAP
AW, I THINK HE BROKE A HIP.
AND HERE I THOUGHT THIS PLACE WAS HOT. COME ON.
ALLOW ME, MR. PRESTON.
AND JUST HOW IS IT YOU KNOW...

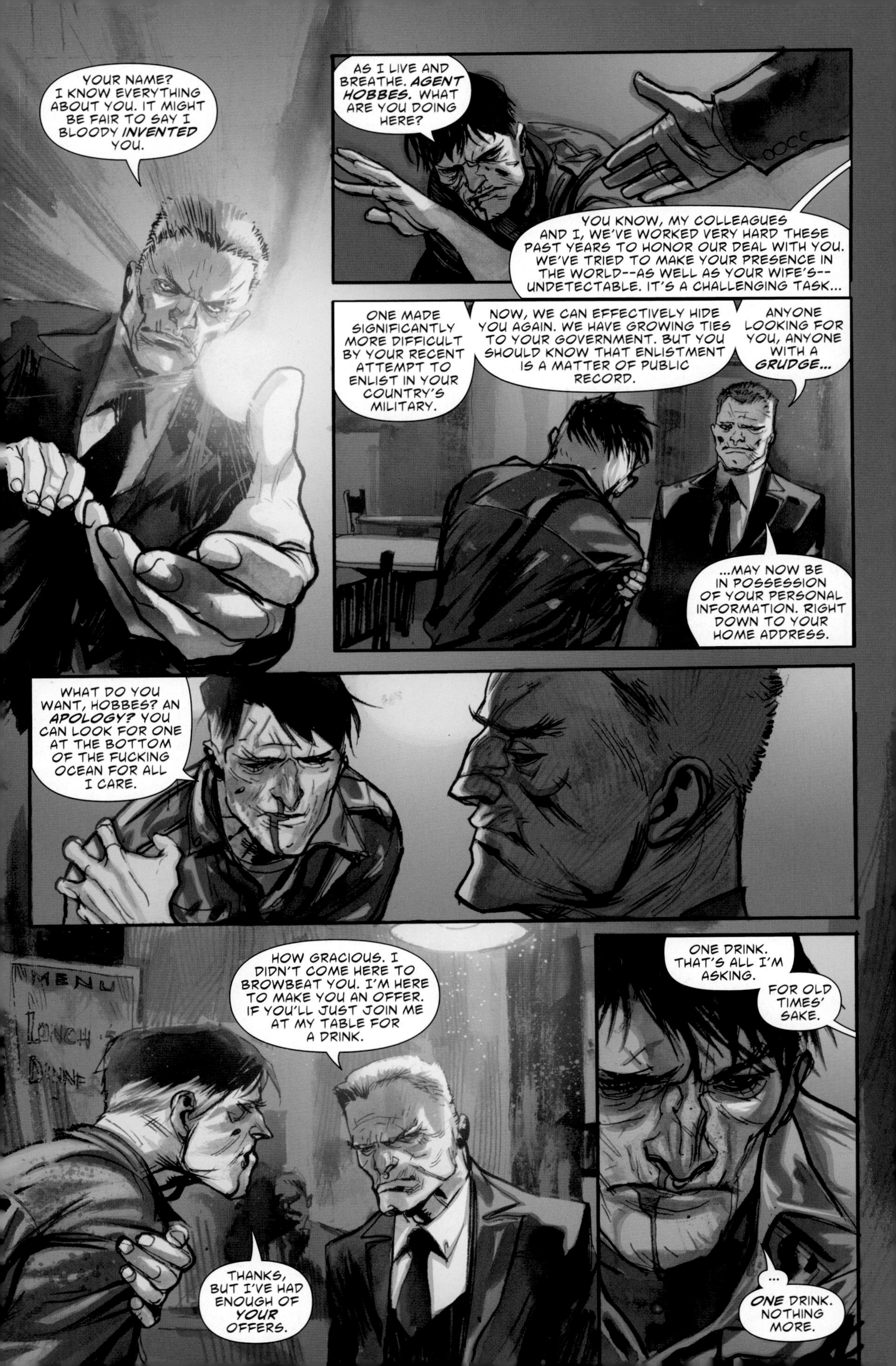
YOUR NAME? I KNOW EVERYTHING ABOUT YOU. IT MIGHT BE FAIR TO SAY I BLOODY INVENTED YOU.
AS I LIVE AND BREATHE. AGENT HOBBES. WHAT ARE YOU DOING HERE?
YOU KNOW, MY COLLEAGUES AND I, WE'VE WORKED VERY HARD THESE PAST YEARS TO HONOR OUR DEAL WITH YOU. WE'VE TRIED TO MAKE YOUR PRESENCE IN THE WORLD--AS WELL AS YOUR WIFE'S--UNDETECTABLE. IT'S A CHALLENGING TASK...
ONE MADE SIGNIFICANTLY MORE DIFFICULT BY YOUR RECENT ATTEMPT TO ENLIST IN YOUR COUNTRY'S MILITARY.
NOW, WE CAN EFFECTIVELY HIDE YOU AGAIN. WE HAVE GROWING TIES TO YOUR GOVERNMENT. BUT YOU SHOULD KNOW THAT ENLISTMENT IS A MATTER OF PUBLIC RECORD.
ANYONE LOOKING FOR YOU, ANYONE WITH A GRUDGE...
...MAY NOW BE IN POSSESSION OF YOUR PERSONAL INFORMATION. RIGHT DOWN TO YOUR HOME ADDRESS.
WHAT DO YOU WANT, HOBBES? AN APOLOGY? YOU CAN LOOK FOR ONE AT THE BOTTOM OF THE FUCKING OCEAN FOR ALL I CARE.
HOW GRACIOUS. I DIDN'T COME HERE TO BROWBEAT YOU. I'M HERE TO MAKE YOU AN OFFER. IF YOU'LL JUST JOIN ME AT MY TABLE FOR A DRINK.
MENU
THANKS, BUT I'VE HAD ENOUGH OF YOUR OFFERS.
ONE DRINK. THAT'S ALL I'M ASKING.
FOR OLD TIMES' SAKE.
...
ONE DRINK. NOTHING MORE.

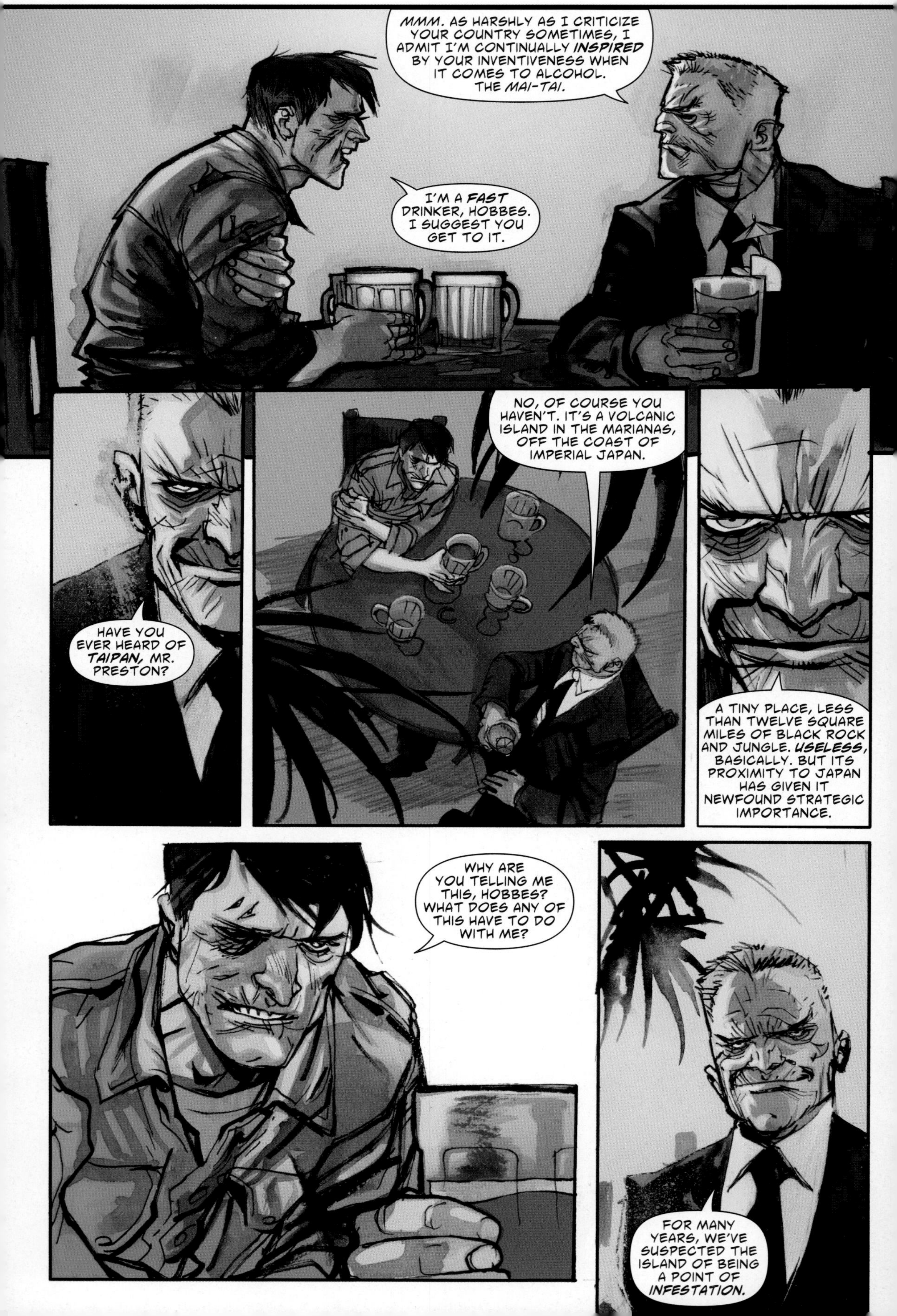

MMM. AS HARSHLY AS I CRITICIZE YOUR COUNTRY SOMETIMES, I ADMIT I'M CONTINUALLY INSPIRED BY YOUR INVENTIVENESS WHEN IT COMES TO ALCOHOL. THE MAI-TAI.
I'M A FAST DRINKER, HOBBES. I SUGGEST YOU GET TO IT.
HAVE YOU EVER HEARD OF TAIPAN, MR. PRESTON?
NO, OF COURSE YOU HAVEN'T. IT'S A VOLCANIC ISLAND IN THE MARIANAS, OFF THE COAST OF IMPERIAL JAPAN.
A TINY PLACE, LESS THAN TWELVE SQUARE MILES OF BLACK ROCK AND JUNGLE. USELESS, BASICALLY. BUT ITS PROXIMITY TO JAPAN HAS GIVEN IT NEWFOUND STRATEGIC IMPORTANCE.
WHY ARE YOU TELLING ME THIS, HOBBES? WHAT DOES ANY OF THIS HAVE TO DO WITH ME?
FOR MANY YEARS, WE'VE SUSPECTED THE ISLAND OF BEING A POINT OF INFESTATION.

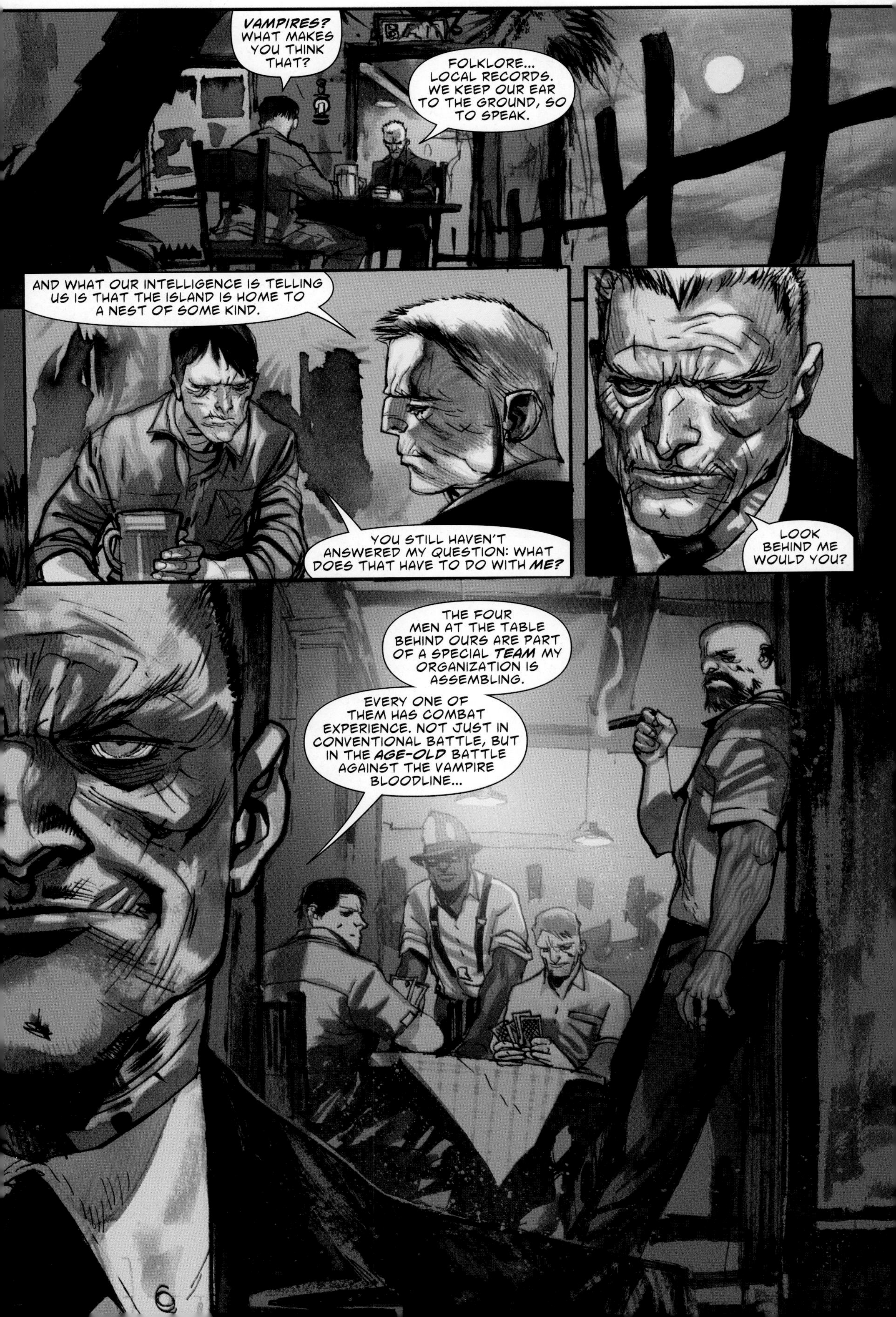

VAMPIRES? WHAT MAKES YOU THINK THAT?
FOLKLORE... LOCAL RECORDS. WE KEEP OUR EAR TO THE GROUND, SO TO SPEAK.
AND WHAT OUR INTELLIGENCE IS TELLING US IS THAT THE ISLAND IS HOME TO A NEST OF SOME KIND.
YOU STILL HAVEN'T ANSWERED MY QUESTION: WHAT DOES THAT HAVE TO DO WITH ME?
LOOK BEHIND ME WOULD YOU?
THE FOUR MEN AT THE TABLE BEHIND OURS ARE PART OF A SPECIAL TEAM MY ORGANIZATION IS ASSEMBLING.
EVERY ONE OF THEM HAS COMBAT EXPERIENCE. NOT JUST IN CONVENTIONAL BATTLE, BUT IN THE AGE-OLD BATTLE AGAINST THE VAMPIRE BLOODLINE...

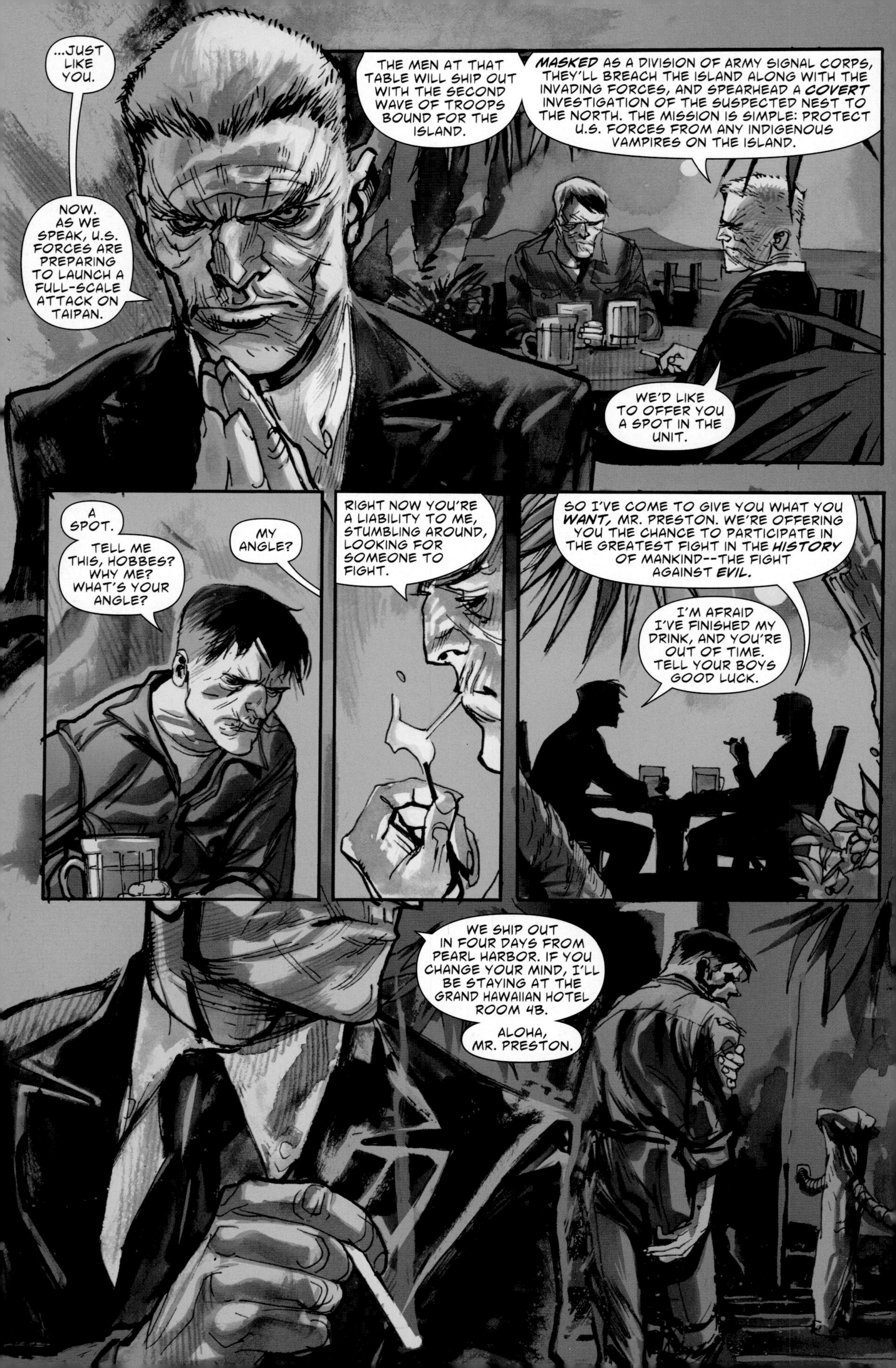
...JUST LIKE YOU.
NOW. AS WE SPEAK, U.S. FORCES ARE PREPARING TO LAUNCH A FULL-SCALE ATTACK ON TAIPAN.
THE MEN AT THAT TABLE WILL SHIP OUT WITH THE SECOND WAVE OF TROOPS BOUND FOR THE ISLAND.
MASKED AS A DIVISION OF ARMY SIGNAL CORPS, THEY'LL BREACH THE ISLAND ALONG WITH THE INVADING FORCES, AND SPEARHEAD A COVERT INVESTIGATION OF THE SUSPECTED NEST TO THE NORTH. THE MISSION IS SIMPLE: PROTECT U.S. FORCES FROM ANY INDIGENOUS VAMPIRES ON THE ISLAND.
WE'D LIKE TO OFFER YOU A SPOT IN THE UNIT.
A SPOT.
TELL ME THIS, HOBBES? WHY ME? WHAT'S YOUR ANGLE?
MY ANGLE?
RIGHT NOW YOU'RE A LIABILITY TO ME, STUMBLING AROUND, LOOKING FOR SOMEONE TO FIGHT.
SO I'VE COME TO GIVE YOU WHAT YOU WANT, MR. PRESTON. WE'RE OFFERING YOU THE CHANCE TO PARTICIPATE IN THE GREATEST FIGHT IN THE HISTORY OF MANKIND--THE FIGHT AGAINST EVIL.
I'M AFRAID I'VE FINISHED MY DRINK, AND YOU'RE OUT OF TIME. TELL YOUR BOYS GOOD LUCK.
WE SHIP OUT IN FOUR DAYS FROM PEARL HARBOR. IF YOU CHANGE YOUR MIND, I'LL BE STAYING AT THE GRAND HAWAIIAN HOTEL ROOM 4B.
ALOHA, MR. PRESTON.

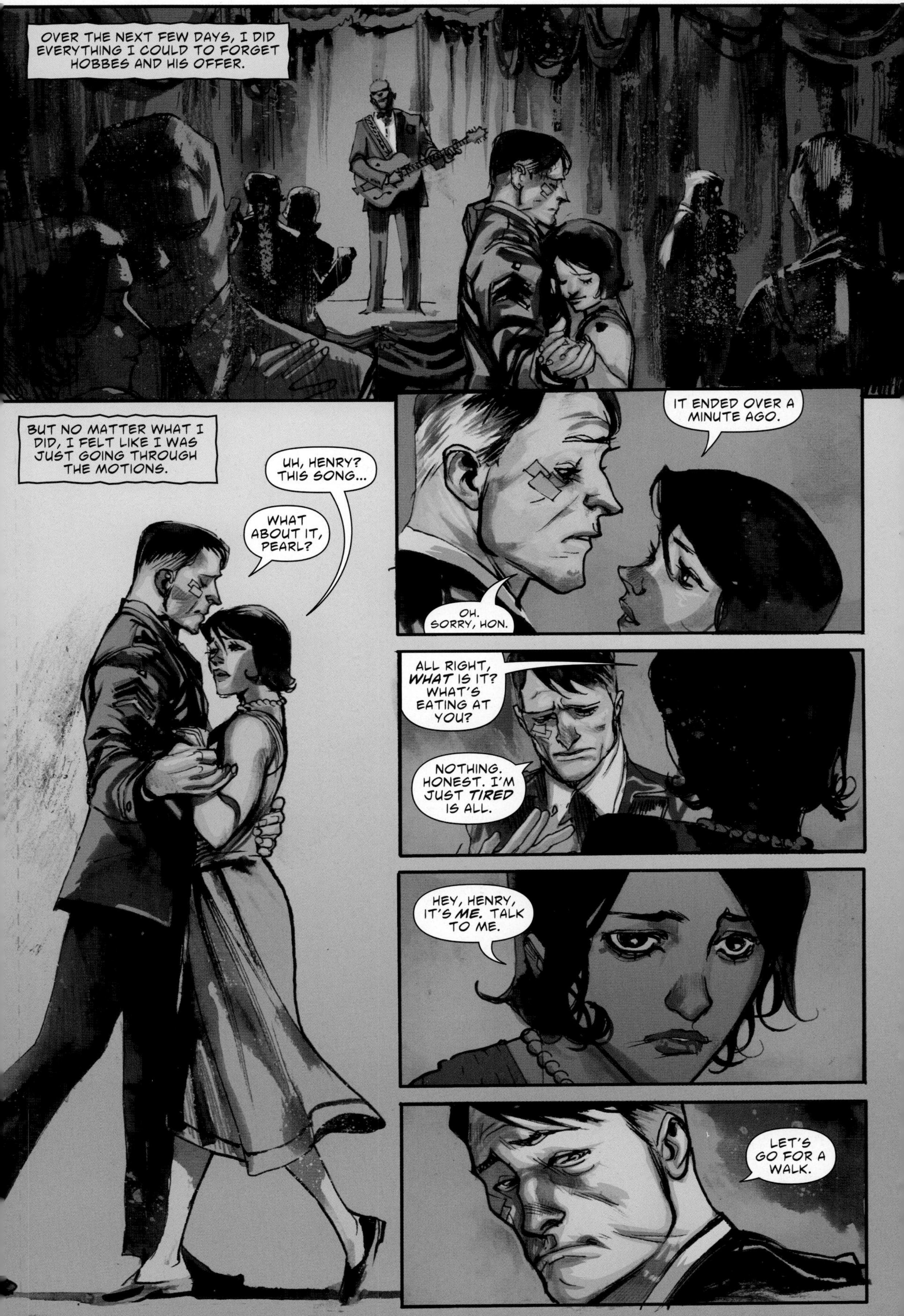
OVER THE NEXT FEW DAYS, I DID EVERYTHING I COULD TO FORGET HOBBES AND HIS OFFER.
BUT NO MATTER WHAT I DID, I FELT LIKE I WAS JUST GOING THROUGH THE MOTIONS.
UH, HENRY? THIS SONG...
WHAT ABOUT IT, PEARL?
IT ENDED OVER A MINUTE AGO.
OH. SORRY, HON.
ALL RIGHT, WHAT IS IT? WHAT'S EATING AT YOU?
NOTHING. HONEST. I'M JUST TIRED IS ALL.
HEY, HENRY, IT'S ME. TALK TO ME.
LET'S GO FOR A WALK.

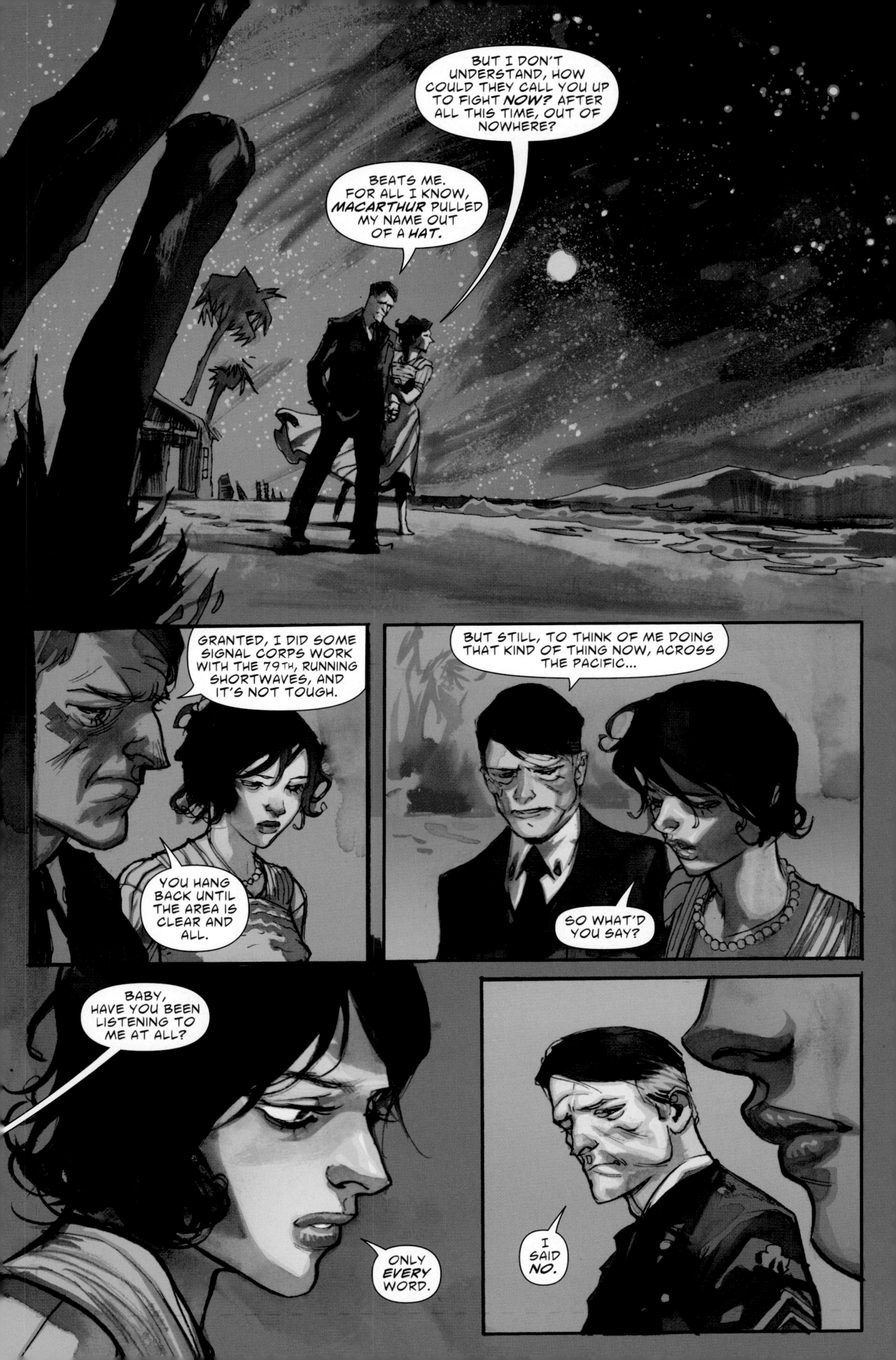
BUT I DON'T UNDERSTAND, HOW COULD THEY CALL YOU UP TO FIGHT NOW? AFTER ALL THIS TIME, OUT OF NOWHERE?
BEATS ME. FOR ALL I KNOW, MACARTHUR PULLED MY NAME OUT OF A HAT.
GRANTED, I DID SOME SIGNAL CORPS WORK WITH THE 79TH, RUNNING SHORTWAVES, AND IT'S NOT TOUGH.
YOU HANG BACK UNTIL THE AREA IS CLEAR AND ALL.
BUT STILL, TO THINK OF ME DOING THAT KIND OF THING NOW, ACROSS THE PACIFIC...
SO WHAT'D YOU SAY?
BABY, HAVE YOU BEEN LISTENING TO ME AT ALL?
ONLY EVERY WORD.
I SAID NO.

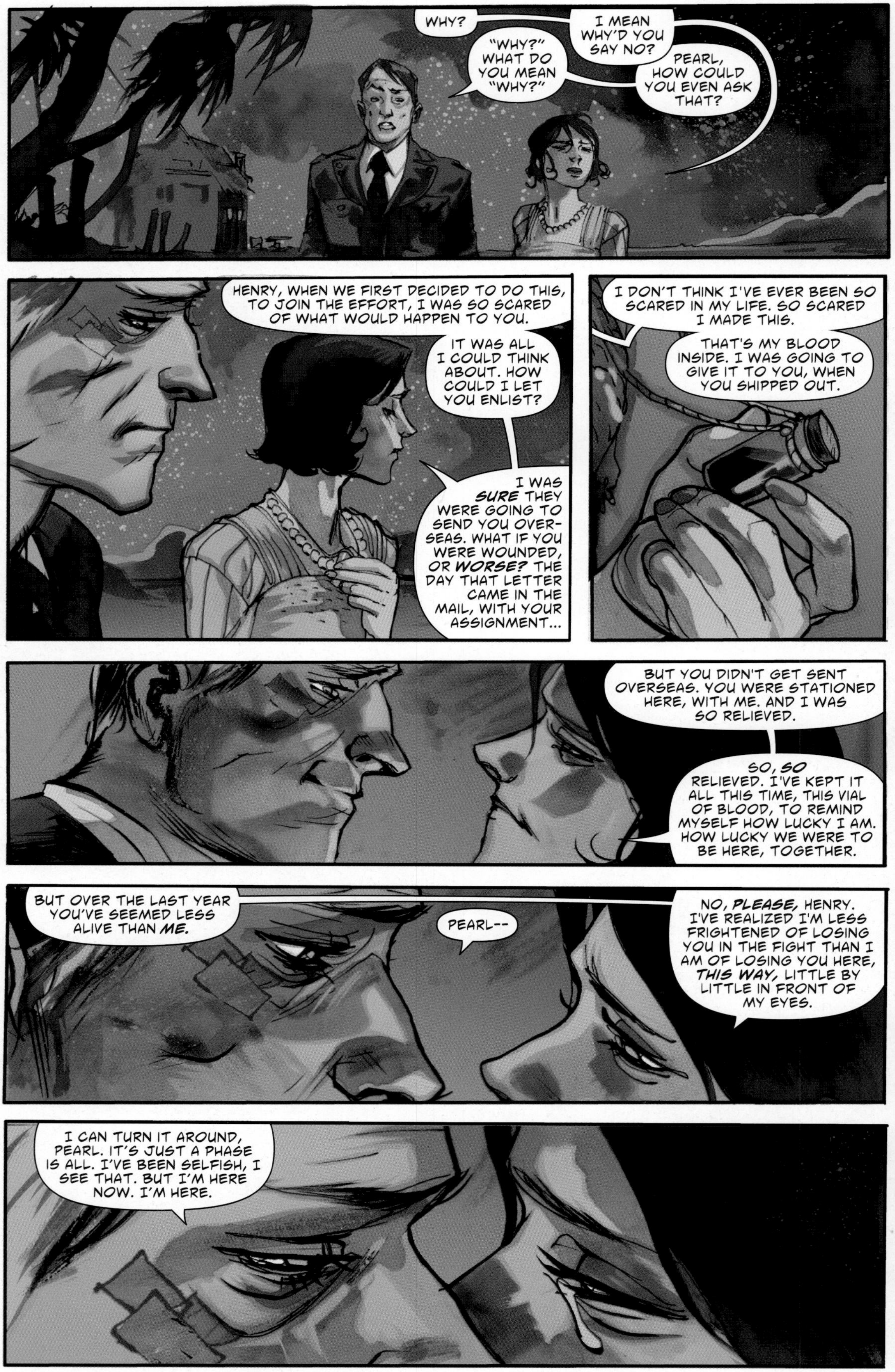
WHY?
I MEAN WHY'D YOU SAY NO?
"WHY?" WHAT DO YOU MEAN "WHY?"
PEARL, HOW COULD YOU EVEN ASK THAT?
HENRY, WHEN WE FIRST DECIDED TO DO THIS, TO JOIN THE EFFORT, I WAS SO SCARED OF WHAT WOULD HAPPEN TO YOU.
IT WAS ALL I COULD THINK ABOUT. HOW COULD I LET YOU ENLIST?
I WAS ***SURE*** THEY WERE GOING TO SEND YOU OVER-SEAS. WHAT IF YOU WERE WOUNDED, OR ***WORSE?*** THE DAY THAT LETTER CAME IN THE MAIL, WITH YOUR ASSIGNMENT...
I DON'T THINK I'VE EVER BEEN SO SCARED IN MY LIFE. SO SCARED I MADE THIS.
THAT'S MY BLOOD INSIDE. I WAS GOING TO GIVE IT TO YOU, WHEN YOU SHIPPED OUT.
BUT YOU DIDN'T GET SENT OVERSEAS. YOU WERE STATIONED HERE, WITH ME. AND I WAS SO RELIEVED.
SO, ***SO*** RELIEVED. I'VE KEPT IT ALL THIS TIME, THIS VIAL OF BLOOD, TO REMIND MYSELF HOW LUCKY I AM. HOW LUCKY WE WERE TO BE HERE, TOGETHER.
BUT OVER THE LAST YEAR YOU'VE SEEMED LESS ALIVE THAN ***ME.***
PEARL--
NO, ***PLEASE,*** HENRY. I'VE REALIZED I'M LESS FRIGHTENED OF LOSING YOU IN THE FIGHT THAN I AM OF LOSING YOU HERE, ***THIS WAY,*** LITTLE BY LITTLE IN FRONT OF MY EYES.
I CAN TURN IT AROUND, PEARL. IT'S JUST A PHASE IS ALL. I'VE BEEN SELFISH, I SEE THAT. BUT I'M HERE NOW. I'M HERE.

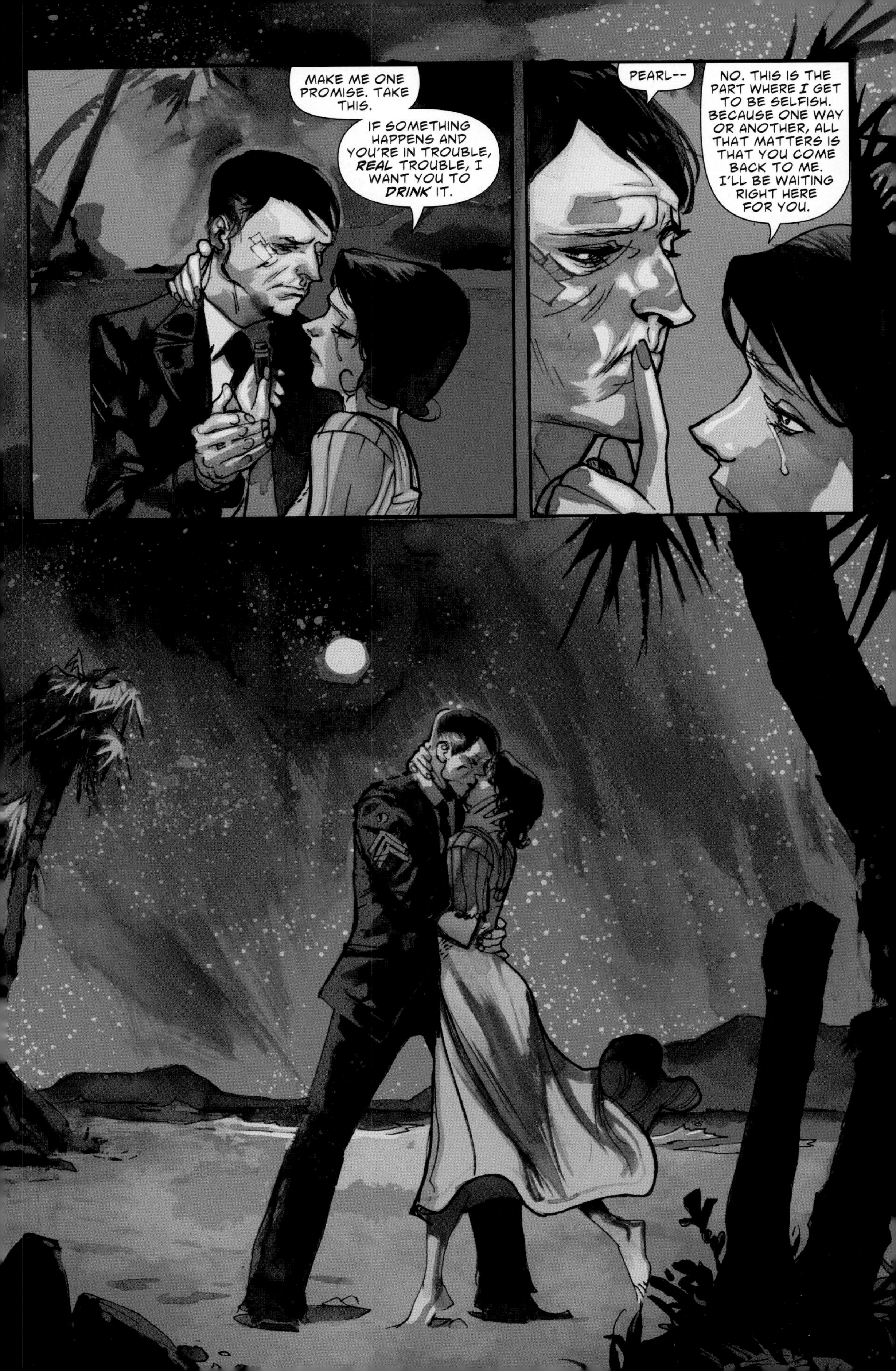
MAKE ME ONE PROMISE. TAKE THIS.
IF SOMETHING HAPPENS AND YOU'RE IN TROUBLE, REAL TROUBLE, I WANT YOU TO DRINK IT.
PEARL--
NO. THIS IS THE PART WHERE I GET TO BE SELFISH. BECAUSE ONE WAY OR ANOTHER, ALL THAT MATTERS IS THAT YOU COME BACK TO ME. I'LL BE WAITING RIGHT HERE FOR YOU.

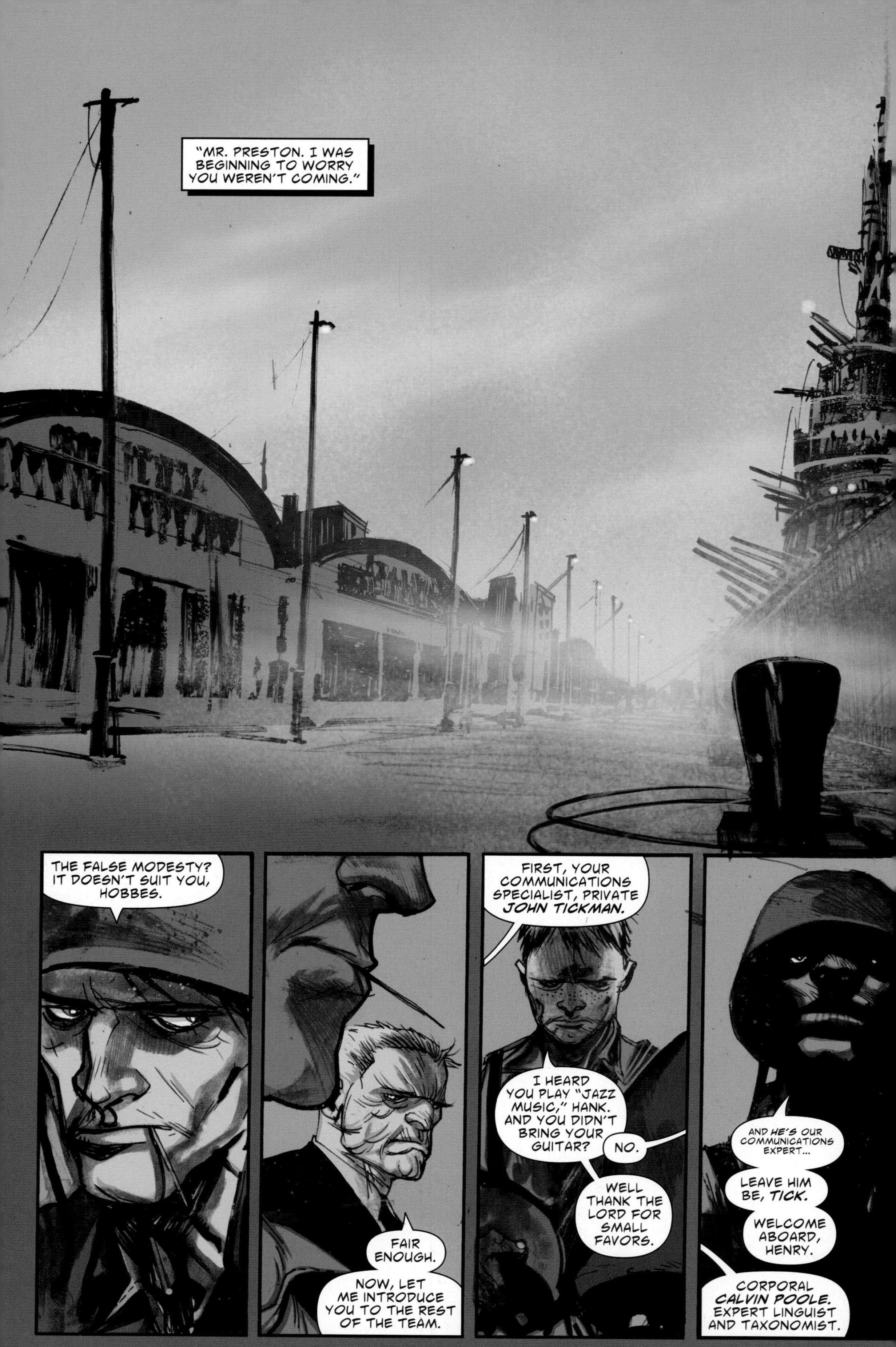
"MR. PRESTON. I WAS BEGINNING TO WORRY YOU WEREN'T COMING."
THE FALSE MODESTY? IT DOESN'T SUIT YOU, HOBBES.
FAIR ENOUGH.
NOW, LET ME INTRODUCE YOU TO THE REST OF THE TEAM.
FIRST, YOUR COMMUNICATIONS SPECIALIST, PRIVATE JOHN TICKMAN.
I HEARD YOU PLAY "JAZZ MUSIC," HANK. AND YOU DIDN'T BRING YOUR GUITAR?
NO.
WELL THANK THE LORD FOR SMALL FAVORS.
AND HE'S OUR COMMUNICATIONS EXPERT...
LEAVE HIM BE, TICK.
WELCOME ABOARD, HENRY.
CORPORAL CALVIN POOLE. EXPERT LINGUIST AND TAXONOMIST.

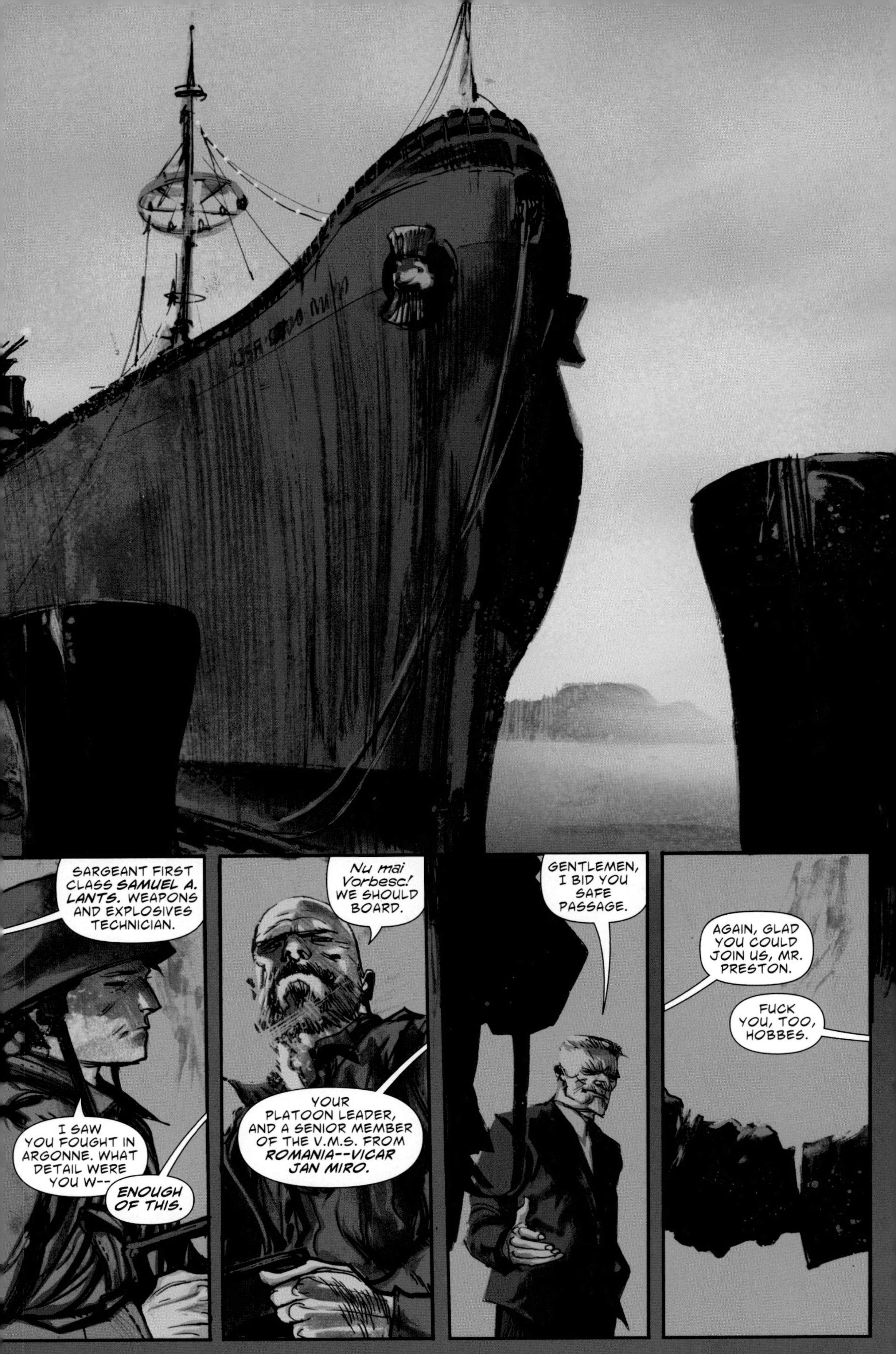
SARGEANT FIRST CLASS **SAMUEL A. LANTS.** WEAPONS AND EXPLOSIVES TECHNICIAN.
I SAW YOU FOUGHT IN ARGONNE. WHAT DETAIL WERE YOU W--
ENOUGH OF THIS.
Nu mai Vorbesc! WE SHOULD BOARD.
YOUR PLATOON LEADER, AND A SENIOR MEMBER OF THE V.M.S. FROM ***ROMANIA--VICAR JAN MIRO.***
GENTLEMEN, I BID YOU SAFE PASSAGE.
AGAIN, GLAD YOU COULD JOIN US, MR. PRESTON.
FUCK YOU, TOO, HOBBES.

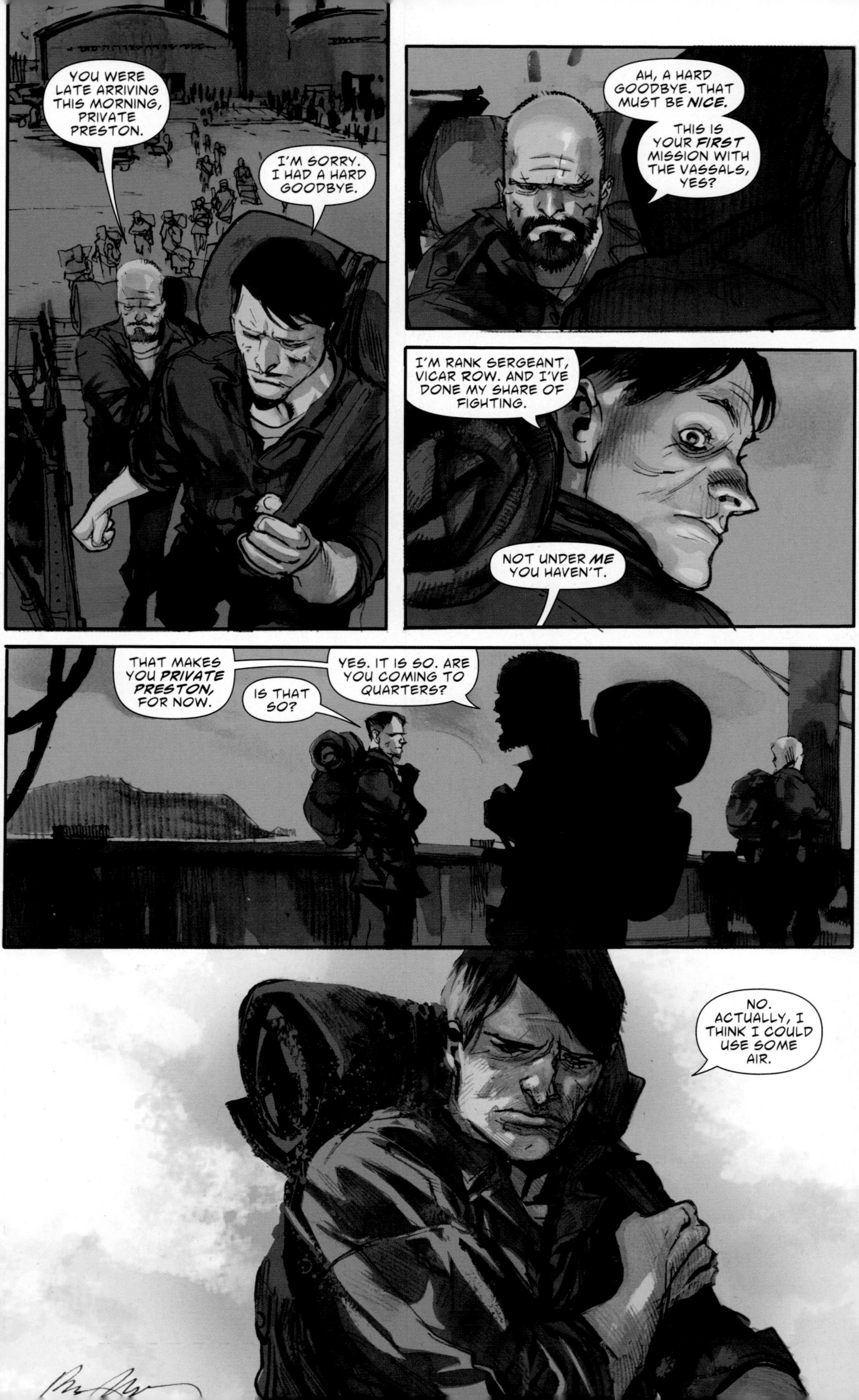
YOU WERE LATE ARRIVING THIS MORNING, PRIVATE PRESTON.
I'M SORRY. I HAD A HARD GOODBYE.
AH, A HARD GOODBYE. THAT MUST BE NICE.
THIS IS YOUR FIRST MISSION WITH THE VASSALS, YES?
I'M RANK SERGEANT, VICAR ROW. AND I'VE DONE MY SHARE OF FIGHTING.
NOT UNDER ME YOU HAVEN'T.
THAT MAKES YOU PRIVATE PRESTON, FOR NOW.
IS THAT SO?
YES. IT IS SO. ARE YOU COMING TO QUARTERS?
NO. ACTUALLY, I THINK I COULD USE SOME AIR.

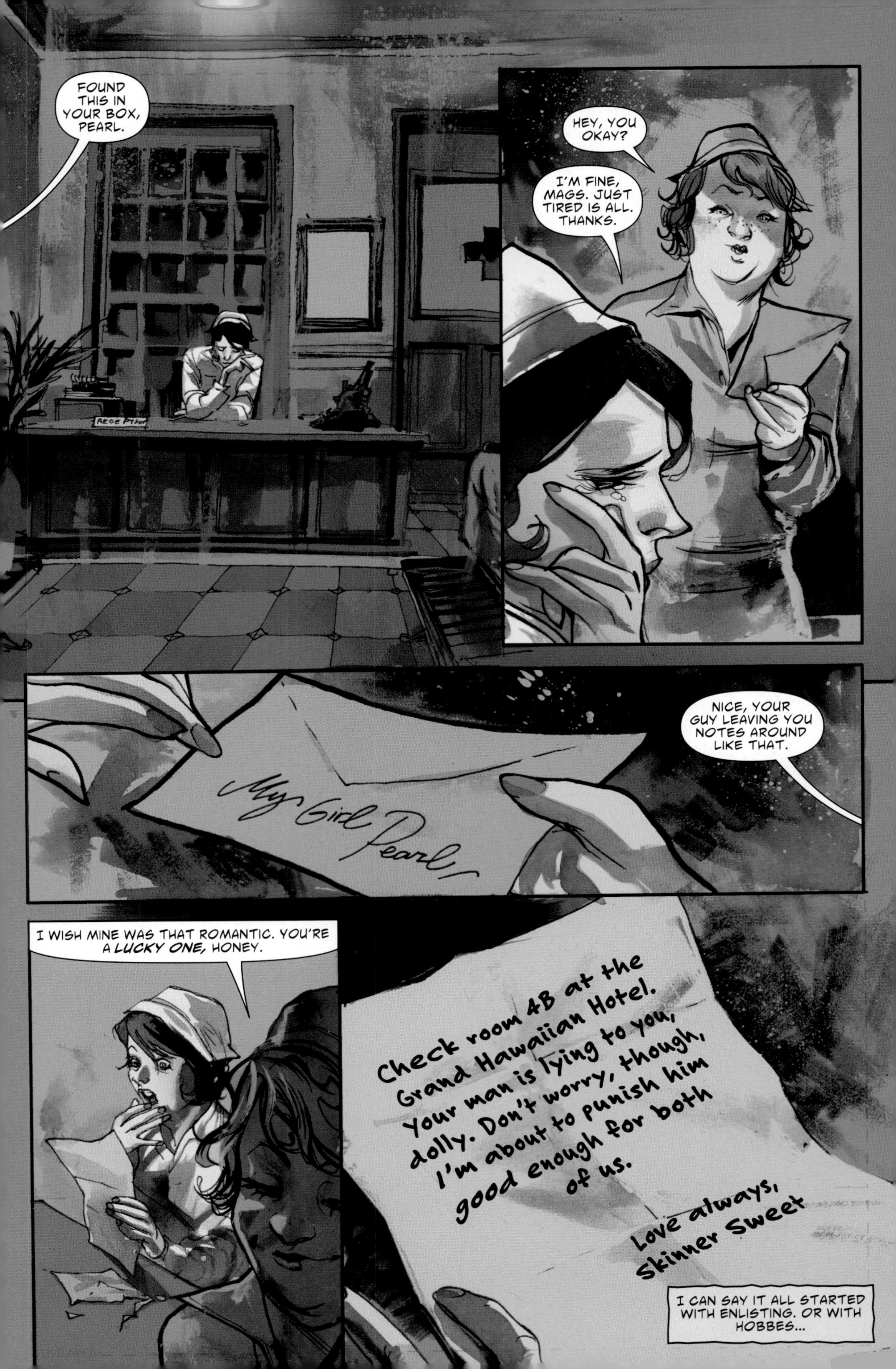

FOUND THIS IN YOUR BOX, PEARL.
HEY, YOU OKAY?
I'M FINE, MAGS. JUST TIRED IS ALL. THANKS.
NICE, YOUR GUY LEAVING YOU NOTES AROUND LIKE THAT.
My Girl Pearl
I WISH MINE WAS THAT ROMANTIC. YOU'RE A LUCKY ONE, HONEY.
Check room 4B at the Grand Hawaiian Hotel. Your man is lying to you, dolly. Don't worry, though, I'm about to punish him good enough for both of us.
Love always, Skinner Sweet
I CAN SAY IT ALL STARTED WITH ENLISTING. OR WITH HOBBES...

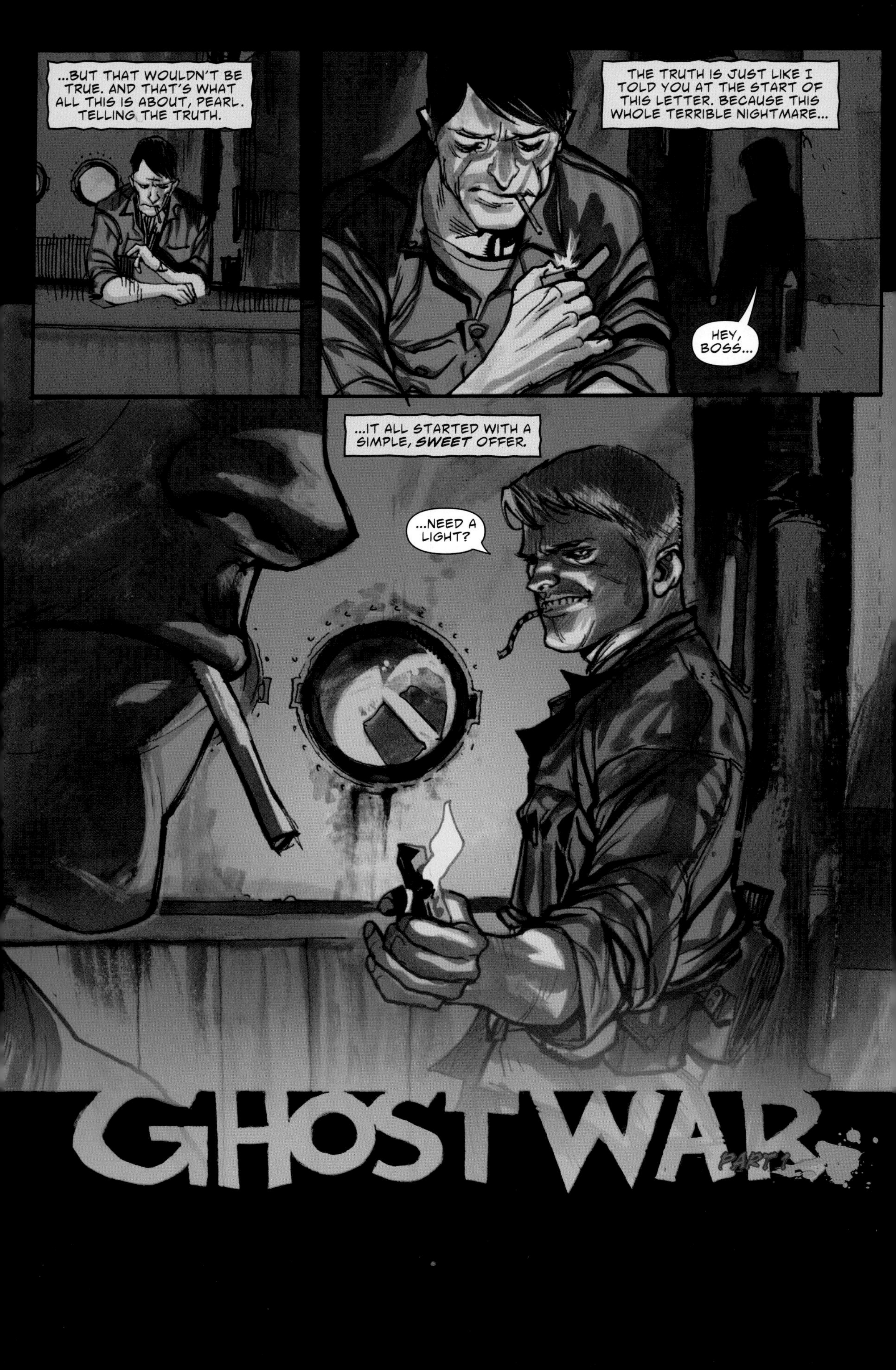
...BUT THAT WOULDN'T BE TRUE. AND THAT'S WHAT ALL THIS IS ABOUT, PEARL. TELLING THE TRUTH.
THE TRUTH IS JUST LIKE I TOLD YOU AT THE START OF THIS LETTER. BECAUSE THIS WHOLE TERRIBLE NIGHTMARE...
HEY, BOSS...
...IT ALL STARTED WITH A SIMPLE, SWEET OFFER.
...NEED A LIGHT?
GHOST WAR
PART 1

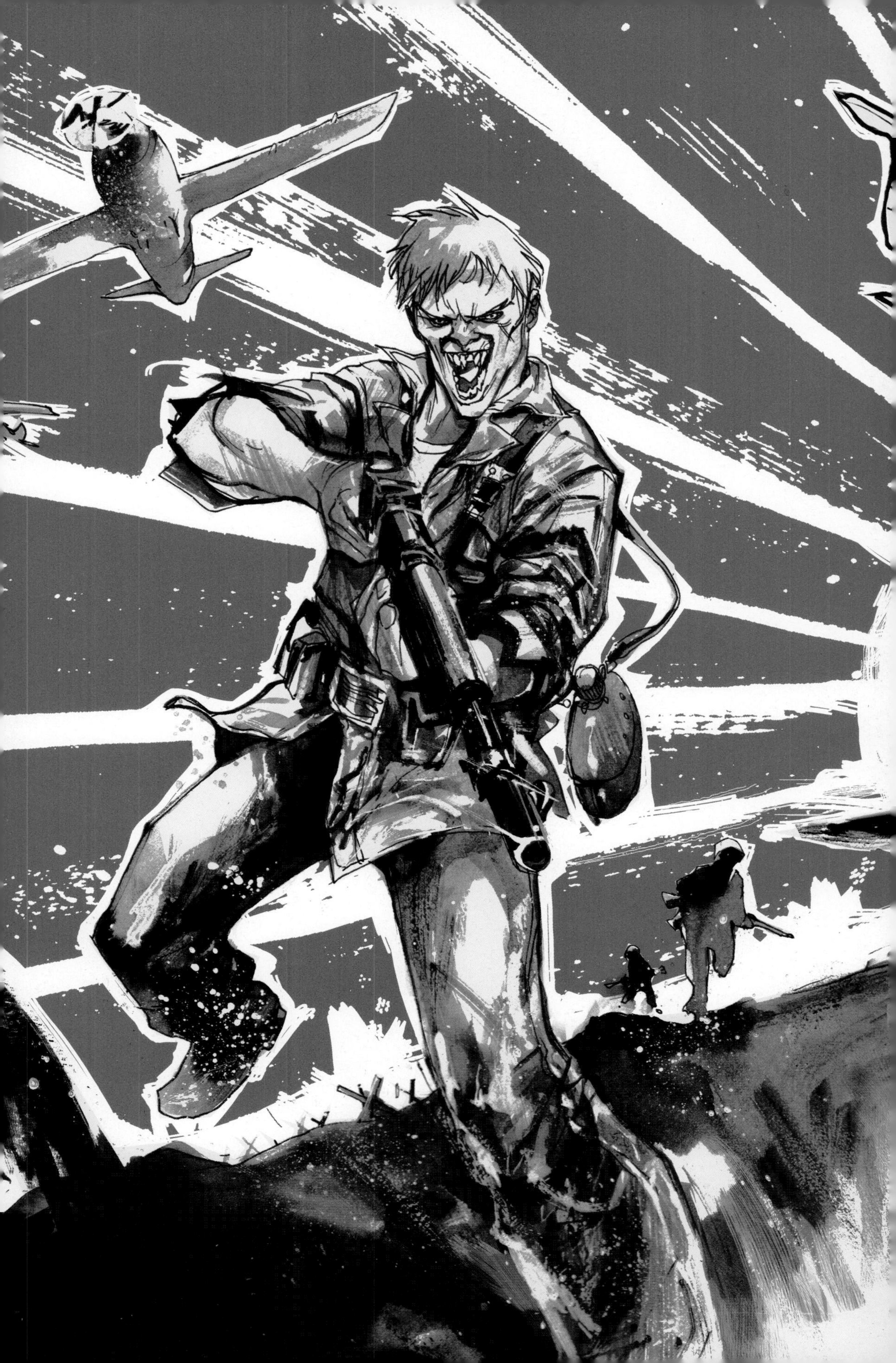

Ghost War

Part Two

Rafael Albuquerque
Artist and cover

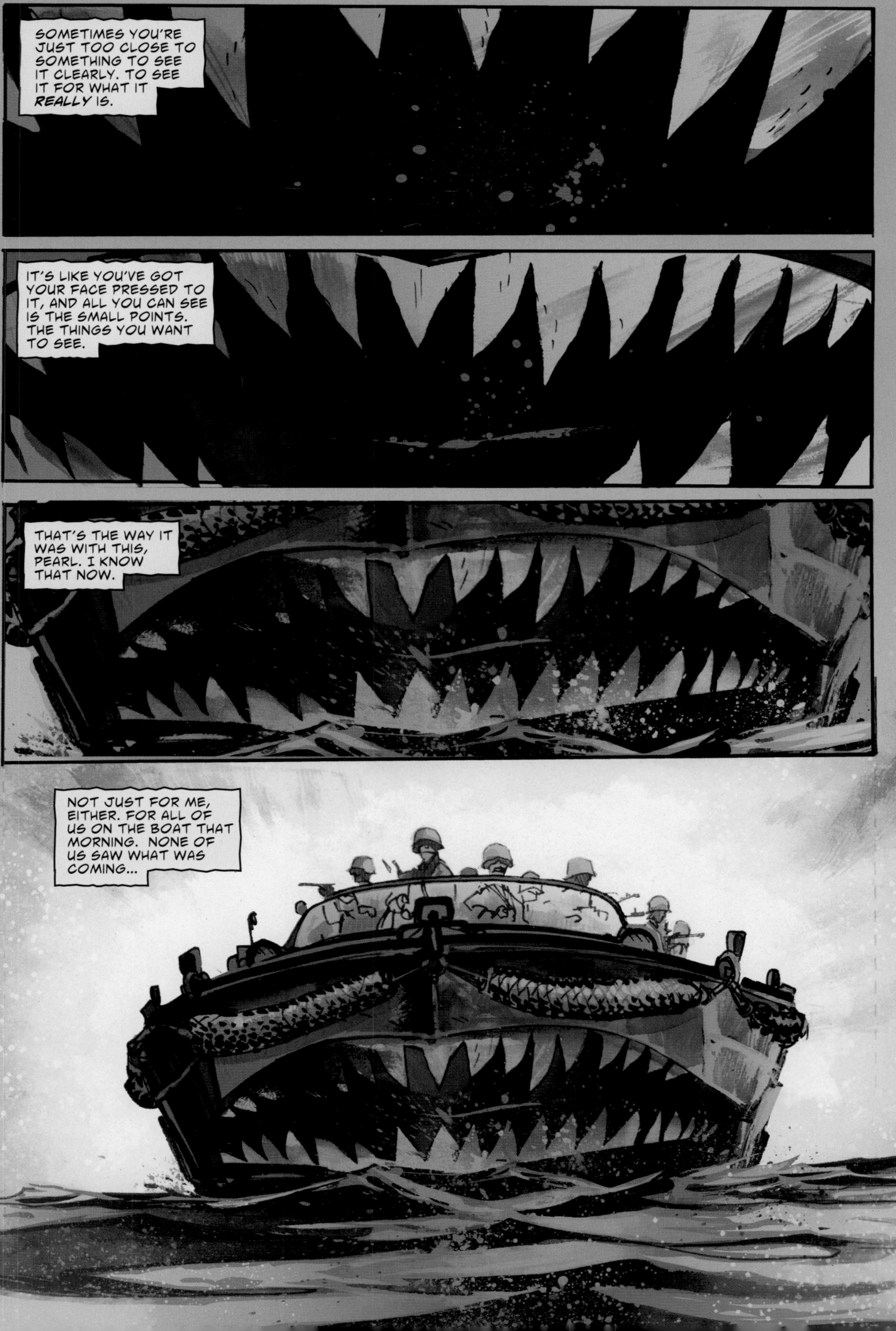
SOMETIMES YOU'RE JUST TOO CLOSE TO SOMETHING TO SEE IT CLEARLY. TO SEE IT FOR WHAT IT *REALLY* IS.
IT'S LIKE YOU'VE GOT YOUR FACE PRESSED TO IT, AND ALL YOU CAN SEE IS THE SMALL POINTS. THE THINGS YOU WANT TO SEE.
THAT'S THE WAY IT WAS WITH THIS, PEARL. I KNOW THAT NOW.
NOT JUST FOR ME, EITHER. FOR ALL OF US ON THE BOAT THAT MORNING. NONE OF US SAW WHAT WAS COMING...

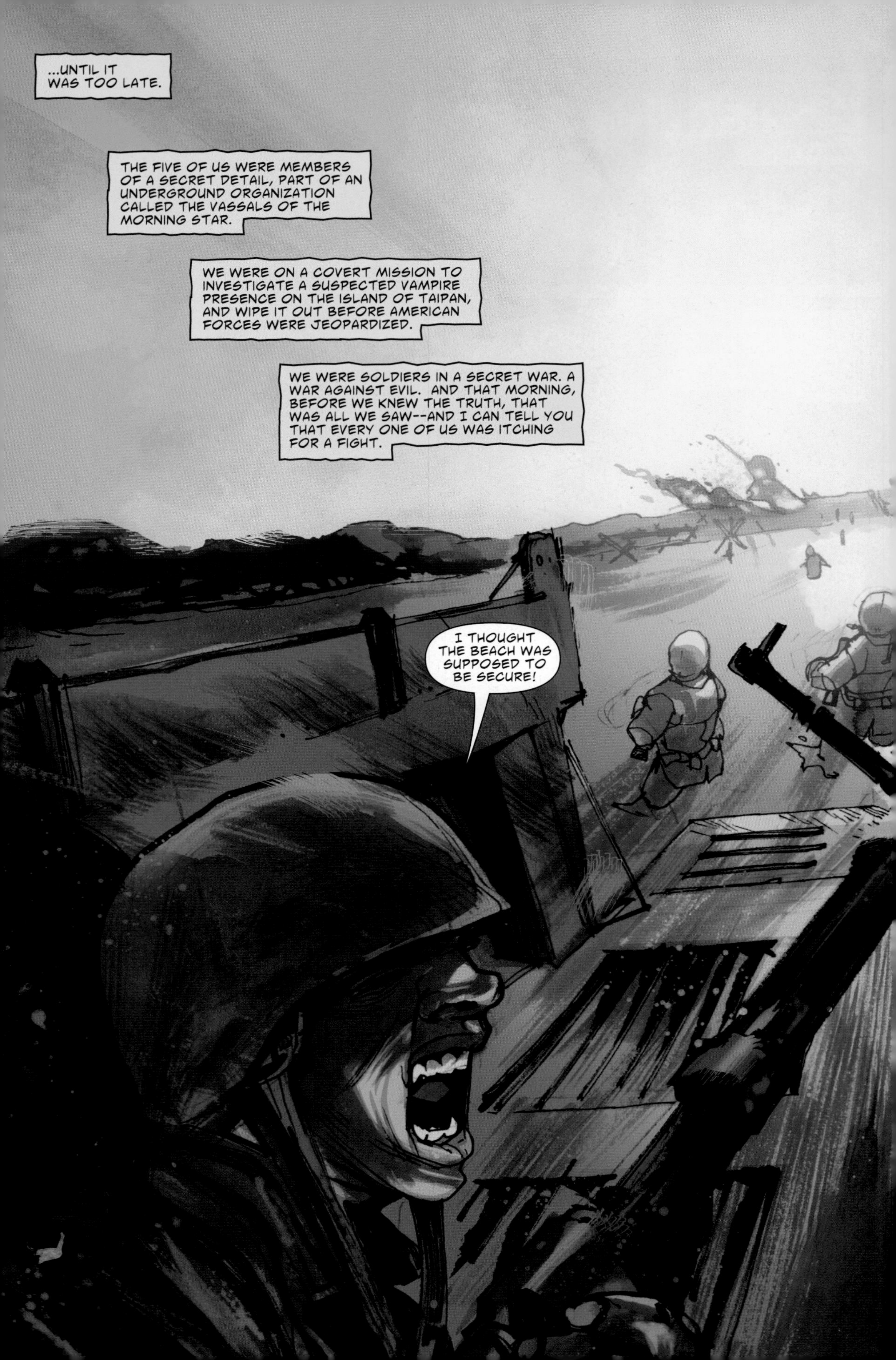
...UNTIL IT WAS TOO LATE.
THE FIVE OF US WERE MEMBERS OF A SECRET DETAIL, PART OF AN UNDERGROUND ORGANIZATION CALLED THE VASSALS OF THE MORNING STAR.
WE WERE ON A COVERT MISSION TO INVESTIGATE A SUSPECTED VAMPIRE PRESENCE ON THE ISLAND OF TAIPAN, AND WIPE IT OUT BEFORE AMERICAN FORCES WERE JEOPARDIZED.
WE WERE SOLDIERS IN A SECRET WAR. A WAR AGAINST EVIL. AND THAT MORNING, BEFORE WE KNEW THE TRUTH, THAT WAS ALL WE SAW--AND I CAN TELL YOU THAT EVERY ONE OF US WAS ITCHING FOR A FIGHT.
I THOUGHT THE BEACH WAS SUPPOSED TO BE SECURE!

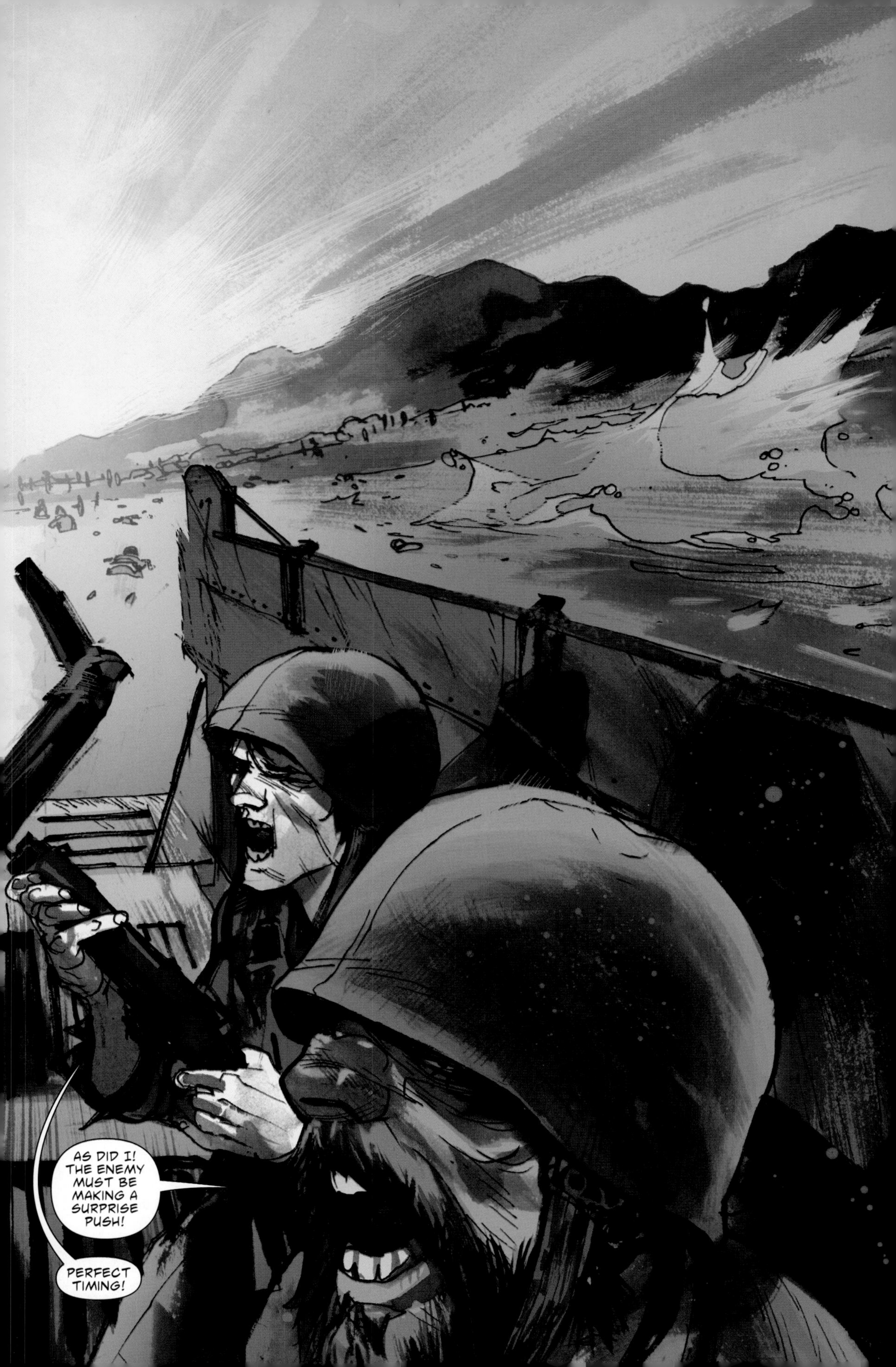
AS DID I! THE ENEMY MUST BE MAKING A SURPRISE PUSH!
PERFECT TIMING!

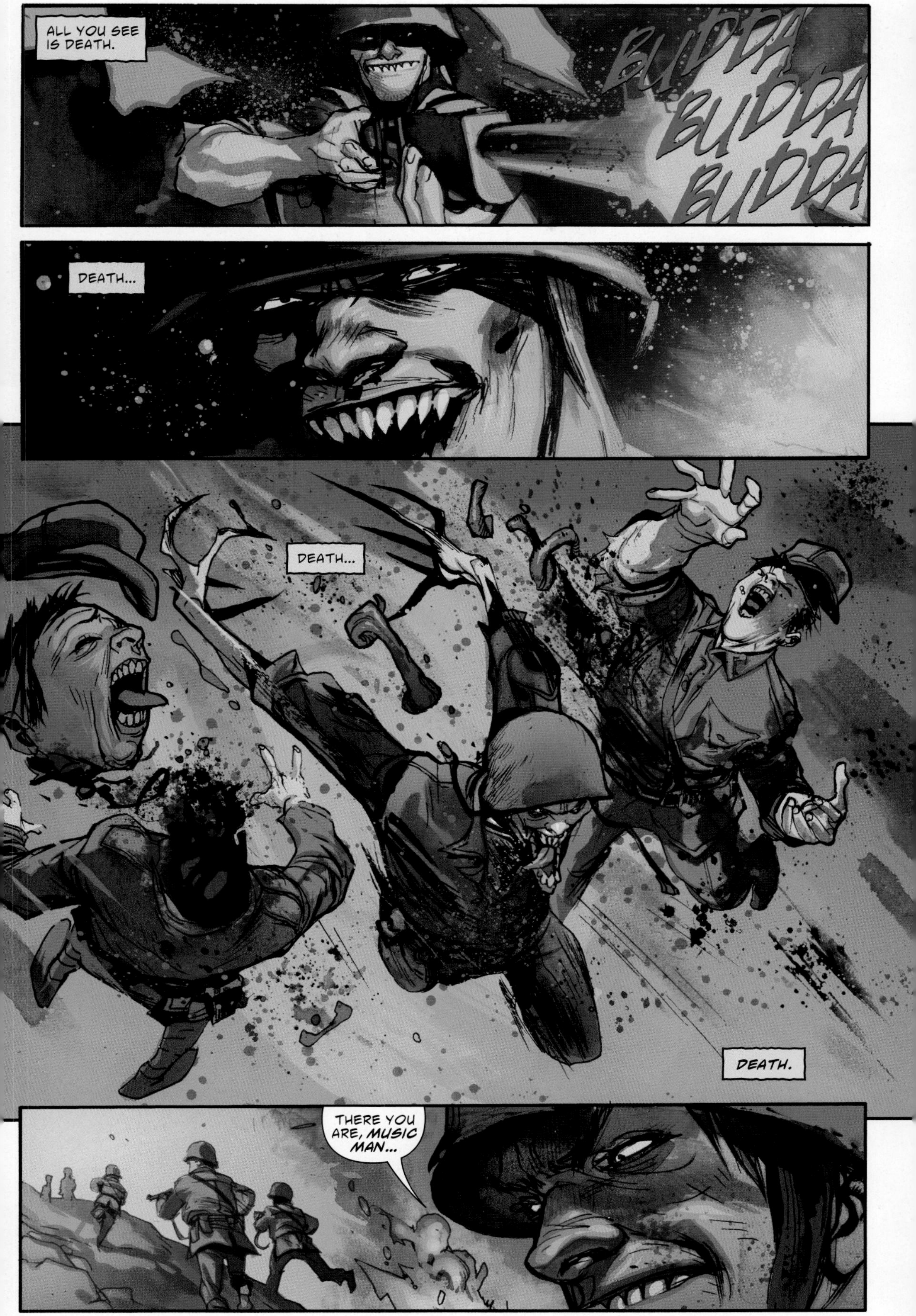

ALL YOU SEE IS DEATH.
BUDDA BUDDA BUDDA
DEATH...
DEATH...
DEATH.
THERE YOU ARE, MUSIC MAN...

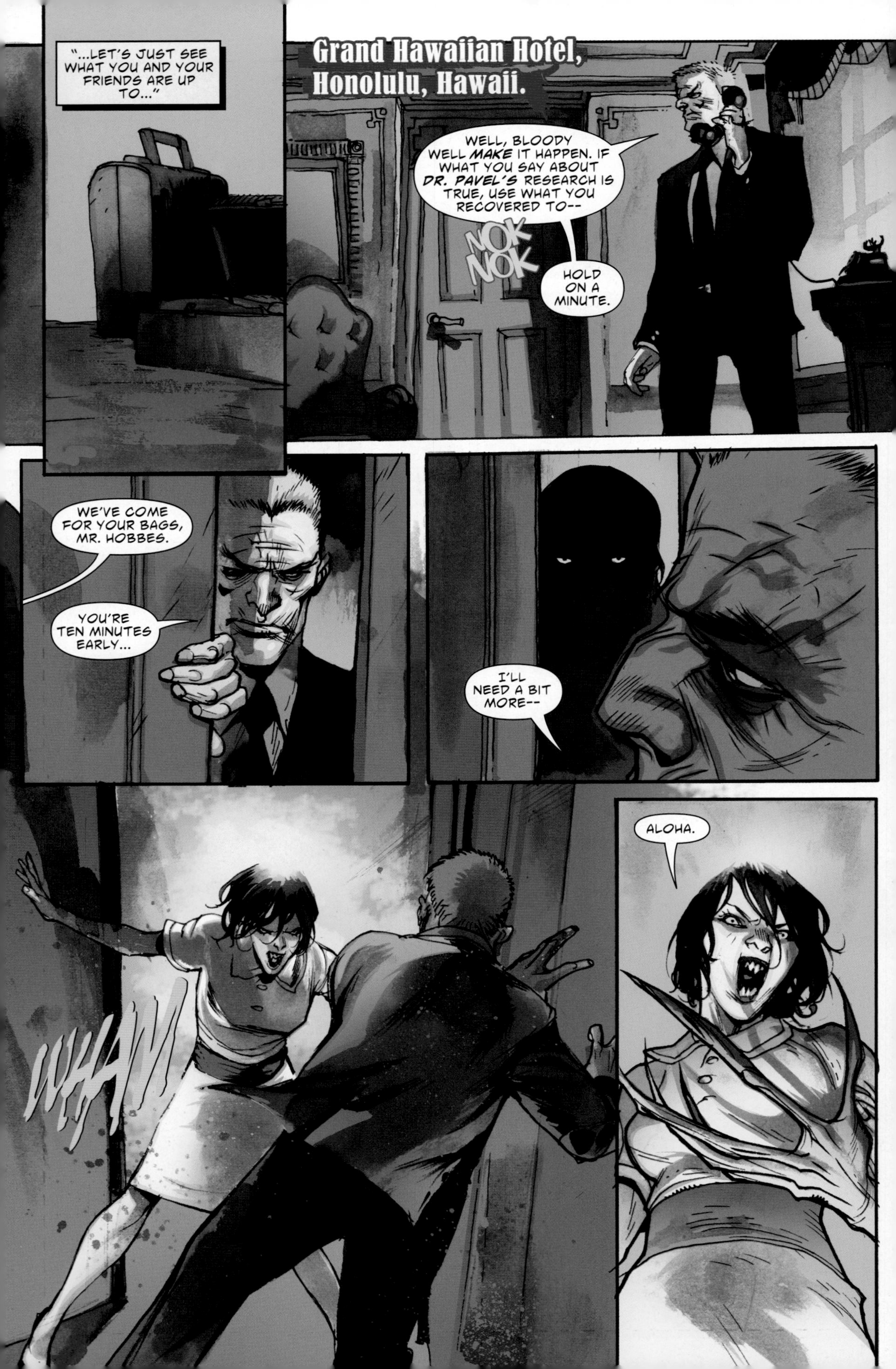

"...LET'S JUST SEE WHAT YOU AND YOUR FRIENDS ARE UP TO..."
Grand Hawaiian Hotel, Honolulu, Hawaii.
WELL, BLOODY WELL MAKE IT HAPPEN. IF WHAT YOU SAY ABOUT DR. PAVEL'S RESEARCH IS TRUE, USE WHAT YOU RECOVERED TO--
NOK NOK
HOLD ON A MINUTE.
WE'VE COME FOR YOUR BAGS, MR. HOBBES.
YOU'RE TEN MINUTES EARLY...
I'LL NEED A BIT MORE--
WHAM
ALOHA.

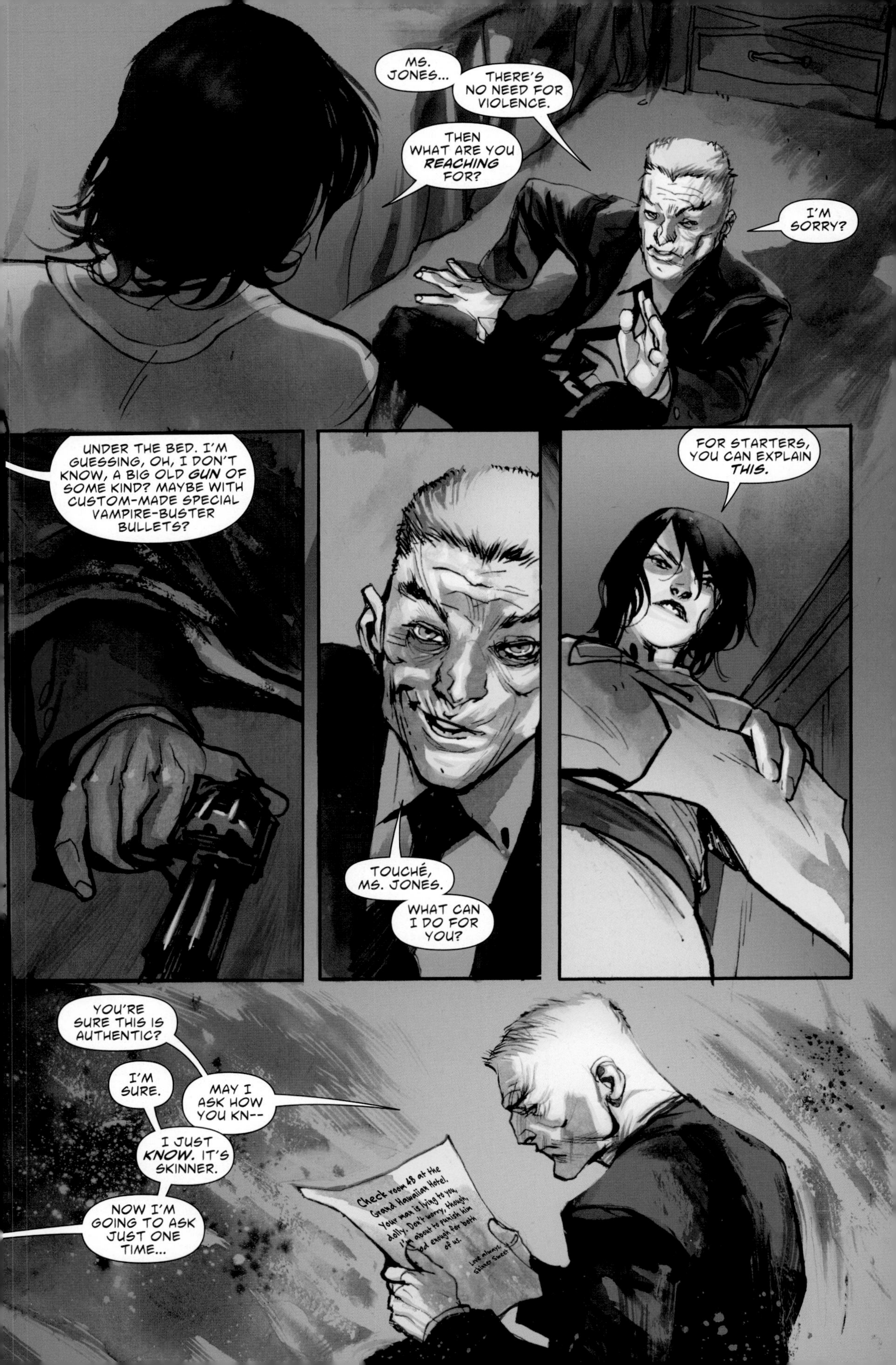
MS. JONES...
THERE'S NO NEED FOR VIOLENCE.
THEN WHAT ARE YOU *REACHING* FOR?
I'M SORRY?
UNDER THE BED. I'M GUESSING, OH, I DON'T KNOW, A BIG OLD *GUN* OF SOME KIND? MAYBE WITH CUSTOM-MADE SPECIAL VAMPIRE-BUSTER BULLETS?
TOUCHÉ, MS. JONES.
WHAT CAN I DO FOR YOU?
FOR STARTERS, YOU CAN EXPLAIN *THIS.*
YOU'RE SURE THIS IS AUTHENTIC?
I'M SURE.
MAY I ASK HOW YOU KN--
I JUST *KNOW.* IT'S SKINNER.
NOW I'M GOING TO ASK JUST ONE TIME...
Check room 48 at the Grand Hawaiian Hotel. Your man is lying to you, dolly. Don't worry, though, I'm about to punish him od enough for both of us.
Love always, Skinner Sweet

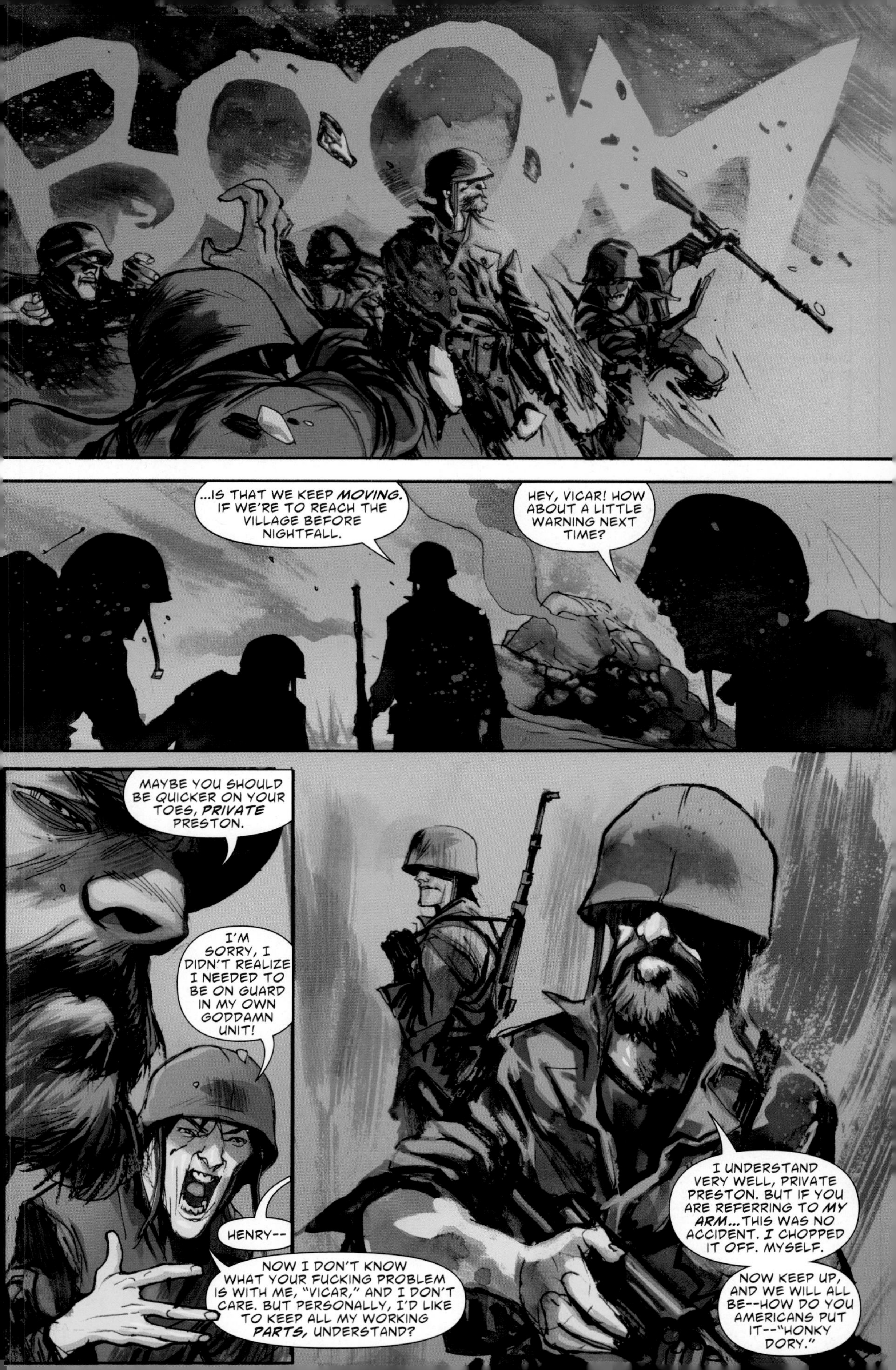
...IS THAT WE KEEP *MOVING.* IF WE'RE TO REACH THE VILLAGE BEFORE NIGHTFALL.
HEY, VICAR! HOW ABOUT A LITTLE WARNING NEXT TIME?
MAYBE YOU SHOULD BE QUICKER ON YOUR TOES, *PRIVATE* PRESTON.
I'M SORRY, I DIDN'T REALIZE I NEEDED TO BE ON GUARD IN MY OWN GODDAMN UNIT!
HENRY--
NOW I DON'T KNOW WHAT YOUR FUCKING PROBLEM IS WITH ME, "VICAR," AND I DON'T CARE. BUT PERSONALLY, I'D LIKE TO KEEP ALL MY WORKING *PARTS,* UNDERSTAND?
I UNDERSTAND VERY WELL, PRIVATE PRESTON. BUT IF YOU ARE REFERRING TO *MY ARM...* THIS WAS NO ACCIDENT. *I* CHOPPED IT OFF. MYSELF.
NOW KEEP UP, AND WE WILL ALL BE--HOW DO YOU AMERICANS PUT IT--"HONKY DORY."

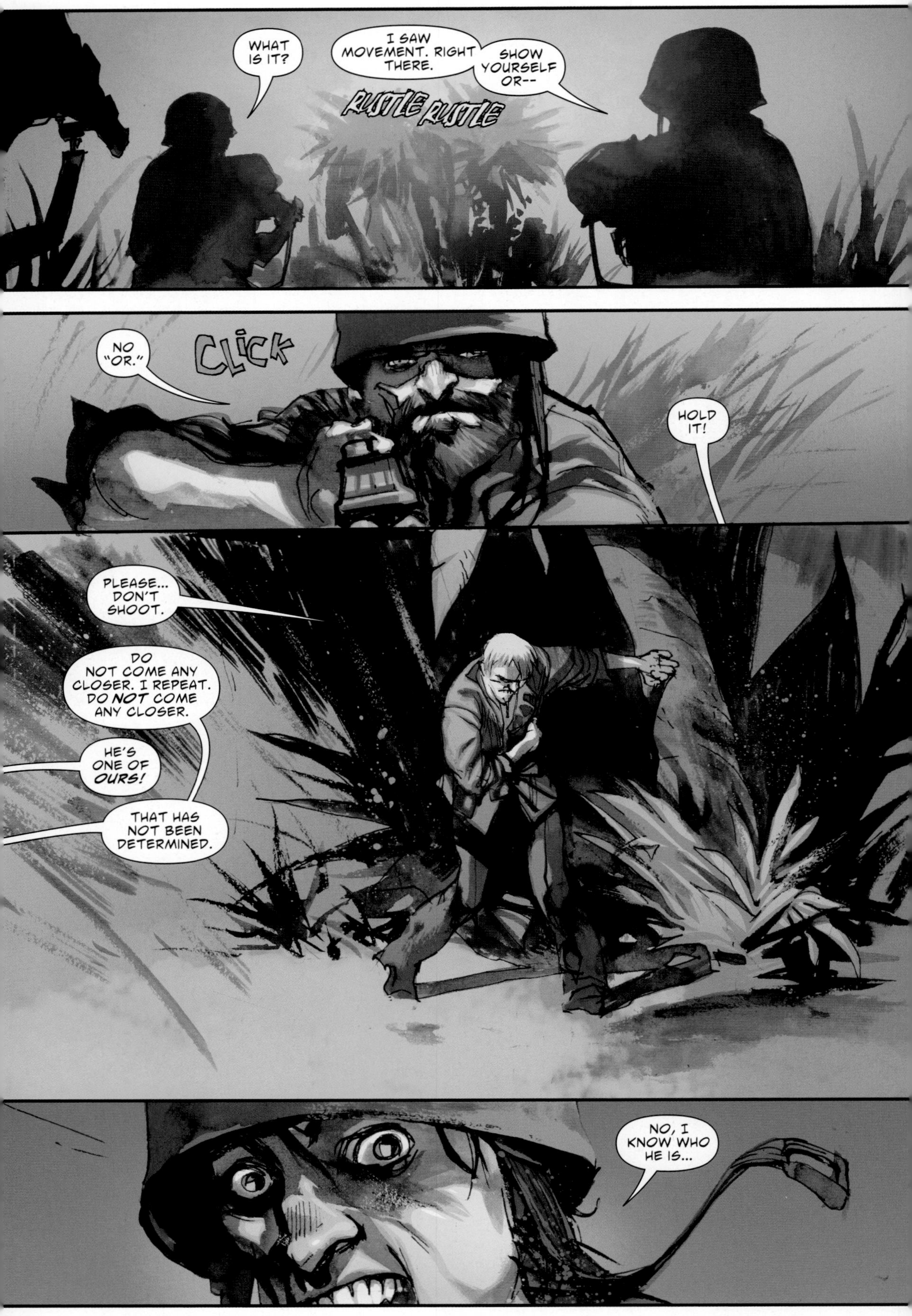
WHAT IS IT?
I SAW MOVEMENT. RIGHT THERE.
SHOW YOURSELF OR--
RUSTLE RUSTLE
NO "OR."
CLICK
HOLD IT!
PLEASE... DON'T SHOOT.
DO NOT COME ANY CLOSER. I REPEAT. DO NOT COME ANY CLOSER.
HE'S ONE OF OURS!
THAT HAS NOT BEEN DETERMINED.
NO, I KNOW WHO HE IS...

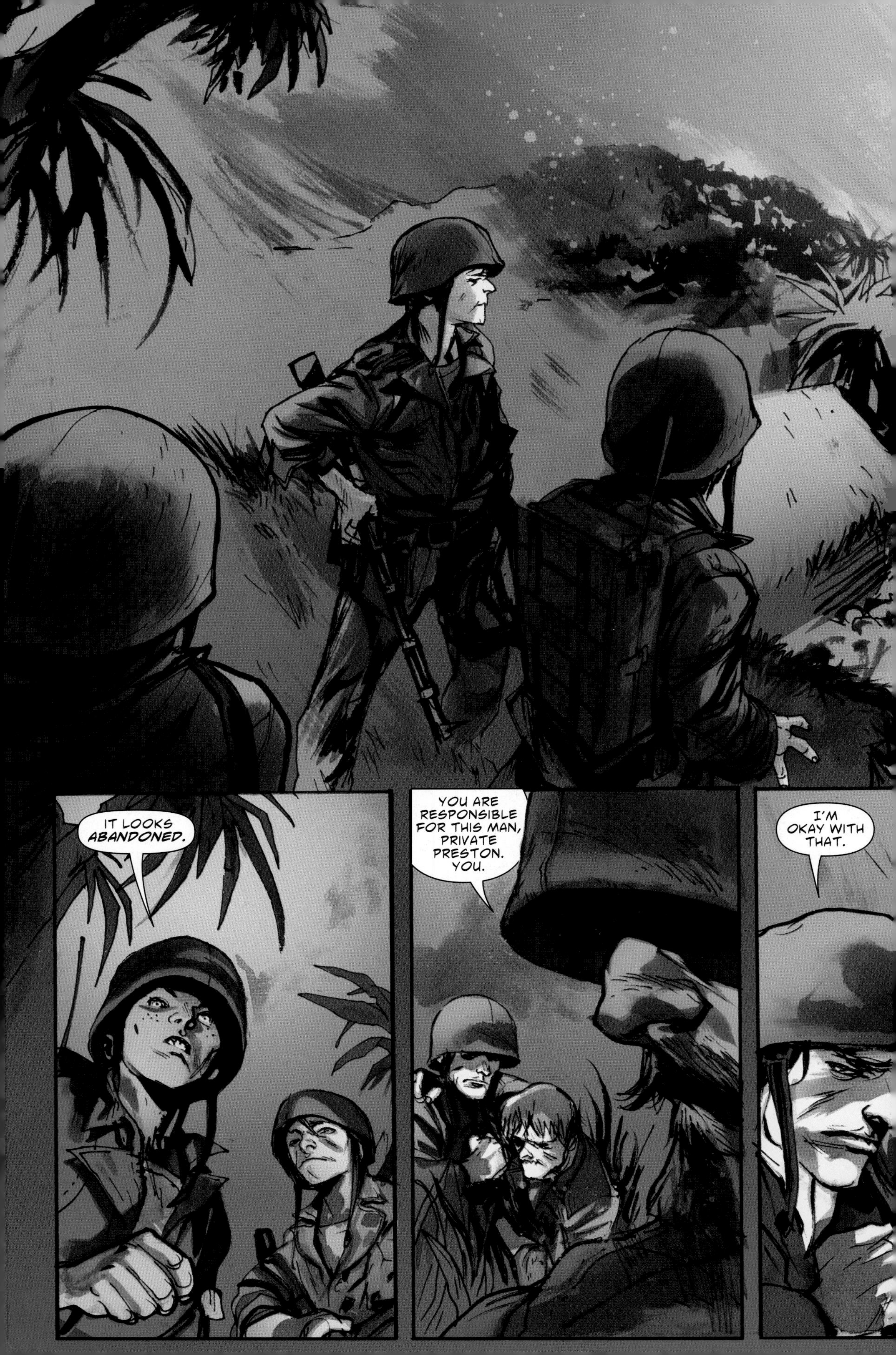
IT LOOKS ABANDONED.
YOU ARE RESPONSIBLE FOR THIS MAN, PRIVATE PRESTON. YOU.
I'M OKAY WITH THAT.

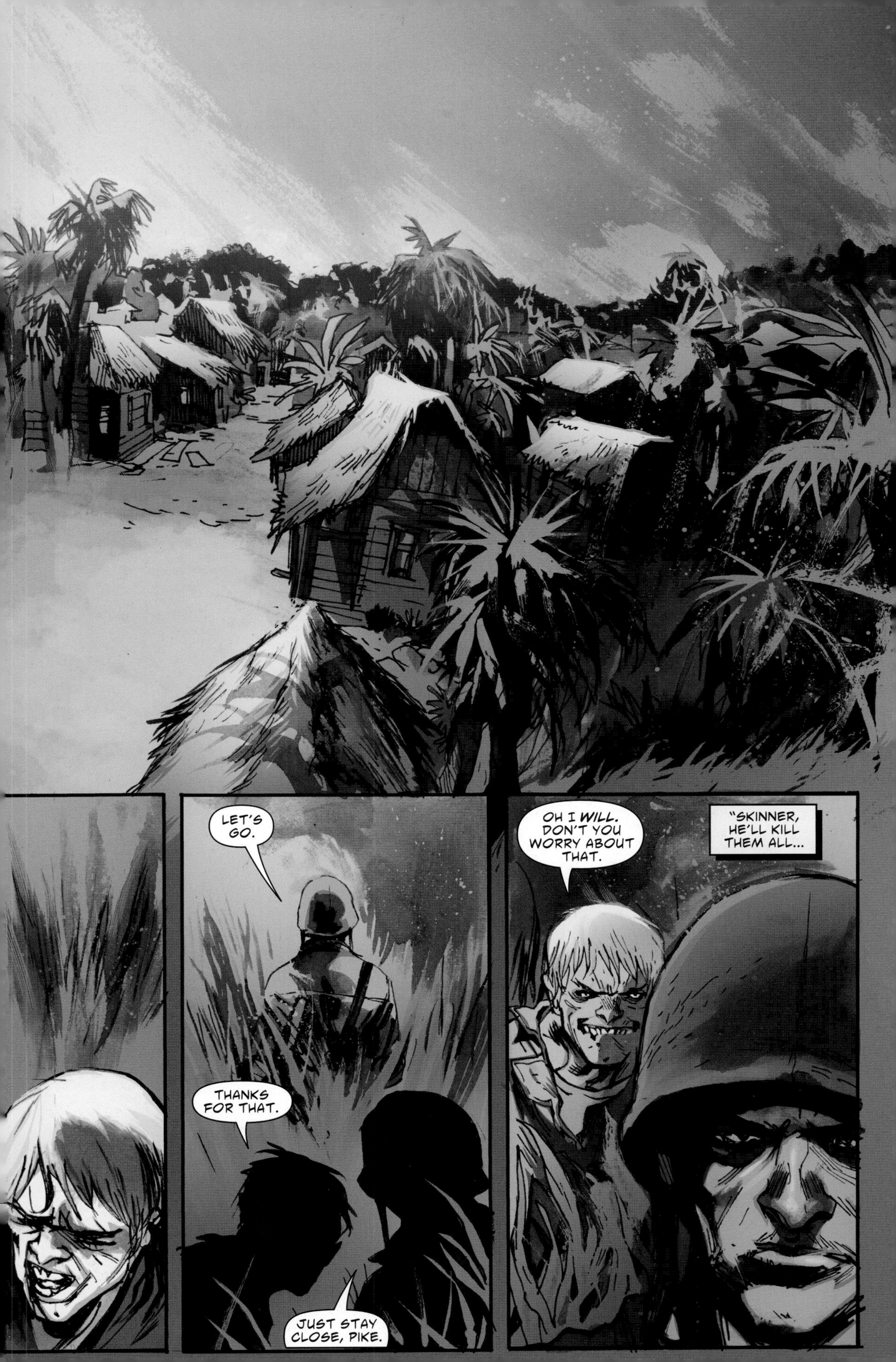
LET'S GO.
THANKS FOR THAT.
JUST STAY CLOSE, PIKE.
OH I WILL. DON'T YOU WORRY ABOUT THAT.
"SKINNER, HE'LL KILL THEM ALL...

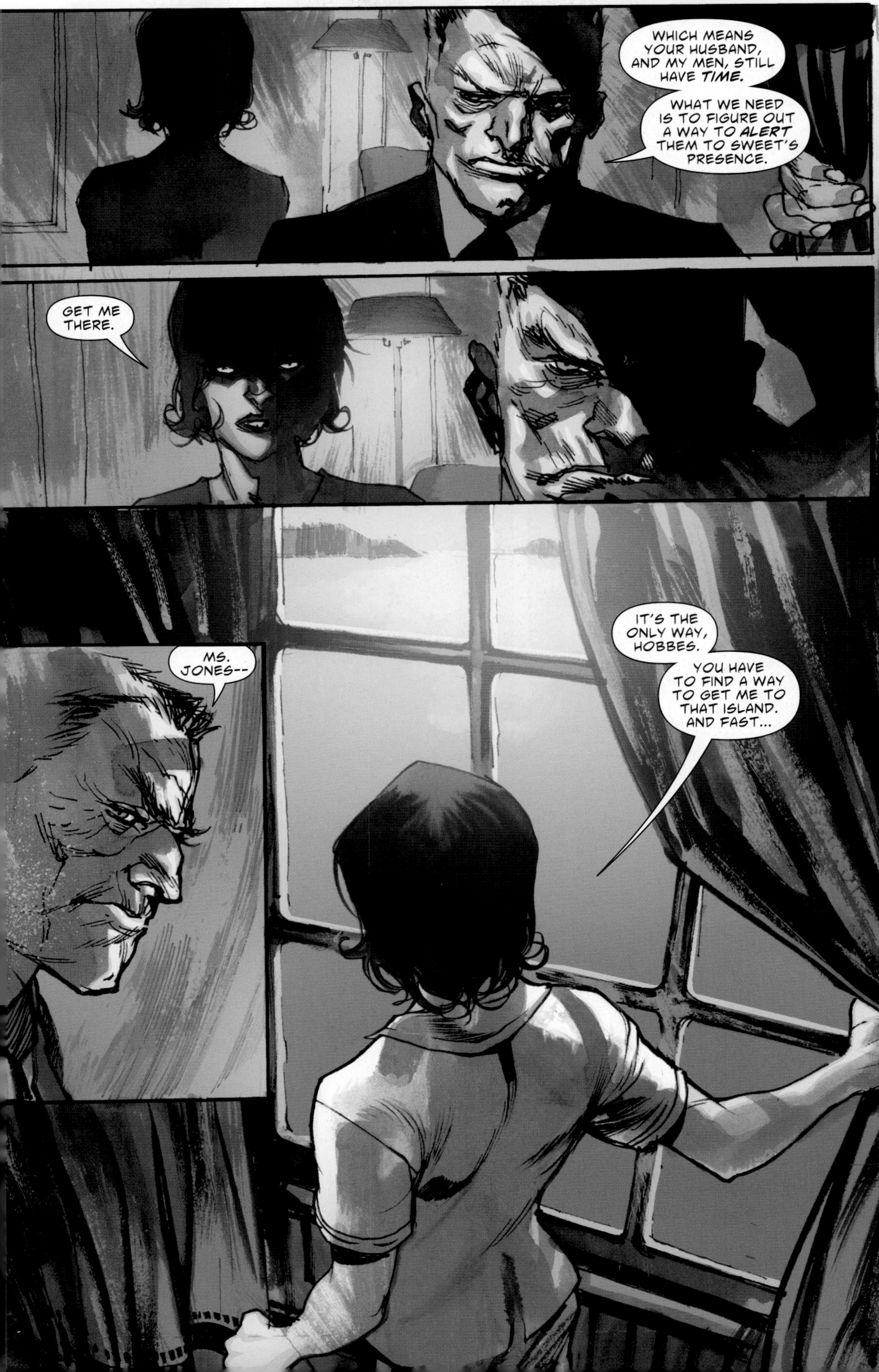
WHICH MEANS YOUR HUSBAND, AND MY MEN, STILL HAVE *TIME.*
WHAT WE NEED IS TO FIGURE OUT A WAY TO *ALERT* THEM TO SWEET'S PRESENCE.
GET ME THERE.
IT'S THE ONLY WAY, HOBBES.
YOU HAVE TO FIND A WAY TO GET ME TO THAT ISLAND. AND FAST...
MS. JONES--

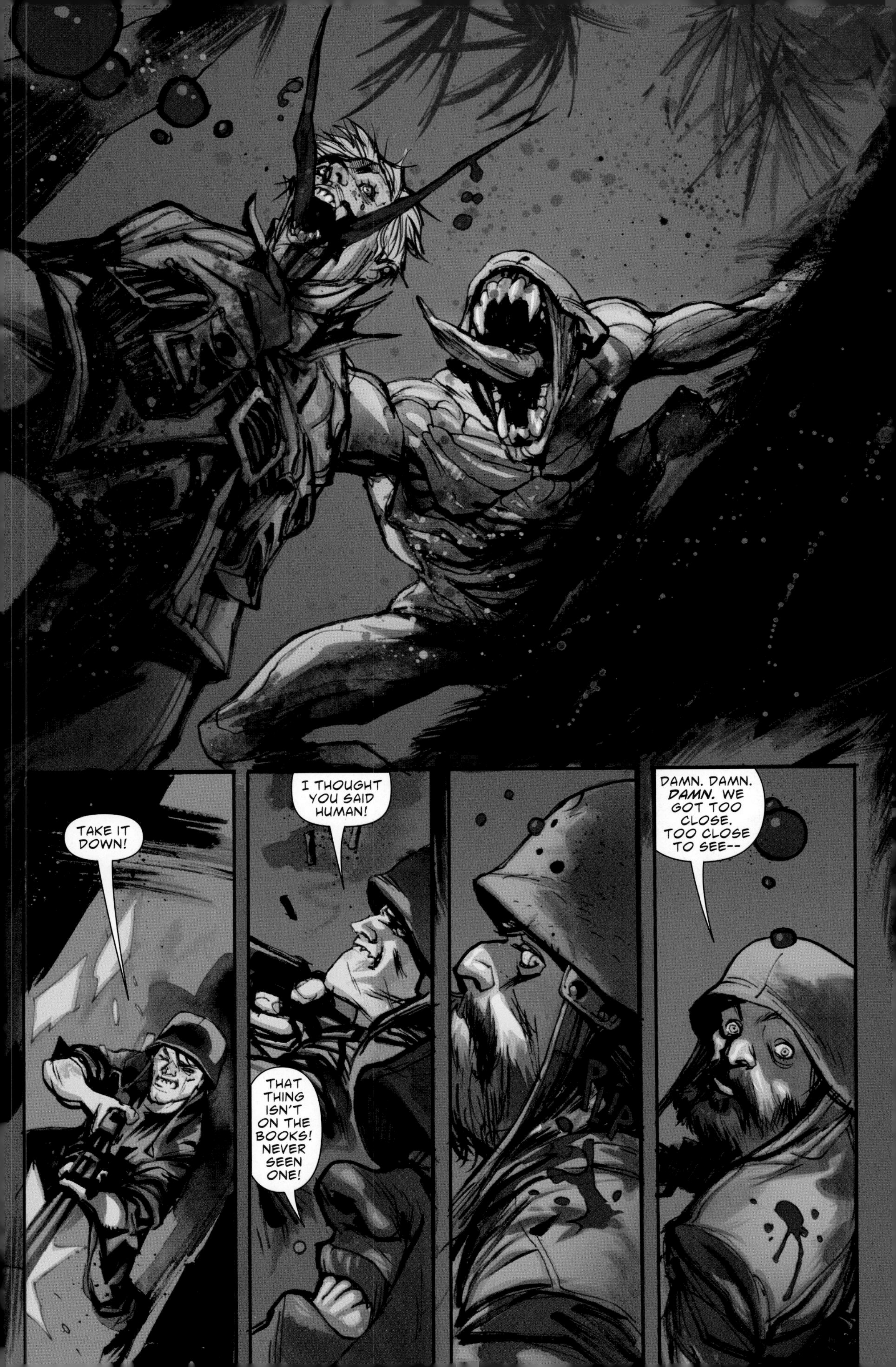
TAKE IT DOWN!
I THOUGHT YOU SAID HUMAN!
THAT THING ISN'T ON THE BOOKS! NEVER SEEN ONE!
DAMN. DAMN. DAMN. WE GOT TOO CLOSE. TOO CLOSE TO SEE--

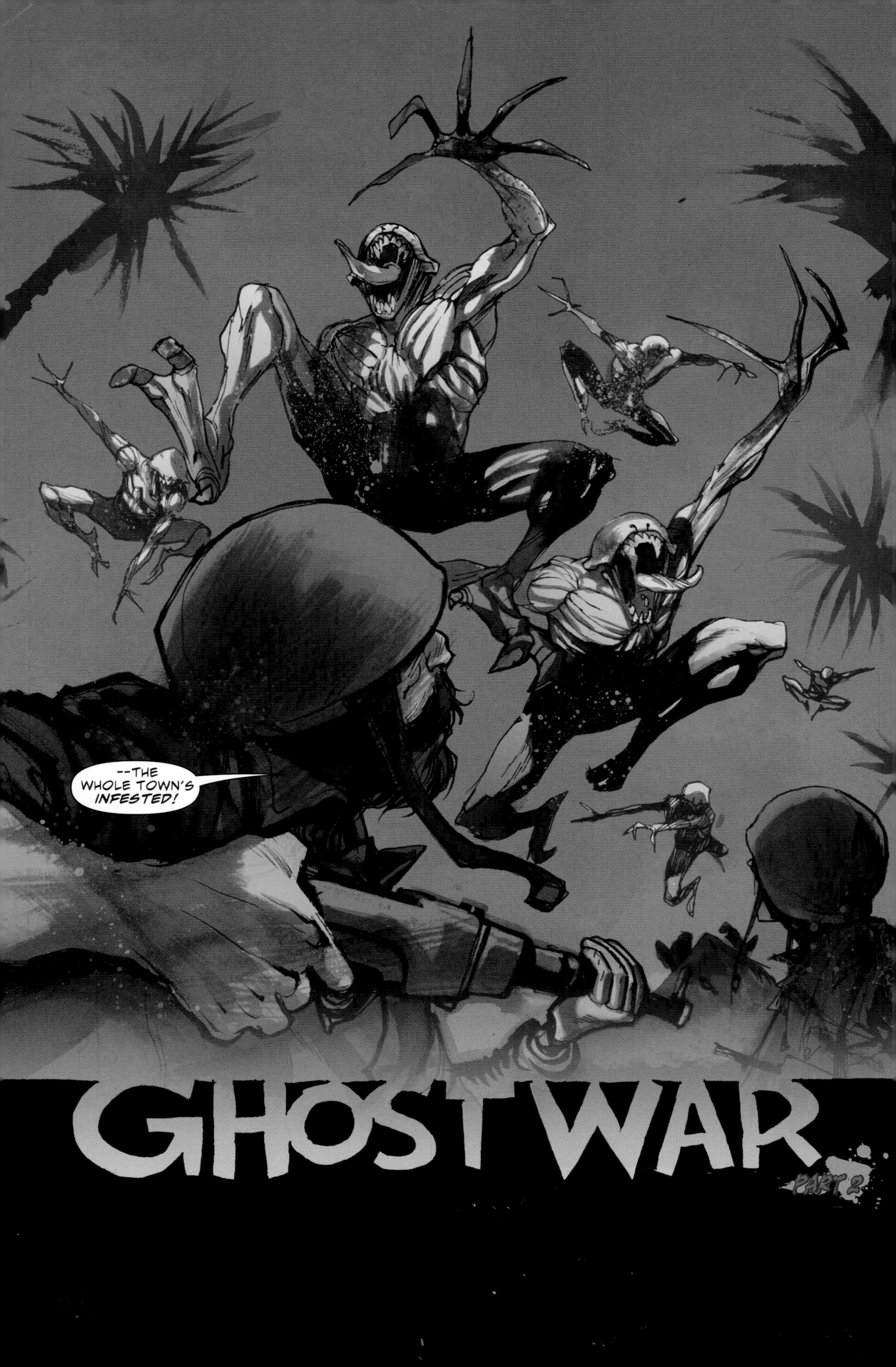
--THE WHOLE TOWN'S INFESTED!
GHOST WAR
PART 2

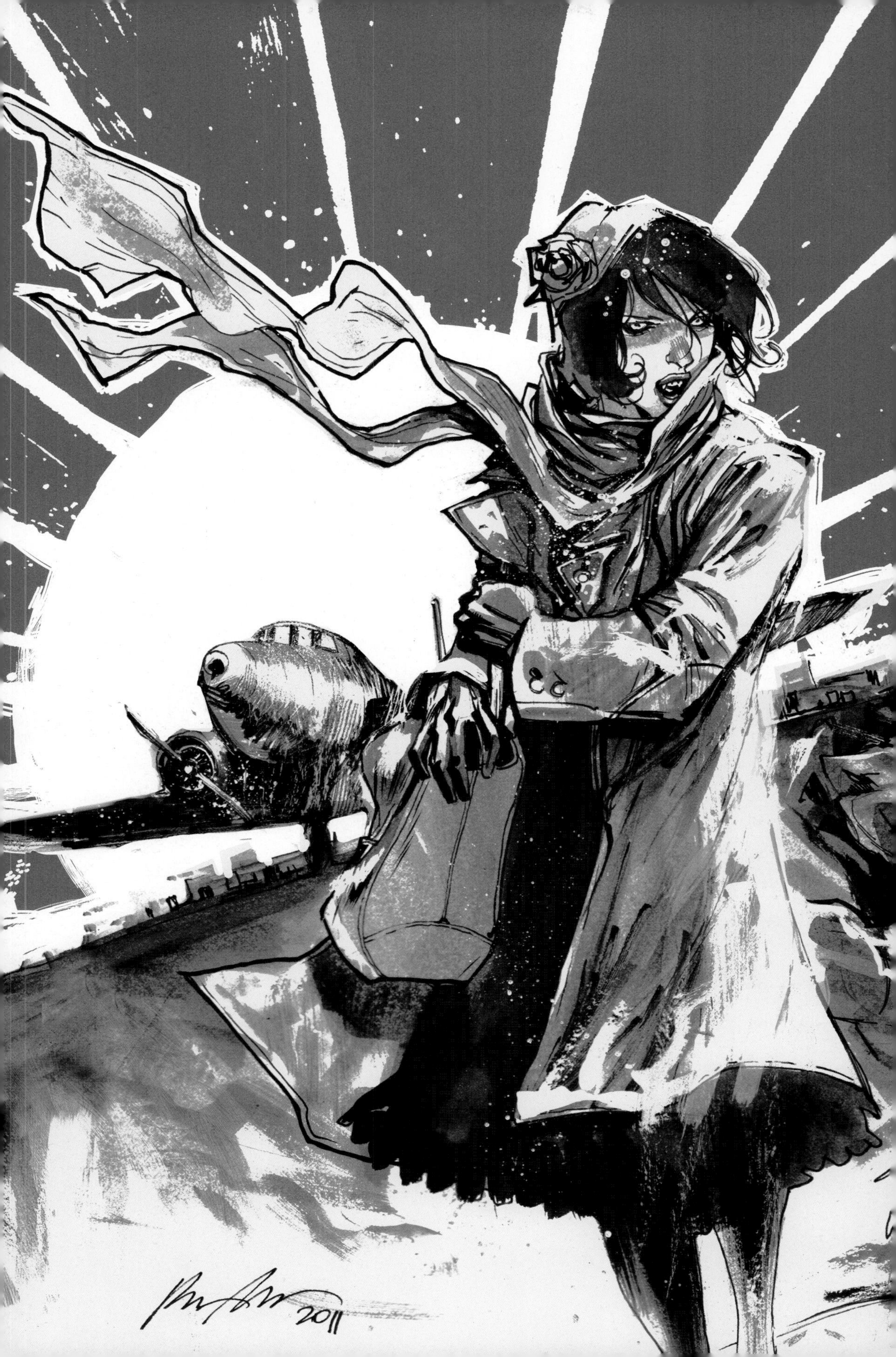

Ghost War

Part Three

Rafael Albuquerque
Artist and cover

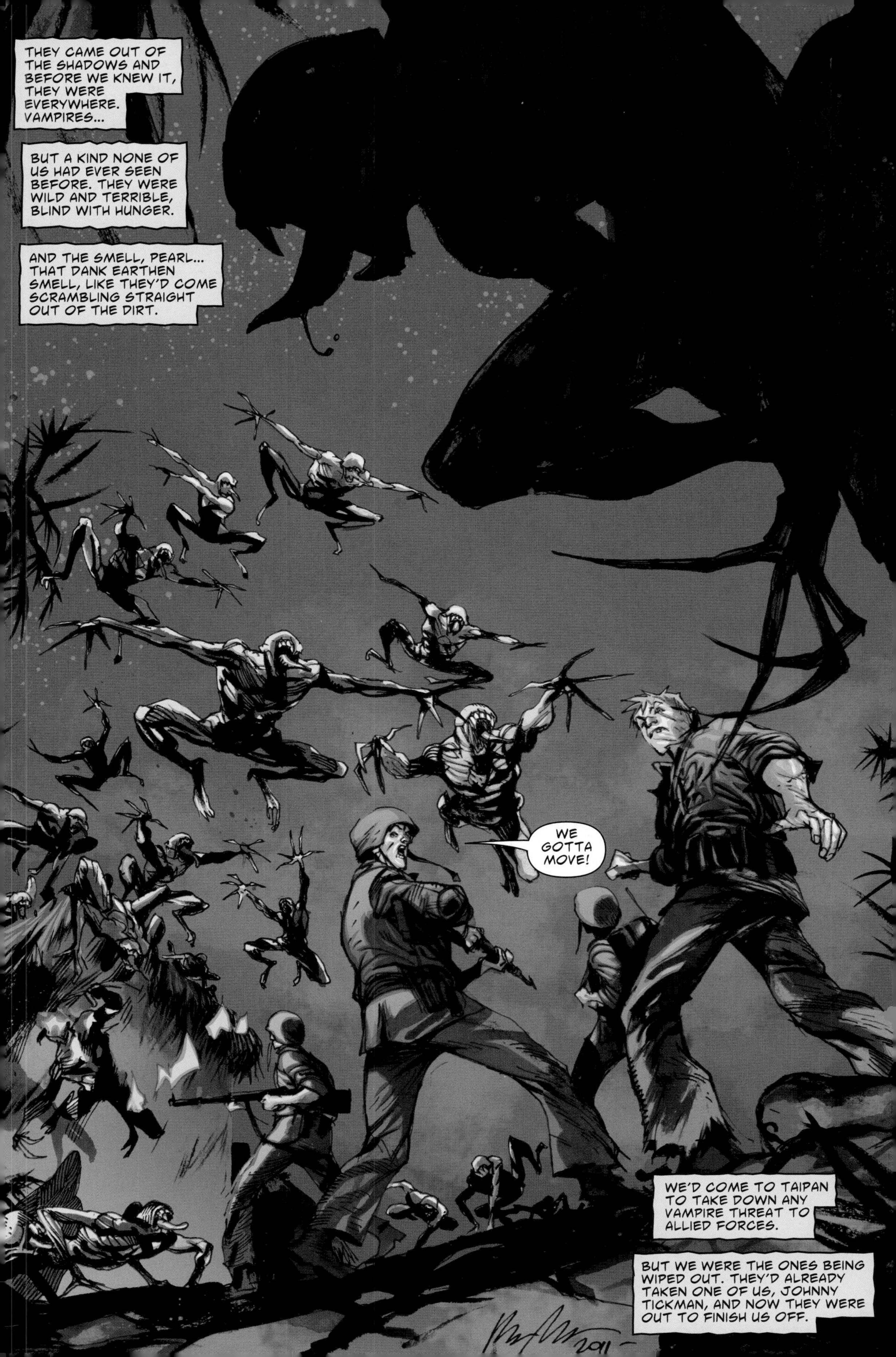
THEY CAME OUT OF THE SHADOWS AND BEFORE WE KNEW IT, THEY WERE EVERYWHERE. VAMPIRES...
BUT A KIND NONE OF US HAD EVER SEEN BEFORE. THEY WERE WILD AND TERRIBLE, BLIND WITH HUNGER.
AND THE SMELL, PEARL... THAT DANK EARTHEN SMELL, LIKE THEY'D COME SCRAMBLING STRAIGHT OUT OF THE DIRT.
WE GOTTA MOVE!
WE'D COME TO TAIPAN TO TAKE DOWN ANY VAMPIRE THREAT TO ALLIED FORCES.
BUT WE WERE THE ONES BEING WIPED OUT. THEY'D ALREADY TAKEN ONE OF US, JOHNNY TICKMAN, AND NOW THEY WERE OUT TO FINISH US OFF.

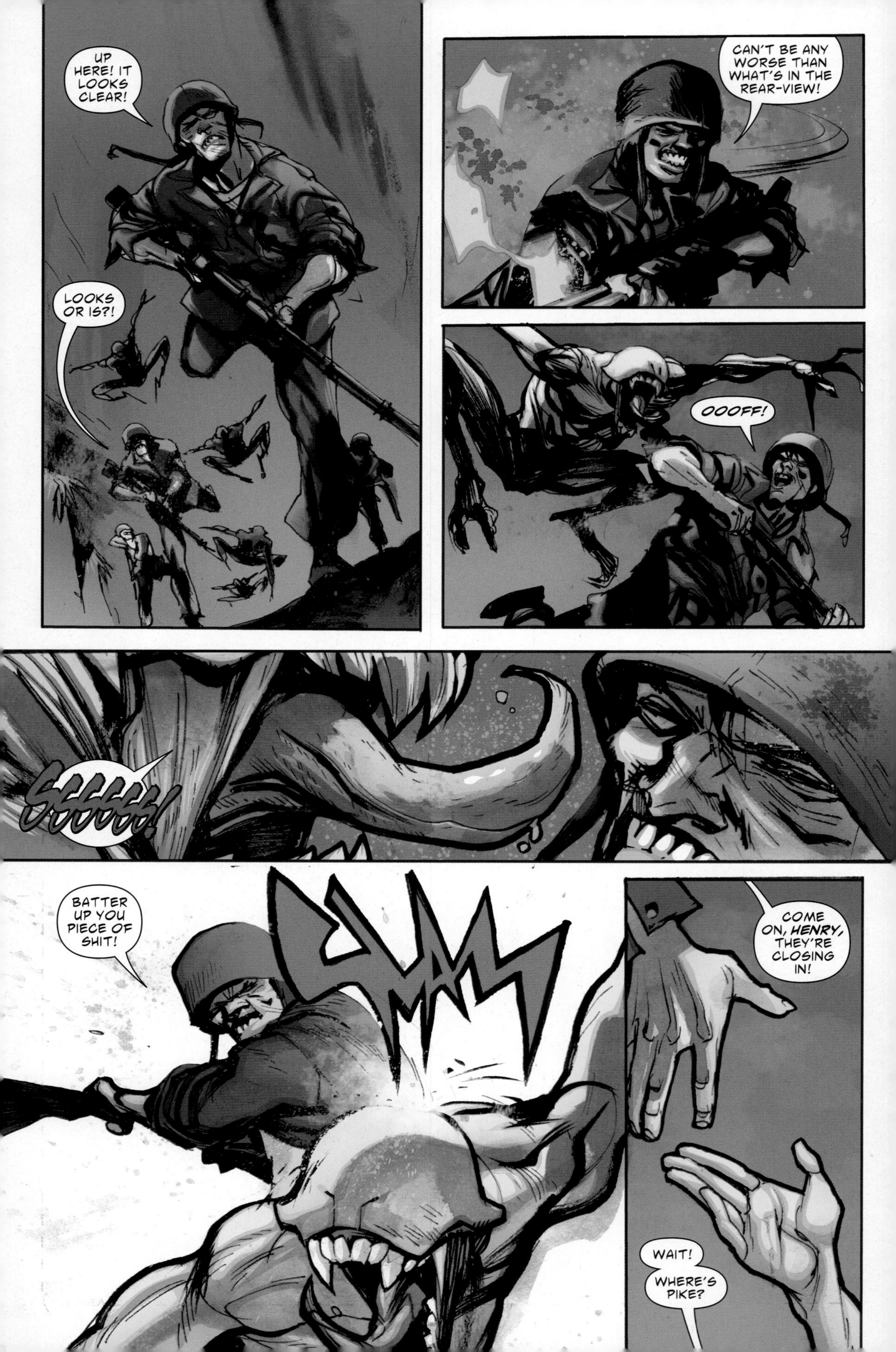
UP HERE! IT LOOKS CLEAR!
LOOKS OR IS?!
CAN'T BE ANY WORSE THAN WHAT'S IN THE REAR-VIEW!
OOOFF!
SSSSSS!
BATTER UP YOU PIECE OF SHIT!
COME ON, HENRY, THEY'RE CLOSING IN!
WAIT!
WHERE'S PIKE?

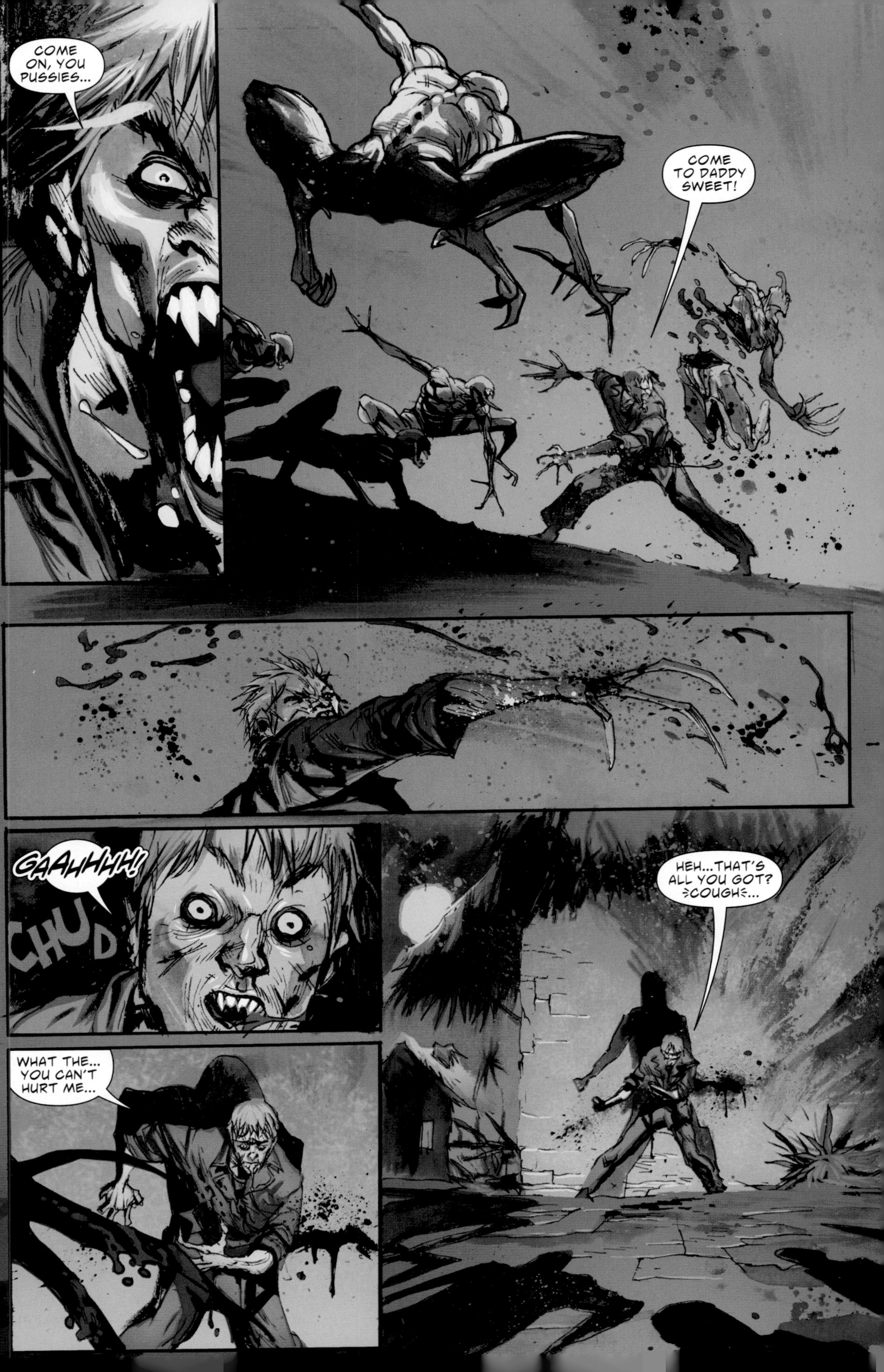

COME ON, YOU PUSSIES...
COME TO DADDY SWEET!
GAAHHHH!
CHUD
HEH...THAT'S ALL YOU GOT? ≥COUGH≤...
WHAT THE... YOU CAN'T HURT ME...

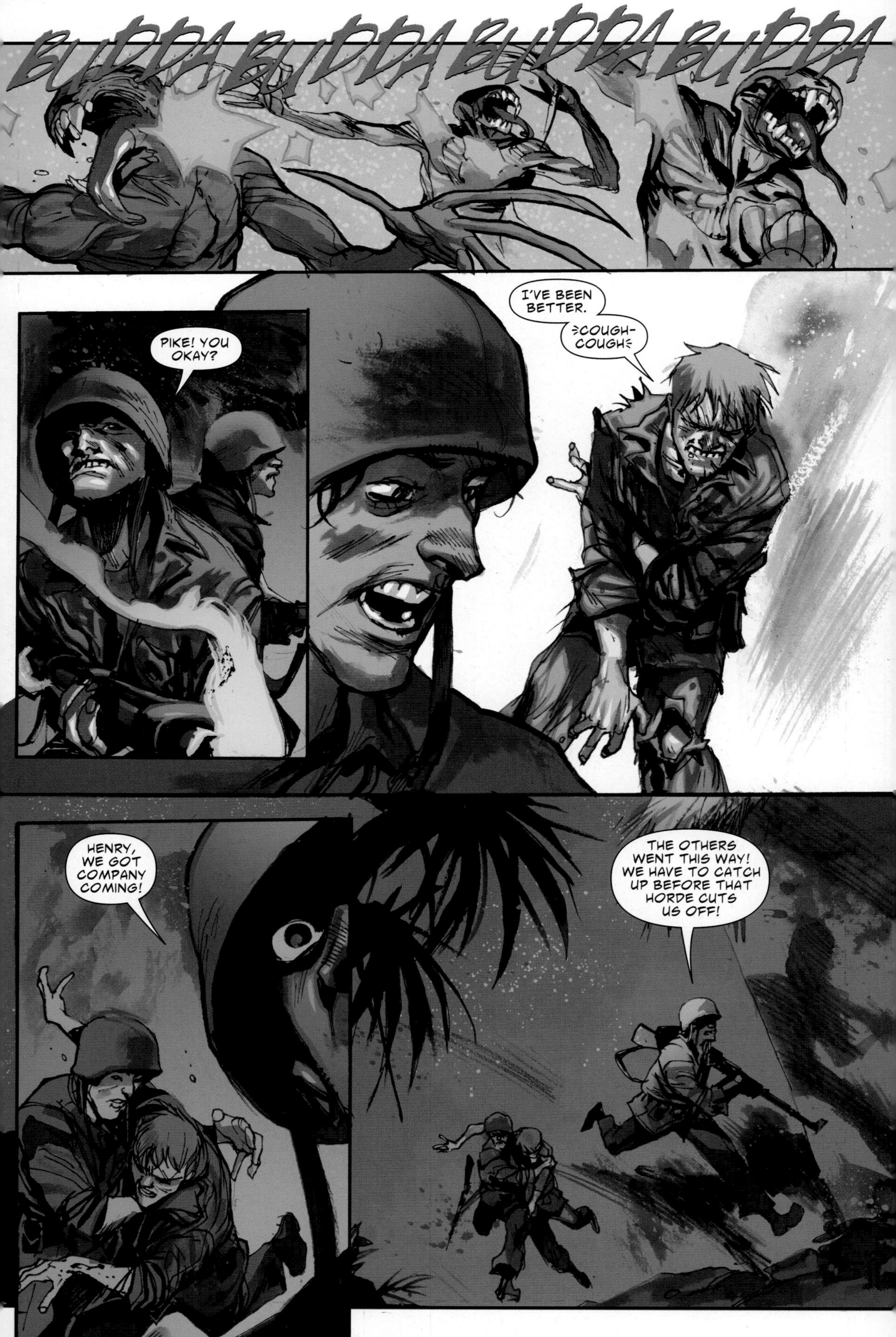
BUDDA BUDDA BUDDA BUDDA
PIKE! YOU OKAY?
I'VE BEEN BETTER.
COUGH-COUGH
HENRY, WE GOT COMPANY COMING!
THE OTHERS WENT THIS WAY! WE HAVE TO CATCH UP BEFORE THAT HORDE CUTS US OFF!

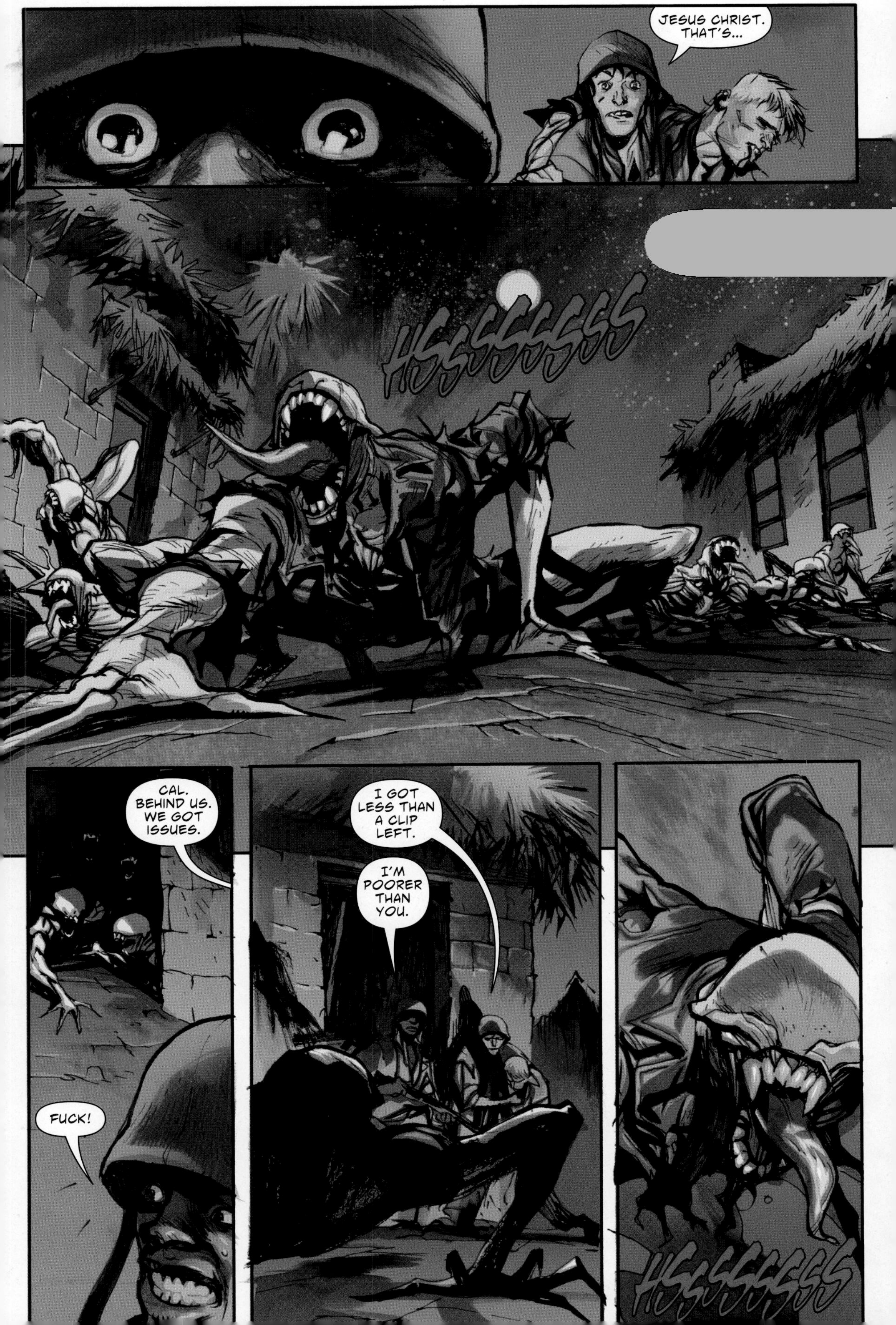
JESUS CHRIST. THAT'S...
HSSSSSSSSS
CAL. BEHIND US. WE GOT ISSUES.
FUCK!
I GOT LESS THAN A CLIP LEFT.
I'M POORER THAN YOU.
HSSSSSSSS

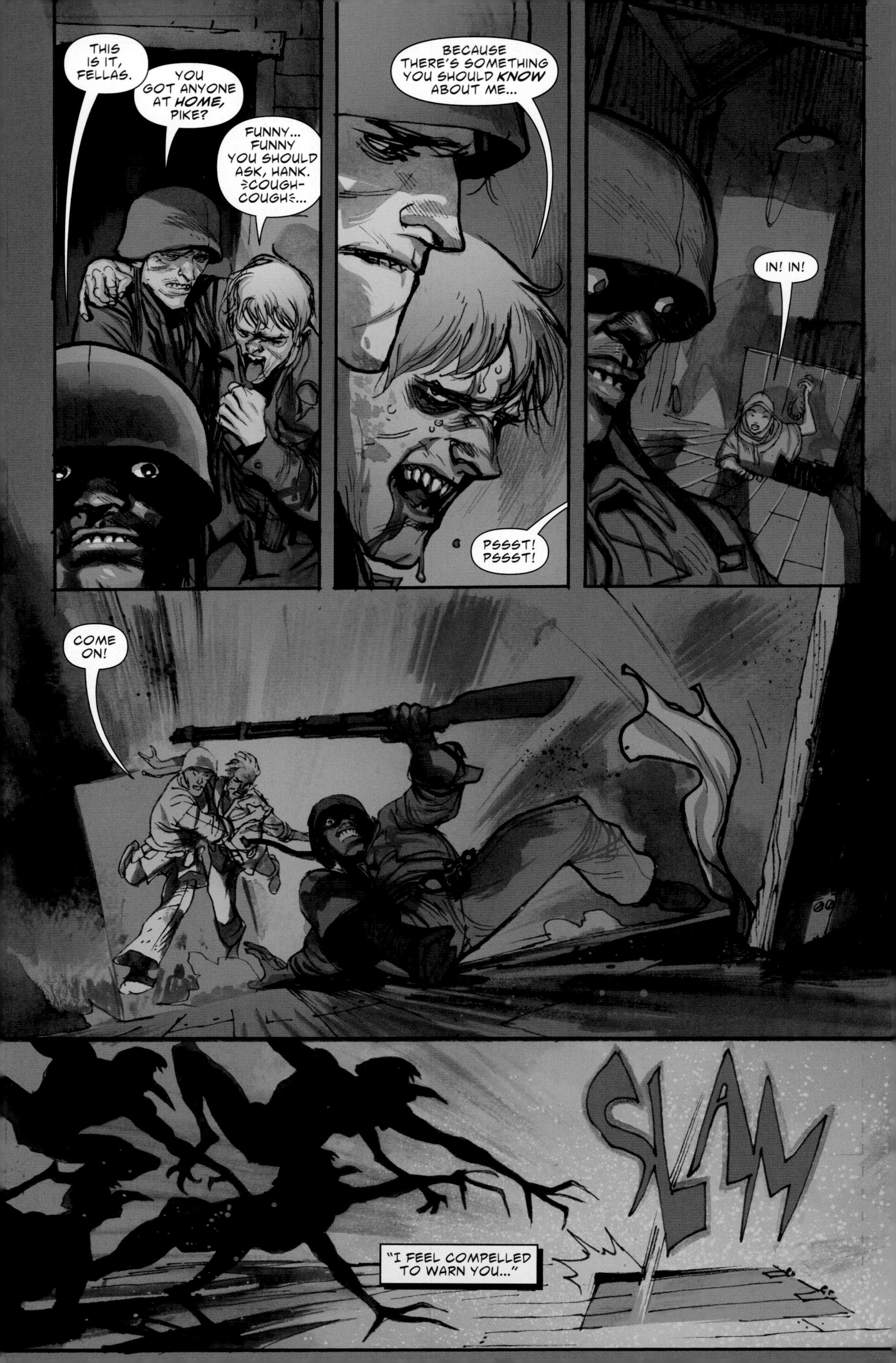
THIS IS IT, FELLAS.
YOU GOT ANYONE AT *HOME,* PIKE?
FUNNY... FUNNY YOU SHOULD ASK, HANK. ≥COUGH-COUGH≤...
BECAUSE THERE'S SOMETHING YOU SHOULD *KNOW* ABOUT ME...
PSSST! PSSST!
IN! IN!
COME ON!
SLAM
"I FEEL COMPELLED TO WARN YOU..."

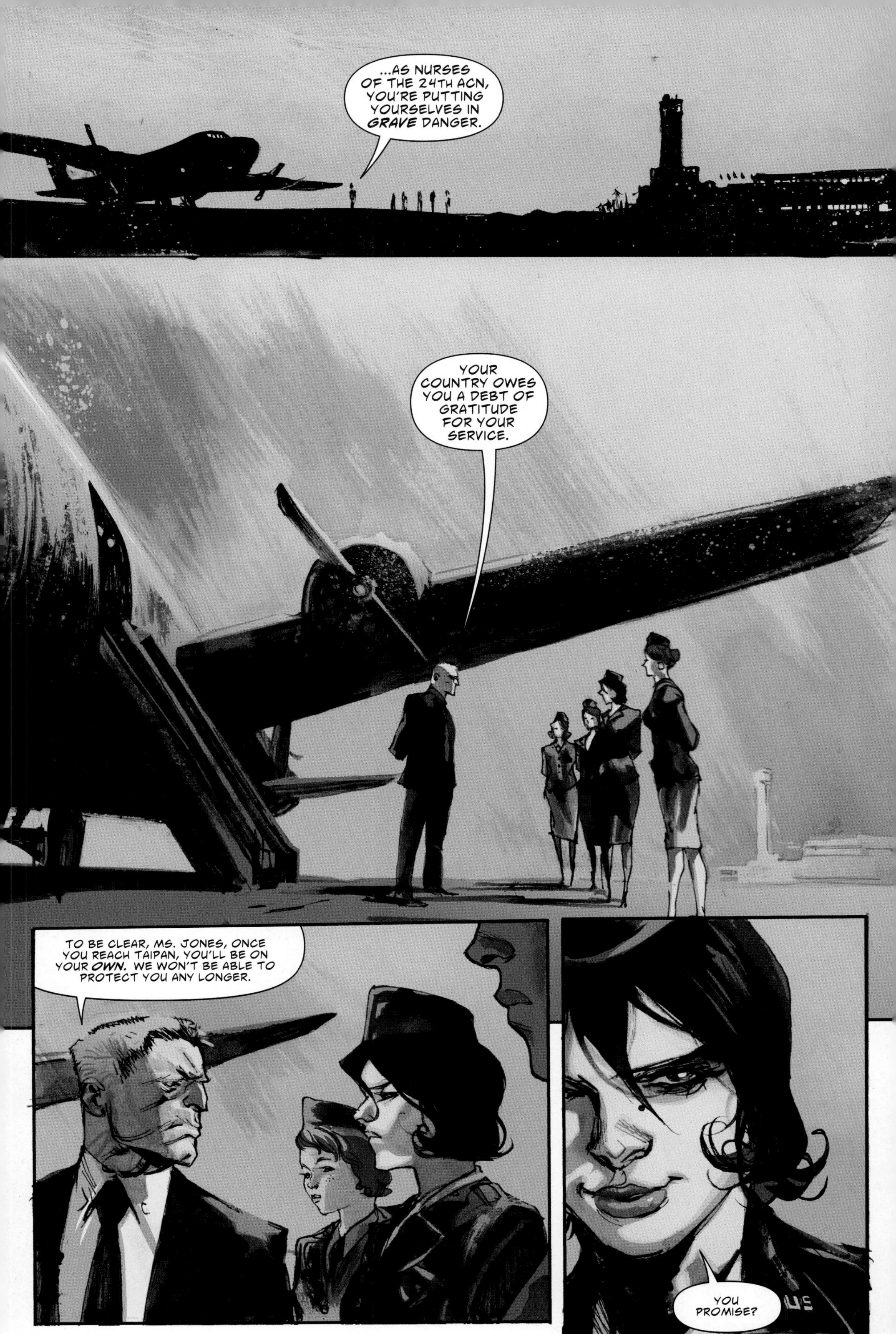
...AS NURSES OF THE 24TH ACN, YOU'RE PUTTING YOURSELVES IN *GRAVE* DANGER.
YOUR COUNTRY OWES YOU A DEBT OF GRATITUDE FOR YOUR SERVICE.
TO BE CLEAR, MS. JONES, ONCE YOU REACH TAIPAN, YOU'LL BE ON YOUR *OWN.* WE WON'T BE ABLE TO PROTECT YOU ANY LONGER.
YOU PROMISE?

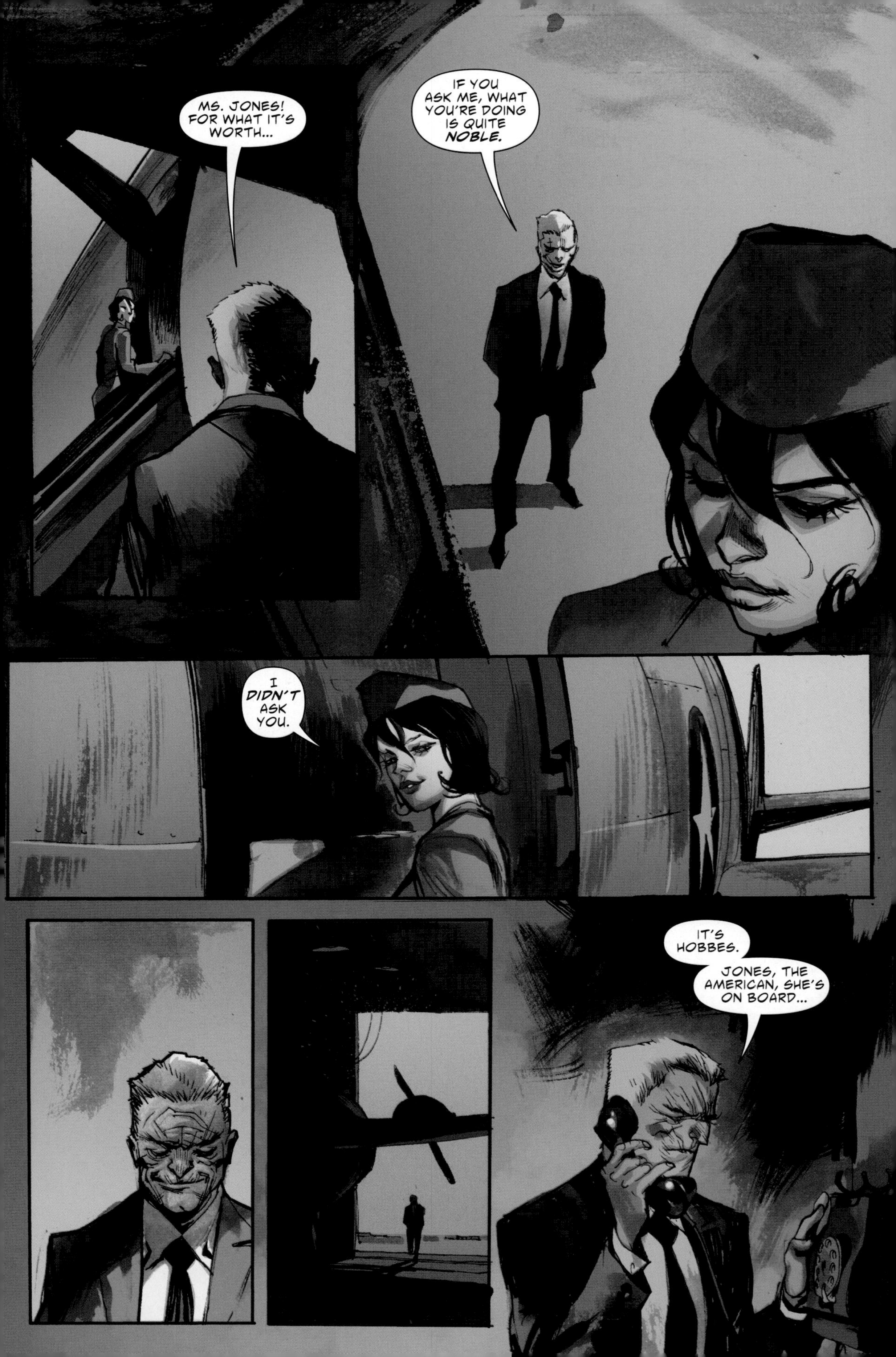
MS. JONES! FOR WHAT IT'S WORTH...
IF YOU ASK ME, WHAT YOU'RE DOING IS QUITE NOBLE.
I DIDN'T ASK YOU.
IT'S HOBBES.
JONES, THE AMERICAN, SHE'S ON BOARD...

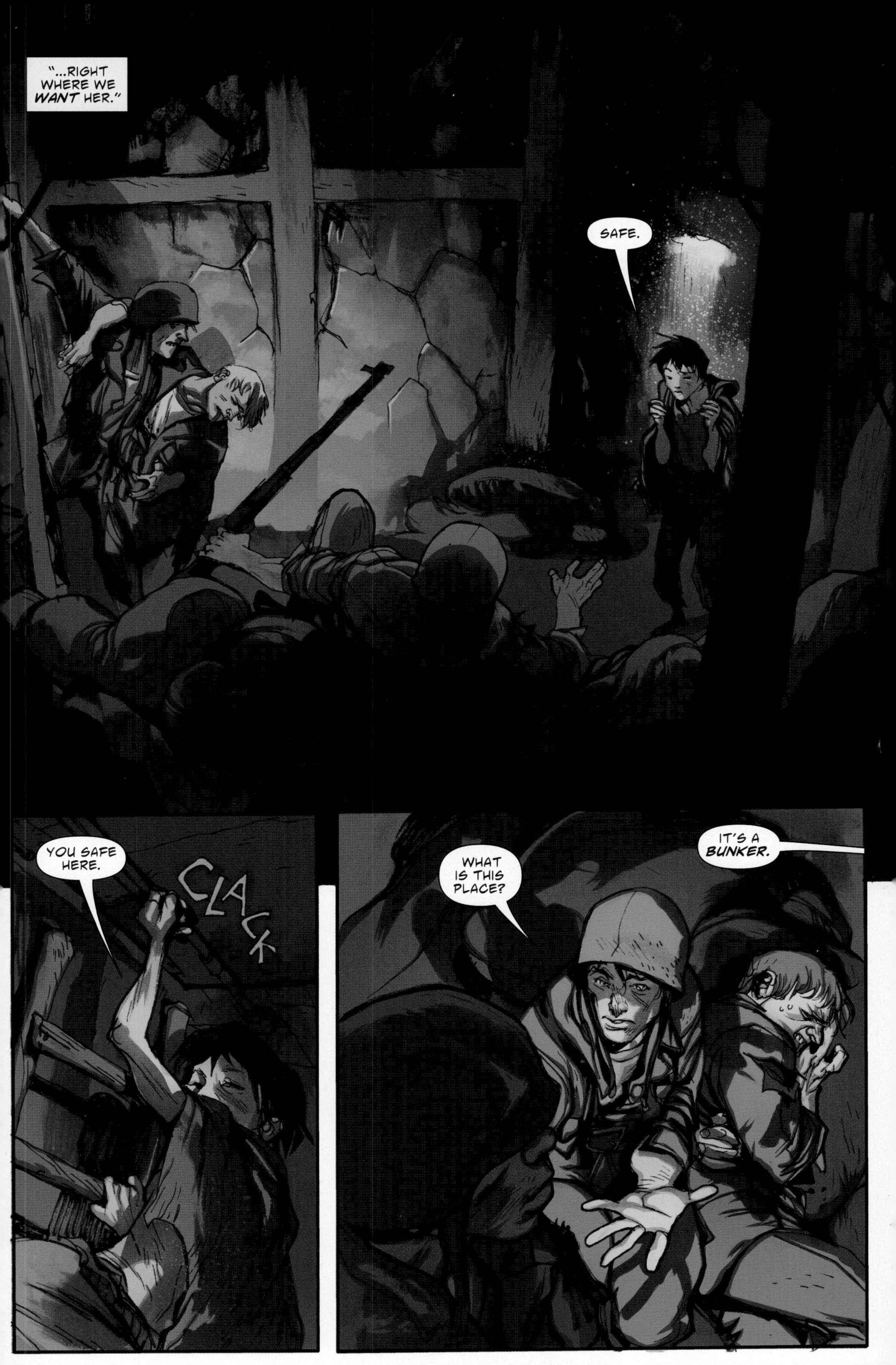
"...RIGHT WHERE WE WANT HER."
SAFE.
YOU SAFE HERE.
CLACK
WHAT IS THIS PLACE?
IT'S A BUNKER.

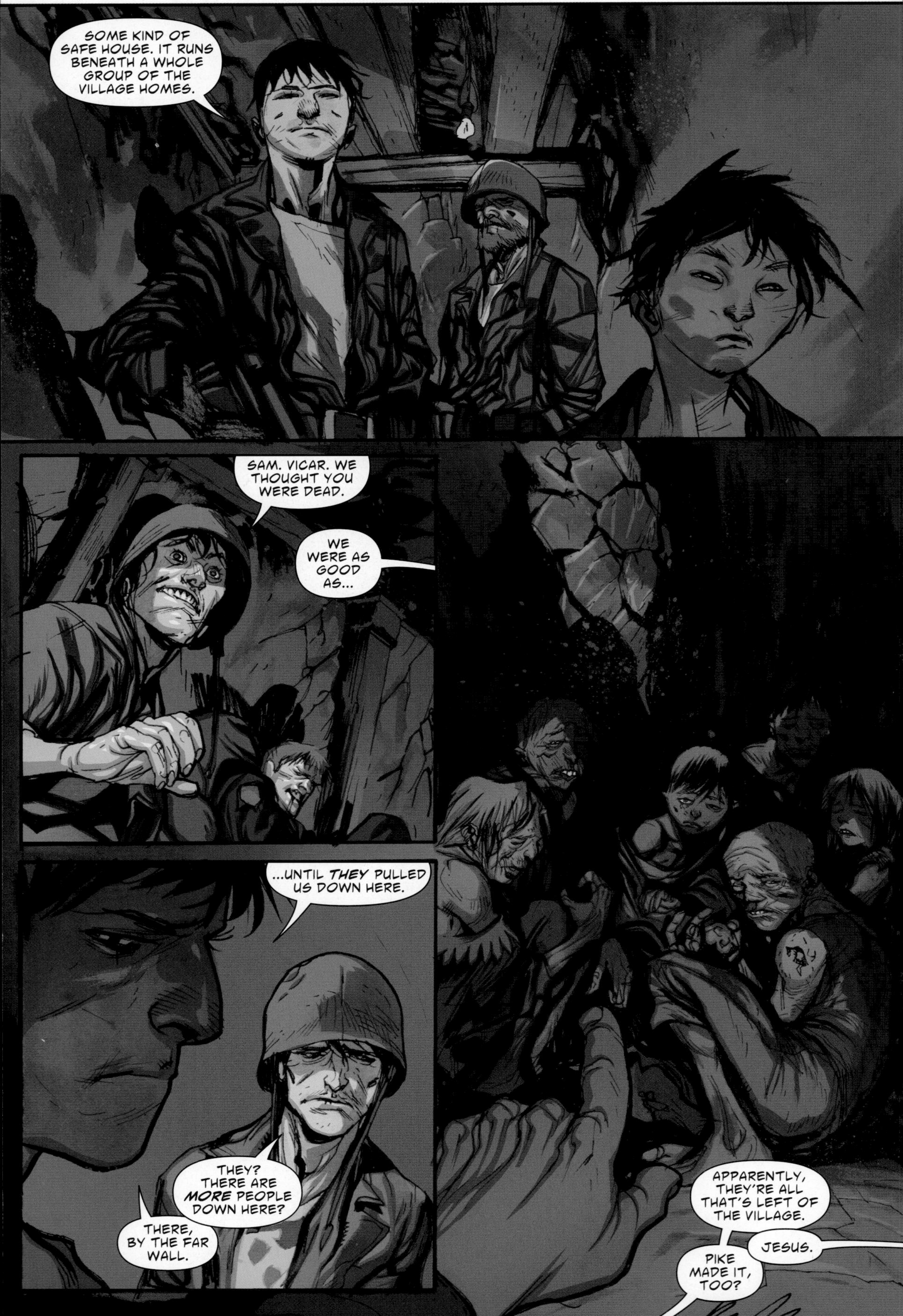
SOME KIND OF SAFE HOUSE. IT RUNS BENEATH A WHOLE GROUP OF THE VILLAGE HOMES.
SAM. VICAR. WE THOUGHT YOU WERE DEAD.
WE WERE AS GOOD AS...
...UNTIL *THEY* PULLED US DOWN HERE.
THEY? THERE ARE *MORE* PEOPLE DOWN HERE?
THERE, BY THE FAR WALL.
APPARENTLY, THEY'RE ALL THAT'S LEFT OF THE VILLAGE.
JESUS.
PIKE MADE IT, TOO?

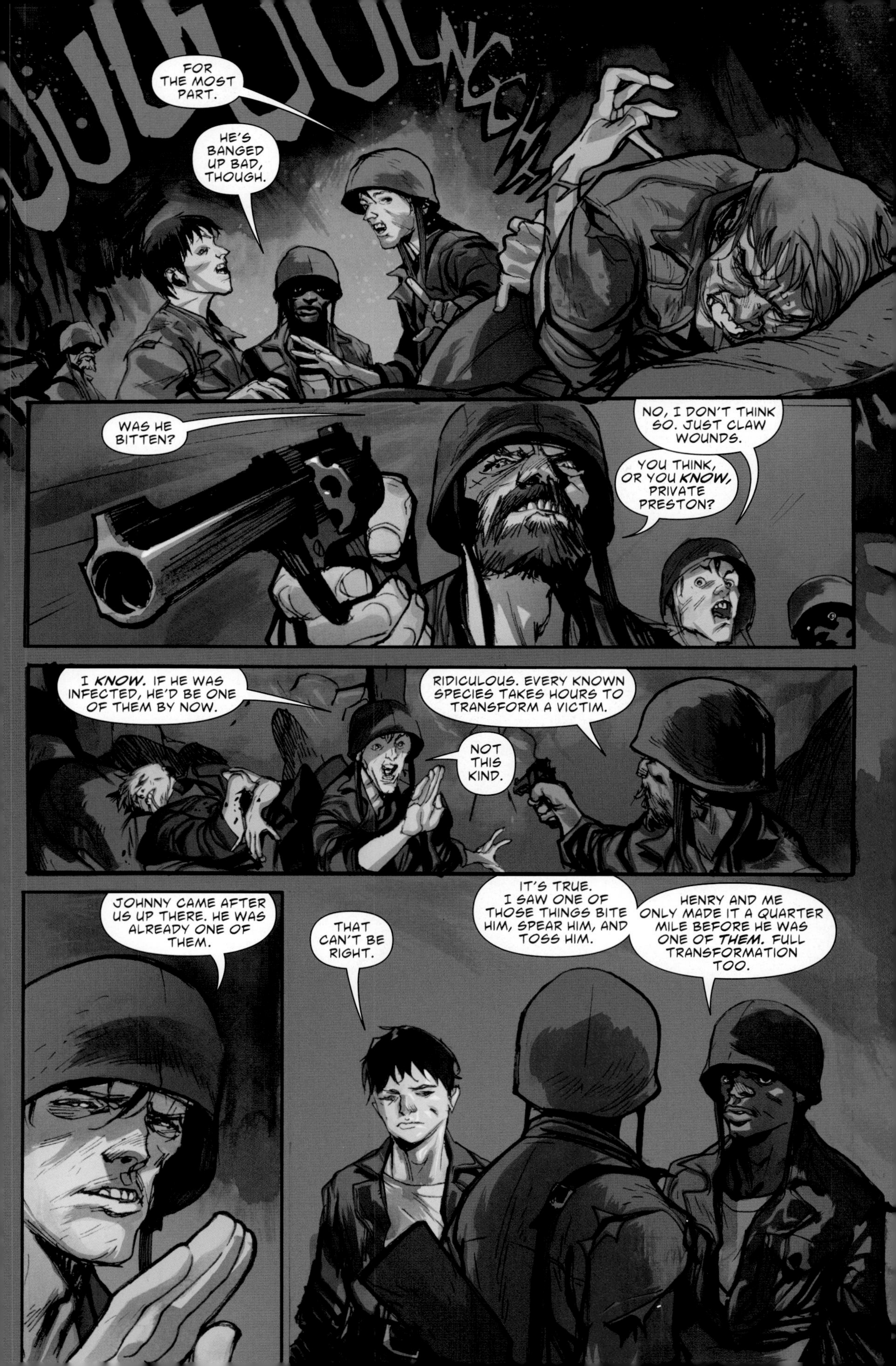
FOR THE MOST PART.
HE'S BANGED UP BAD, THOUGH.
WAS HE BITTEN?
NO, I DON'T THINK SO. JUST CLAW WOUNDS.
YOU THINK, OR YOU KNOW, PRIVATE PRESTON?
I KNOW. IF HE WAS INFECTED, HE'D BE ONE OF THEM BY NOW.
RIDICULOUS. EVERY KNOWN SPECIES TAKES HOURS TO TRANSFORM A VICTIM.
NOT THIS KIND.
JOHNNY CAME AFTER US UP THERE. HE WAS ALREADY ONE OF THEM.
THAT CAN'T BE RIGHT.
IT'S TRUE. I SAW ONE OF THOSE THINGS BITE HIM, SPEAR HIM, AND TOSS HIM.
HENRY AND ME ONLY MADE IT A QUARTER MILE BEFORE HE WAS ONE OF THEM. FULL TRANSFORMATION TOO.

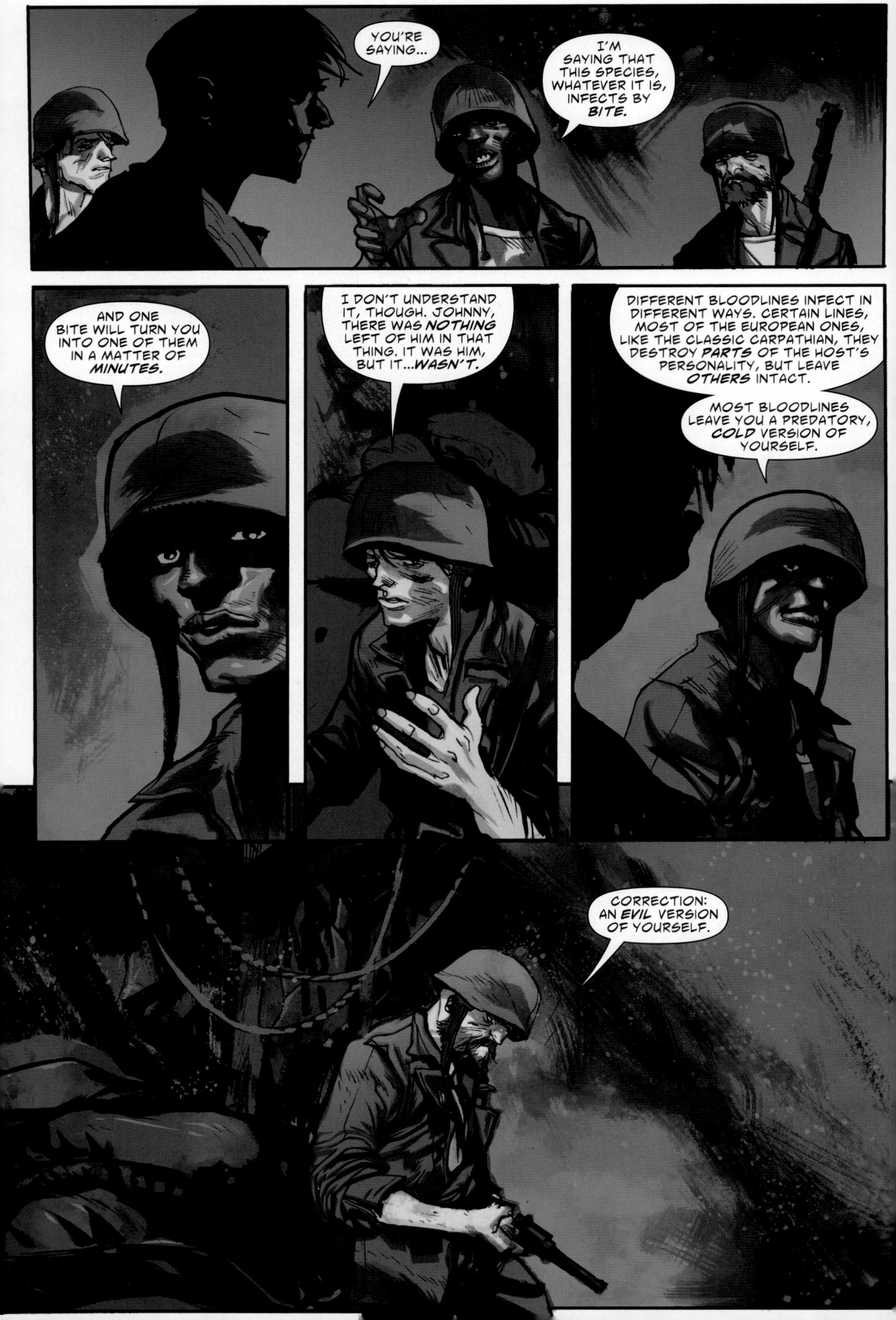
YOU'RE SAYING...
I'M SAYING THAT THIS SPECIES, WHATEVER IT IS, INFECTS BY BITE.
AND ONE BITE WILL TURN YOU INTO ONE OF THEM IN A MATTER OF MINUTES.
I DON'T UNDERSTAND IT, THOUGH. JOHNNY, THERE WAS NOTHING LEFT OF HIM IN THAT THING. IT WAS HIM, BUT IT...WASN'T.
DIFFERENT BLOODLINES INFECT IN DIFFERENT WAYS. CERTAIN LINES, MOST OF THE EUROPEAN ONES, LIKE THE CLASSIC CARPATHIAN, THEY DESTROY PARTS OF THE HOST'S PERSONALITY, BUT LEAVE OTHERS INTACT.
MOST BLOODLINES LEAVE YOU A PREDATORY, COLD VERSION OF YOURSELF.
CORRECTION: AN EVIL VERSION OF YOURSELF.

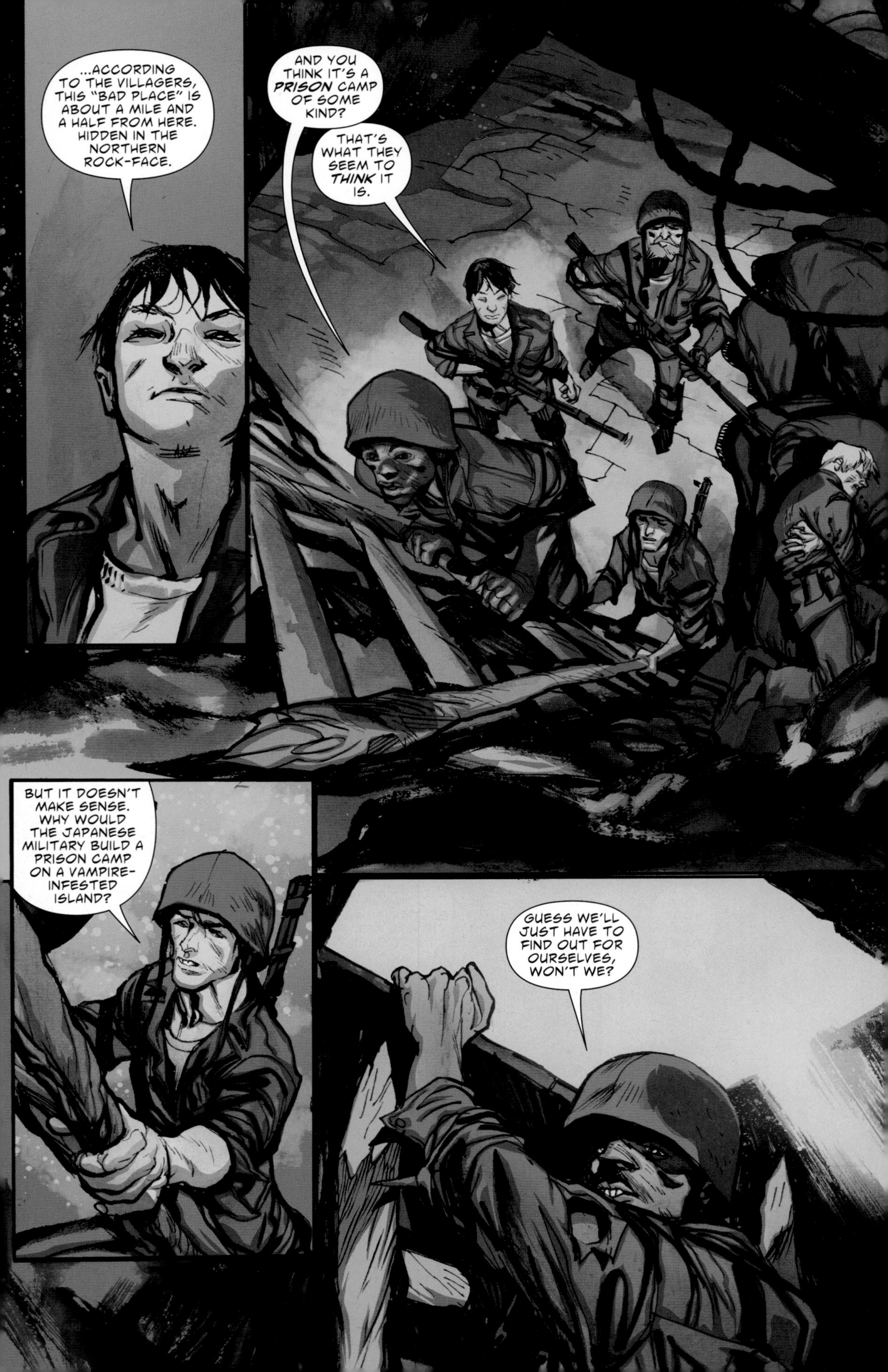
...ACCORDING TO THE VILLAGERS, THIS "BAD PLACE" IS ABOUT A MILE AND A HALF FROM HERE. HIDDEN IN THE NORTHERN ROCK-FACE.
AND YOU THINK IT'S A PRISON CAMP OF SOME KIND?
THAT'S WHAT THEY SEEM TO THINK IT IS.
BUT IT DOESN'T MAKE SENSE. WHY WOULD THE JAPANESE MILITARY BUILD A PRISON CAMP ON A VAMPIRE-INFESTED ISLAND?
GUESS WE'LL JUST HAVE TO FIND OUT FOR OURSELVES, WON'T WE?

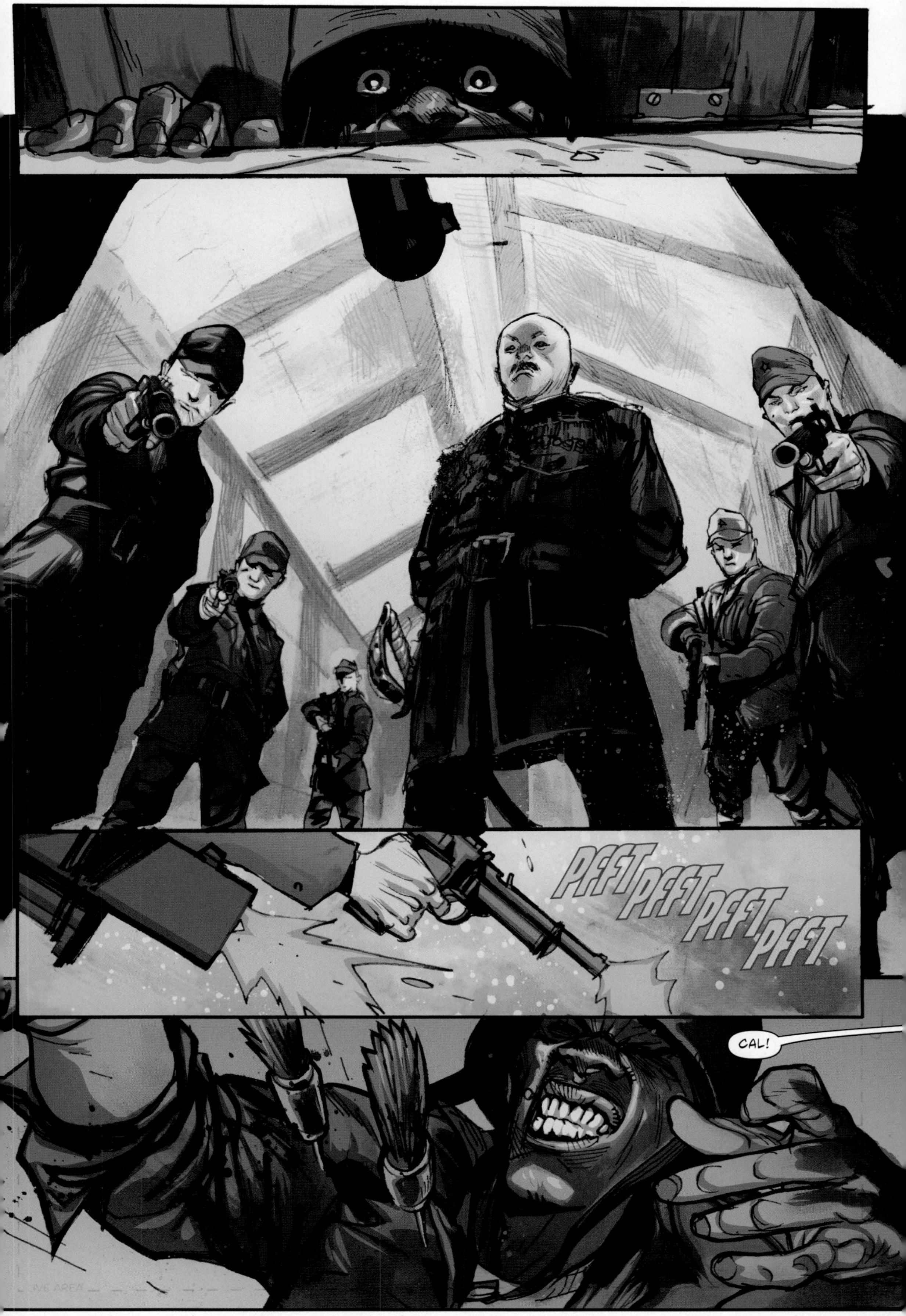
PFFT PFFT PFFT PFFT
CAL!

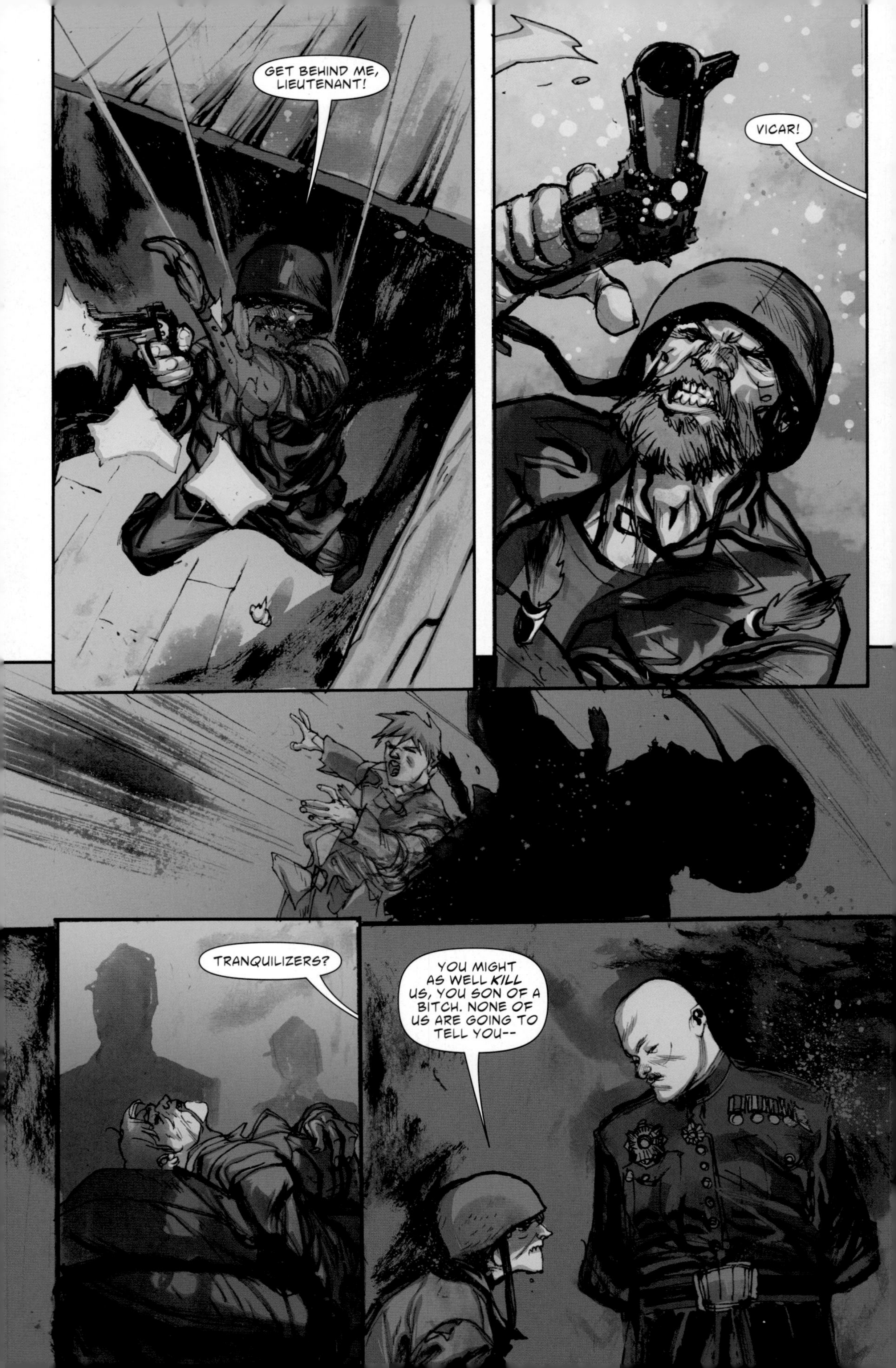
GET BEHIND ME, LIEUTENANT!
VICAR!
TRANQUILIZERS?
YOU MIGHT AS WELL KILL US, YOU SON OF A BITCH. NONE OF US ARE GOING TO TELL YOU--

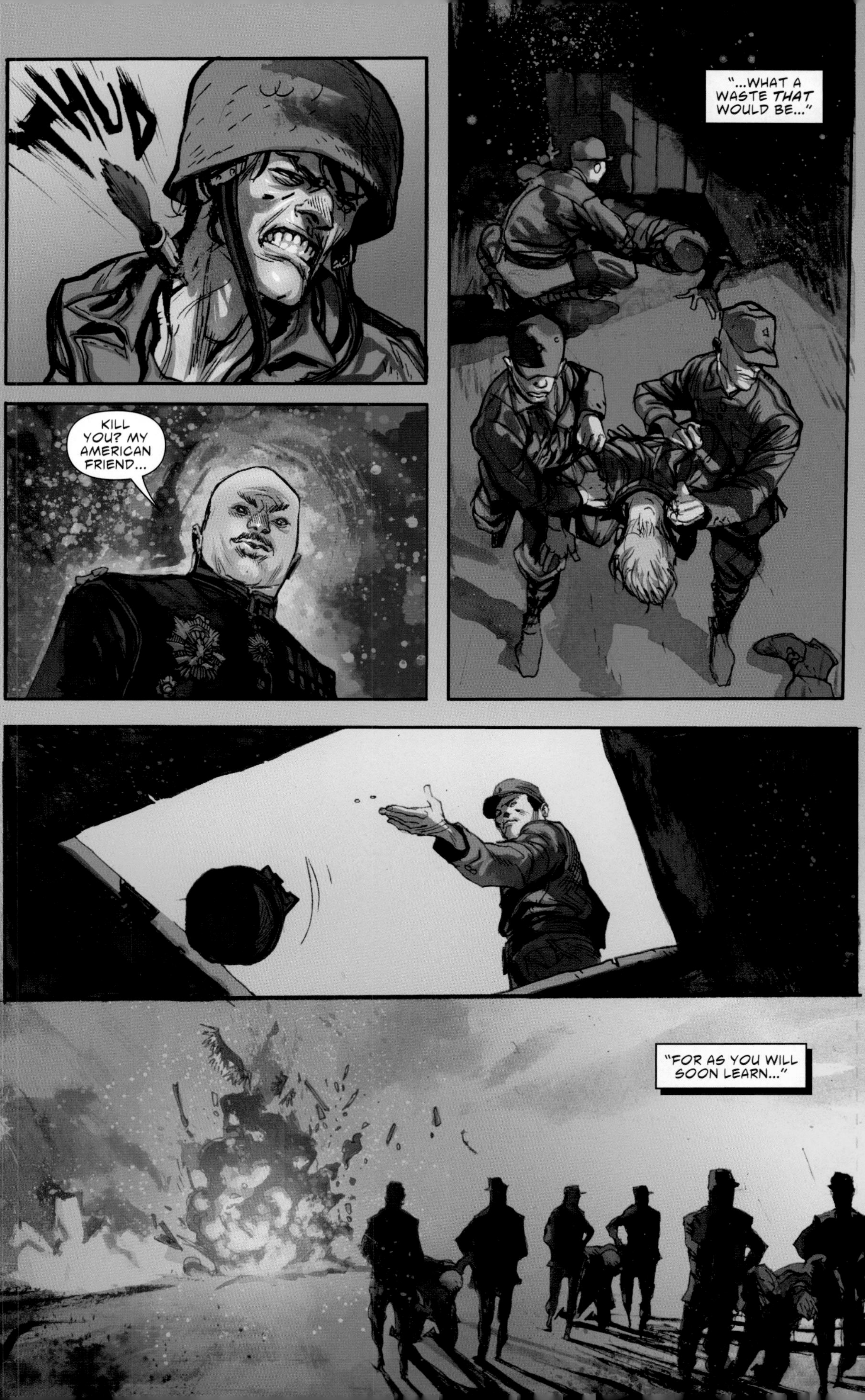
THUD
"...WHAT A WASTE THAT WOULD BE..."
KILL YOU? MY AMERICAN FRIEND...
"FOR AS YOU WILL SOON LEARN..."

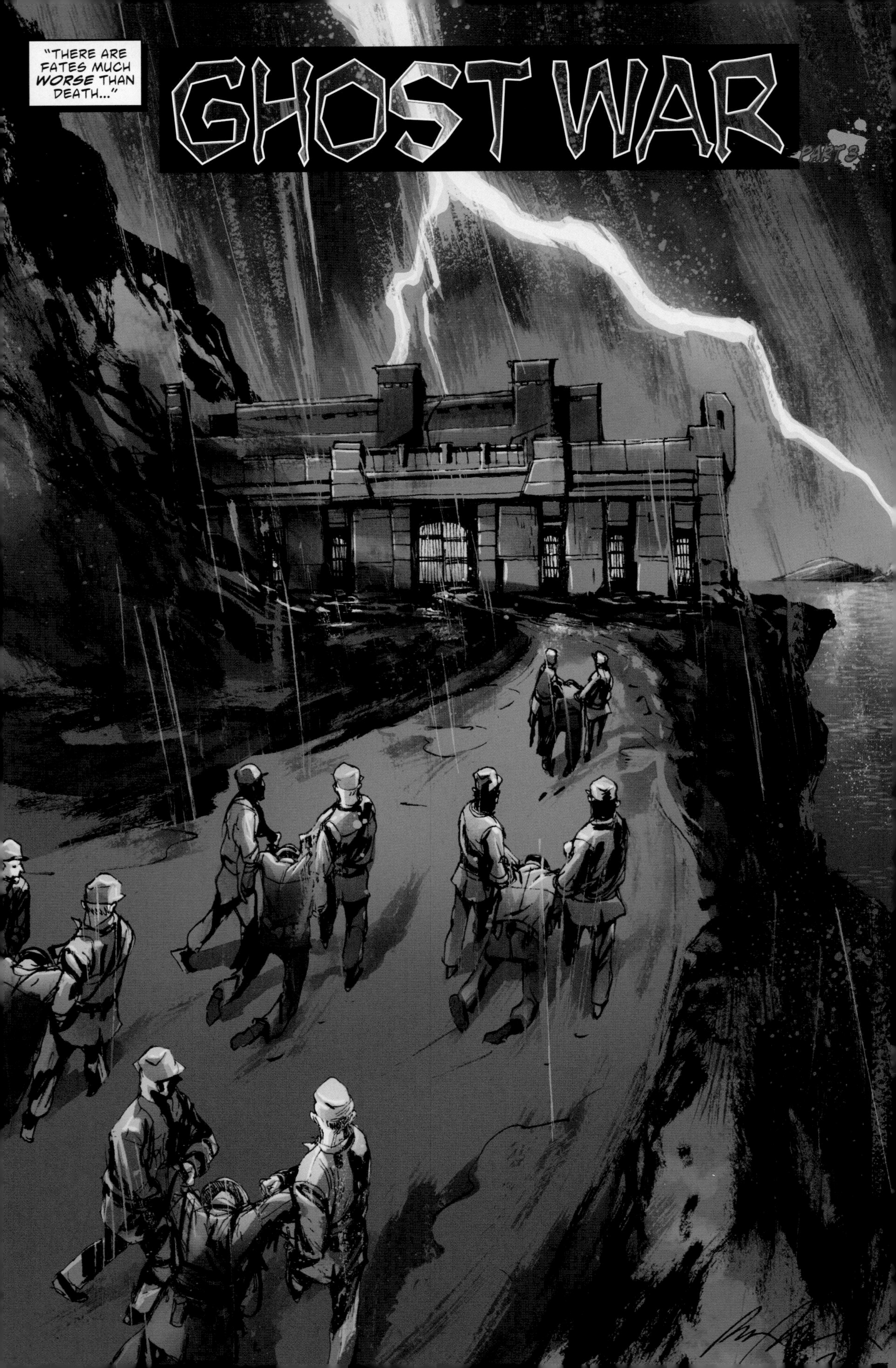
"THERE ARE FATES MUCH WORSE THAN DEATH..."
GHOST WAR
PART 3

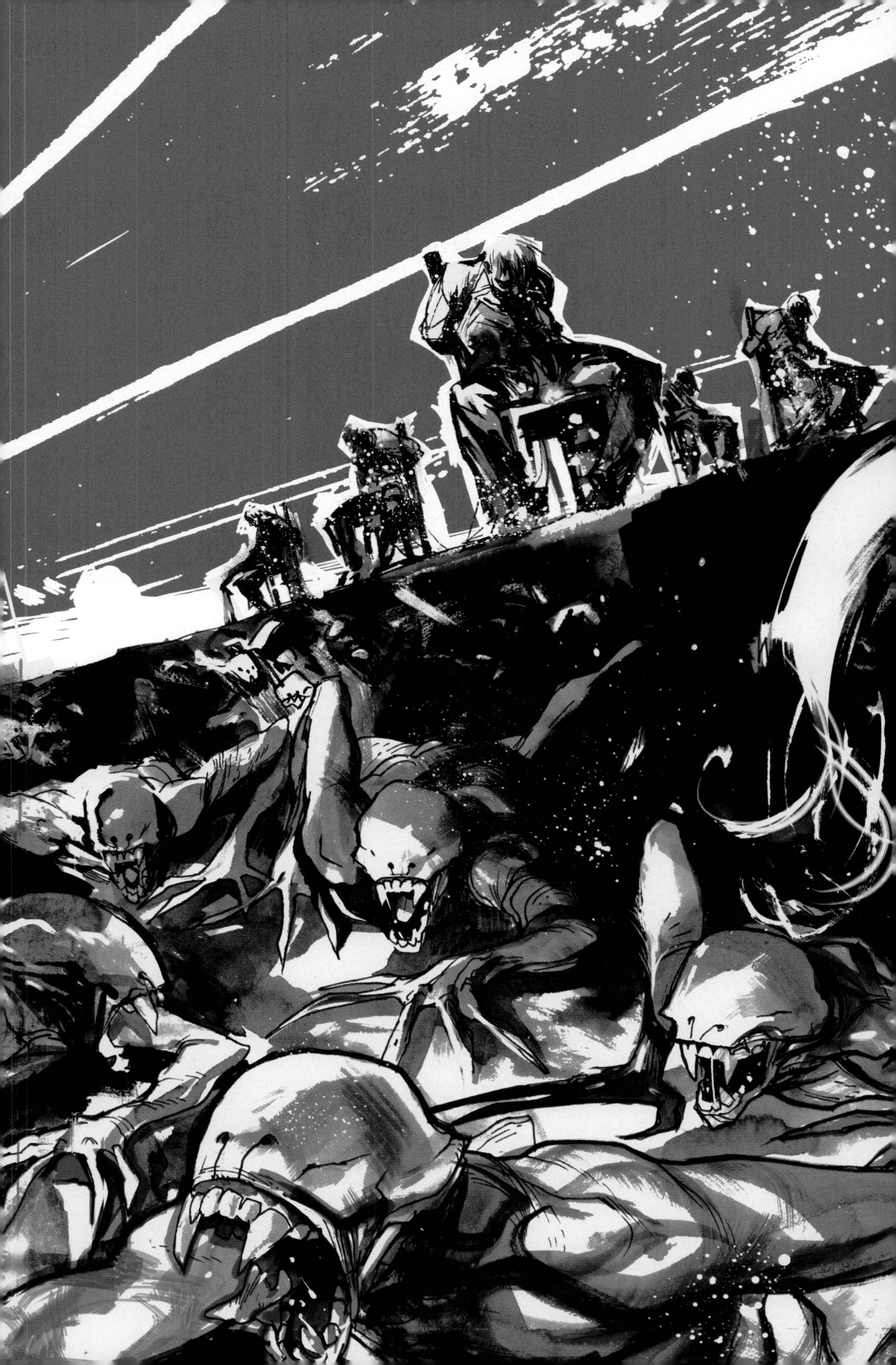

Ghost War

Part Four

Rafael Albuquerque
Artist and cover

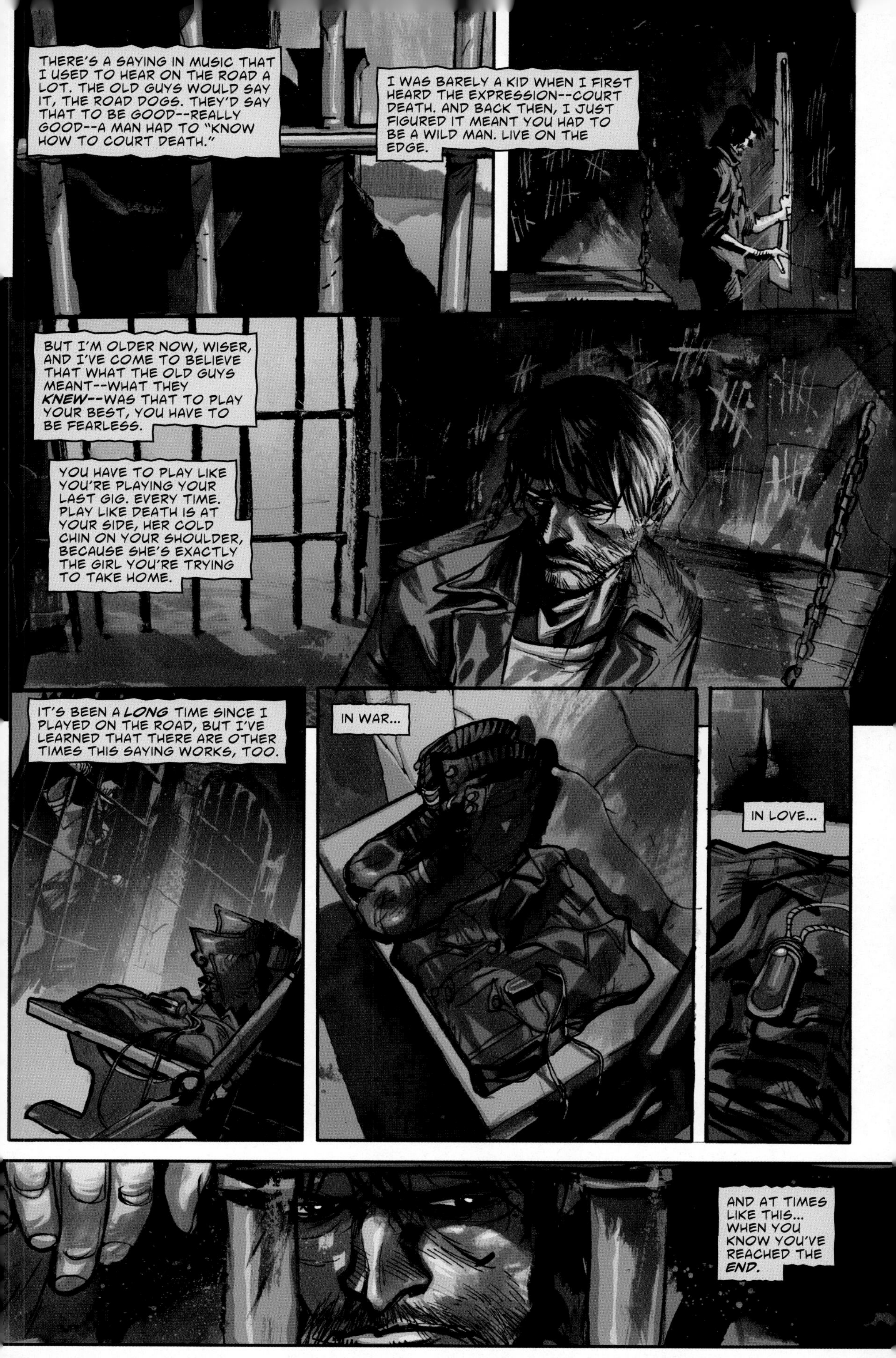
THERE'S A SAYING IN MUSIC THAT I USED TO HEAR ON THE ROAD A LOT. THE OLD GUYS WOULD SAY IT, THE ROAD DOGS. THEY'D SAY THAT TO BE GOOD--REALLY GOOD--A MAN HAD TO "KNOW HOW TO COURT DEATH."
I WAS BARELY A KID WHEN I FIRST HEARD THE EXPRESSION--COURT DEATH. AND BACK THEN, I JUST FIGURED IT MEANT YOU HAD TO BE A WILD MAN. LIVE ON THE EDGE.
BUT I'M OLDER NOW, WISER, AND I'VE COME TO BELIEVE THAT WHAT THE OLD GUYS MEANT--WHAT THEY *KNEW*--WAS THAT TO PLAY YOUR BEST, YOU HAVE TO BE FEARLESS.
YOU HAVE TO PLAY LIKE YOU'RE PLAYING YOUR LAST GIG. EVERY TIME. PLAY LIKE DEATH IS AT YOUR SIDE, HER COLD CHIN ON YOUR SHOULDER, BECAUSE SHE'S EXACTLY THE GIRL YOU'RE TRYING TO TAKE HOME.
IT'S BEEN A *LONG* TIME SINCE I PLAYED ON THE ROAD, BUT I'VE LEARNED THAT THERE ARE OTHER TIMES THIS SAYING WORKS, TOO.
IN WAR...
IN LOVE...
AND AT TIMES LIKE THIS... WHEN YOU KNOW YOU'VE REACHED THE *END*.

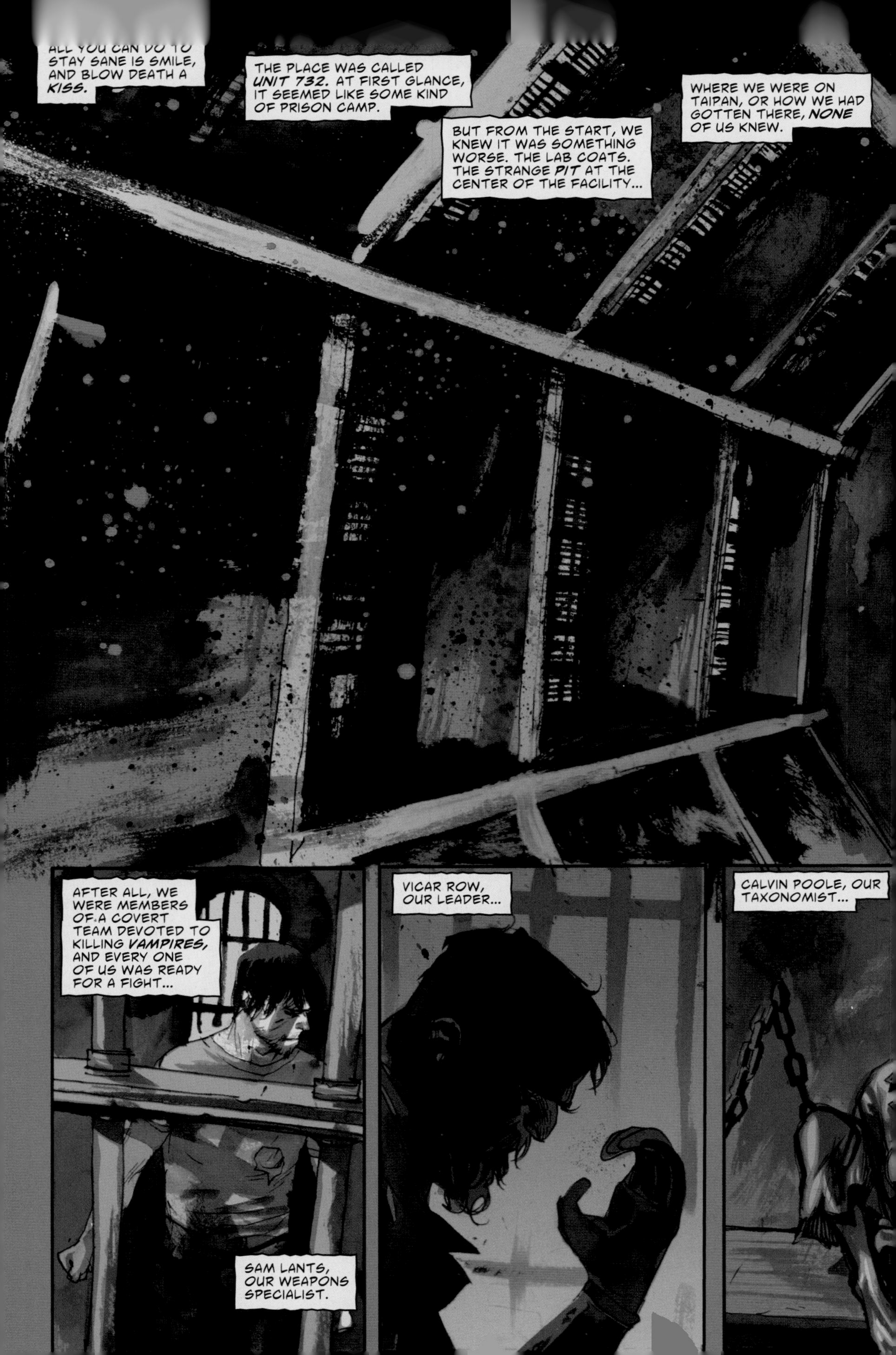
ALL YOU CAN DO TO STAY SANE IS SMILE, AND BLOW DEATH A KISS.
THE PLACE WAS CALLED UNIT 732. AT FIRST GLANCE, IT SEEMED LIKE SOME KIND OF PRISON CAMP.
BUT FROM THE START, WE KNEW IT WAS SOMETHING WORSE. THE LAB COATS. THE STRANGE PIT AT THE CENTER OF THE FACILITY...
WHERE WE WERE ON TAIPAN, OR HOW WE HAD GOTTEN THERE, NONE OF US KNEW.
AFTER ALL, WE WERE MEMBERS OF A COVERT TEAM DEVOTED TO KILLING VAMPIRES, AND EVERY ONE OF US WAS READY FOR A FIGHT...
SAM LANTS, OUR WEAPONS SPECIALIST.
VICAR ROW, OUR LEADER...
CALVIN POOLE, OUR TAXONOMIST...

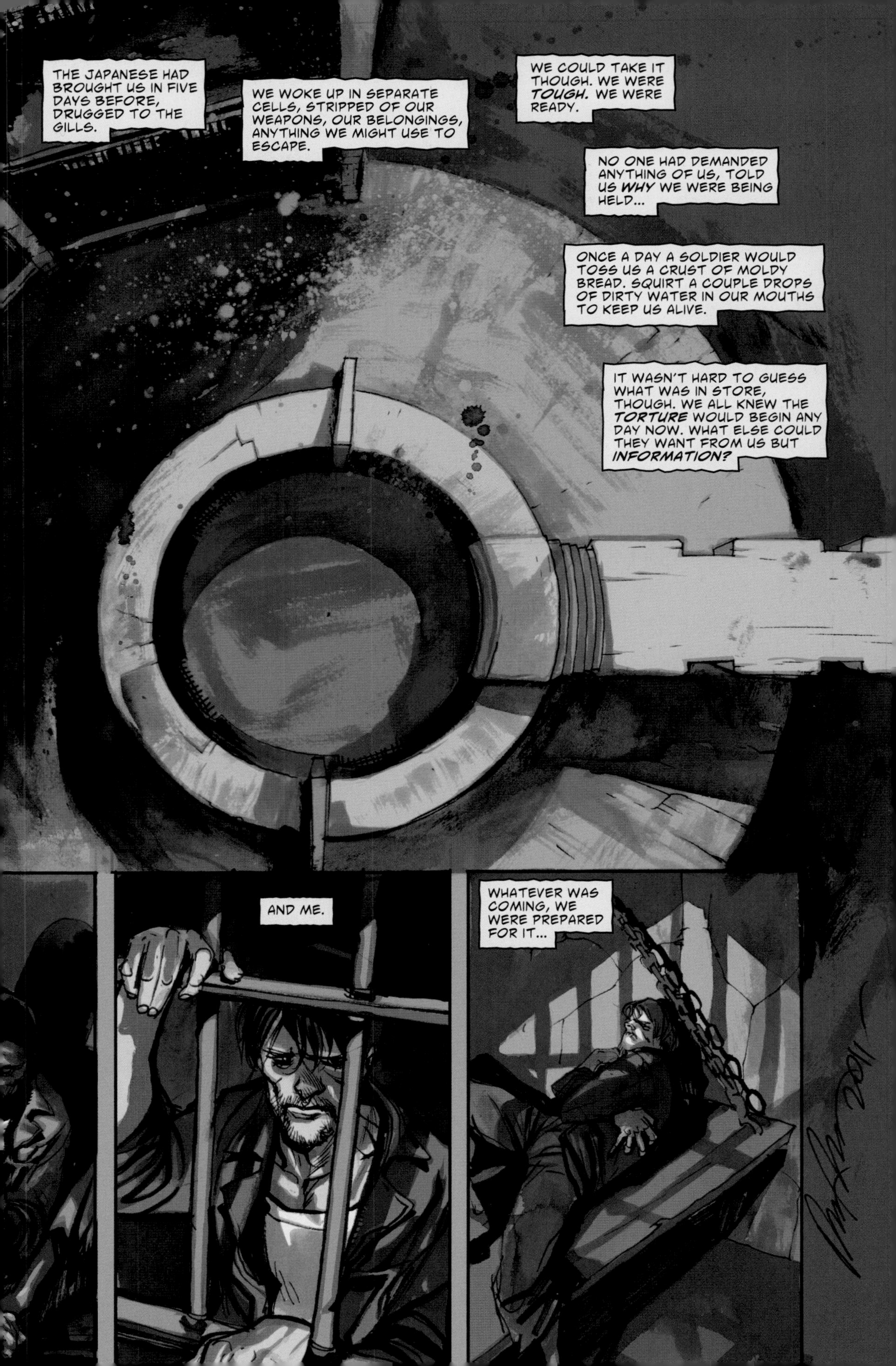
THE JAPANESE HAD BROUGHT US IN FIVE DAYS BEFORE, DRUGGED TO THE GILLS.
WE WOKE UP IN SEPARATE CELLS, STRIPPED OF OUR WEAPONS, OUR BELONGINGS, ANYTHING WE MIGHT USE TO ESCAPE.
WE COULD TAKE IT THOUGH. WE WERE TOUGH. WE WERE READY.
NO ONE HAD DEMANDED ANYTHING OF US, TOLD US WHY WE WERE BEING HELD...
ONCE A DAY A SOLDIER WOULD TOSS US A CRUST OF MOLDY BREAD. SQUIRT A COUPLE DROPS OF DIRTY WATER IN OUR MOUTHS TO KEEP US ALIVE.
IT WASN'T HARD TO GUESS WHAT WAS IN STORE, THOUGH. WE ALL KNEW THE TORTURE WOULD BEGIN ANY DAY NOW. WHAT ELSE COULD THEY WANT FROM US BUT INFORMATION?
AND ME.
WHATEVER WAS COMING, WE WERE PREPARED FOR IT...

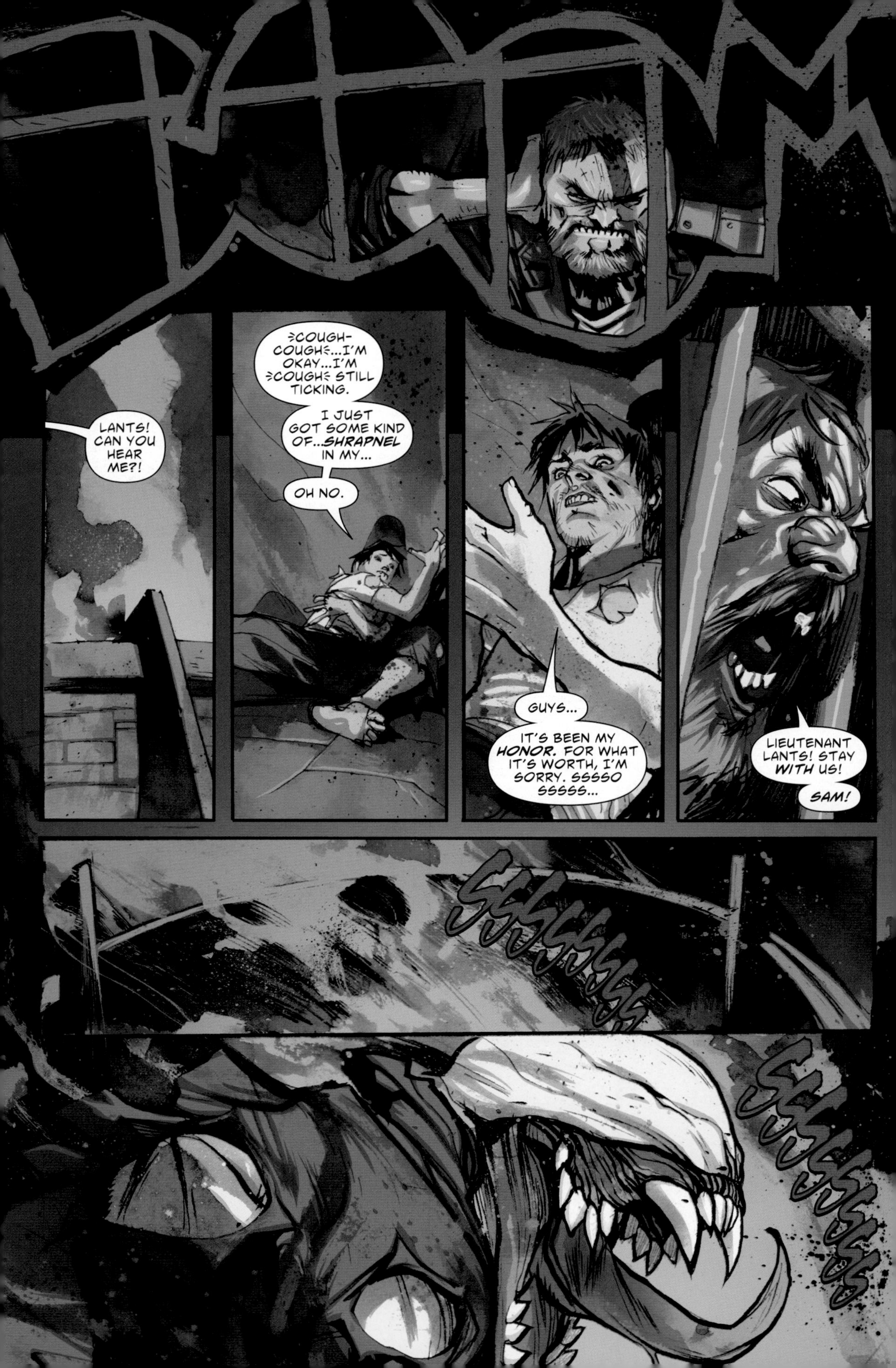
BRA-OOM
LANTS! CAN YOU HEAR ME?!
=COUGH-COUGH=...I'M OKAY...I'M =COUGH= STILL TICKING.
I JUST GOT SOME KIND OF...SHRAPNEL IN MY...
OH NO.
GUYS...
IT'S BEEN MY HONOR. FOR WHAT IT'S WORTH, I'M SORRY. SSSSO SSSSS...
LIEUTENANT LANTS! STAY WITH US!
SAM!
SSSSSSSSS
SSSSSSSSSS

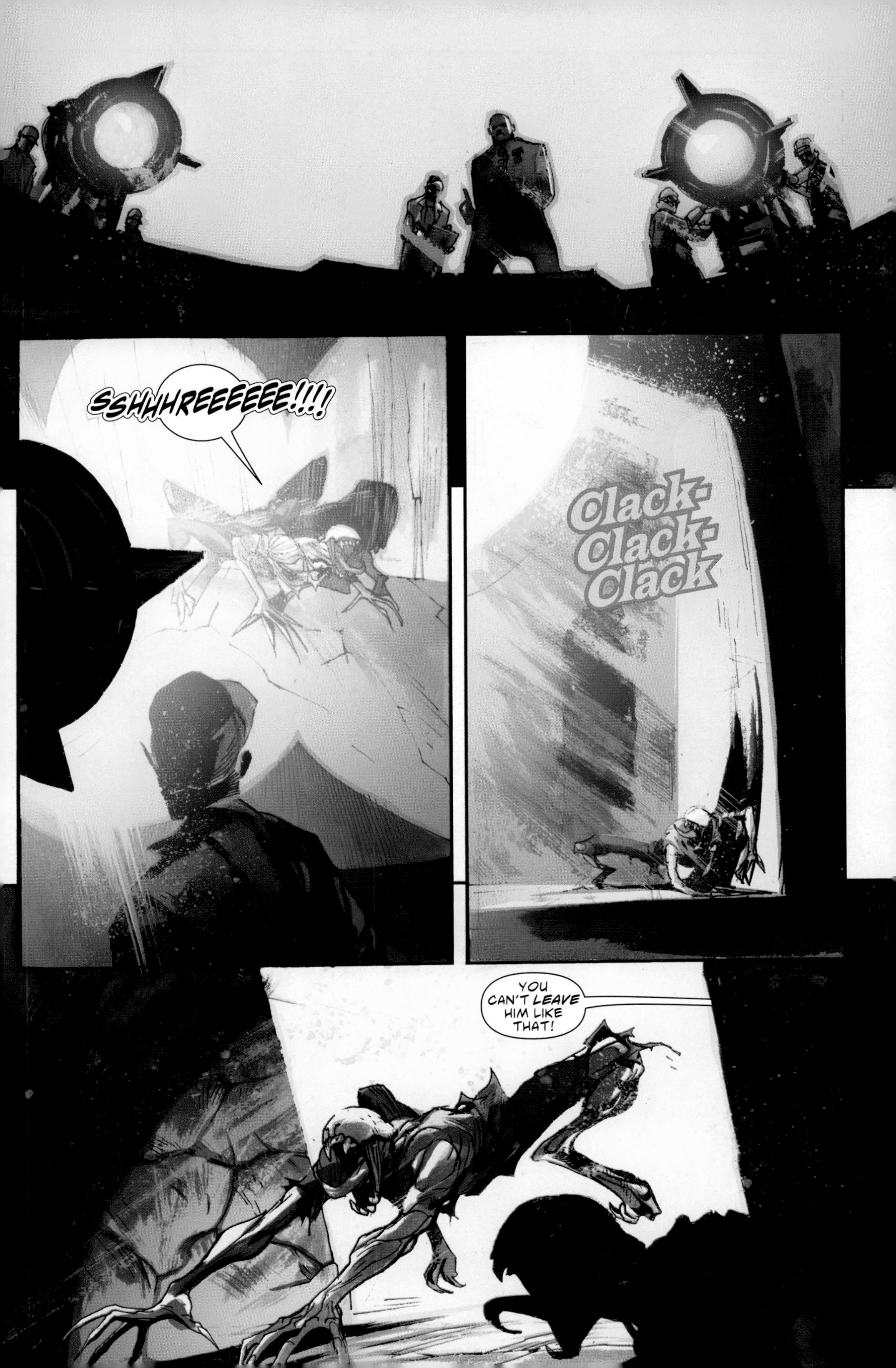
SSHHHREEEEEEE!!!!
Clack-Clack-Clack
YOU CAN'T *LEAVE* HIM LIKE THAT!

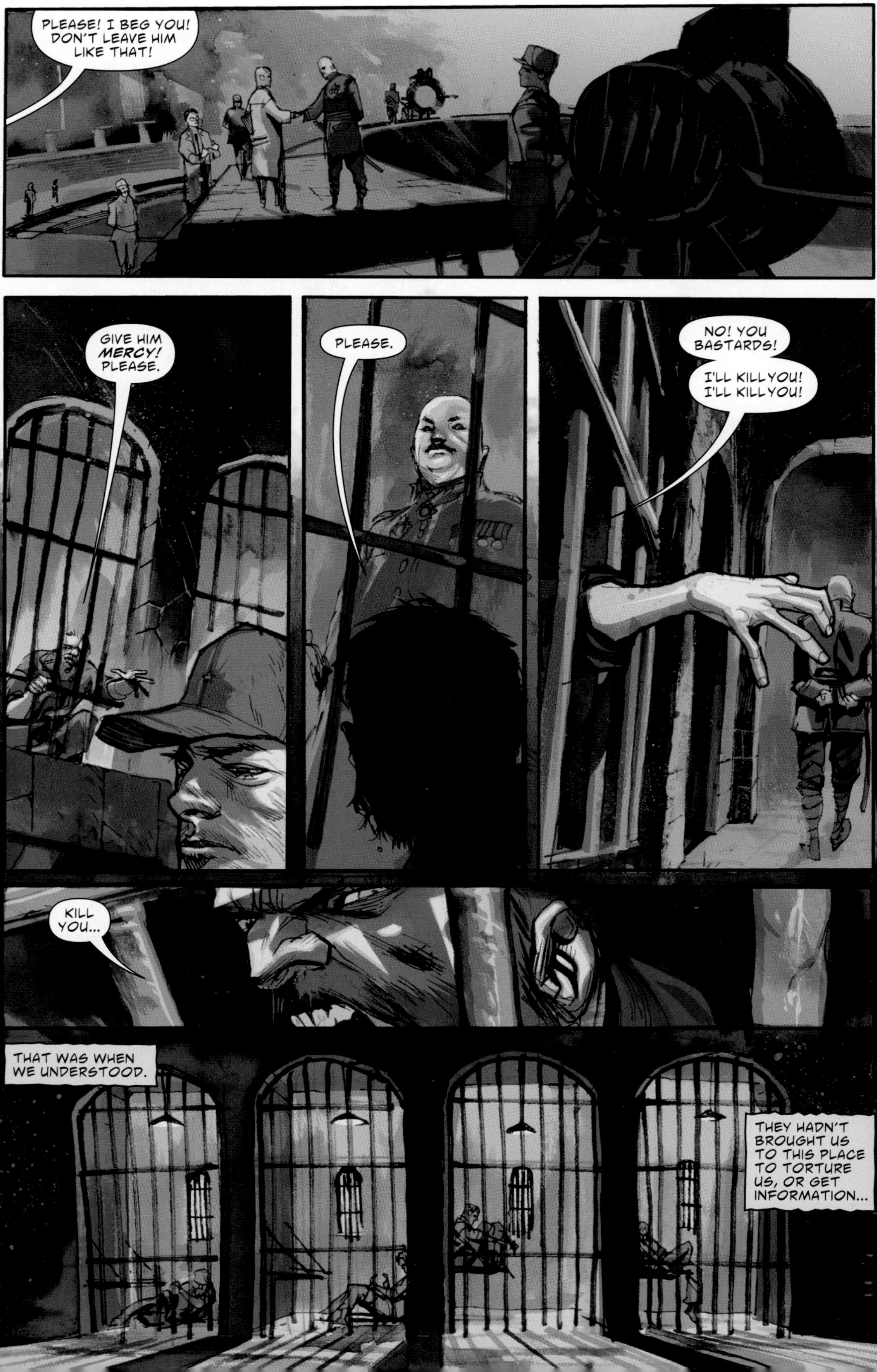
PLEASE! I BEG YOU! DON'T LEAVE HIM LIKE THAT!
GIVE HIM *MERCY!* PLEASE.
PLEASE.
NO! YOU BASTARDS!
I'LL KILL YOU! I'LL KILL YOU!
KILL YOU...
THAT WAS WHEN WE UNDERSTOOD.
THEY HADN'T BROUGHT US TO THIS PLACE TO TORTURE US, OR GET INFORMATION...

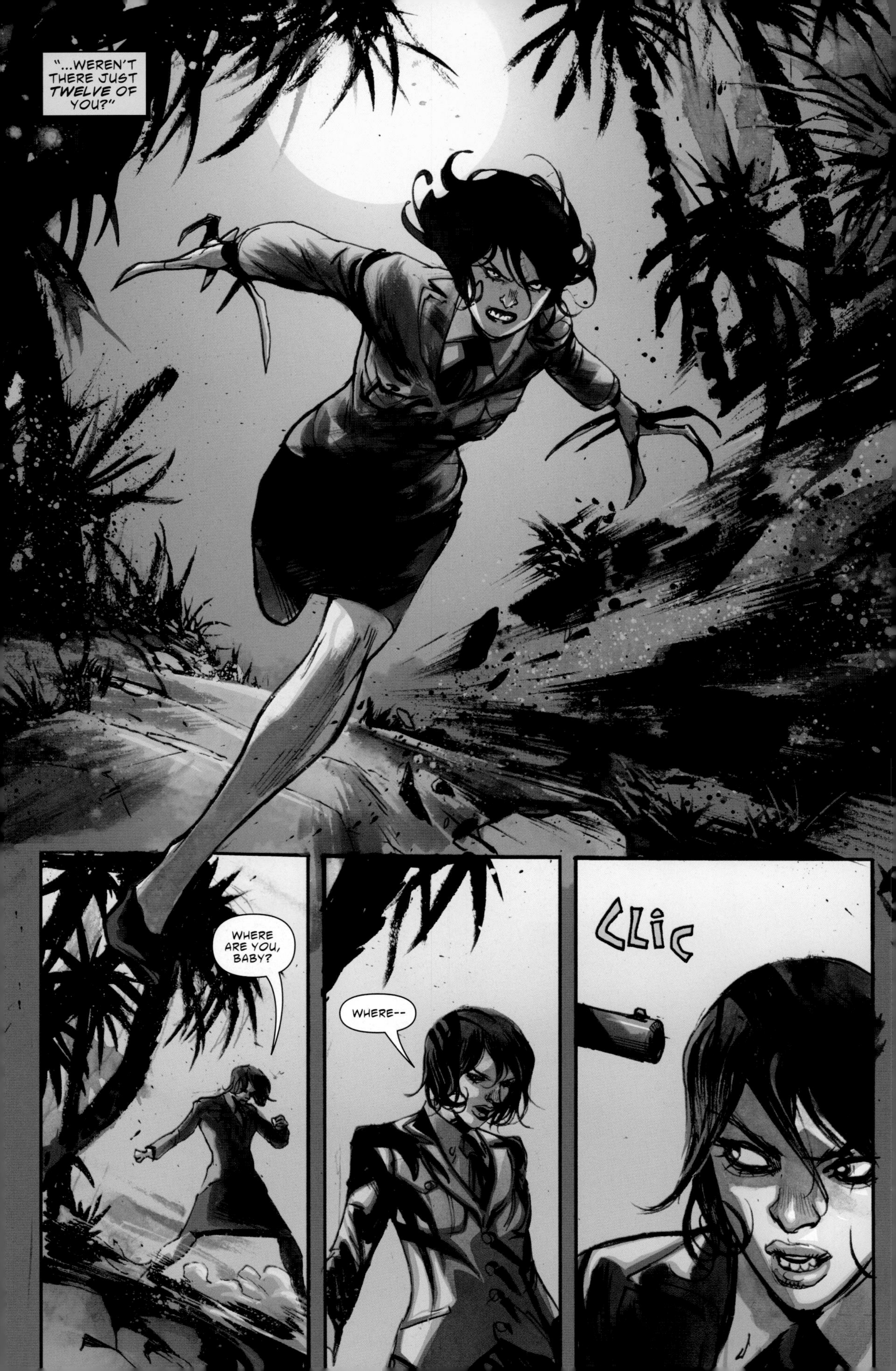
"...WEREN'T THERE JUST *TWELVE* OF YOU?"
WHERE ARE YOU, BABY?
WHERE--
CLIC

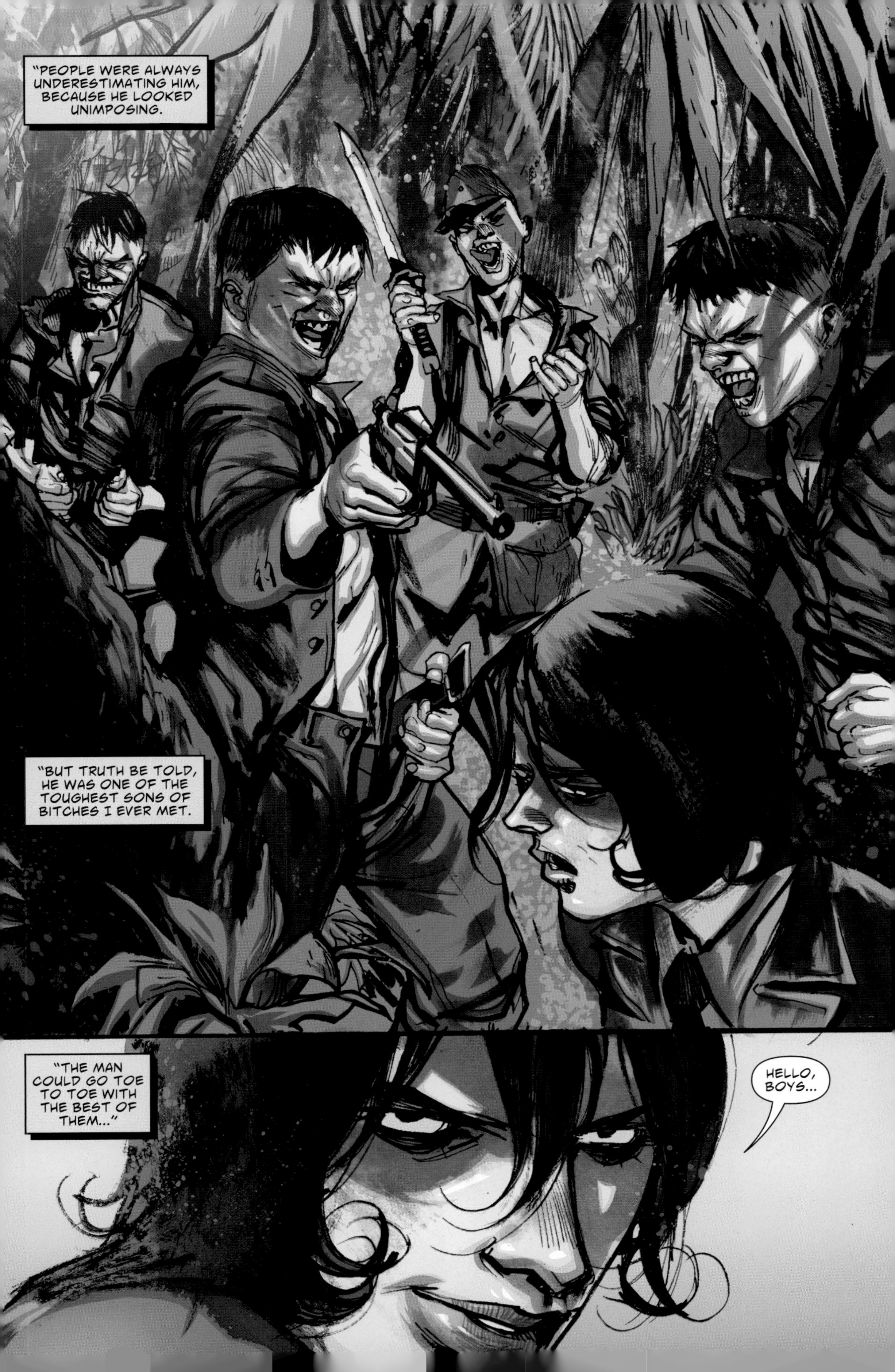
"PEOPLE WERE ALWAYS UNDERESTIMATING HIM, BECAUSE HE LOOKED UNIMPOSING.
"BUT TRUTH BE TOLD, HE WAS ONE OF THE TOUGHEST SONS OF BITCHES I EVER MET.
"THE MAN COULD GO TOE TO TOE WITH THE BEST OF THEM..."
HELLO, BOYS...

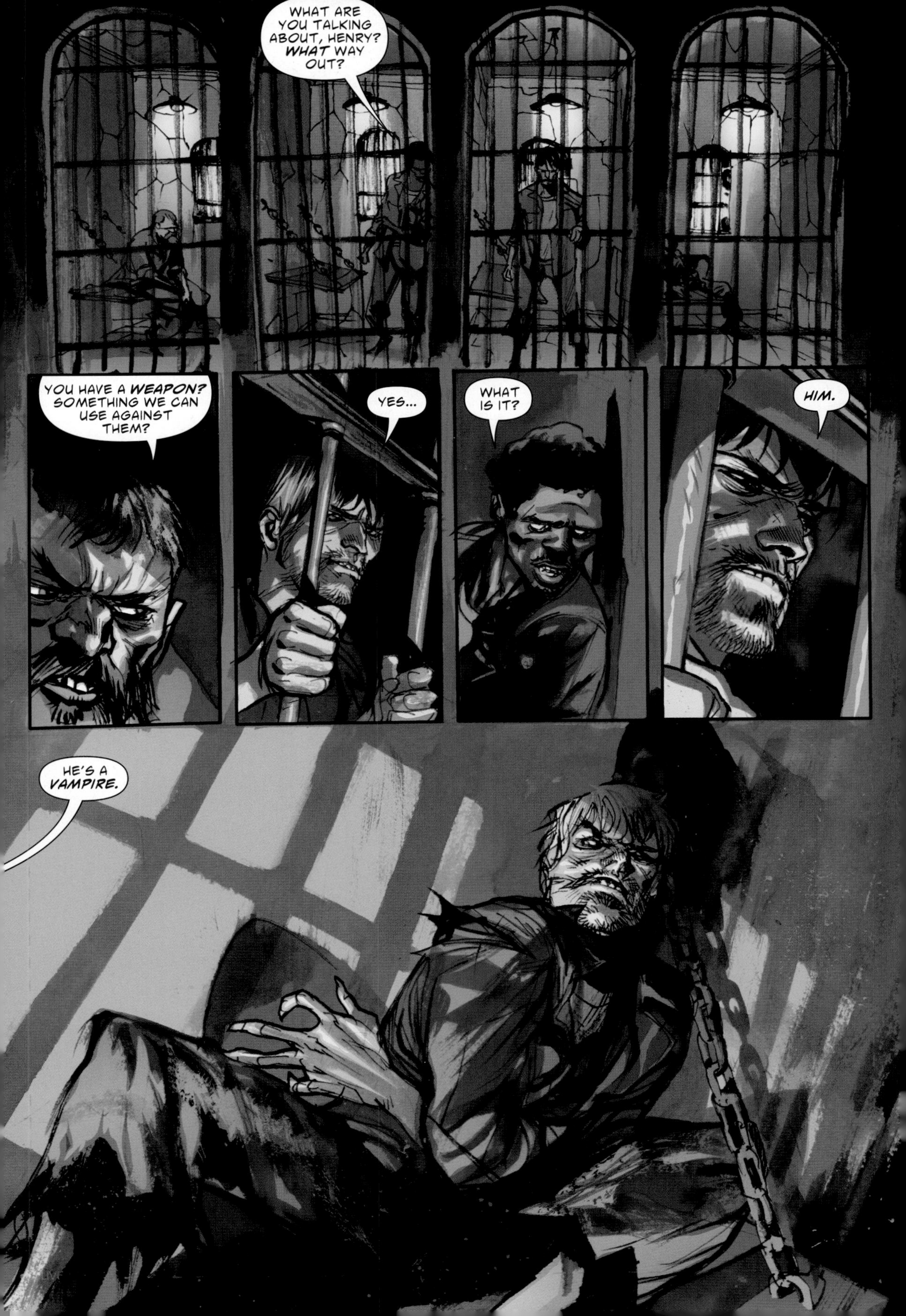
WHAT ARE YOU TALKING ABOUT, HENRY? WHAT WAY OUT?
YOU HAVE A WEAPON? SOMETHING WE CAN USE AGAINST THEM?
YES...
WHAT IS IT?
HIM.
HE'S A VAMPIRE.

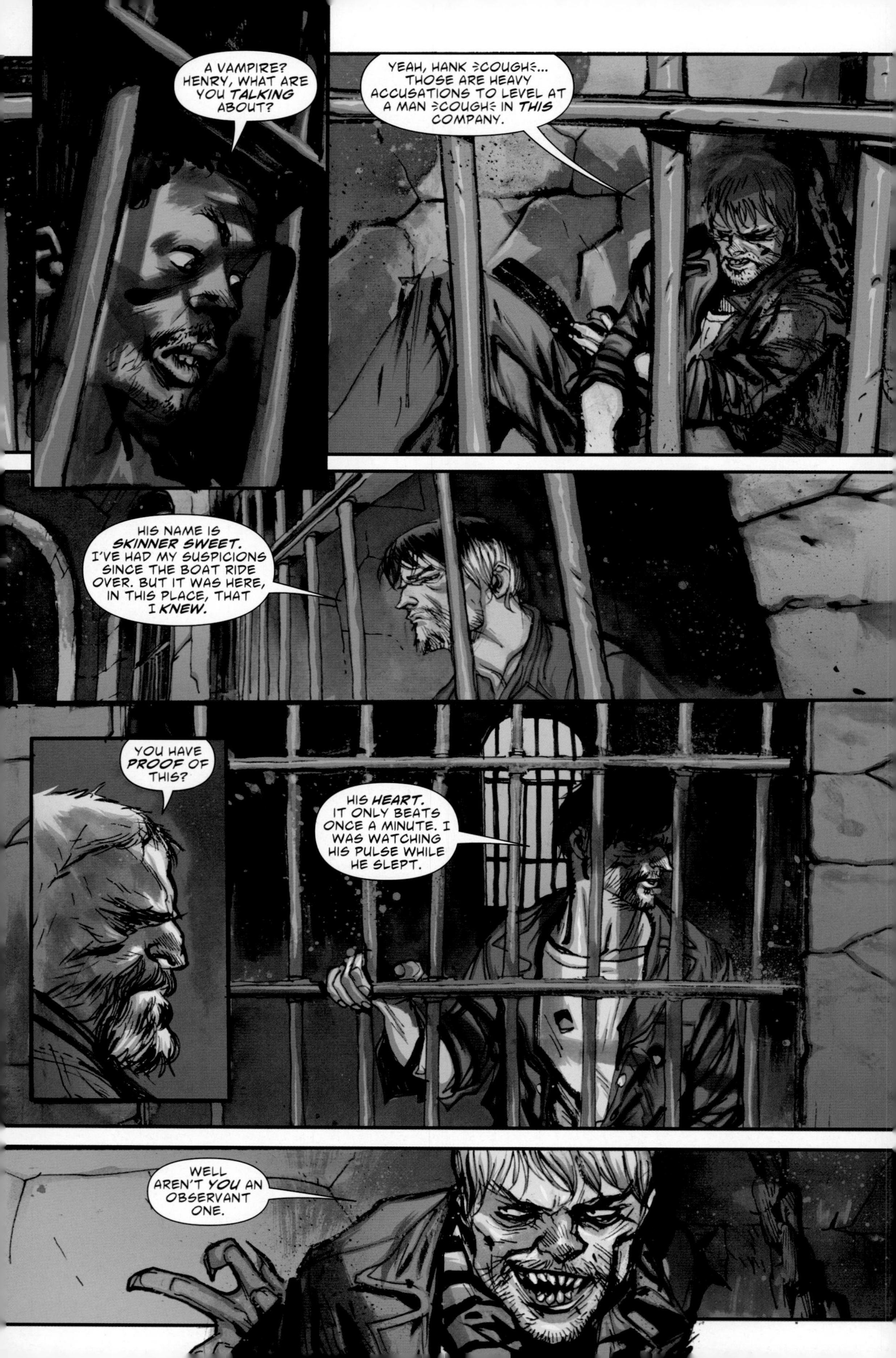
A VAMPIRE? HENRY, WHAT ARE YOU *TALKING* ABOUT?
YEAH, HANK ⪢COUGH⪡... THOSE ARE HEAVY ACCUSATIONS TO LEVEL AT A MAN ⪢COUGH⪡ IN *THIS* COMPANY.
HIS NAME IS *SKINNER SWEET.* I'VE HAD MY SUSPICIONS SINCE THE BOAT RIDE OVER. BUT IT WAS HERE, IN THIS PLACE, THAT I *KNEW.*
YOU HAVE *PROOF* OF THIS?
HIS *HEART.* IT ONLY BEATS ONCE A MINUTE. I WAS WATCHING HIS PULSE WHILE HE SLEPT.
WELL AREN'T *YOU* AN OBSERVANT ONE.

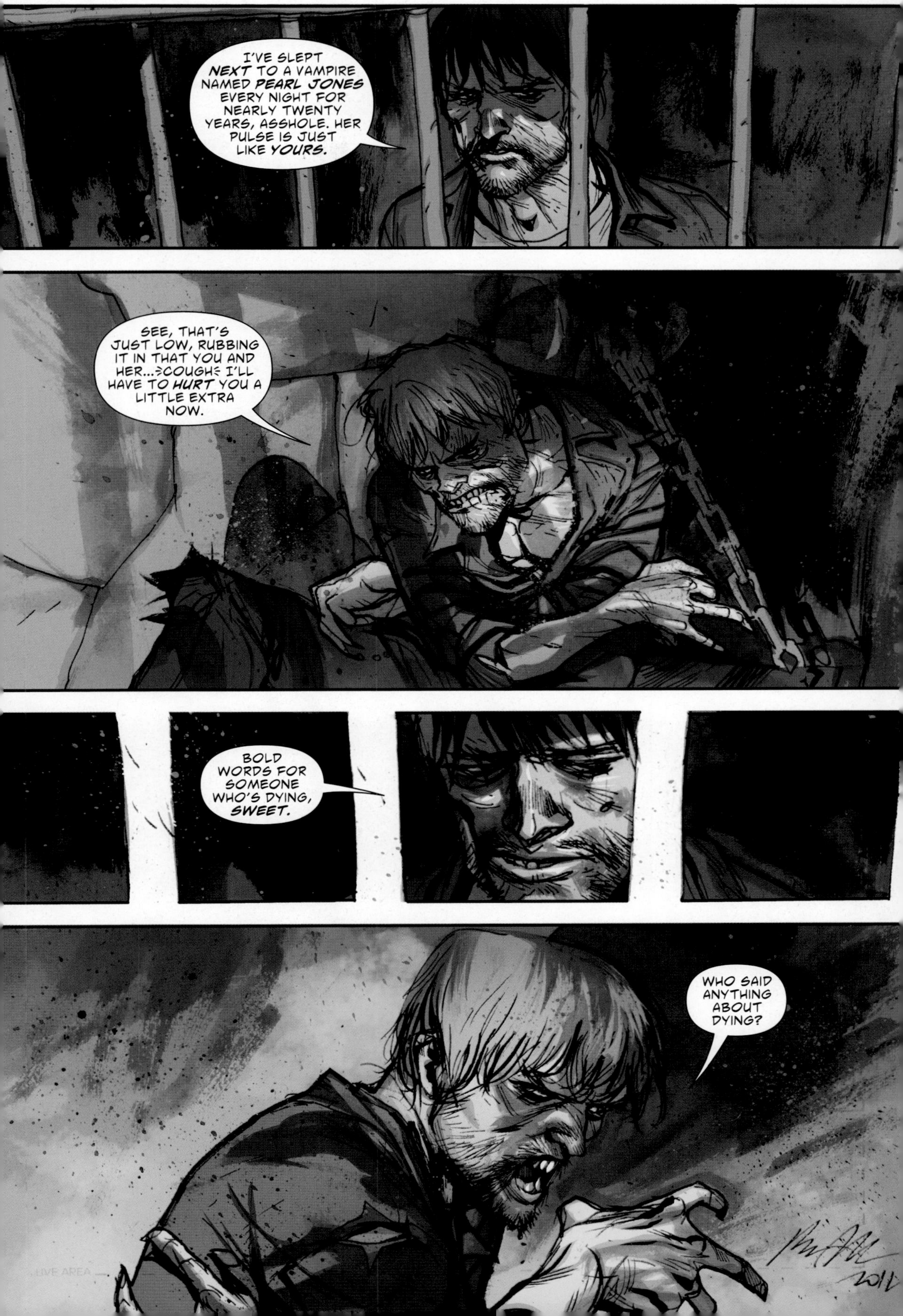
I'VE SLEPT NEXT TO A VAMPIRE NAMED PEARL JONES EVERY NIGHT FOR NEARLY TWENTY YEARS, ASSHOLE. HER PULSE IS JUST LIKE YOURS.
SEE, THAT'S JUST LOW, RUBBING IT IN THAT YOU AND HER... ≥COUGH≤ I'LL HAVE TO HURT YOU A LITTLE EXTRA NOW.
BOLD WORDS FOR SOMEONE WHO'S DYING, SWEET.
WHO SAID ANYTHING ABOUT DYING?

THESE VAMPIRES, THE SPECIES ON THIS ISLAND, WHATEVER THEY ARE, THEY CAN *HURT* YOU, SAME AS US. YOU'RE PRACTICALLY TORN TO PIECES IN THERE. YOU'VE LOST TOO MUCH BLOOD. I DOUBT YOU COULD CHANGE MUCH IF YOU WANTED TO.

IT'S ONLY GOING TO GET WORSE, TOO. DENY IT ALL YOU WANT, BUT ANY MINUTE, YOU'LL COLLAPSE FROM BLOOD LOSS. YOUR BODY WILL GO INTO SHOCK, THEN *HIBERNATION.* FOR ALL INTENTS AND PURPOSES, YOU'LL *DIE,* SKINNER.

NOW I DON'T KNOW WHY YOU'RE HERE, OR WHAT YOU'RE AFTER. MY GUESS IS YOU WERE CLOSING IN ON ME BACK IN *HAWAII,* WHEN YOU CAUGHT WIND OF THIS *MISSION* AND, NOT KNOWING THE OBJECTIVE, DECIDED, HELL, WHY NOT TAG ALONG?

YOU'D GET TO KILL ME, AND AS A BONUS, MAYBE GET YOUR HANDS ON SOMETHING VALUABLE TO THE *VASSALS,* YOUR SWORN ENEMIES.

LIKE I SAID, I DON'T KNOW. AND THE TRUTH IS, I DON'T CARE. BOTTOM LINE: I KNOW ALL TOO WELL WHAT HAPPENS TO PEOPLE WHO MAKE DEALS WITH YOU. IT'S WHY I HAVEN'T CALLED YOU OUT UNTIL NOW.

YOU KNOW ME SO WELL, HANK, THEN WHY ≶COUGH≶ WHY TALK *DEALS* AT ALL?

BECAUSE LIKE I SAID BEFORE, THE VAMPIRES ON THIS ISLAND, THEY CAN HURT YOU, SWEET. KILL YOU.

YOU NEED US TO GET OUT OF HERE, SAME AS WE NEED *YOU.* WE'RE IN IT TOGETHER, AT LEAST UNTIL WE REACH SAFE GROUND. THEN YOU AND ME, WE CAN HAVE IT OUT.

HSSSSS
HSSSSS

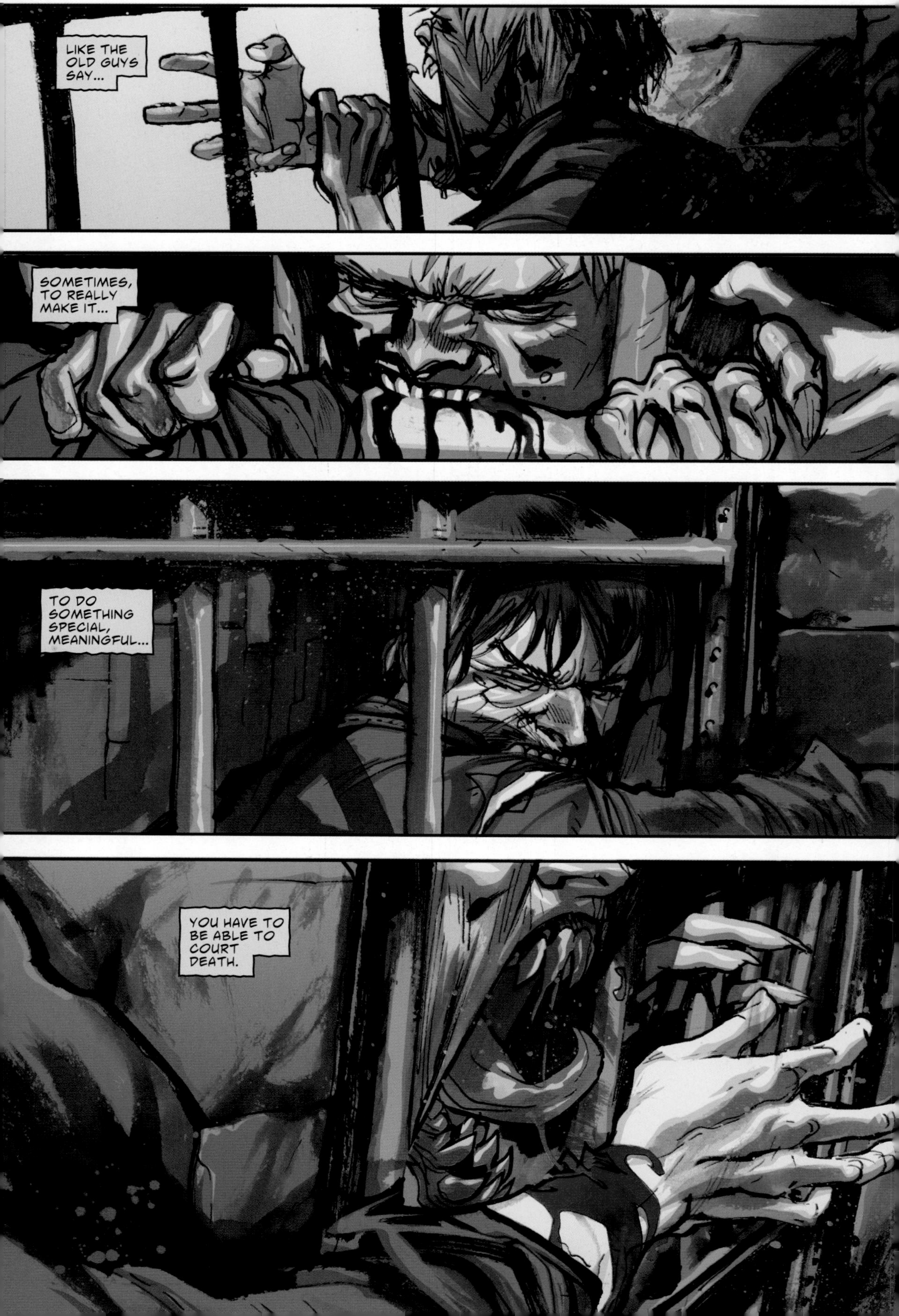
LIKE THE OLD GUYS SAY...
SOMETIMES, TO REALLY MAKE IT...
TO DO SOMETHING SPECIAL, MEANINGFUL...
YOU HAVE TO BE ABLE TO COURT DEATH.

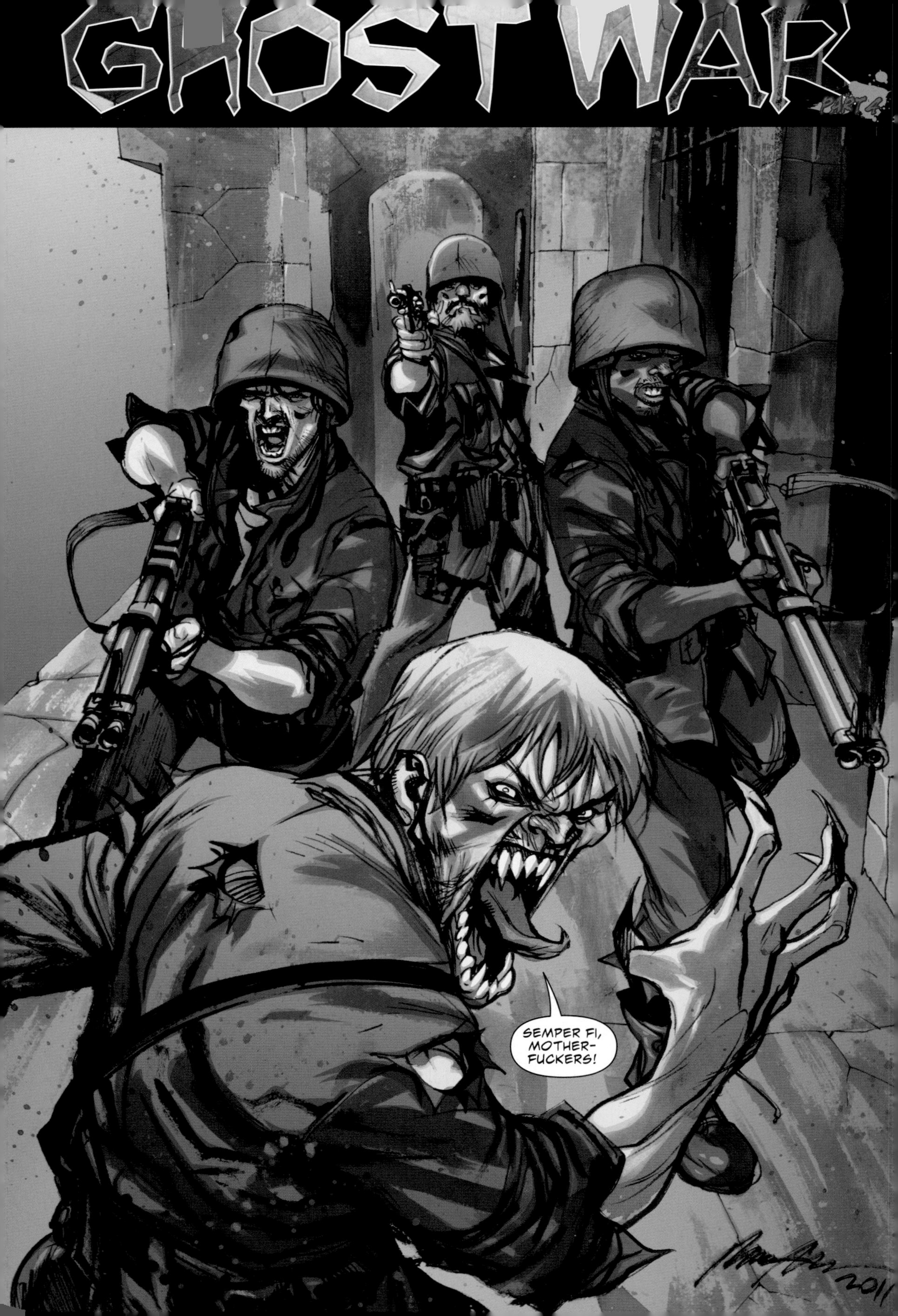
GHOST WAR
PART 4
SEMPER FI, MOTHER-FUCKERS!

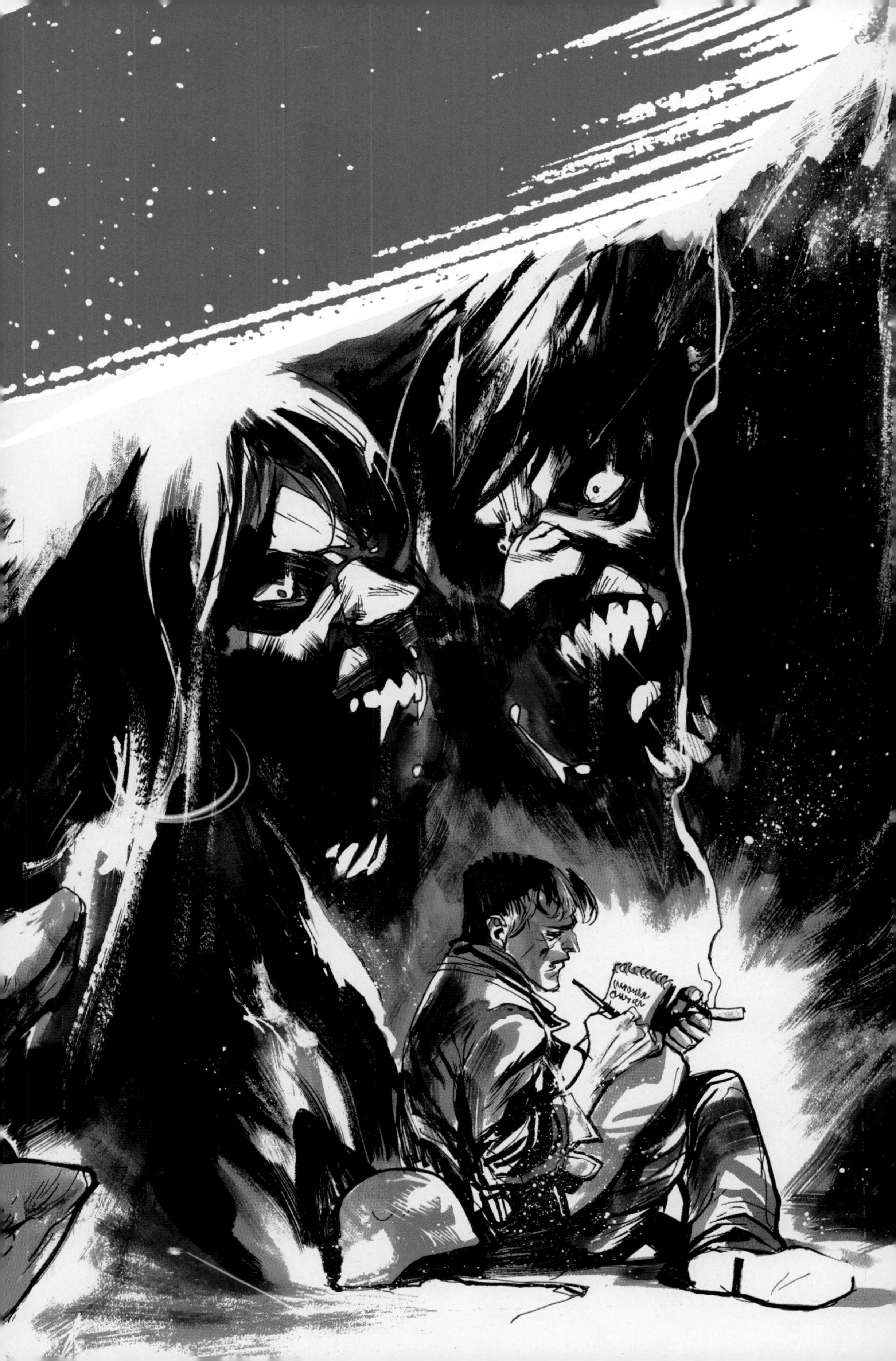

Ghost War

Part Five

Rafael Albuquerque
Artist and cover

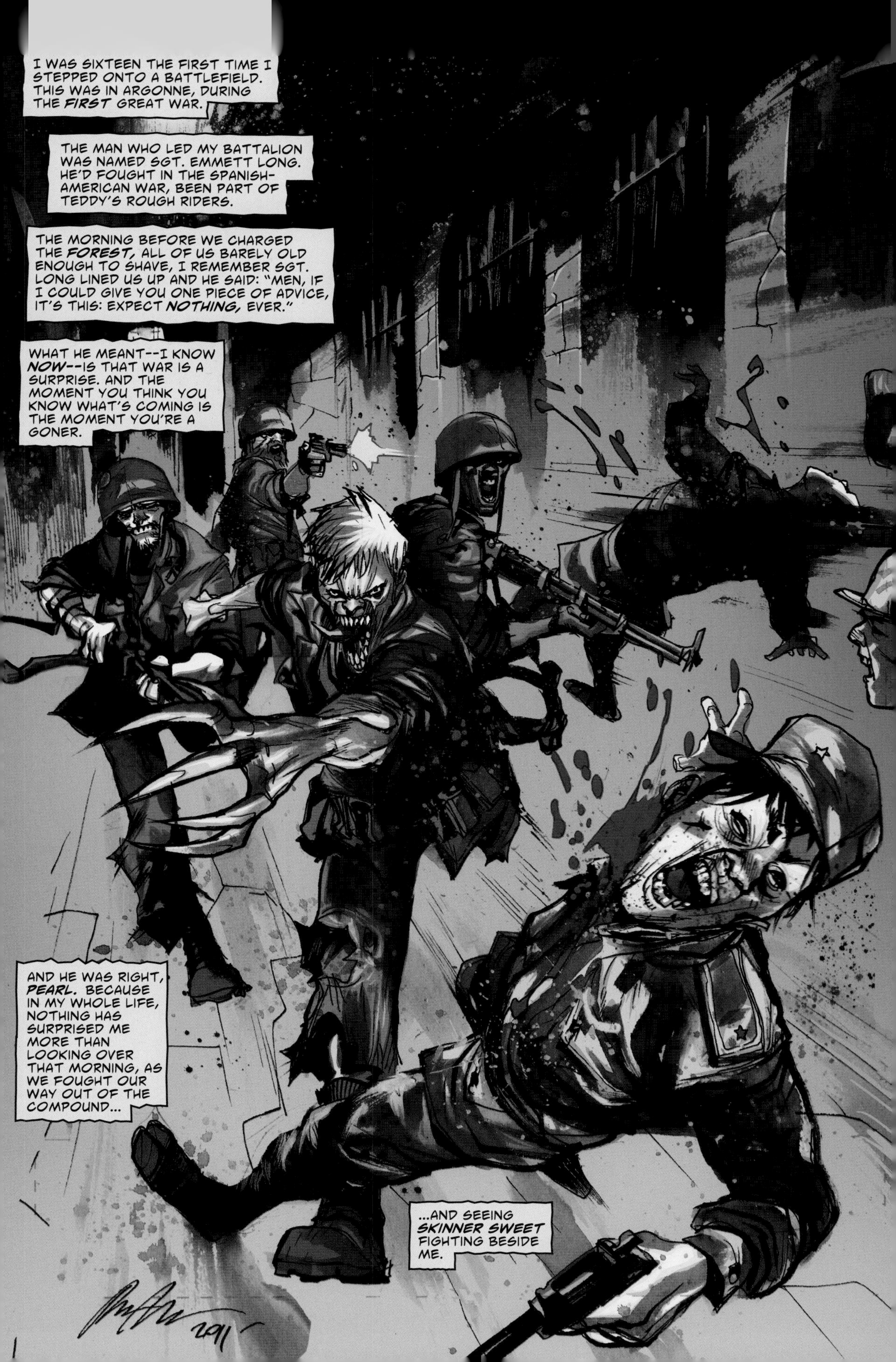
I WAS SIXTEEN THE FIRST TIME I STEPPED ONTO A BATTLEFIELD. THIS WAS IN ARGONNE, DURING THE FIRST GREAT WAR.
THE MAN WHO LED MY BATTALION WAS NAMED SGT. EMMETT LONG. HE'D FOUGHT IN THE SPANISH-AMERICAN WAR, BEEN PART OF TEDDY'S ROUGH RIDERS.
THE MORNING BEFORE WE CHARGED THE FOREST, ALL OF US BARELY OLD ENOUGH TO SHAVE, I REMEMBER SGT. LONG LINED US UP AND HE SAID: "MEN, IF I COULD GIVE YOU ONE PIECE OF ADVICE, IT'S THIS: EXPECT NOTHING, EVER."
WHAT HE MEANT--I KNOW NOW--IS THAT WAR IS A SURPRISE. AND THE MOMENT YOU THINK YOU KNOW WHAT'S COMING IS THE MOMENT YOU'RE A GONER.
AND HE WAS RIGHT, PEARL. BECAUSE IN MY WHOLE LIFE, NOTHING HAS SURPRISED ME MORE THAN LOOKING OVER THAT MORNING, AS WE FOUGHT OUR WAY OUT OF THE COMPOUND...
...AND SEEING SKINNER SWEET FIGHTING BESIDE ME.

CRACK

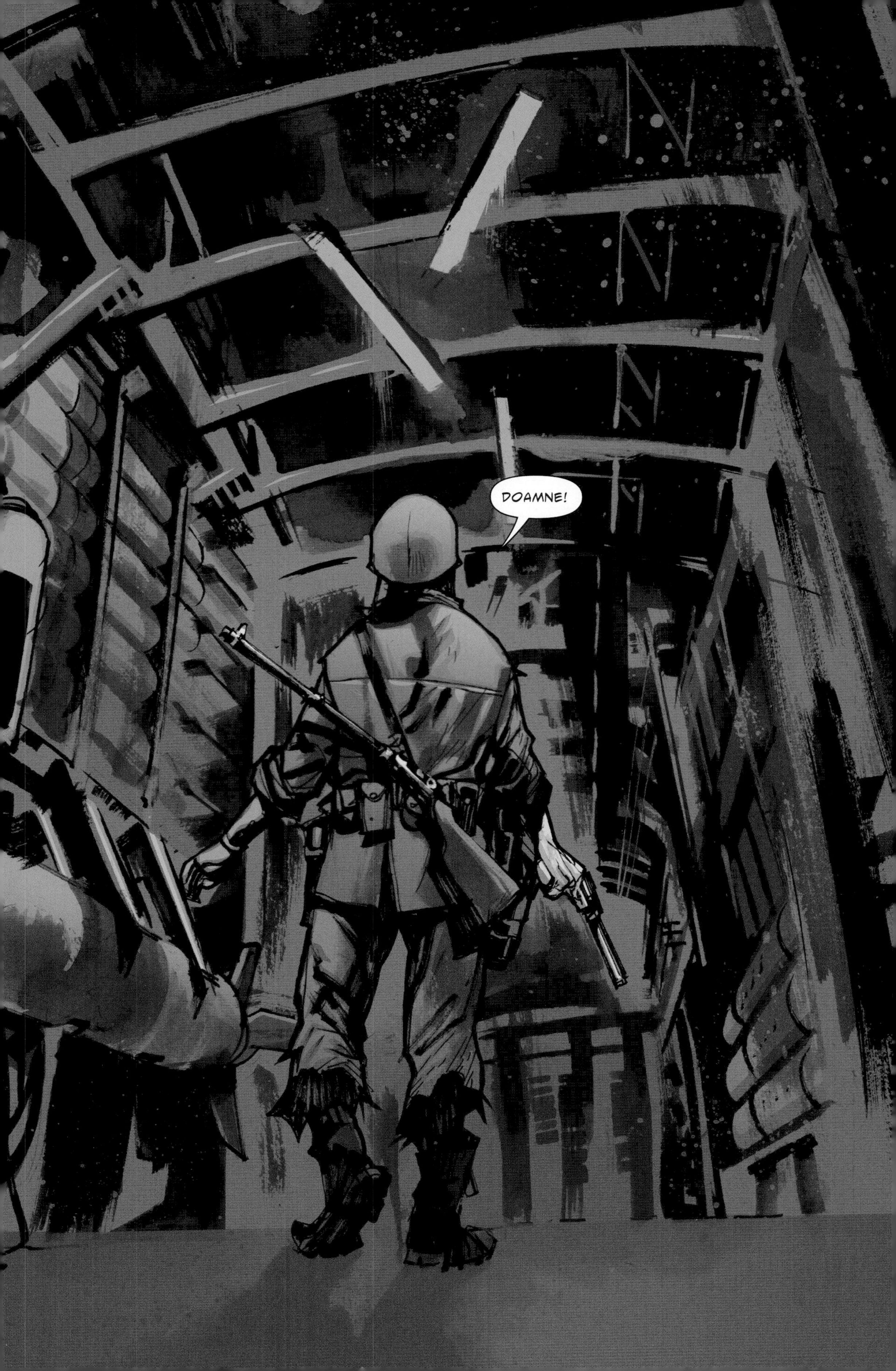
DOAMNE!

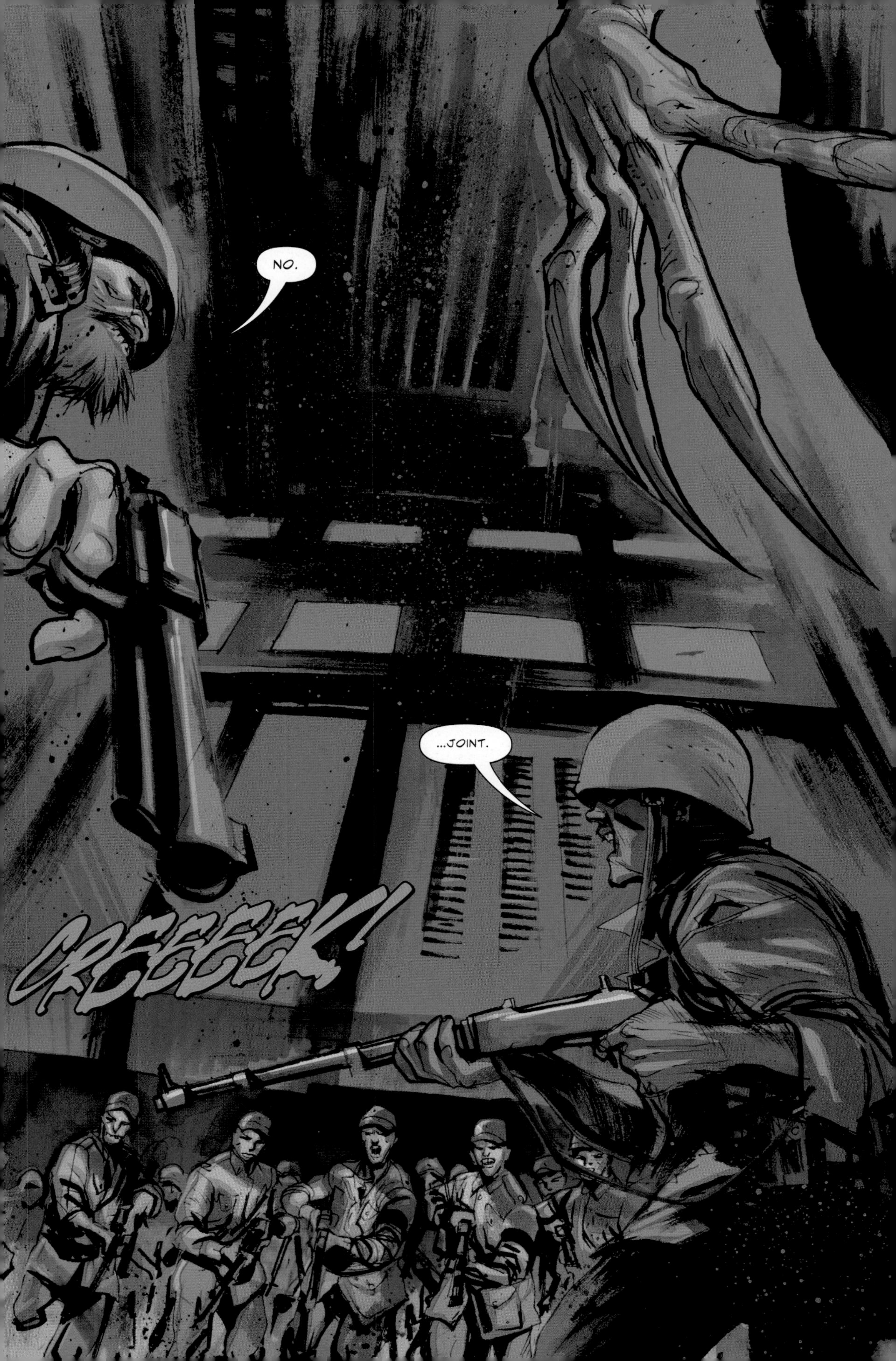
NO.
...JOINT.
CREEEEK!

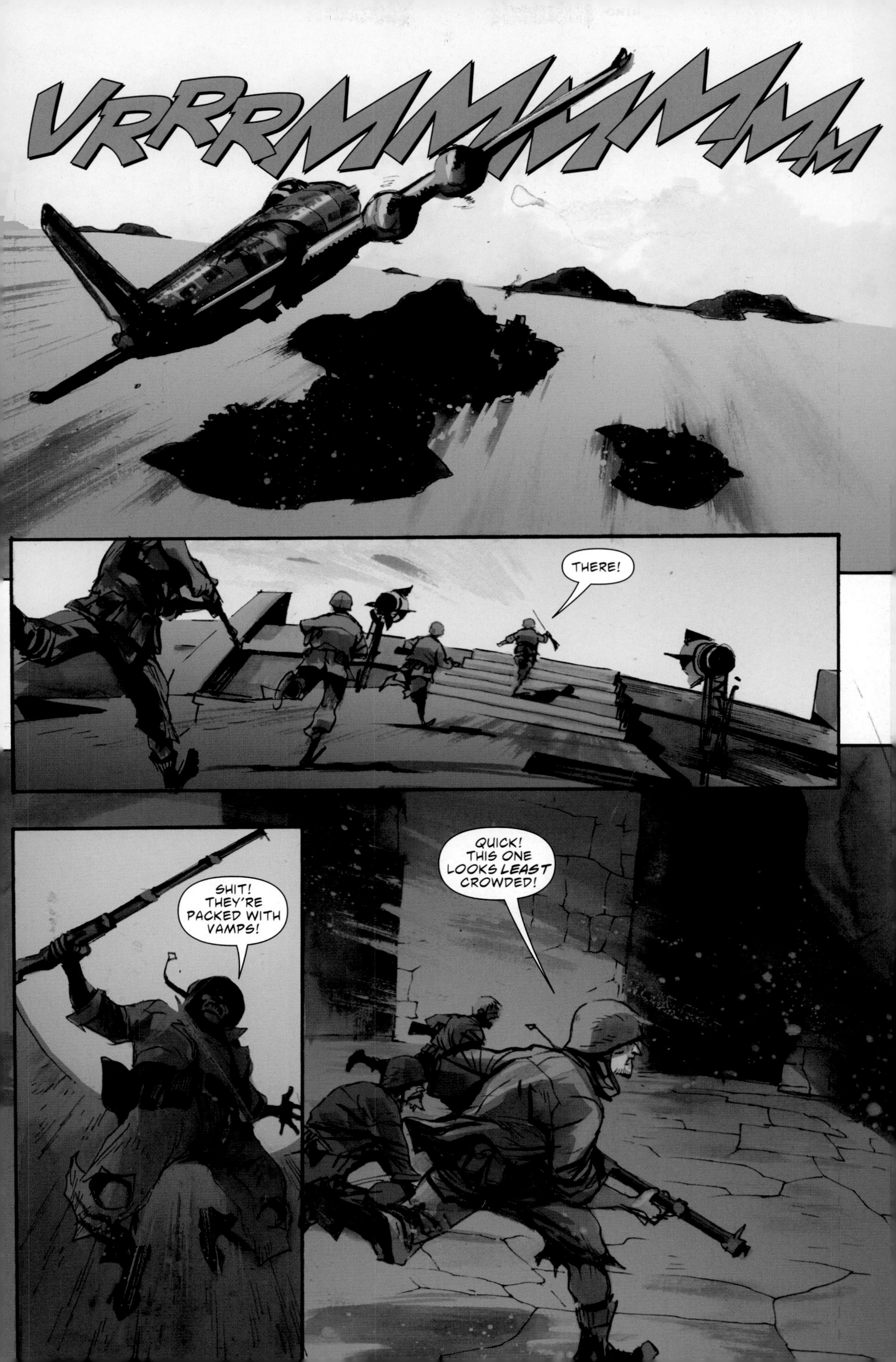
VRRRMMMMMMMm
THERE!
SHIT! THEY'RE PACKED WITH VAMPS!
QUICK! THIS ONE LOOKS LEAST CROWDED!

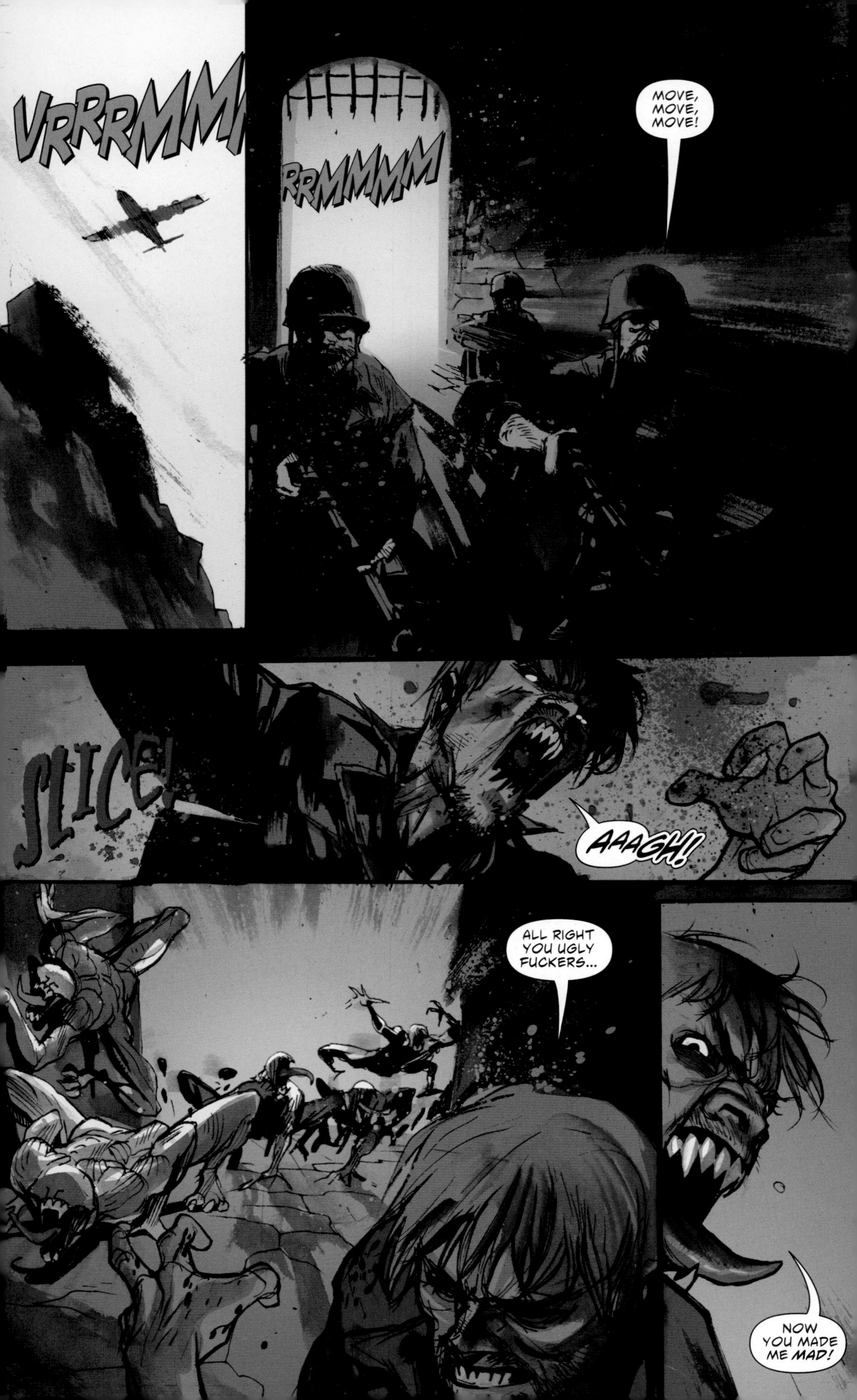
VRRRMMM
RRMMMMM
MOVE, MOVE, MOVE!
SLICE!
AAAGH!
ALL RIGHT YOU UGLY FUCKERS...
NOW YOU MADE ME *MAD!*

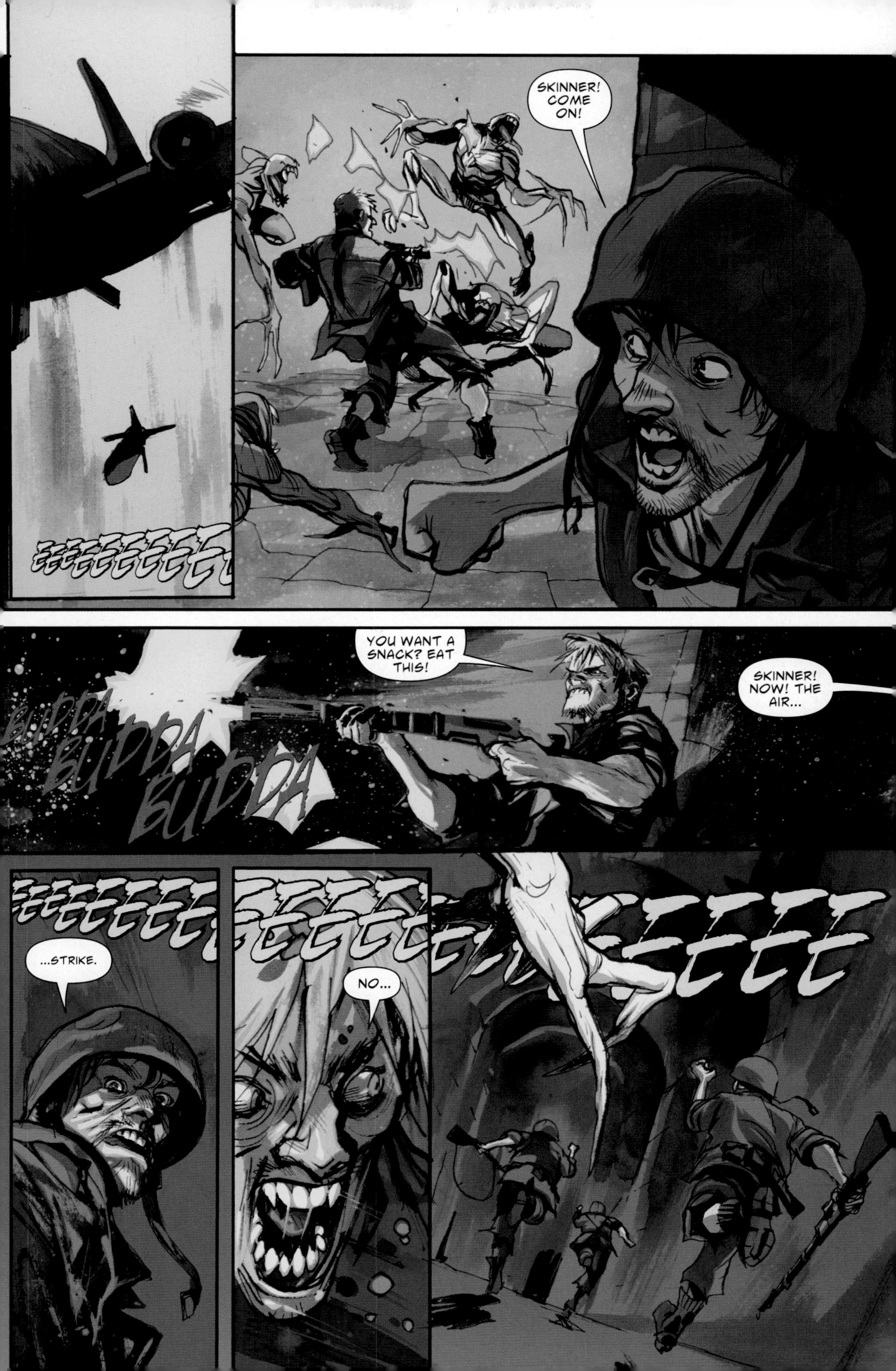
EEEEEEEEEEEE
SKINNER! COME ON!
BUDDA BUDDA BUDDA
YOU WANT A SNACK? EAT THIS!
SKINNER! NOW! THE AIR...
EEEEEEEEEEEEEEEEEEEEEEEEEEEEEEE
...STRIKE.
NO...

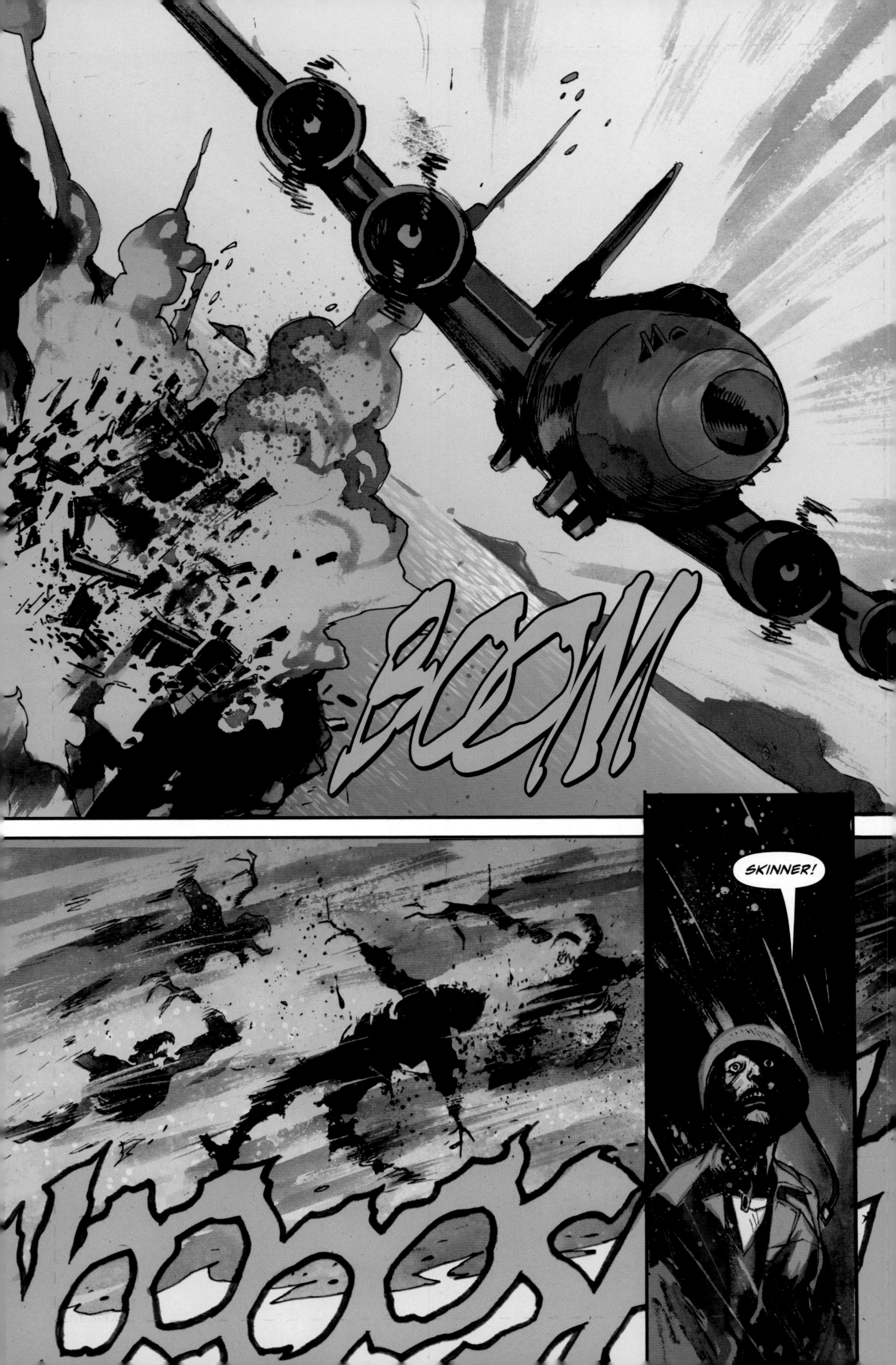
BOOM
SKINNER!

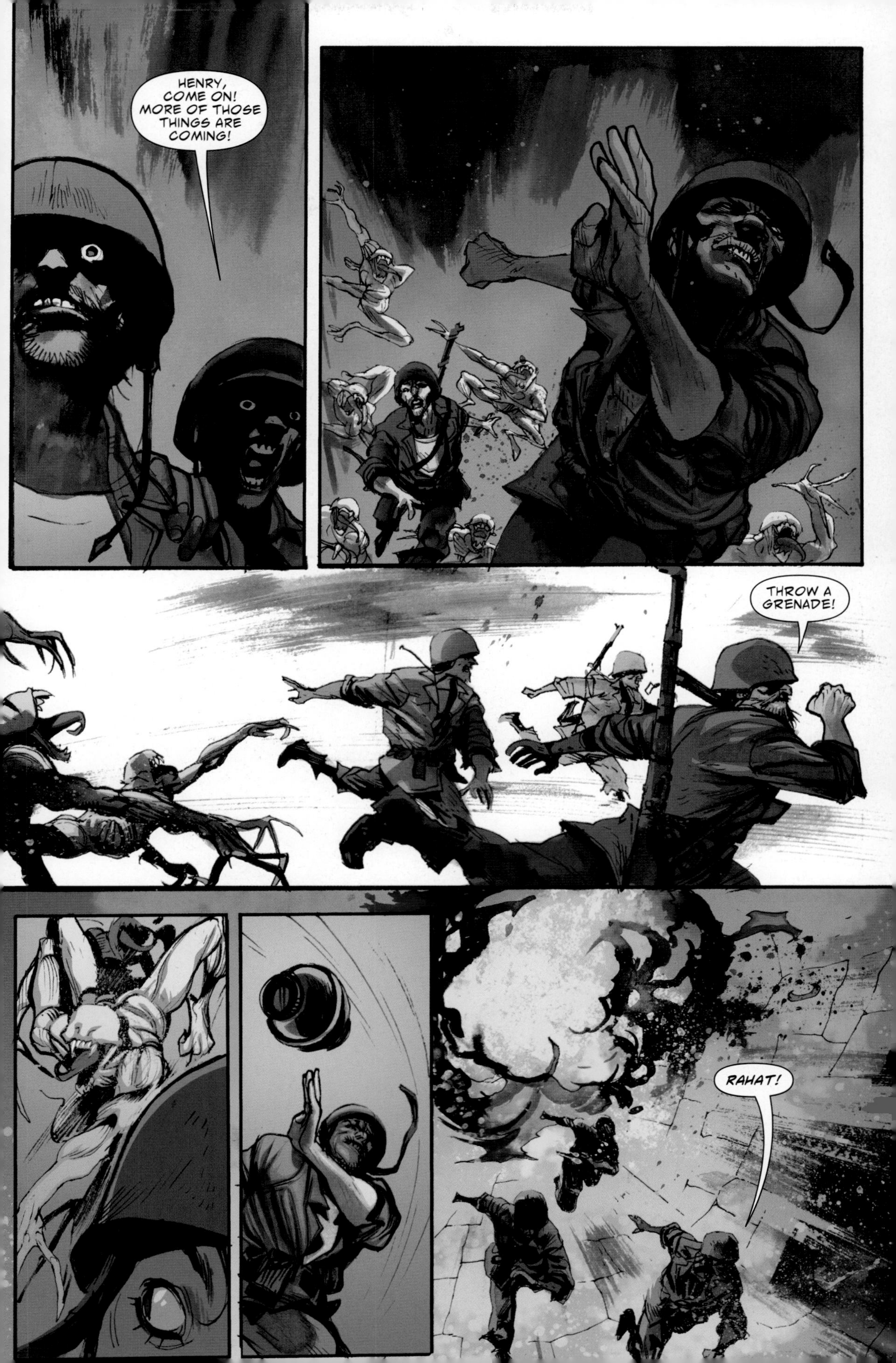
HENRY, COME ON! MORE OF THOSE THINGS ARE COMING!
THROW A GRENADE!
RAHAT!

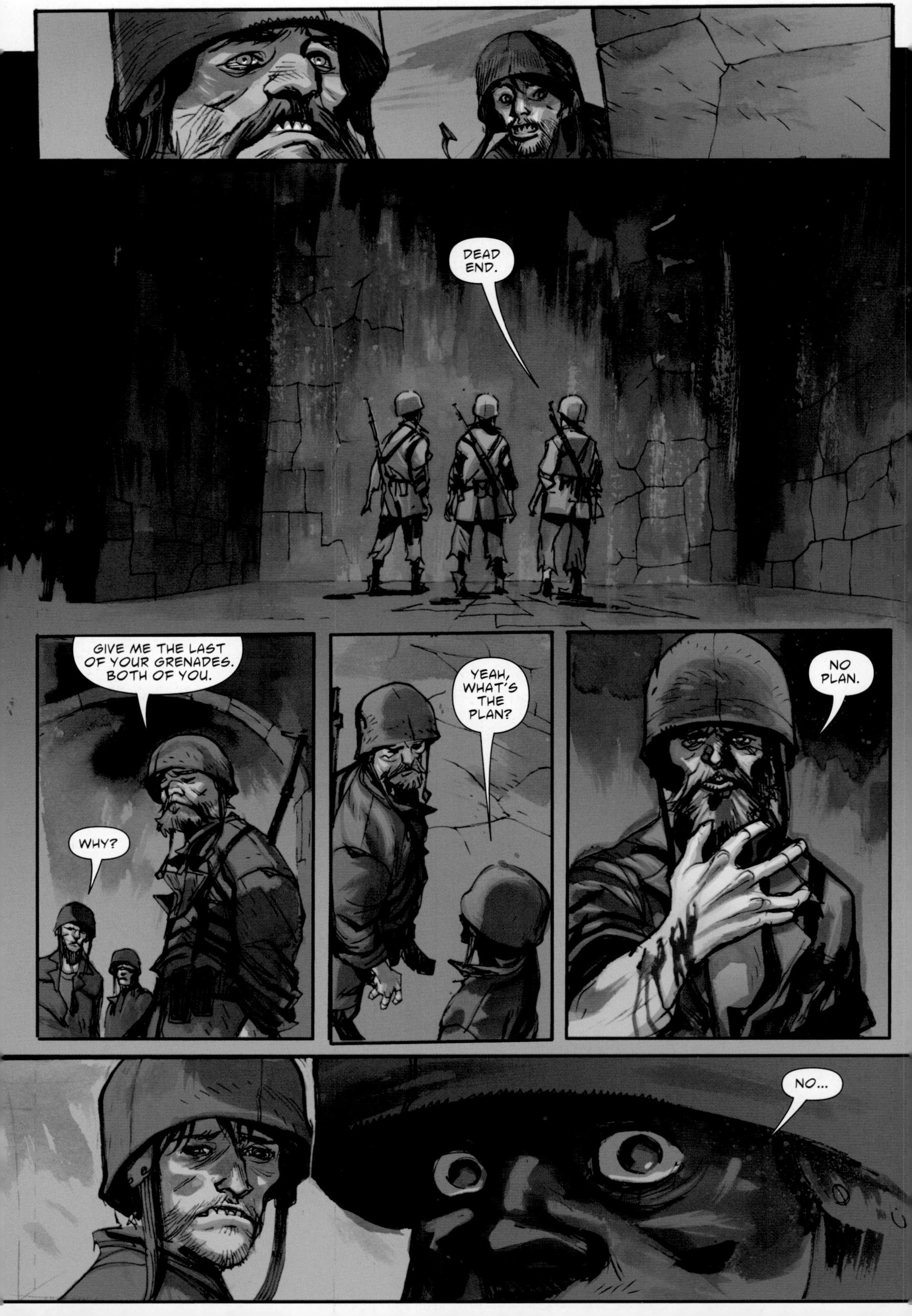
DEAD END.
GIVE ME THE LAST OF YOUR GRENADES. BOTH OF YOU.
WHY?
YEAH, WHAT'S THE PLAN?
NO PLAN.
NO...

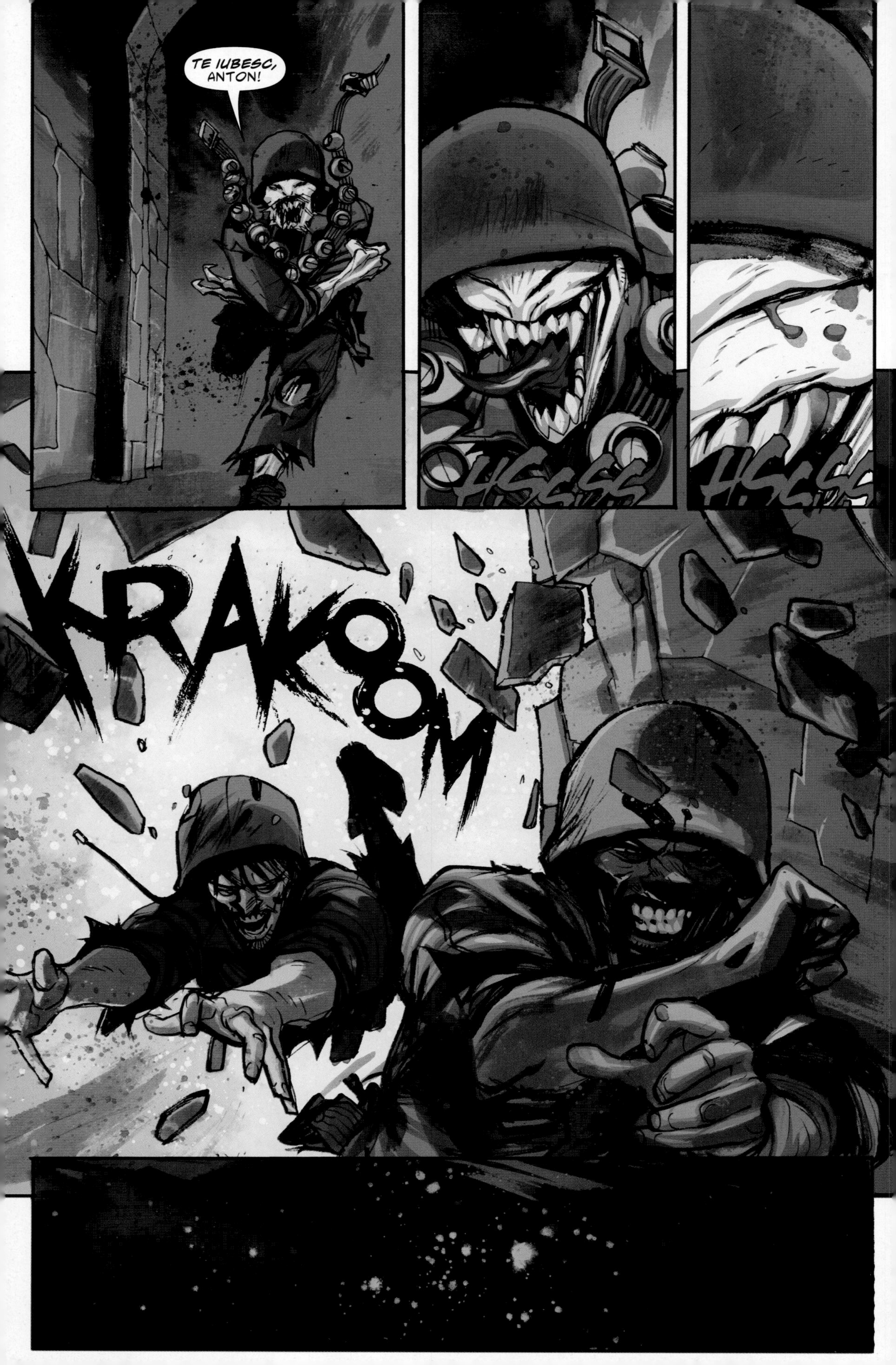
TE IUBESC, ANTON!
HSSSS
HSSSS
KRAKOOM

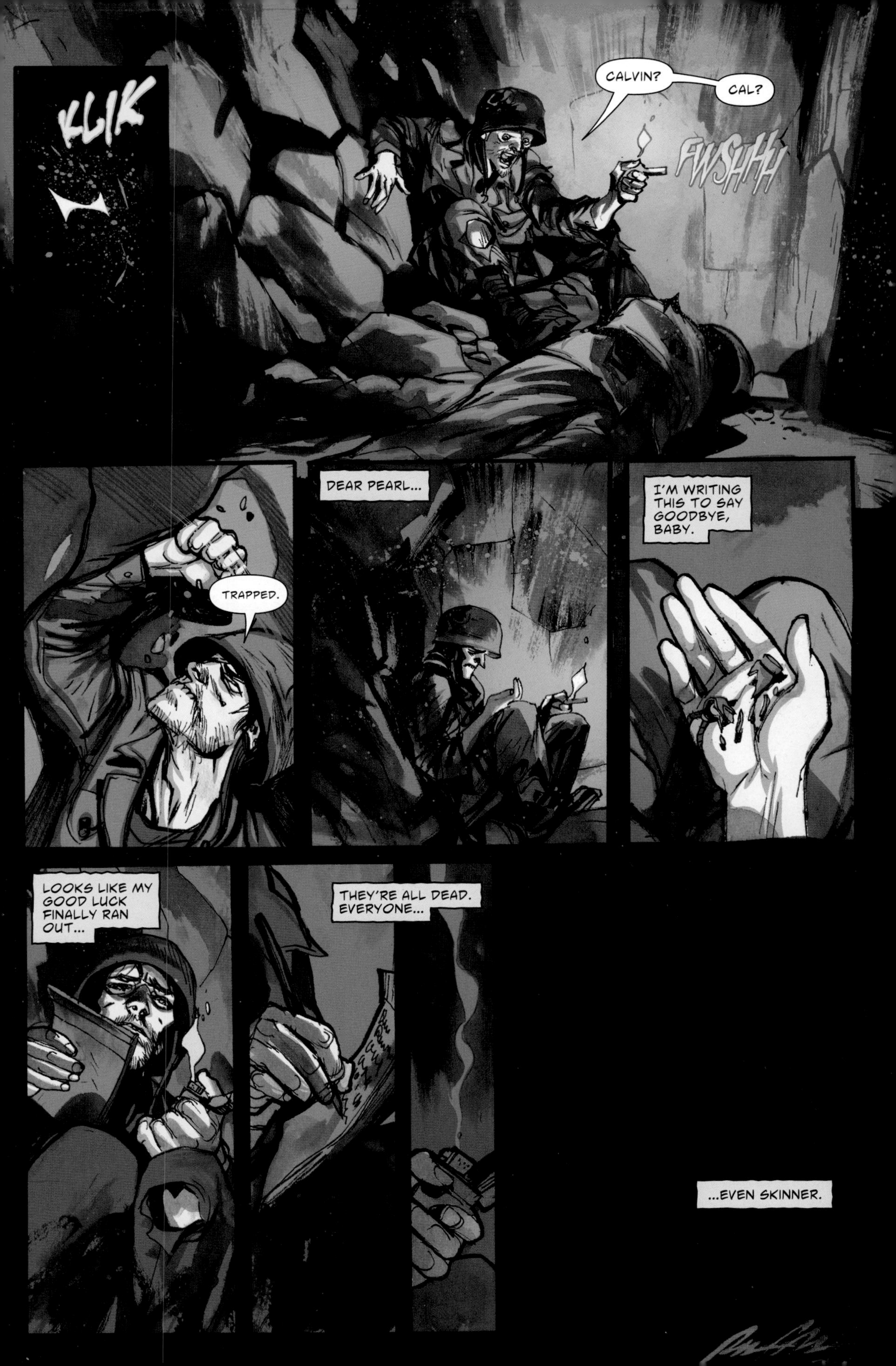
KLIK
CALVIN?
CAL?
FWSHHH
TRAPPED.
DEAR PEARL...
I'M WRITING THIS TO SAY GOODBYE, BABY.
LOOKS LIKE MY GOOD LUCK FINALLY RAN OUT...
THEY'RE ALL DEAD. EVERYONE...
...EVEN SKINNER.

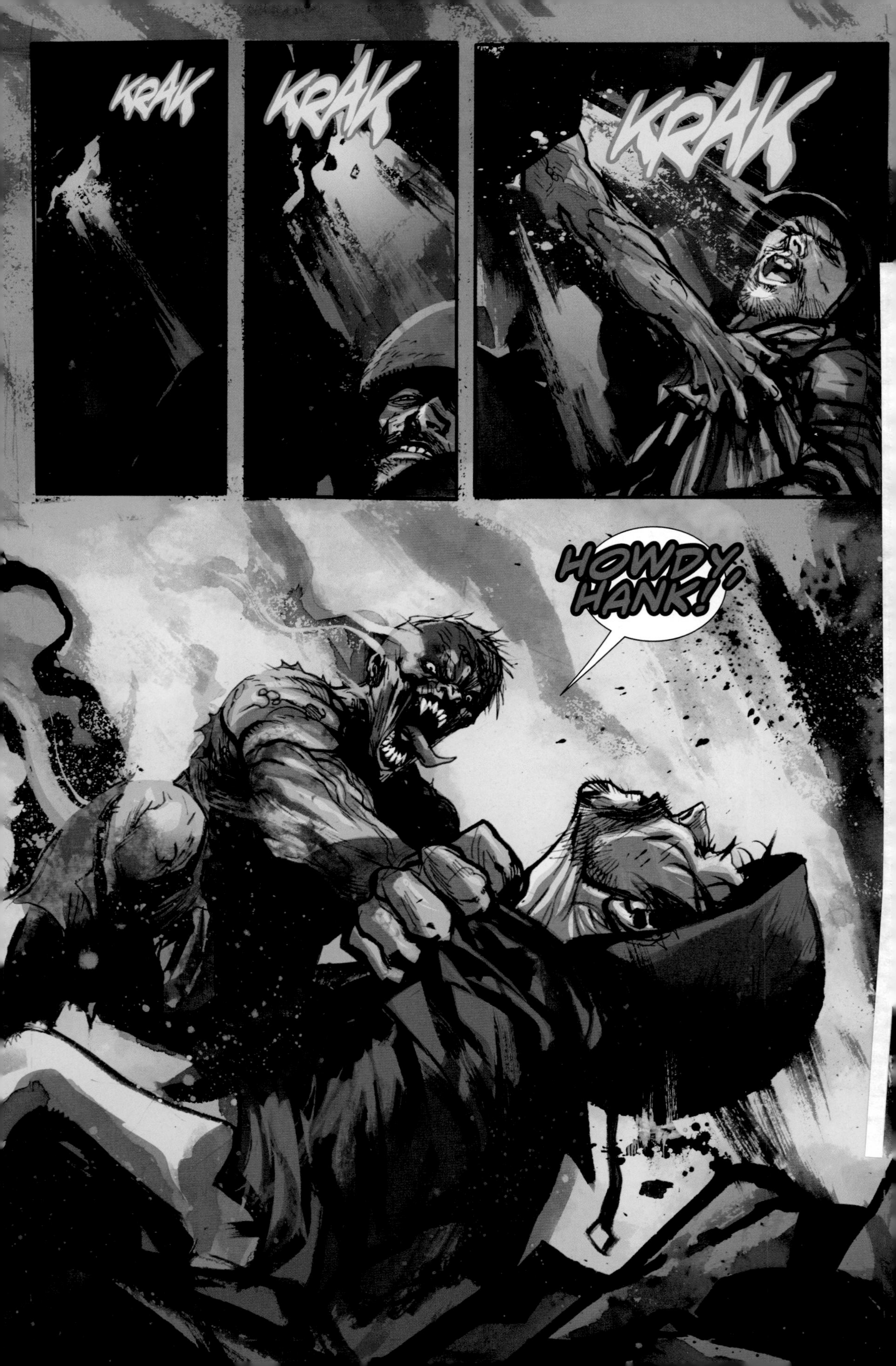
KRAK
KRAK
KRAK
HOWDY, HANK!

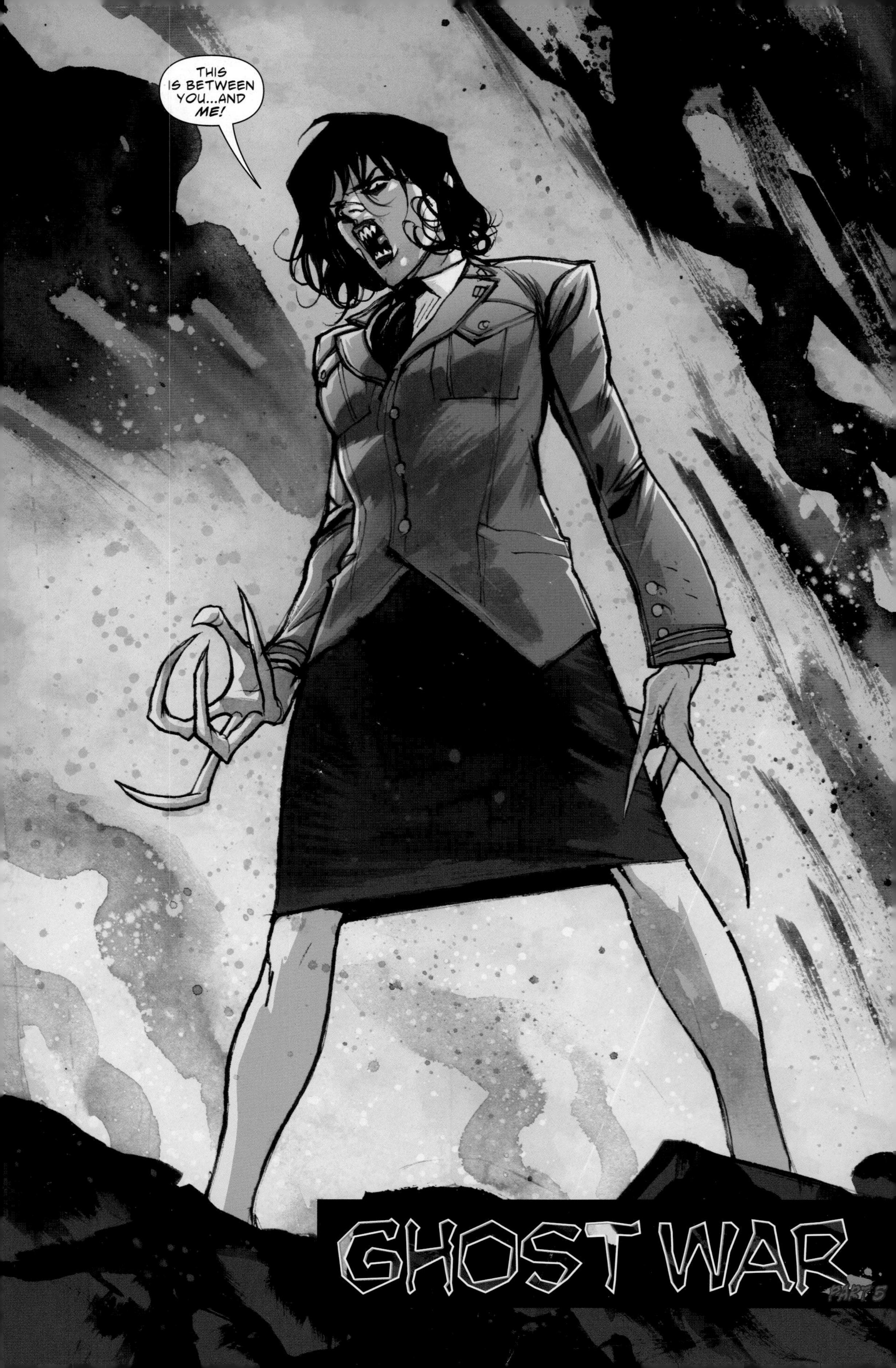
THIS IS BETWEEN YOU...AND *ME!*
GHOST WAR
PART 5

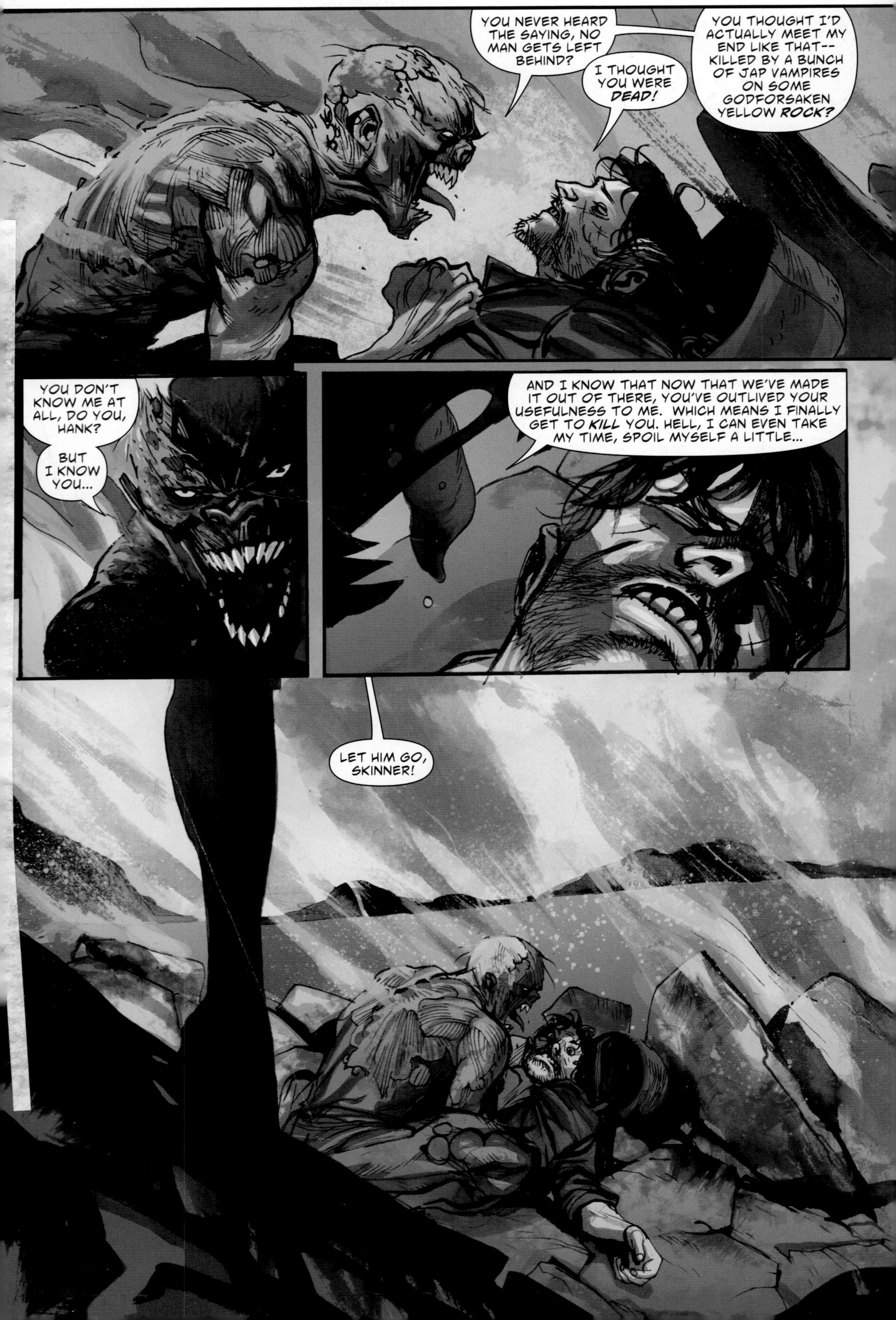
YOU NEVER HEARD THE SAYING, NO MAN GETS LEFT BEHIND?
I THOUGHT YOU WERE DEAD!
YOU THOUGHT I'D ACTUALLY MEET MY END LIKE THAT-- KILLED BY A BUNCH OF JAP VAMPIRES ON SOME GODFORSAKEN YELLOW ROCK?
YOU DON'T KNOW ME AT ALL, DO YOU, HANK?
BUT I KNOW YOU...
AND I KNOW THAT NOW THAT WE'VE MADE IT OUT OF THERE, YOU'VE OUTLIVED YOUR USEFULNESS TO ME. WHICH MEANS I FINALLY GET TO KILL YOU. HELL, I CAN EVEN TAKE MY TIME, SPOIL MYSELF A LITTLE...
LET HIM GO, SKINNER!

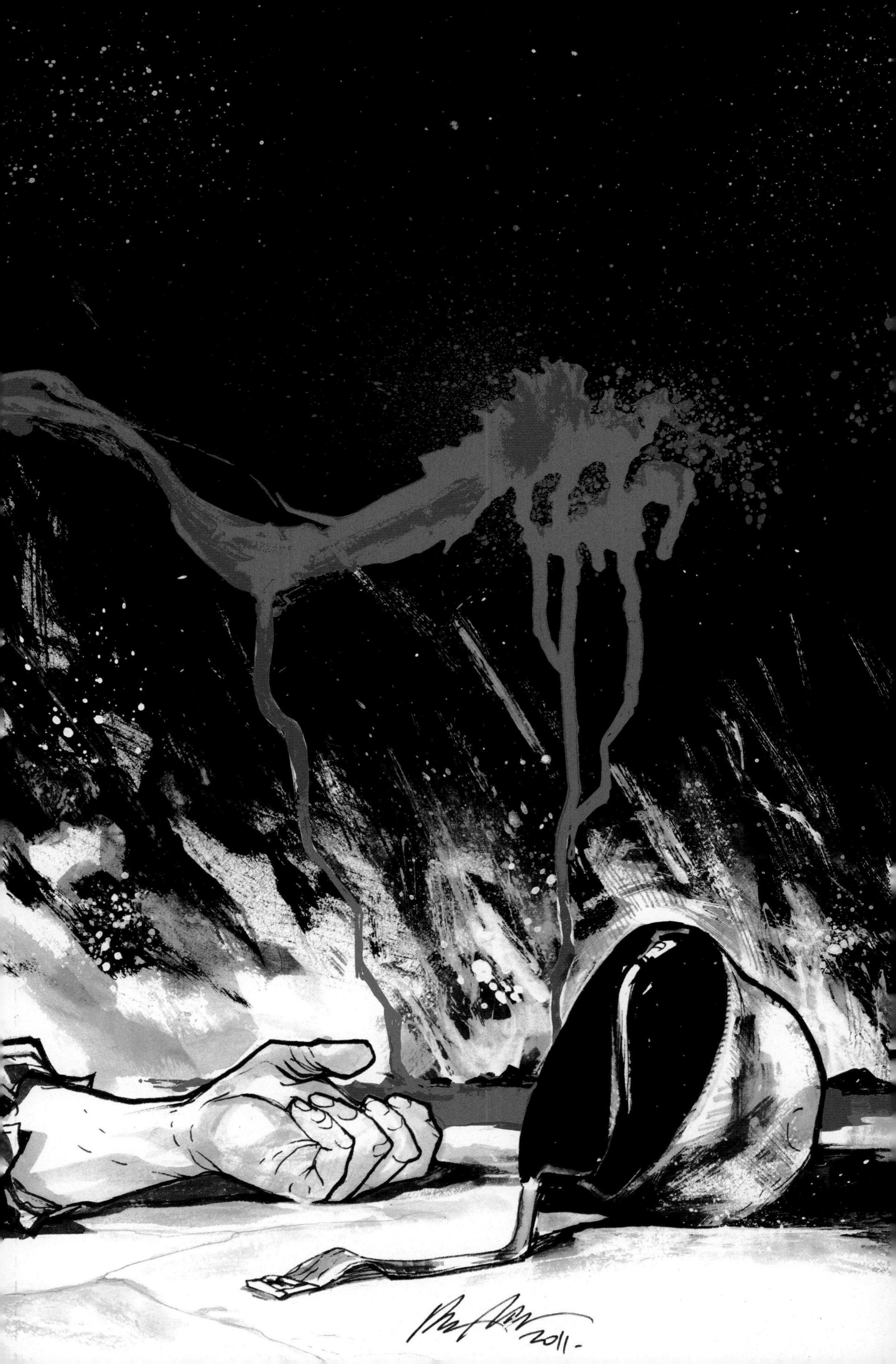

Ghost War
Conclusion

Rafael Albuquerque
Artist and cover

GHOST WAR
CONCLUSION

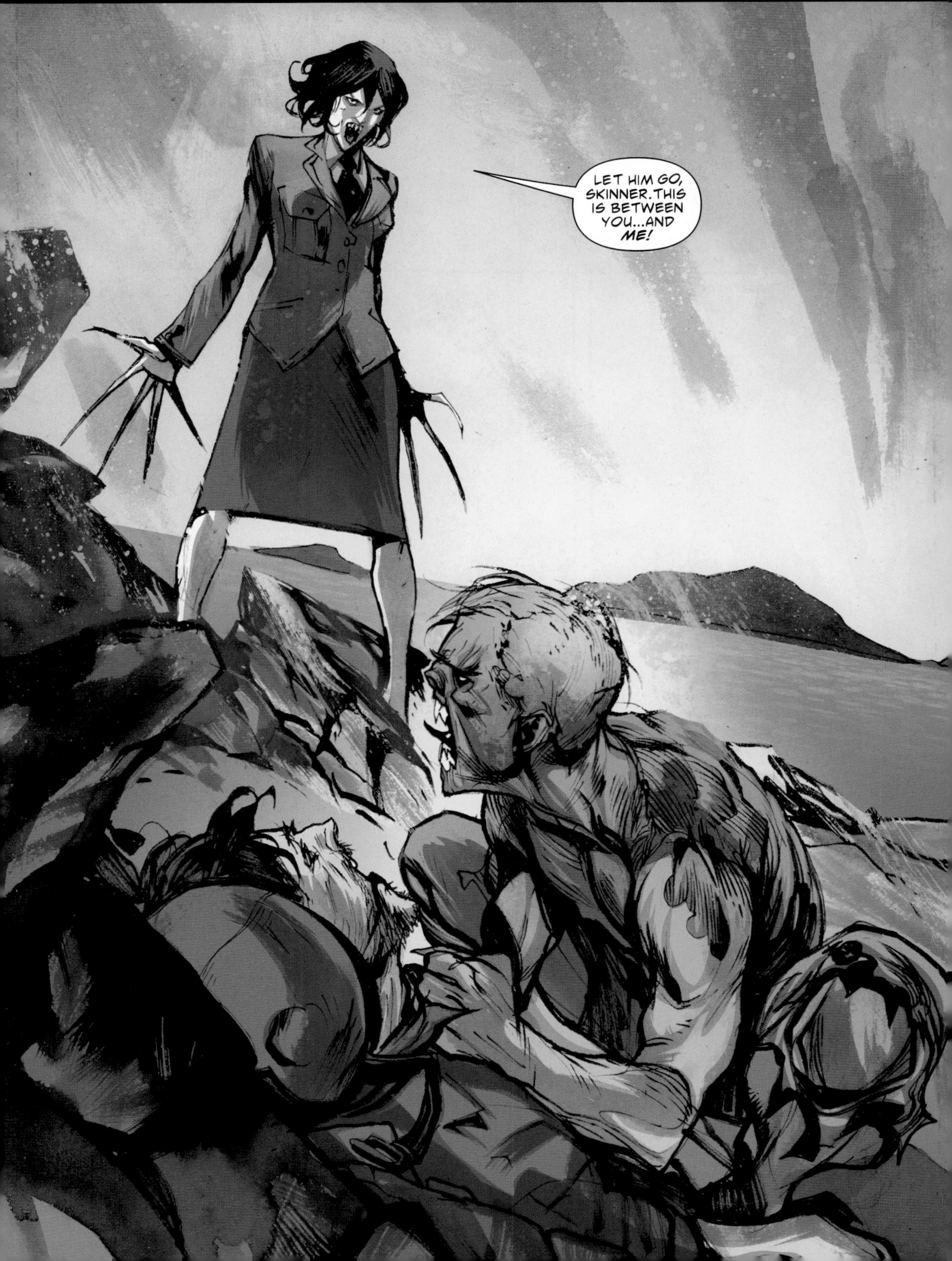
LET HIM GO, SKINNER. THIS IS BETWEEN YOU...AND ME!

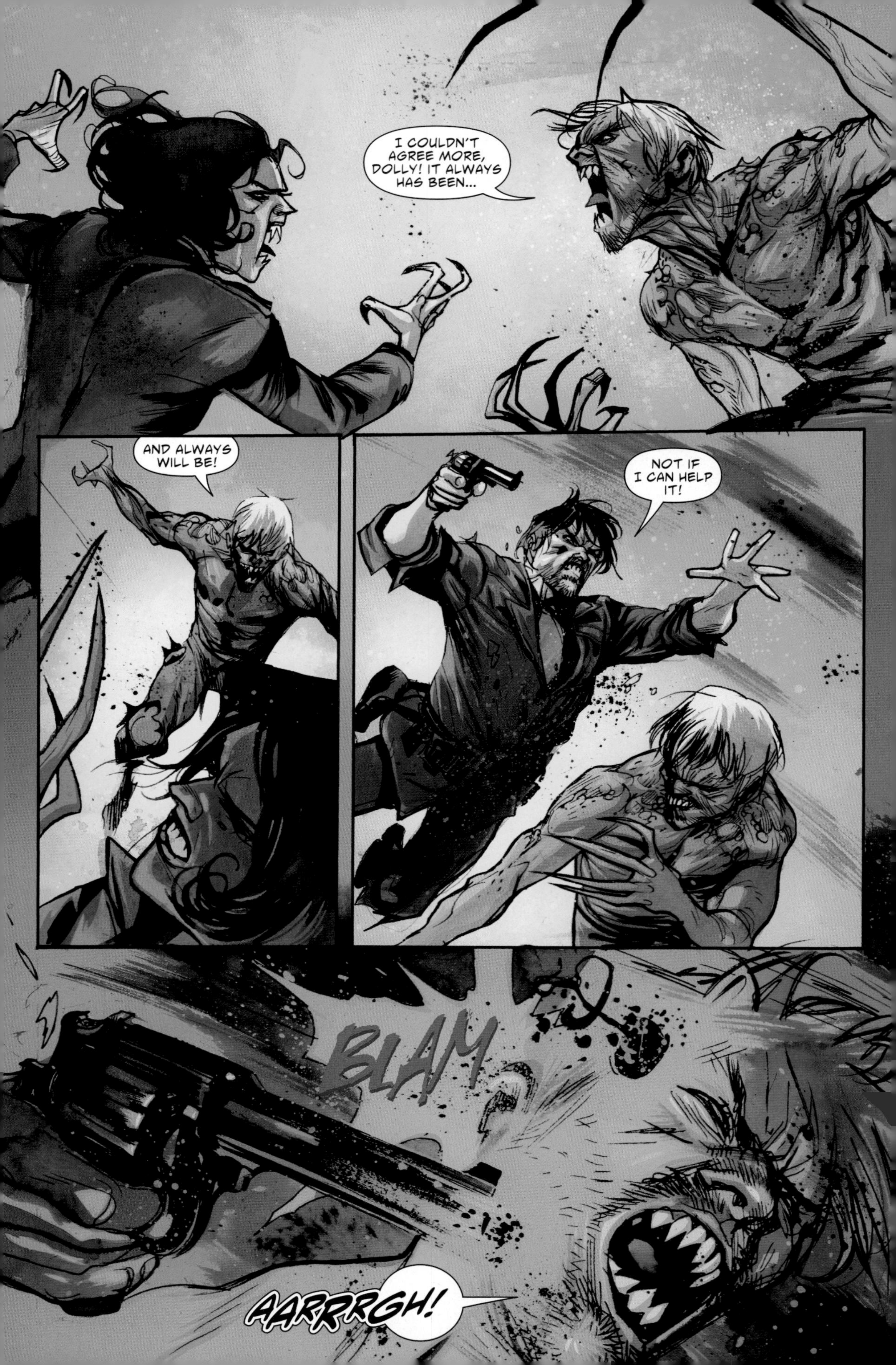
I COULDN'T AGREE MORE, DOLLY! IT ALWAYS HAS BEEN...
AND ALWAYS WILL BE!
NOT IF I CAN HELP IT!
BLAM
AARRRGH!

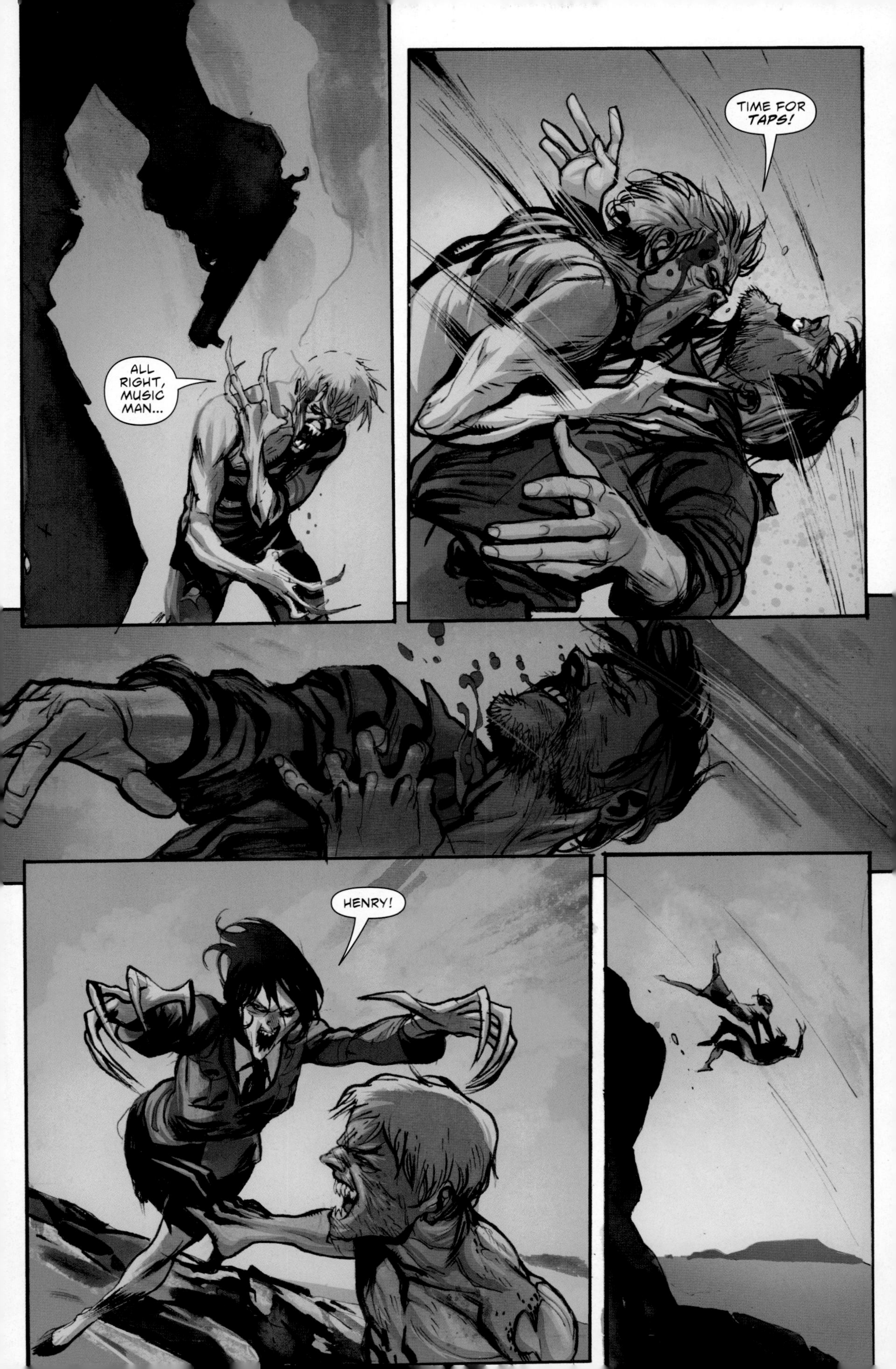
ALL RIGHT, MUSIC MAN...
TIME FOR TAPS!
HENRY!

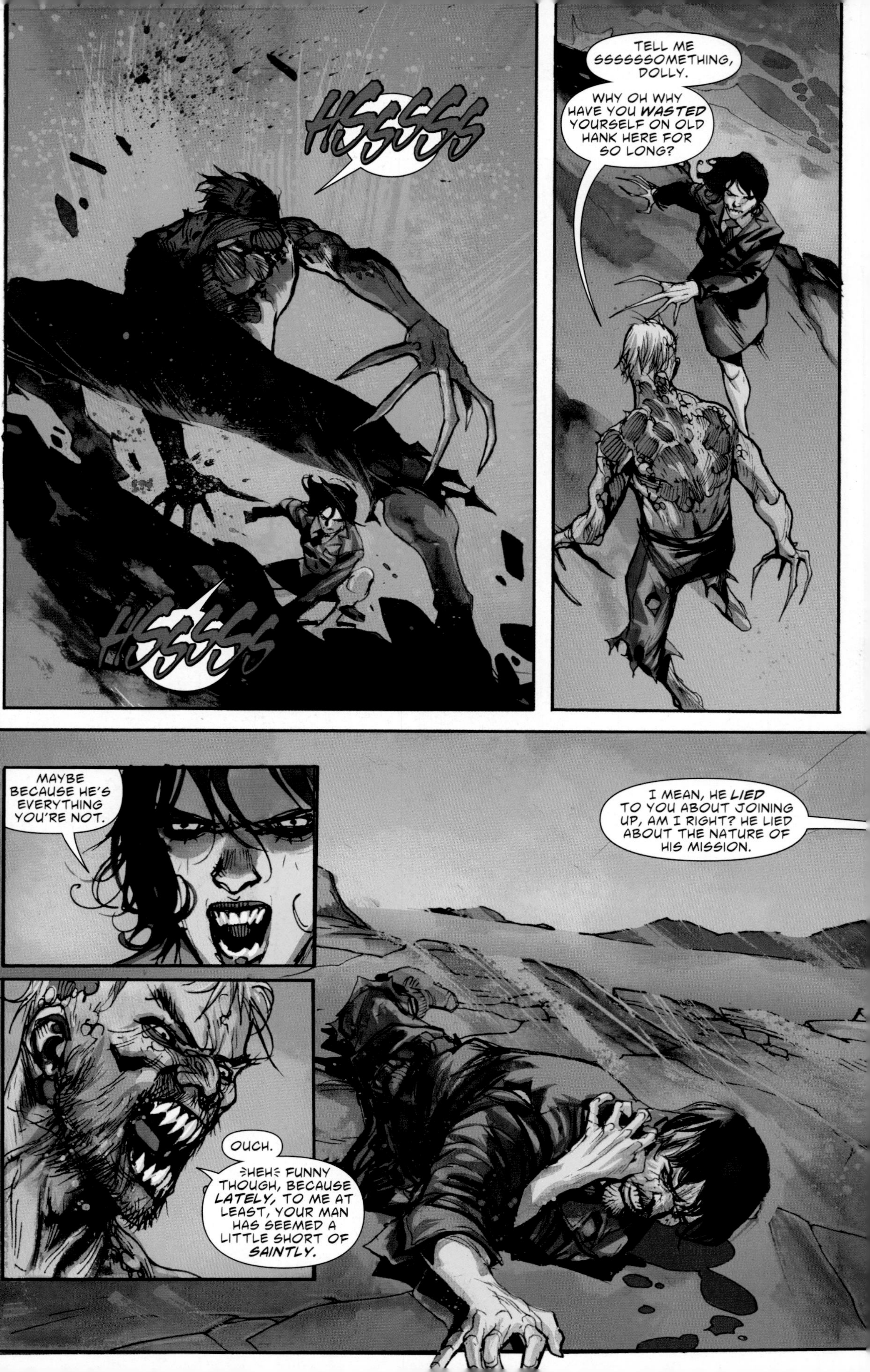

HSSSSS
HSSSSS
TELL ME SSSSSSOMETHING, DOLLY.
WHY OH WHY HAVE YOU WASTED YOURSELF ON OLD HANK HERE FOR SO LONG?
MAYBE BECAUSE HE'S EVERYTHING YOU'RE NOT.
I MEAN, HE LIED TO YOU ABOUT JOINING UP, AM I RIGHT? HE LIED ABOUT THE NATURE OF HIS MISSION.
OUCH.
HEH FUNNY THOUGH, BECAUSE LATELY, TO ME AT LEAST, YOUR MAN HAS SEEMED A LITTLE SHORT OF SAINTLY.

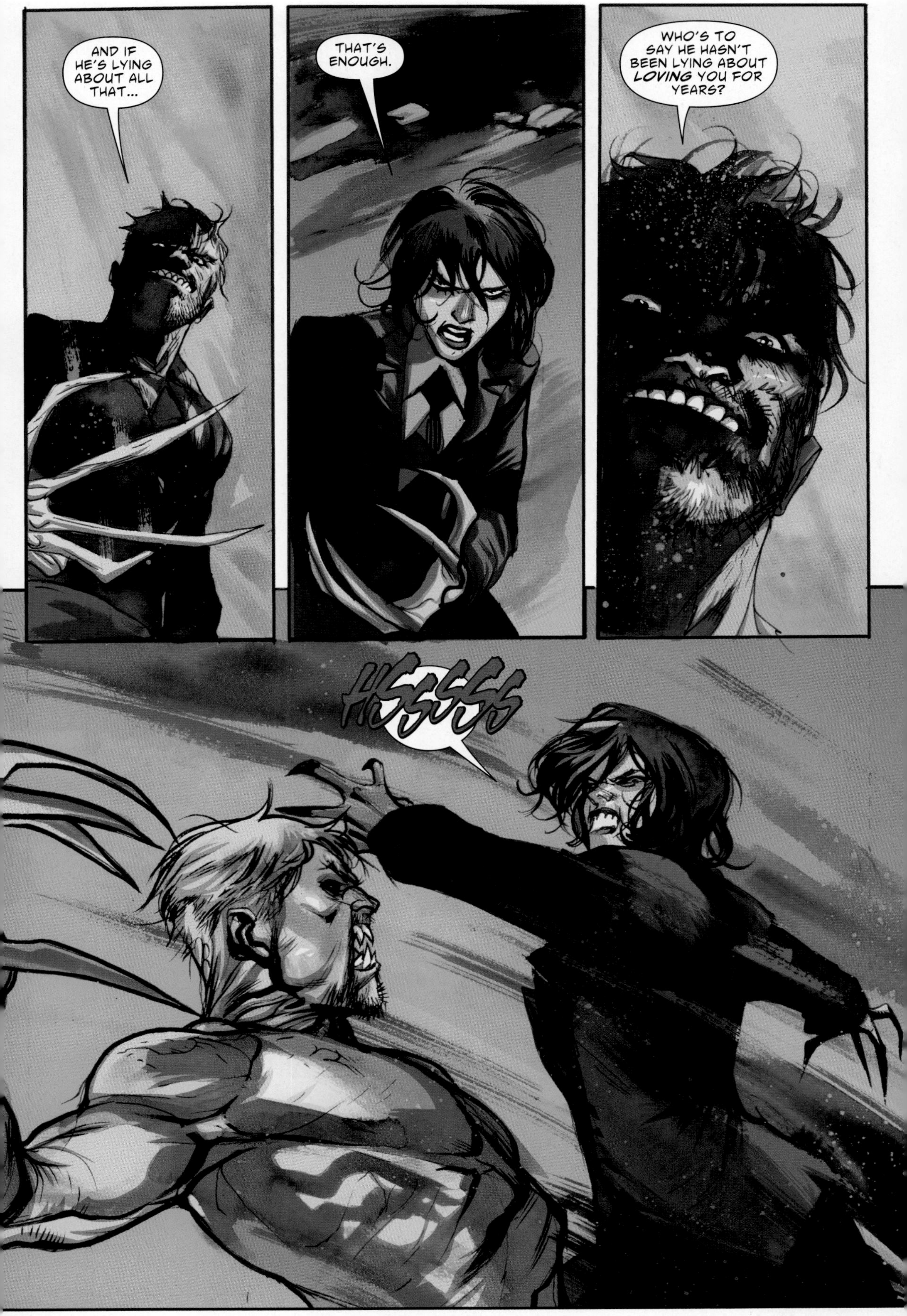
AND IF HE'S LYING ABOUT ALL THAT...
THAT'S ENOUGH.
WHO'S TO SAY HE HASN'T BEEN LYING ABOUT LOVING YOU FOR YEARS?
HSSSSS

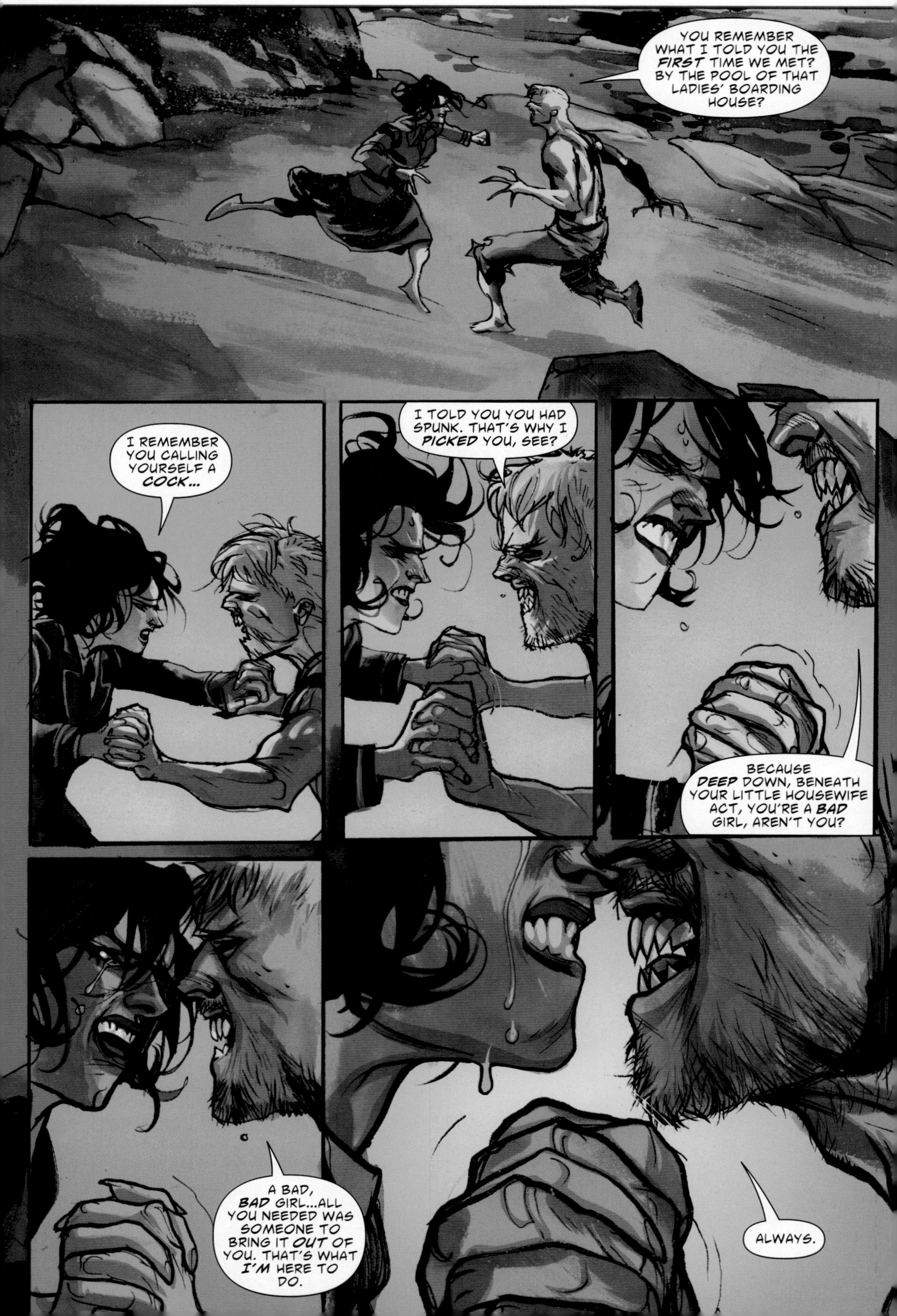
YOU REMEMBER WHAT I TOLD YOU THE FIRST TIME WE MET? BY THE POOL OF THAT LADIES' BOARDING HOUSE?
I REMEMBER YOU CALLING YOURSELF A COCK...
I TOLD YOU YOU HAD SPUNK. THAT'S WHY I PICKED YOU, SEE?
BECAUSE DEEP DOWN, BENEATH YOUR LITTLE HOUSEWIFE ACT, YOU'RE A BAD GIRL, AREN'T YOU?
A BAD, BAD GIRL...ALL YOU NEEDED WAS SOMEONE TO BRING IT OUT OF YOU. THAT'S WHAT I'M HERE TO DO.
ALWAYS.

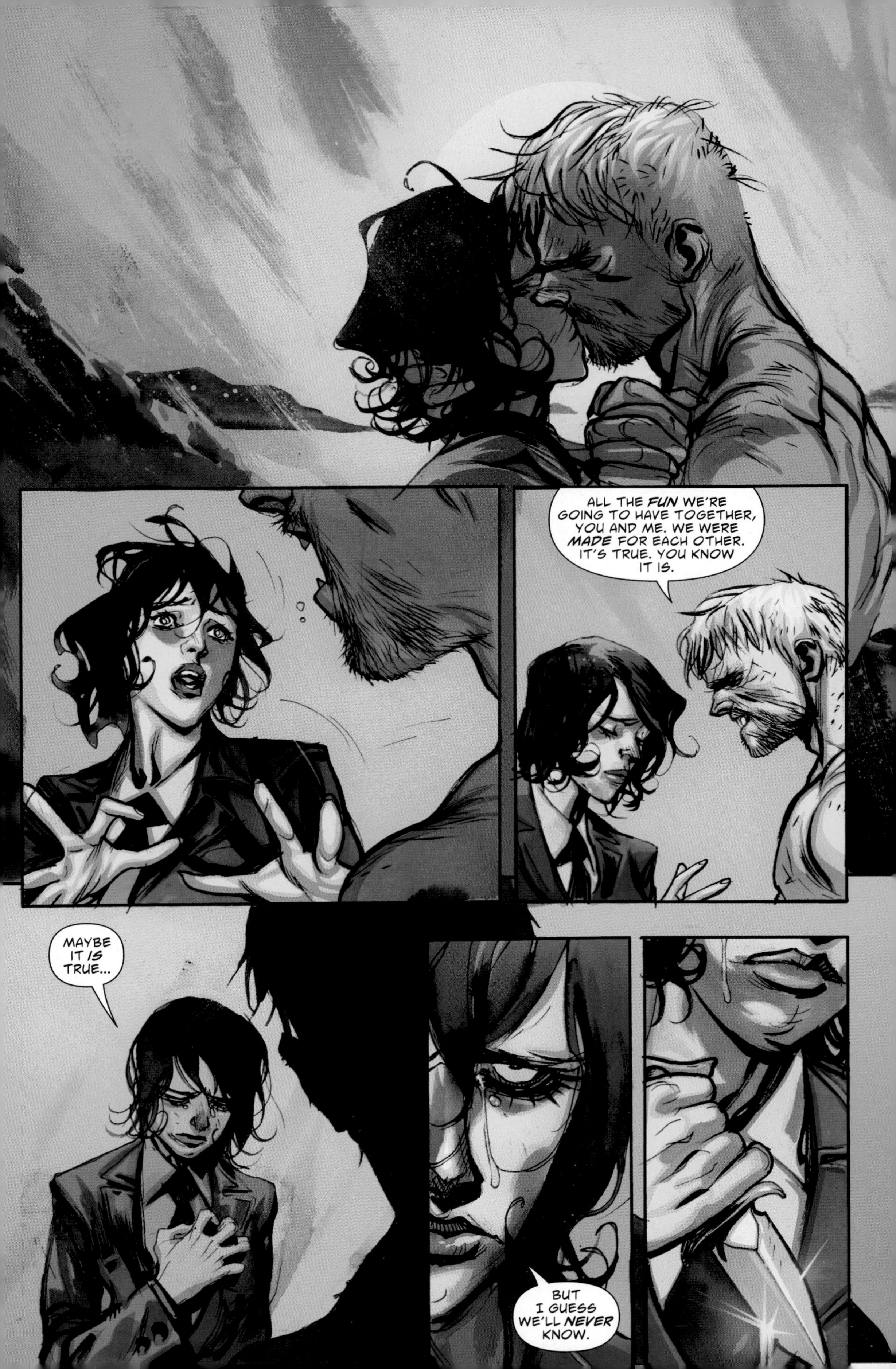
ALL THE FUN WE'RE GOING TO HAVE TOGETHER, YOU AND ME. WE WERE MADE FOR EACH OTHER. IT'S TRUE. YOU KNOW IT IS.
MAYBE IT IS TRUE...
BUT I GUESS WE'LL NEVER KNOW.

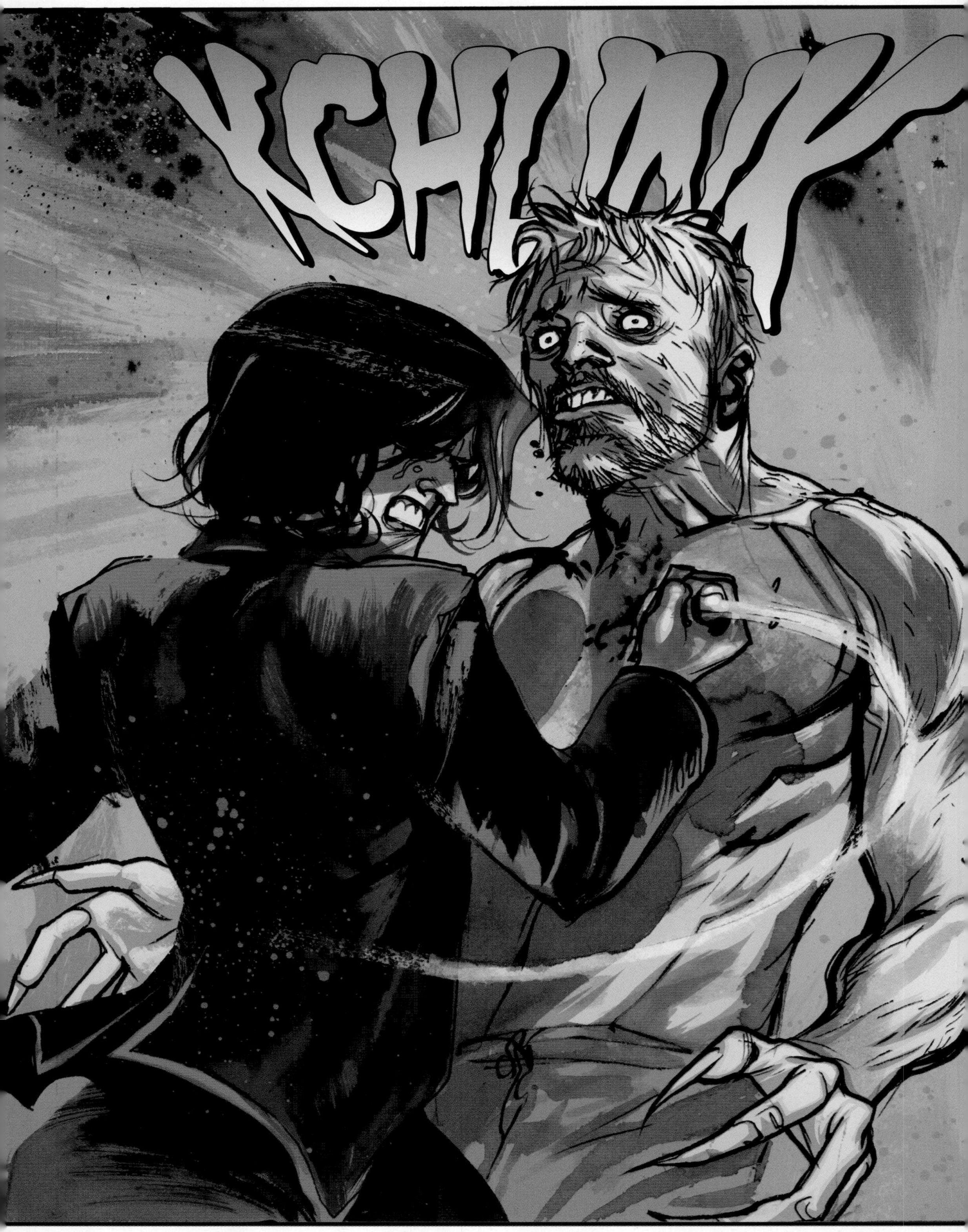
KCHUNK

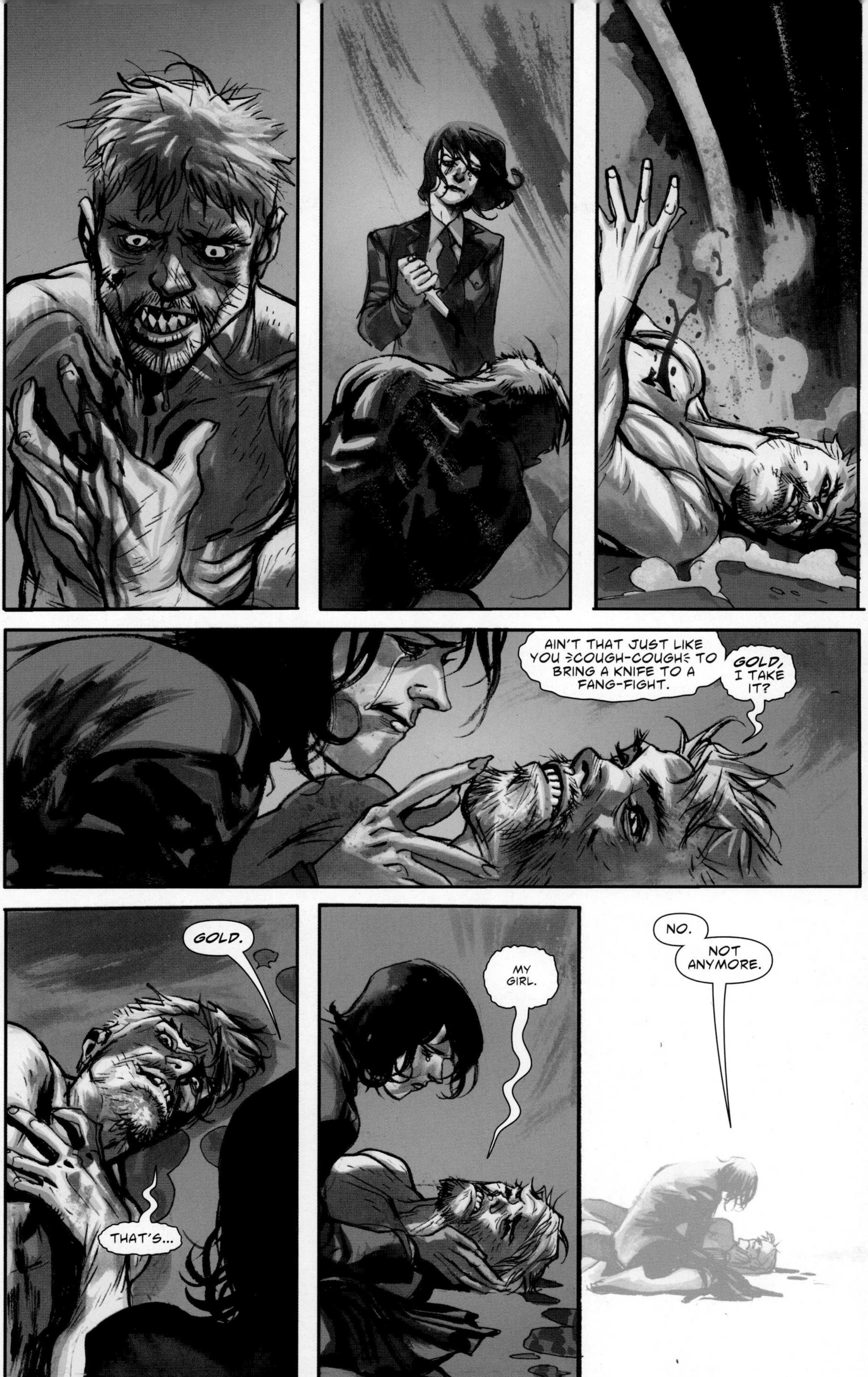
AIN'T THAT JUST LIKE YOU ≶COUGH-COUGH≶ TO BRING A KNIFE TO A FANG-FIGHT.
GOLD, I TAKE IT?
GOLD.
THAT'S...
MY GIRL.
NO.
NOT ANYMORE.

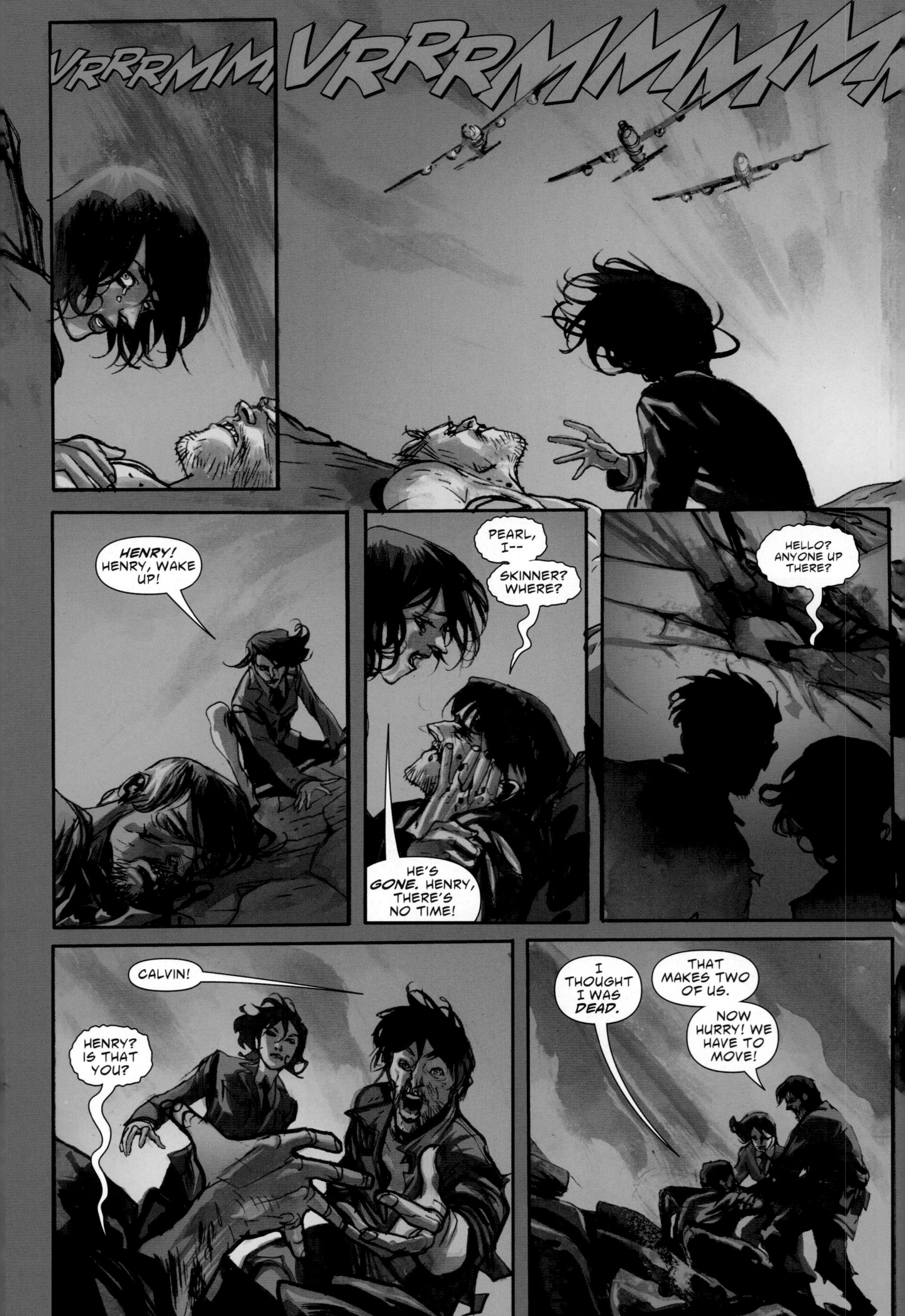
VRRRMMMVRRRMMMMMMM
HENRY! HENRY, WAKE UP!
PEARL, I--
SKINNER? WHERE?
HE'S GONE. HENRY, THERE'S NO TIME!
HELLO? ANYONE UP THERE?
CALVIN!
HENRY? IS THAT YOU?
I THOUGHT I WAS DEAD.
THAT MAKES TWO OF US.
NOW HURRY! WE HAVE TO MOVE!

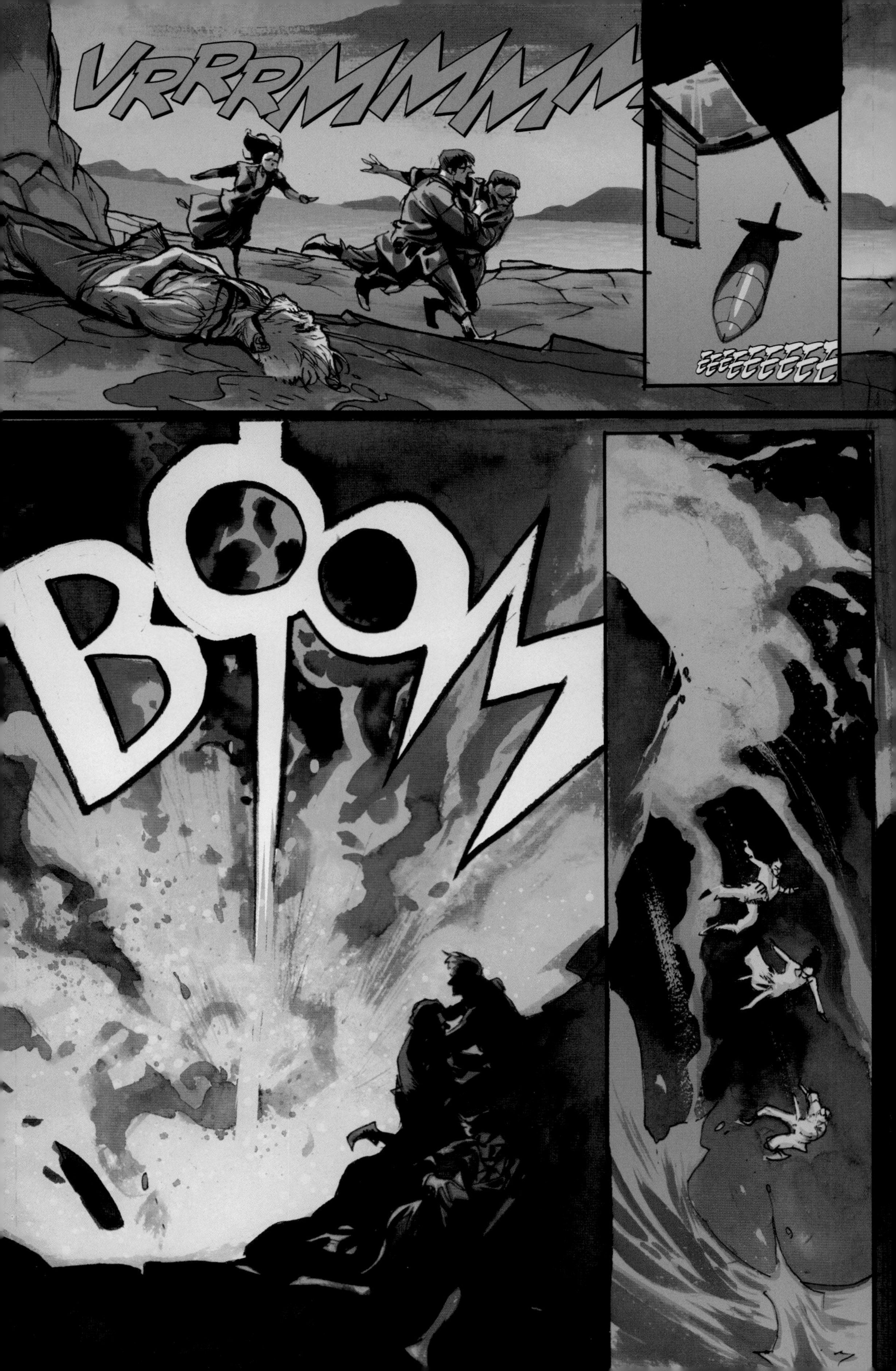
VRRRMMMMM
EEEEEEEEEE
BOOM

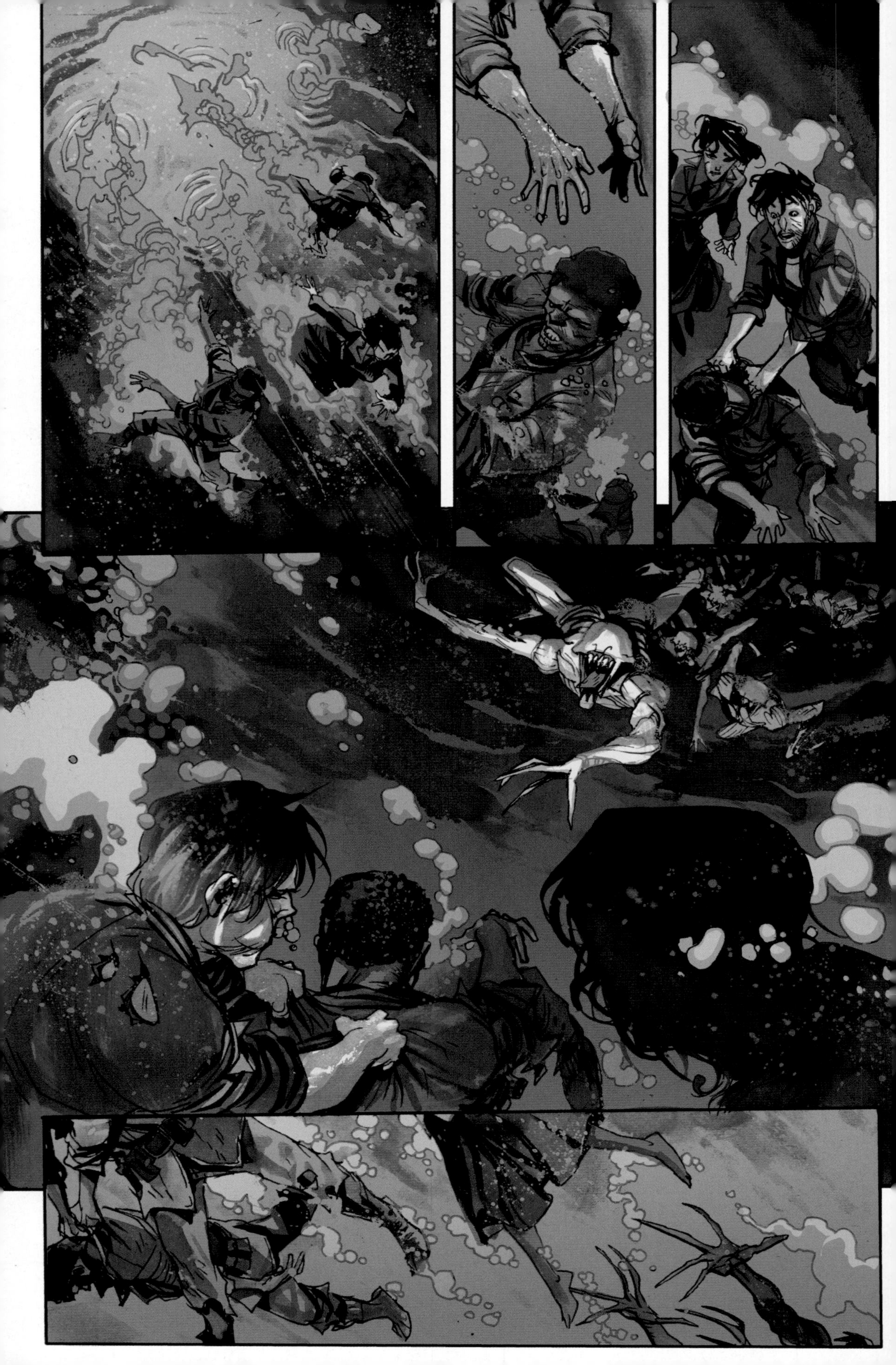

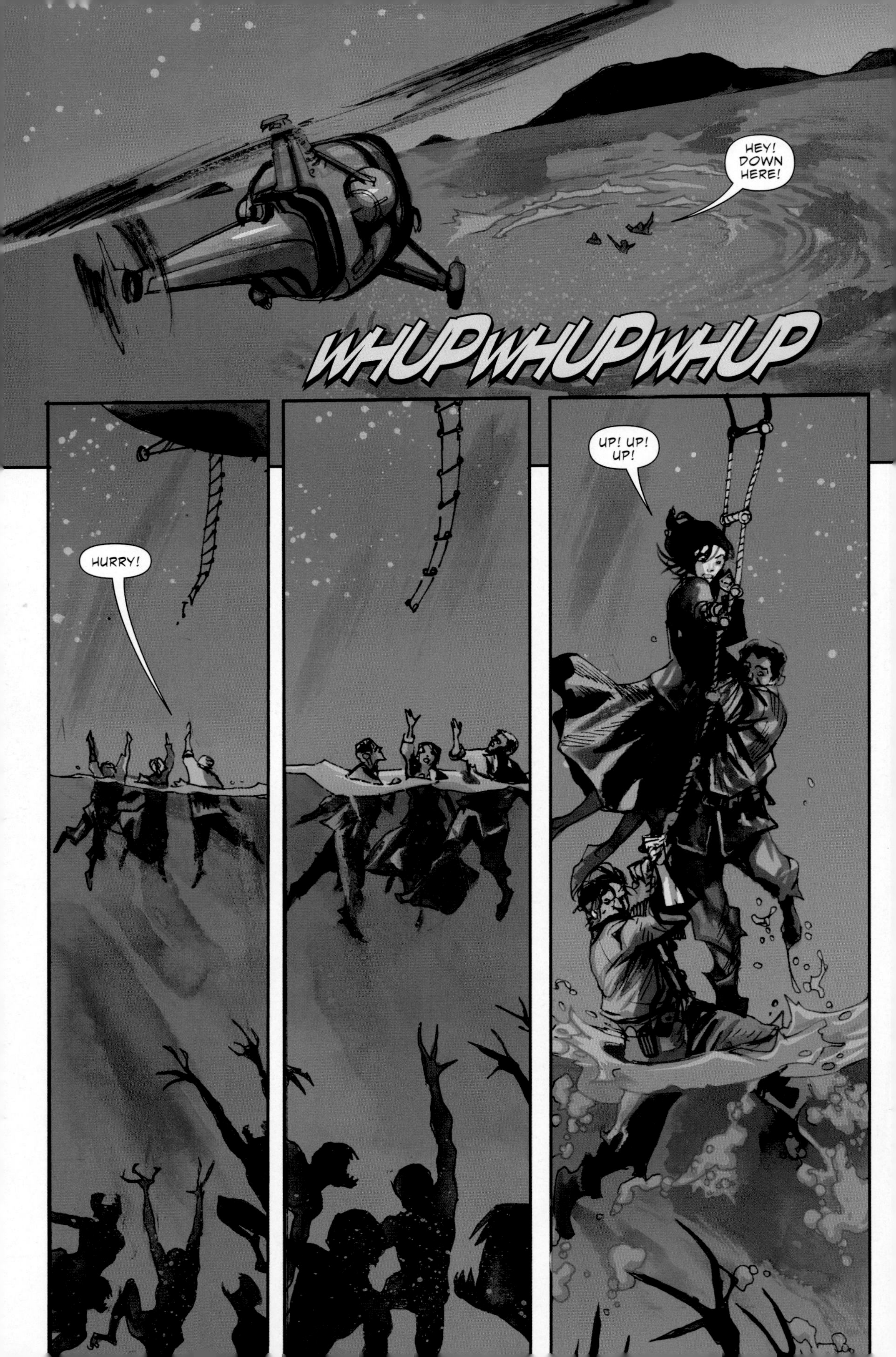
HEY! DOWN HERE!
WHUPWHUPWHUP
HURRY!
UP! UP! UP!

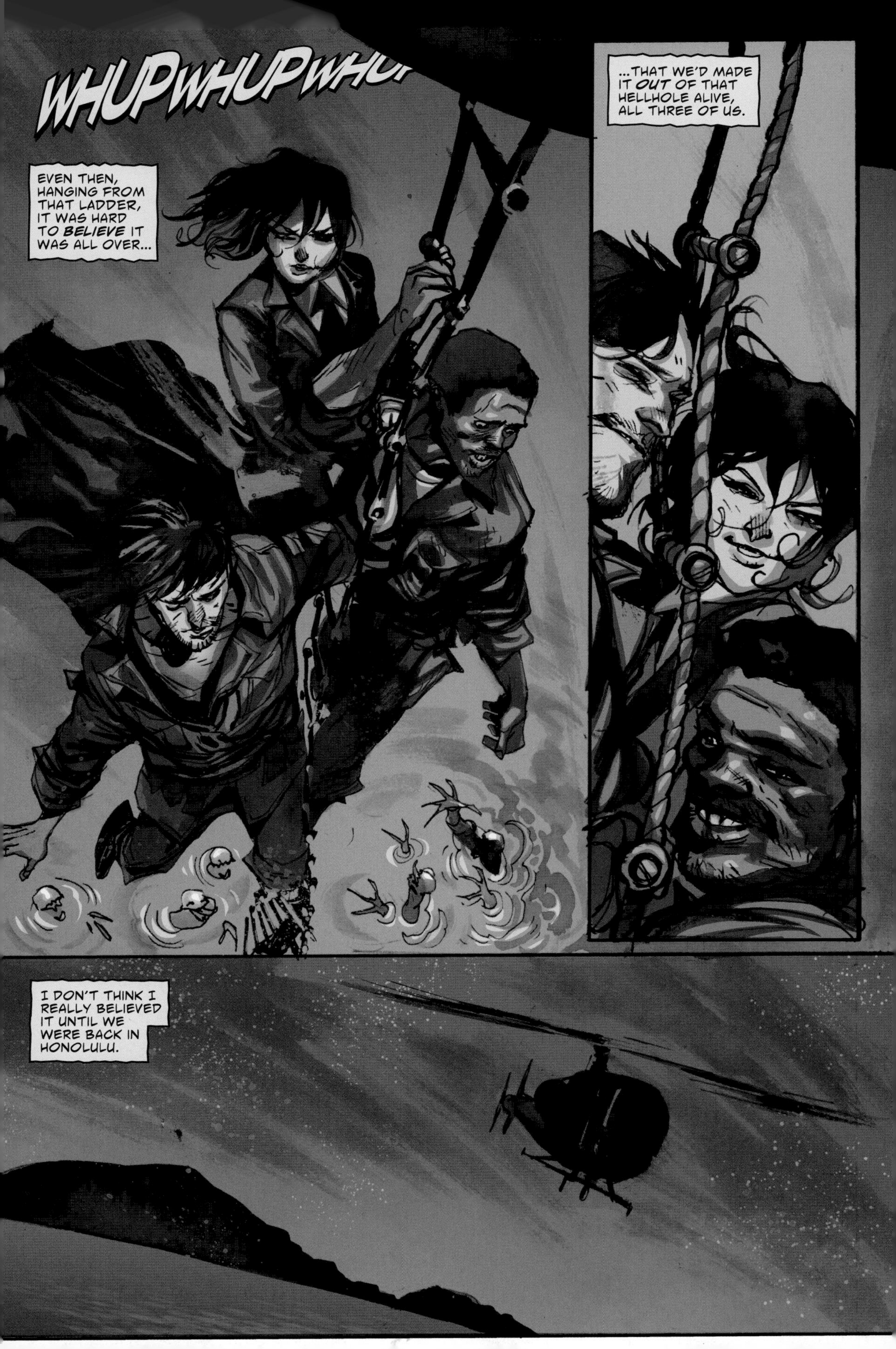
WHUPWHUPWHU
EVEN THEN, HANGING FROM THAT LADDER, IT WAS HARD TO *BELIEVE* IT WAS ALL OVER...
...THAT WE'D MADE IT *OUT* OF THAT HELLHOLE ALIVE, ALL THREE OF US.
I DON'T THINK I REALLY BELIEVED IT UNTIL WE WERE BACK IN HONOLULU.

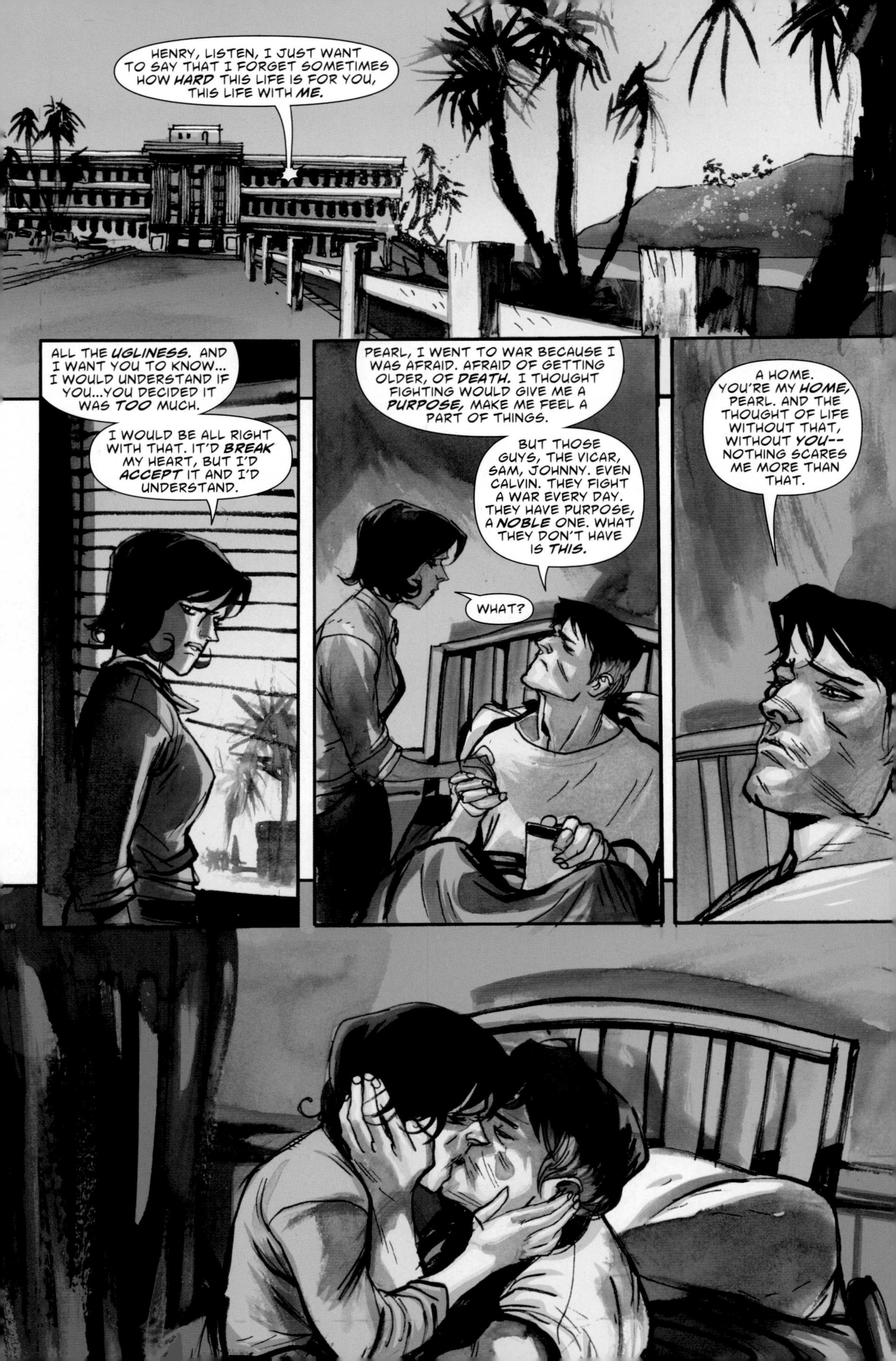
HENRY, LISTEN, I JUST WANT TO SAY THAT I FORGET SOMETIMES HOW HARD THIS LIFE IS FOR YOU, THIS LIFE WITH ME.
ALL THE UGLINESS. AND I WANT YOU TO KNOW... I WOULD UNDERSTAND IF YOU...YOU DECIDED IT WAS TOO MUCH.
I WOULD BE ALL RIGHT WITH THAT. IT'D BREAK MY HEART, BUT I'D ACCEPT IT AND I'D UNDERSTAND.
PEARL, I WENT TO WAR BECAUSE I WAS AFRAID. AFRAID OF GETTING OLDER, OF DEATH. I THOUGHT FIGHTING WOULD GIVE ME A PURPOSE, MAKE ME FEEL A PART OF THINGS.
BUT THOSE GUYS, THE VICAR, SAM, JOHNNY. EVEN CALVIN. THEY FIGHT A WAR EVERY DAY. THEY HAVE PURPOSE, A NOBLE ONE. WHAT THEY DON'T HAVE IS THIS.
WHAT?
A HOME. YOU'RE MY HOME, PEARL. AND THE THOUGHT OF LIFE WITHOUT THAT, WITHOUT YOU-- NOTHING SCARES ME MORE THAN THAT.

End

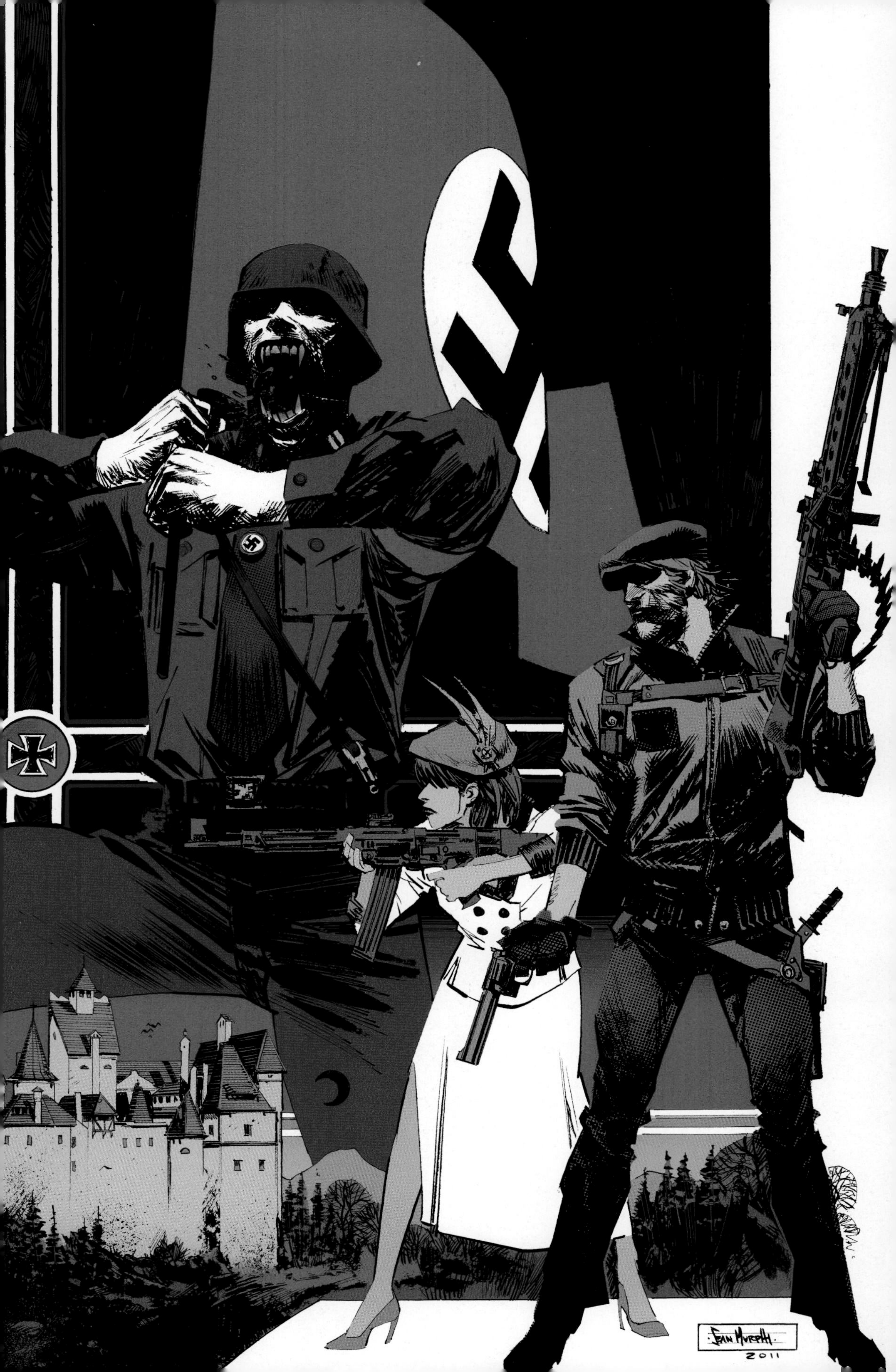
SEAN MURPHY
2011

Survival
of the Fittest
Part One

Sean Murphy
Artist and cover

Dave Stewart
cover color

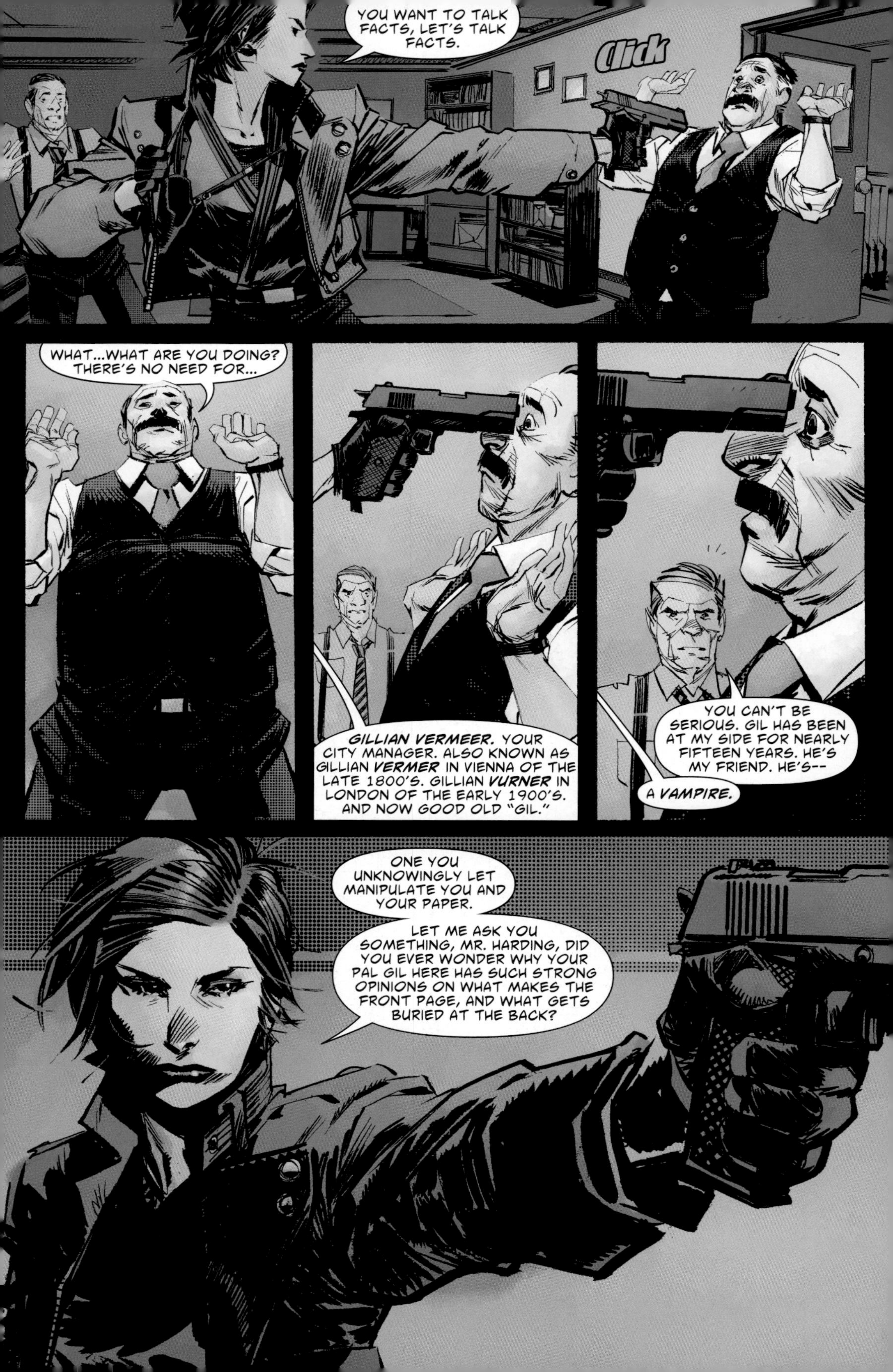
YOU WANT TO TALK FACTS, LET'S TALK FACTS.
Click
WHAT...WHAT ARE YOU DOING? THERE'S NO NEED FOR...
GILLIAN VERMEER. YOUR CITY MANAGER. ALSO KNOWN AS GILLIAN VERMER IN VIENNA OF THE LATE 1800'S. GILLIAN VURNER IN LONDON OF THE EARLY 1900'S. AND NOW GOOD OLD "GIL."
YOU CAN'T BE SERIOUS. GIL HAS BEEN AT MY SIDE FOR NEARLY FIFTEEN YEARS. HE'S MY FRIEND. HE'S--
A VAMPIRE.
ONE YOU UNKNOWINGLY LET MANIPULATE YOU AND YOUR PAPER.
LET ME ASK YOU SOMETHING, MR. HARDING, DID YOU EVER WONDER WHY YOUR PAL GIL HERE HAS SUCH STRONG OPINIONS ON WHAT MAKES THE FRONT PAGE, AND WHAT GETS BURIED AT THE BACK?

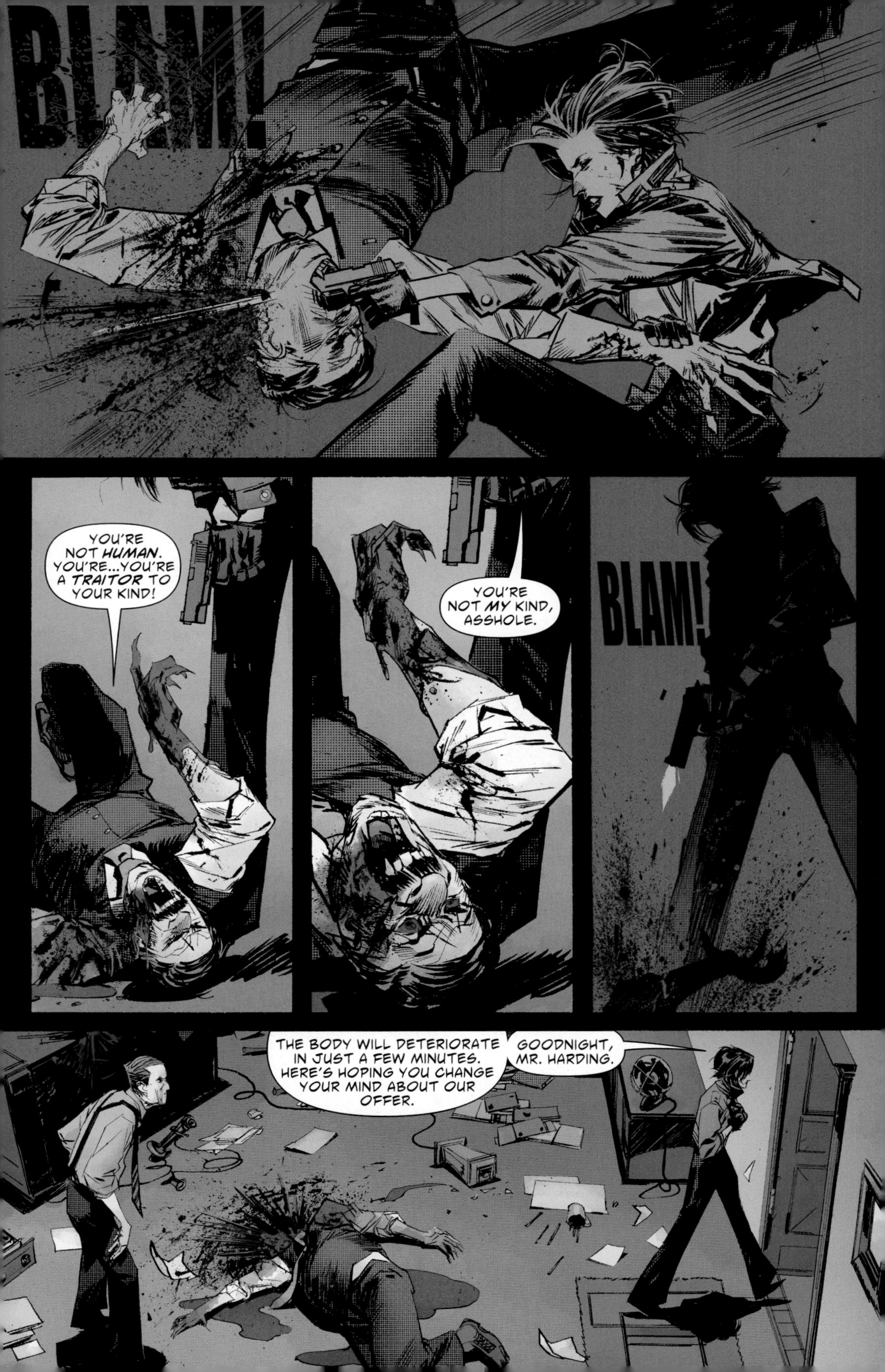
BLAM!
YOU'RE NOT *HUMAN*. YOU'RE...YOU'RE A *TRAITOR* TO YOUR KIND!
YOU'RE NOT *MY* KIND, ASSHOLE.
BLAM!
THE BODY WILL DETERIORATE IN JUST A FEW MINUTES. HERE'S HOPING YOU CHANGE YOUR MIND ABOUT OUR OFFER.
GOODNIGHT, MR. HARDING.

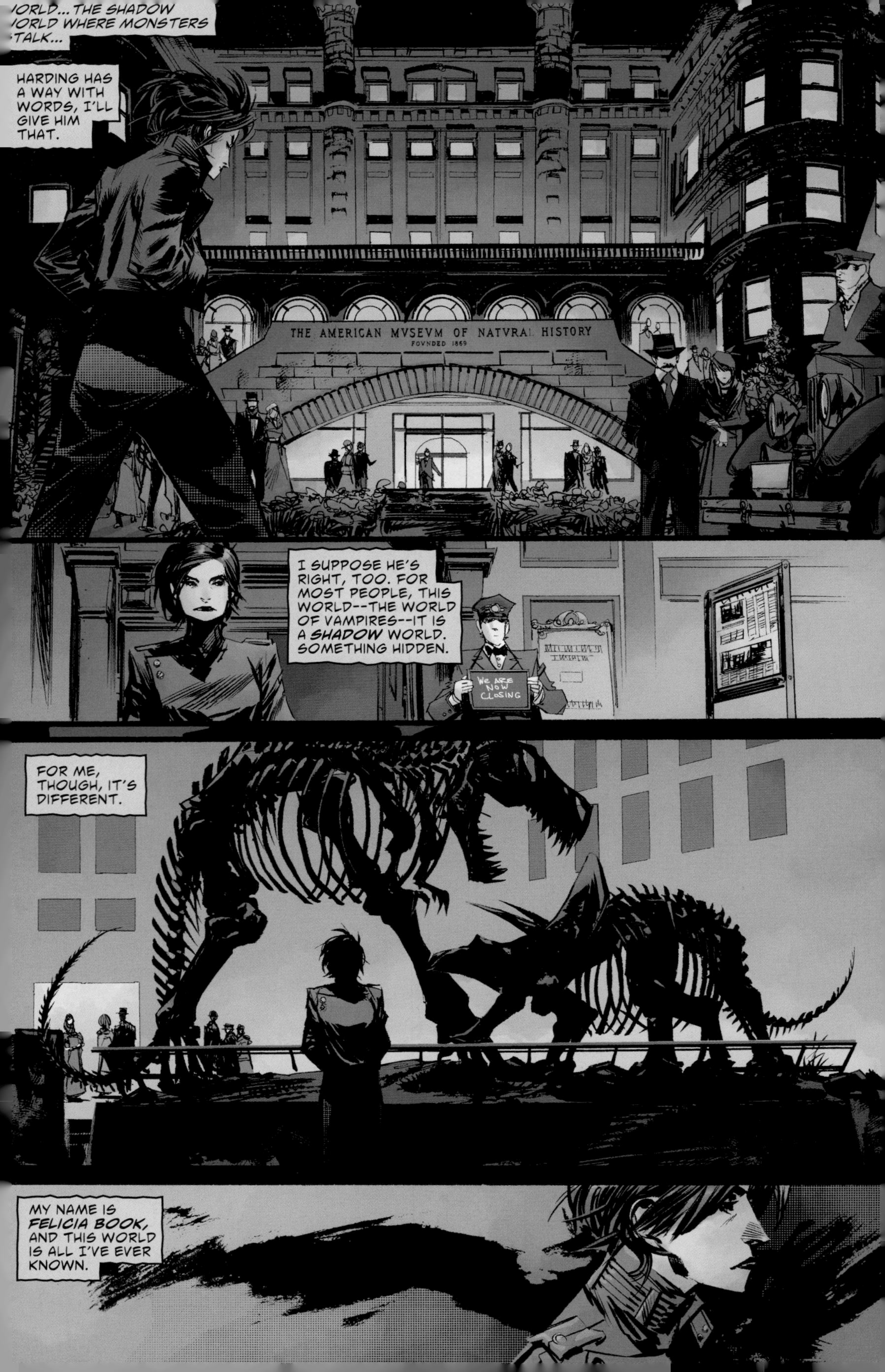
WORLD... THE SHADOW WORLD WHERE MONSTERS STALK...
HARDING HAS A WAY WITH WORDS, I'LL GIVE HIM THAT.
THE AMERICAN MVSEVM OF NATVRAL HISTORY
FOVNDED 1869
I SUPPOSE HE'S RIGHT, TOO. FOR MOST PEOPLE, THIS WORLD--THE WORLD OF VAMPIRES--IT IS A SHADOW WORLD. SOMETHING HIDDEN.
WE ARE NOW CLOSING
FOR ME, THOUGH, IT'S DIFFERENT.
MY NAME IS FELICIA BOOK, AND THIS WORLD IS ALL I'VE EVER KNOWN.

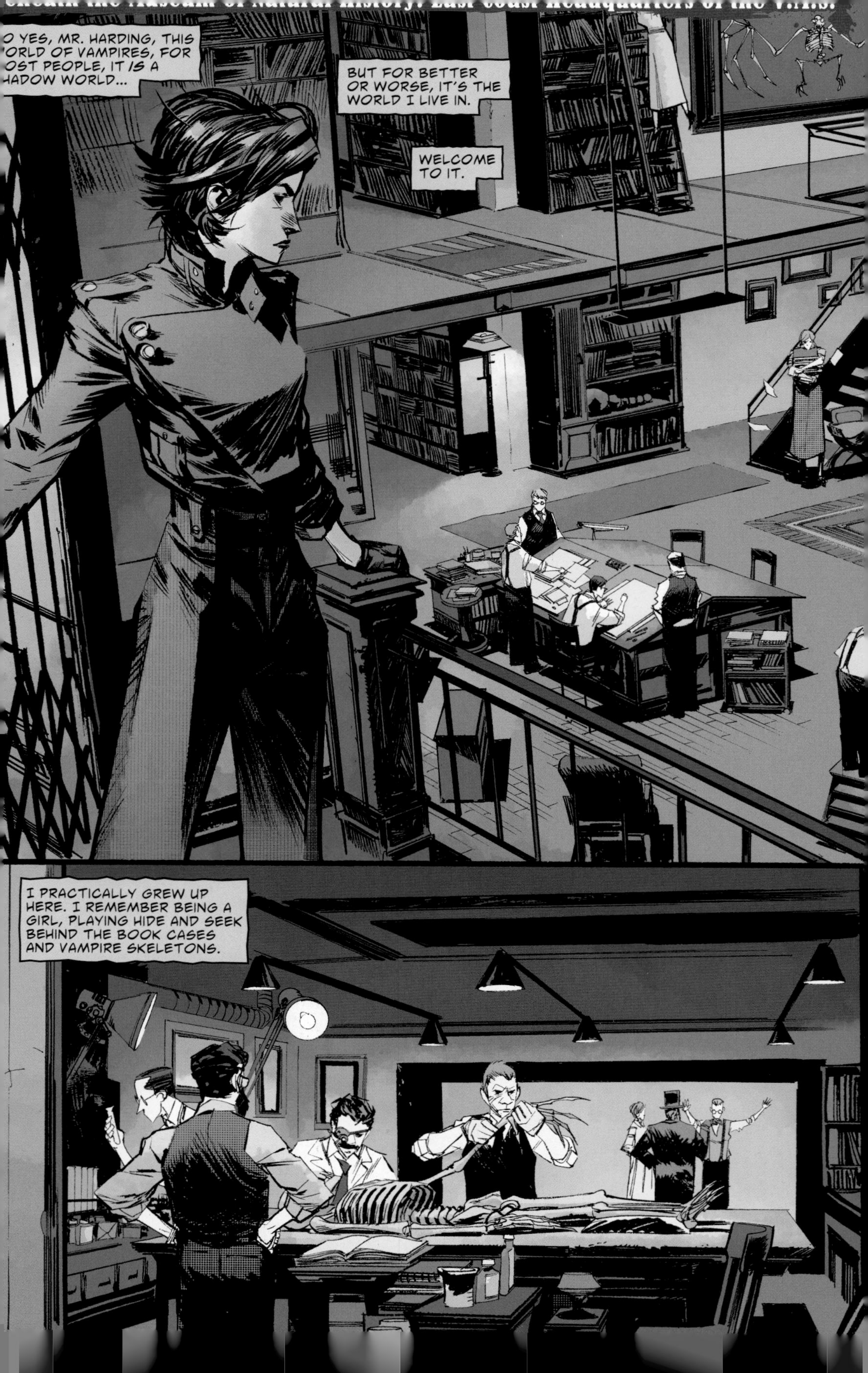
O YES, MR. HARDING, THIS ORLD OF VAMPIRES, FOR OST PEOPLE, IT IS A HADOW WORLD...
BUT FOR BETTER OR WORSE, IT'S THE WORLD I LIVE IN.
WELCOME TO IT.
I PRACTICALLY GREW UP HERE. I REMEMBER BEING A GIRL, PLAYING HIDE AND SEEK BEHIND THE BOOK CASES AND VAMPIRE SKELETONS.

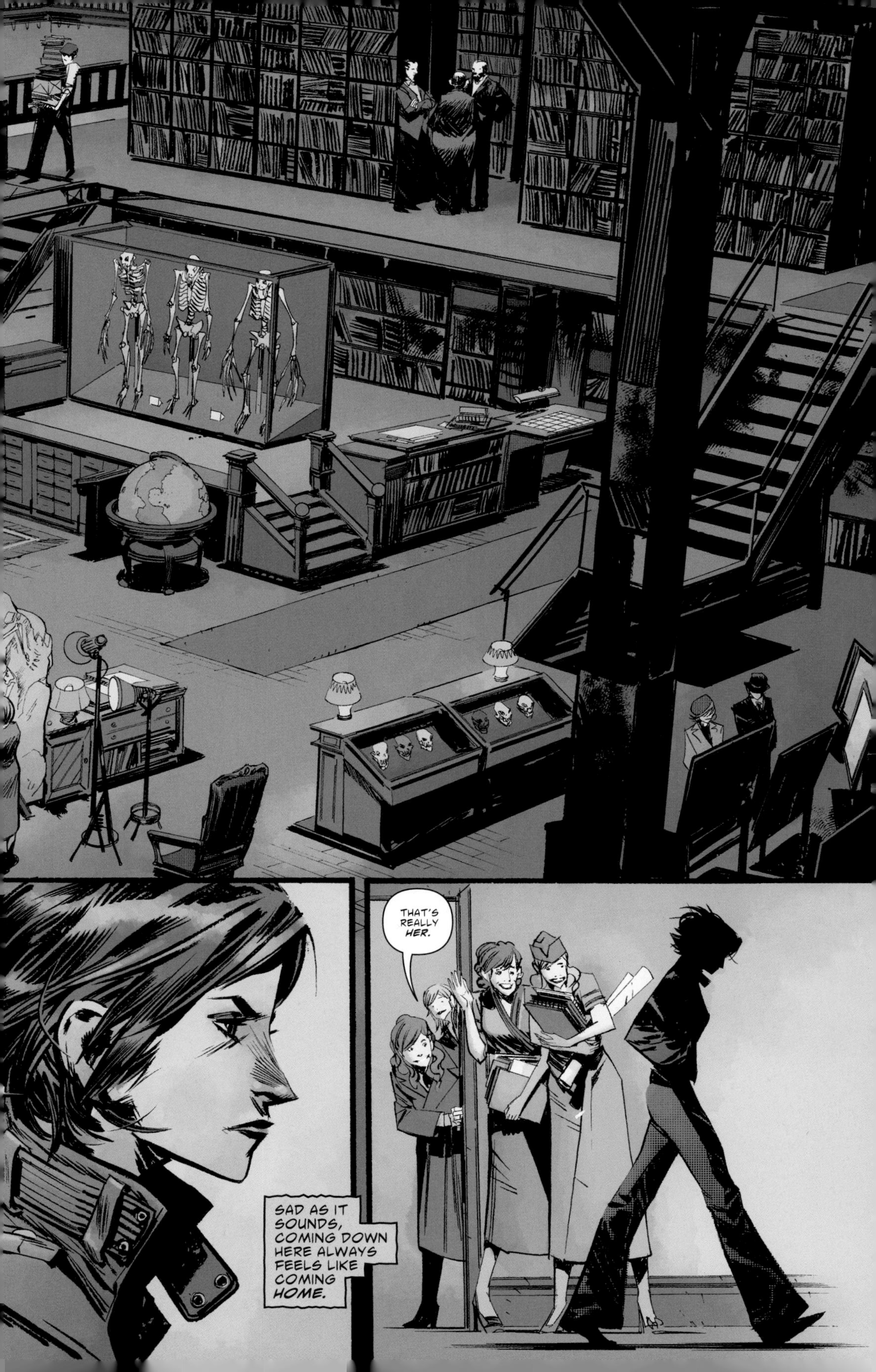
SAD AS IT SOUNDS, COMING DOWN HERE ALWAYS FEELS LIKE COMING HOME.
THAT'S REALLY HER.

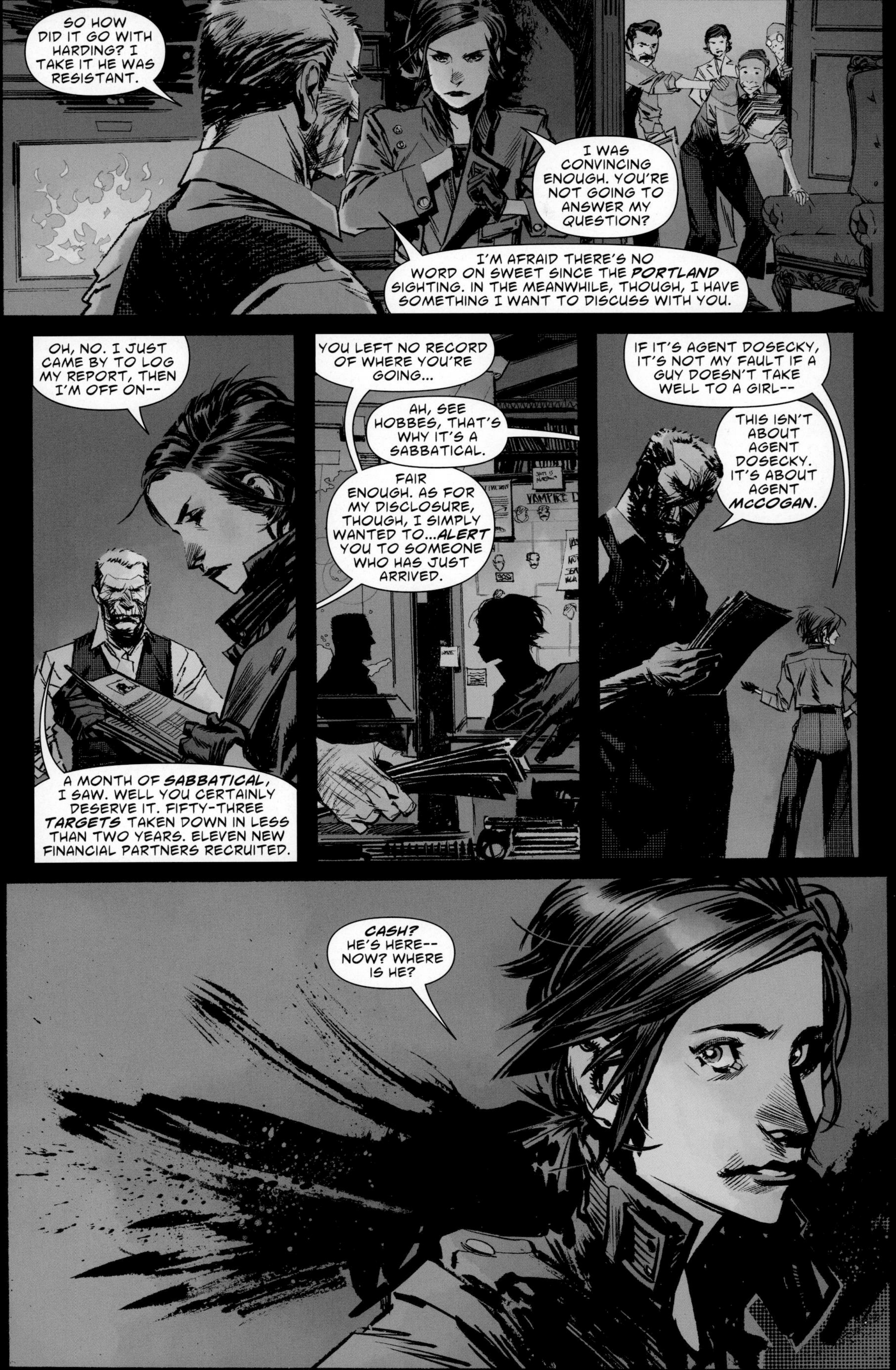
SO HOW DID IT GO WITH HARDING? I TAKE IT HE WAS RESISTANT.
I WAS CONVINCING ENOUGH. YOU'RE NOT GOING TO ANSWER MY QUESTION?
I'M AFRAID THERE'S NO WORD ON SWEET SINCE THE *PORTLAND* SIGHTING. IN THE MEANWHILE, THOUGH, I HAVE SOMETHING I WANT TO DISCUSS WITH YOU.
OH, NO. I JUST CAME BY TO LOG MY REPORT, THEN I'M OFF ON--
A MONTH OF *SABBATICAL*, I SAW. WELL YOU CERTAINLY DESERVE IT. FIFTY-THREE *TARGETS* TAKEN DOWN IN LESS THAN TWO YEARS. ELEVEN NEW FINANCIAL PARTNERS RECRUITED.
YOU LEFT NO RECORD OF WHERE YOU'RE GOING...
AH, SEE HOBBES, THAT'S WHY IT'S A SABBATICAL.
FAIR ENOUGH. AS FOR MY DISCLOSURE, THOUGH, I SIMPLY WANTED TO...*ALERT* YOU TO SOMEONE WHO HAS JUST ARRIVED.
IF IT'S AGENT DOSECKY, IT'S NOT MY FAULT IF A GUY DOESN'T TAKE WELL TO A GIRL--
THIS ISN'T ABOUT AGENT DOSECKY. IT'S ABOUT AGENT *McCOGAN*.
CASH? HE'S HERE-- NOW? WHERE IS HE?

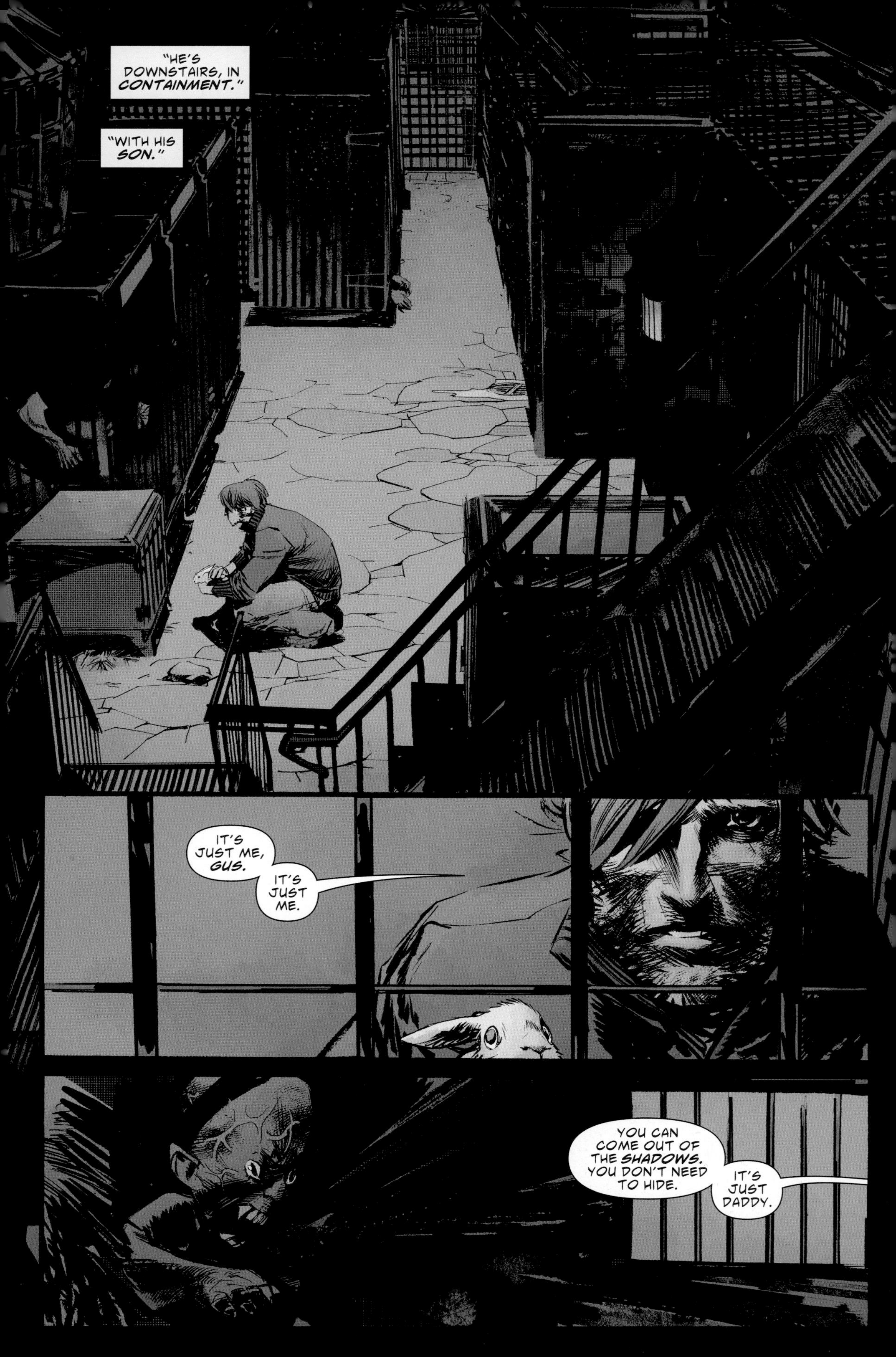
"HE'S DOWNSTAIRS, IN CONTAINMENT."
"WITH HIS SON."
IT'S JUST ME, GUS.
IT'S JUST ME.
YOU CAN COME OUT OF THE SHADOWS. YOU DON'T NEED TO HIDE.
IT'S JUST DADDY.

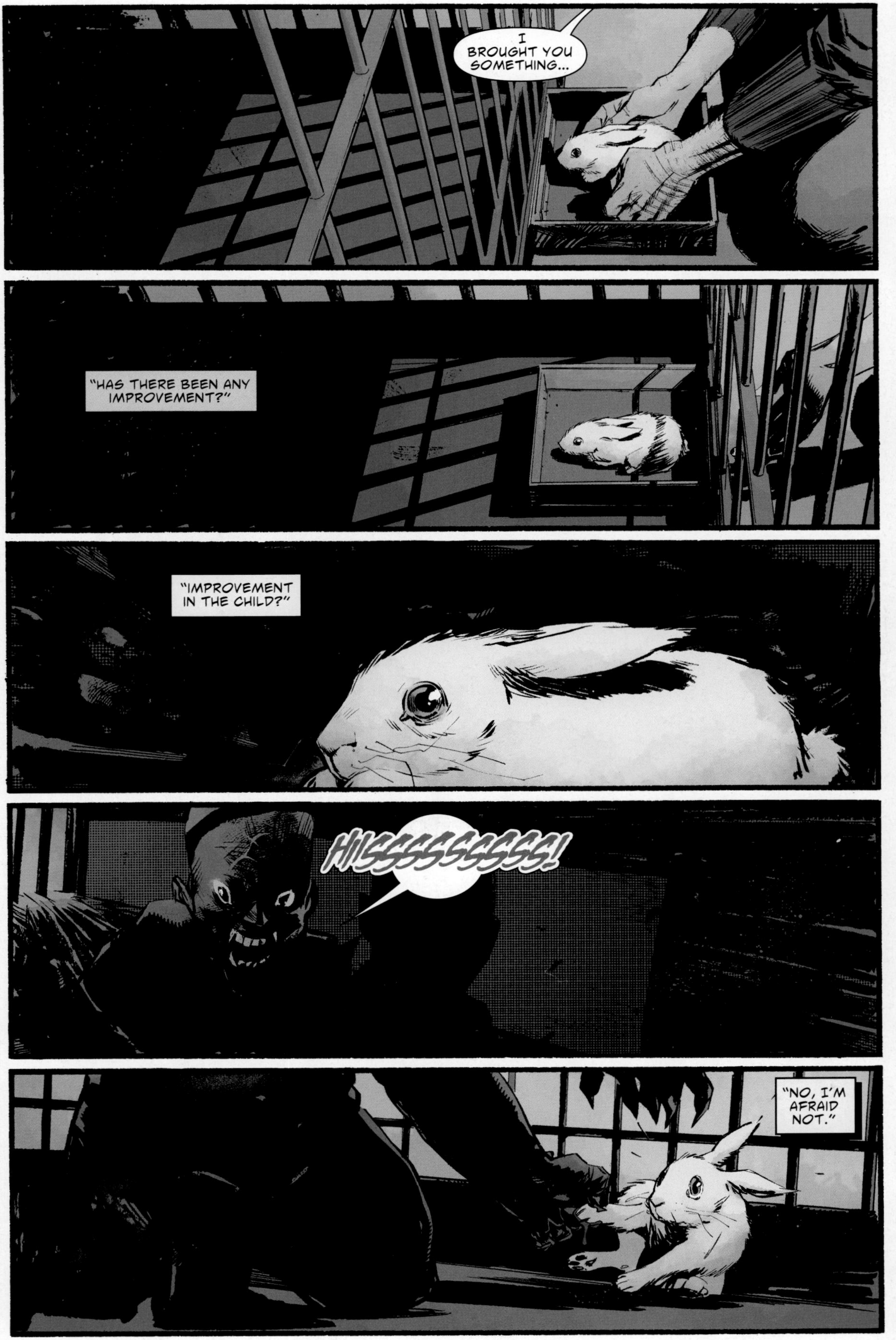
I BROUGHT YOU SOMETHING...
"HAS THERE BEEN ANY IMPROVEMENT?"
"IMPROVEMENT IN THE CHILD?"
HISSSSSSSSSS!
"NO, I'M AFRAID NOT."

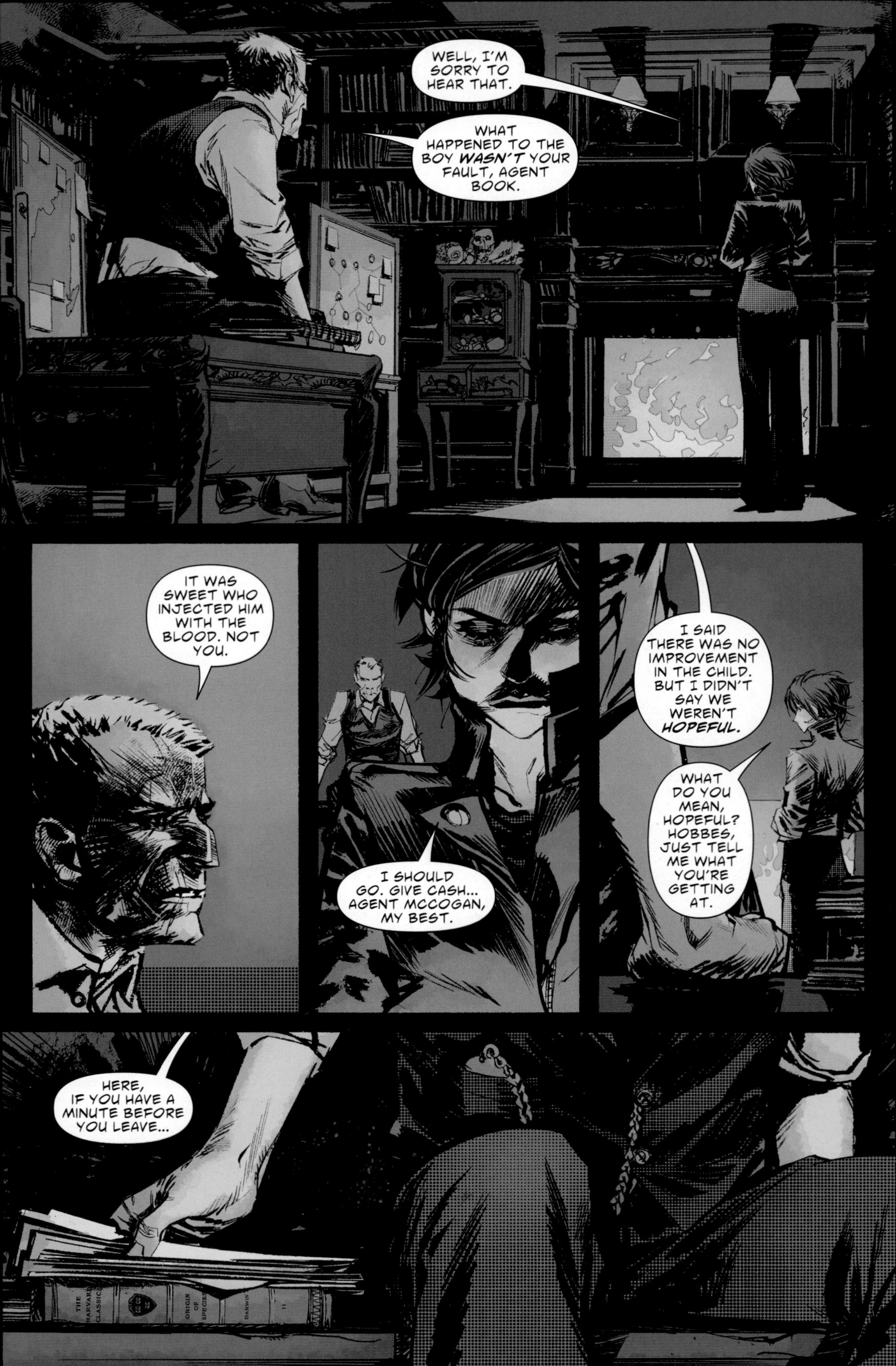
WELL, I'M SORRY TO HEAR THAT.
WHAT HAPPENED TO THE BOY WASN'T YOUR FAULT, AGENT BOOK.
IT WAS SWEET WHO INJECTED HIM WITH THE BLOOD. NOT YOU.
I SHOULD GO. GIVE CASH... AGENT MCCOGAN, MY BEST.
I SAID THERE WAS NO IMPROVEMENT IN THE CHILD. BUT I DIDN'T SAY WE WEREN'T HOPEFUL.
WHAT DO YOU MEAN, HOPEFUL? HOBBES, JUST TELL ME WHAT YOU'RE GETTING AT.
HERE, IF YOU HAVE A MINUTE BEFORE YOU LEAVE...
THE HARVARD CLASSICS
ORIGIN OF SPECIES
DARWIN

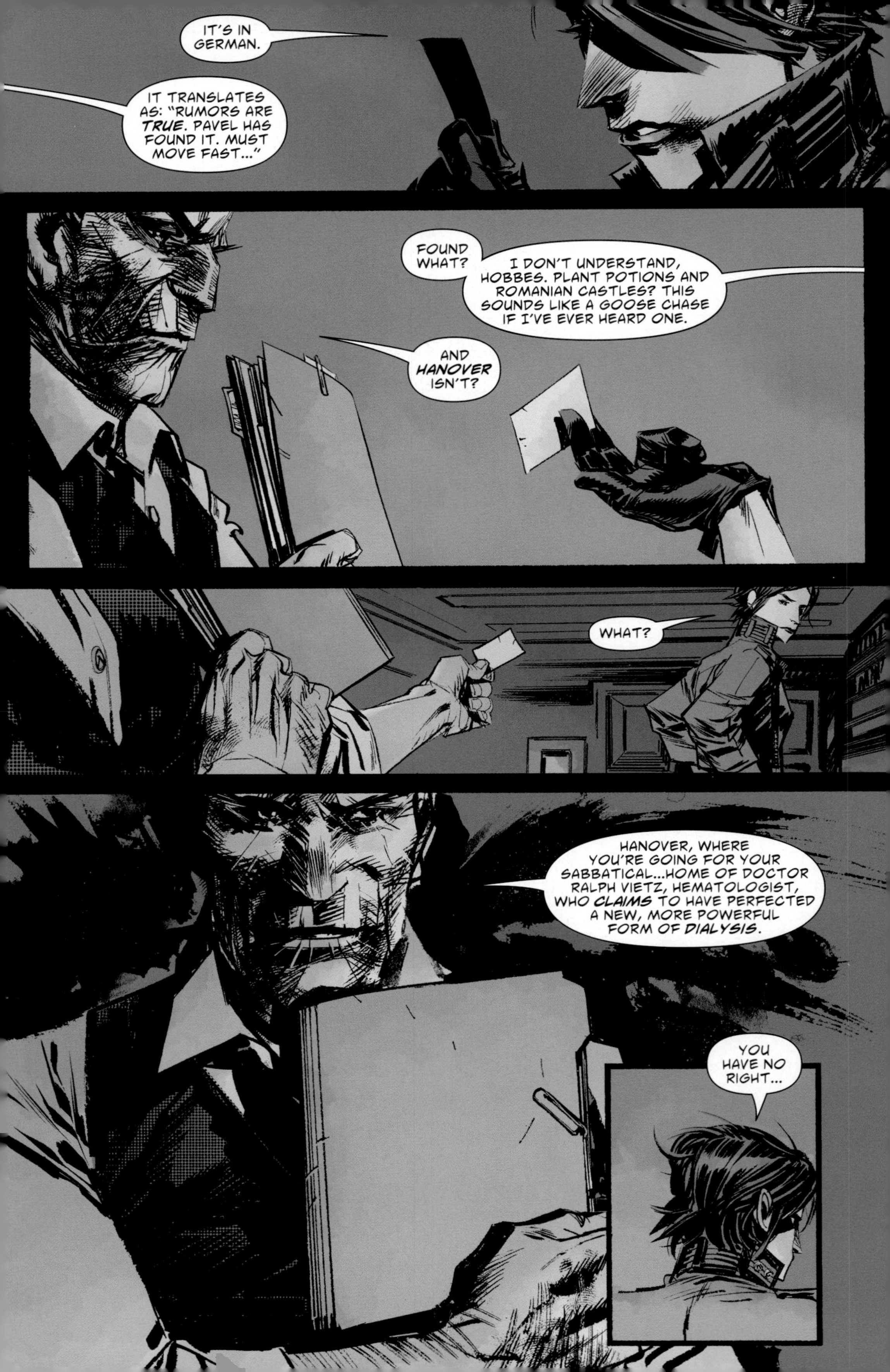
IT'S IN GERMAN.
IT TRANSLATES AS: "RUMORS ARE TRUE. PAVEL HAS FOUND IT. MUST MOVE FAST..."
FOUND WHAT?
I DON'T UNDERSTAND, HOBBES. PLANT POTIONS AND ROMANIAN CASTLES? THIS SOUNDS LIKE A GOOSE CHASE IF I'VE EVER HEARD ONE.
AND HANOVER ISN'T?
WHAT?
HANOVER, WHERE YOU'RE GOING FOR YOUR SABBATICAL...HOME OF DOCTOR RALPH VIETZ, HEMATOLOGIST, WHO CLAIMS TO HAVE PERFECTED A NEW, MORE POWERFUL FORM OF DIALYSIS.
YOU HAVE NO RIGHT...

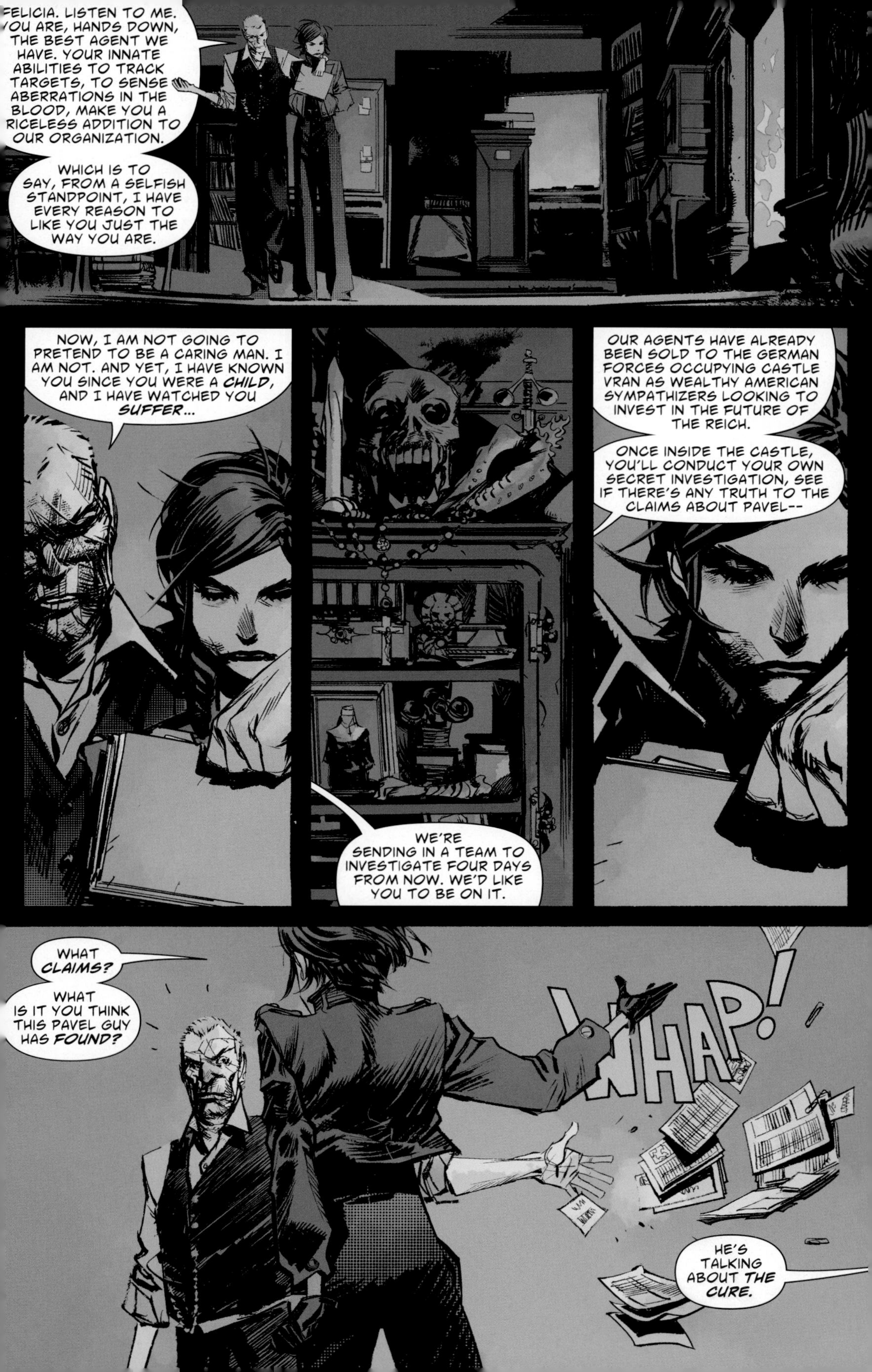
FELICIA. LISTEN TO ME. YOU ARE, HANDS DOWN, THE BEST AGENT WE HAVE. YOUR INNATE ABILITIES TO TRACK TARGETS, TO SENSE ABERRATIONS IN THE BLOOD, MAKE YOU A PRICELESS ADDITION TO OUR ORGANIZATION.
WHICH IS TO SAY, FROM A SELFISH STANDPOINT, I HAVE EVERY REASON TO LIKE YOU JUST THE WAY YOU ARE.
NOW, I AM NOT GOING TO PRETEND TO BE A CARING MAN. I AM NOT. AND YET, I HAVE KNOWN YOU SINCE YOU WERE A *CHILD*, AND I HAVE WATCHED YOU *SUFFER*...
WE'RE SENDING IN A TEAM TO INVESTIGATE FOUR DAYS FROM NOW. WE'D LIKE YOU TO BE ON IT.
OUR AGENTS HAVE ALREADY BEEN SOLD TO THE GERMAN FORCES OCCUPYING CASTLE VRAN AS WEALTHY AMERICAN SYMPATHIZERS LOOKING TO INVEST IN THE FUTURE OF THE REICH.
ONCE INSIDE THE CASTLE, YOU'LL CONDUCT YOUR OWN SECRET INVESTIGATION, SEE IF THERE'S ANY TRUTH TO THE CLAIMS ABOUT PAVEL--
WHAT *CLAIMS?*
WHAT IS IT YOU THINK THIS PAVEL GUY HAS *FOUND?*
WHAP!
HE'S TALKING ABOUT *THE CURE.*

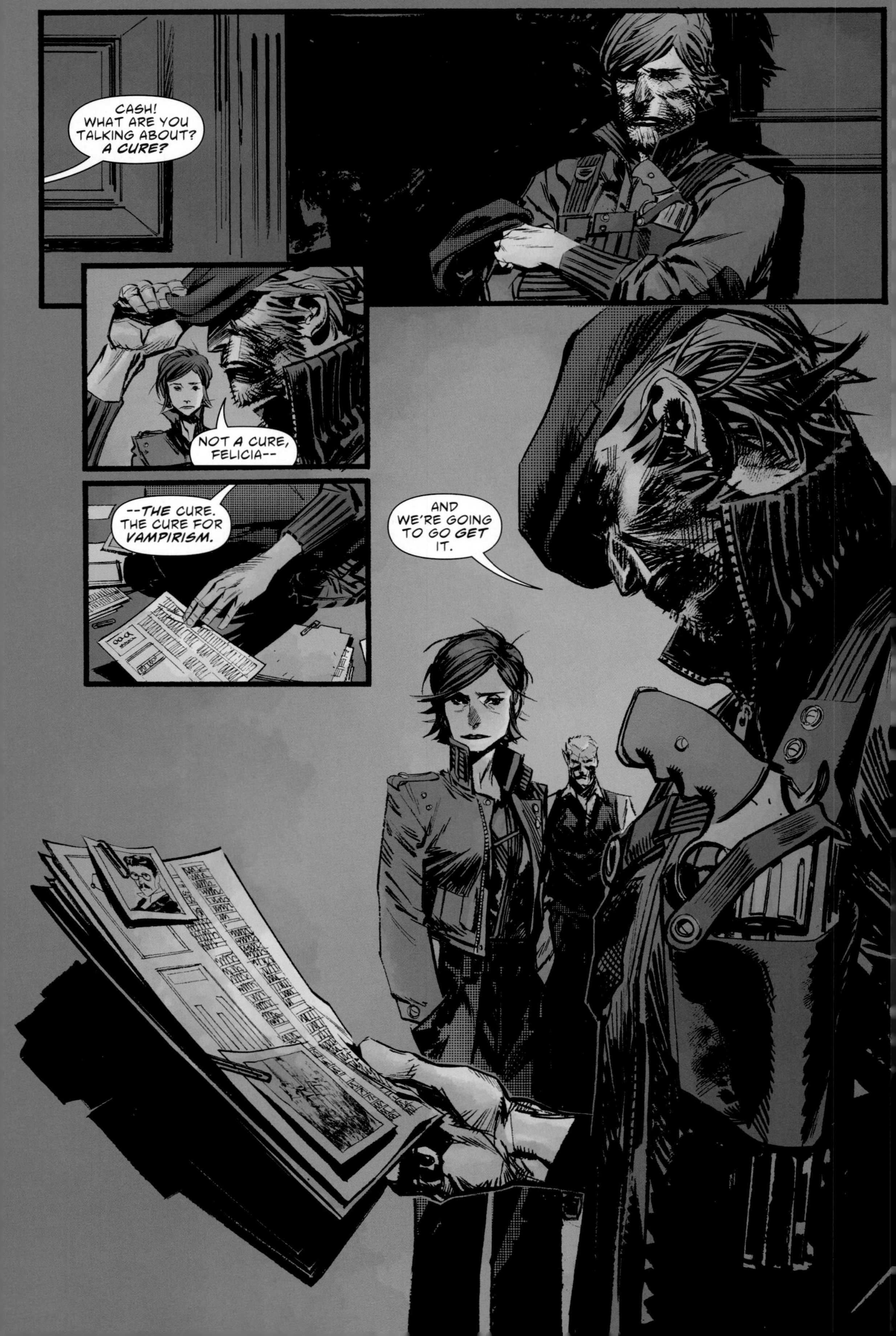
CASH! WHAT ARE YOU TALKING ABOUT? A CURE?
NOT A CURE, FELICIA--
--THE CURE. THE CURE FOR VAMPIRISM.
AND WE'RE GOING TO GO GET IT.

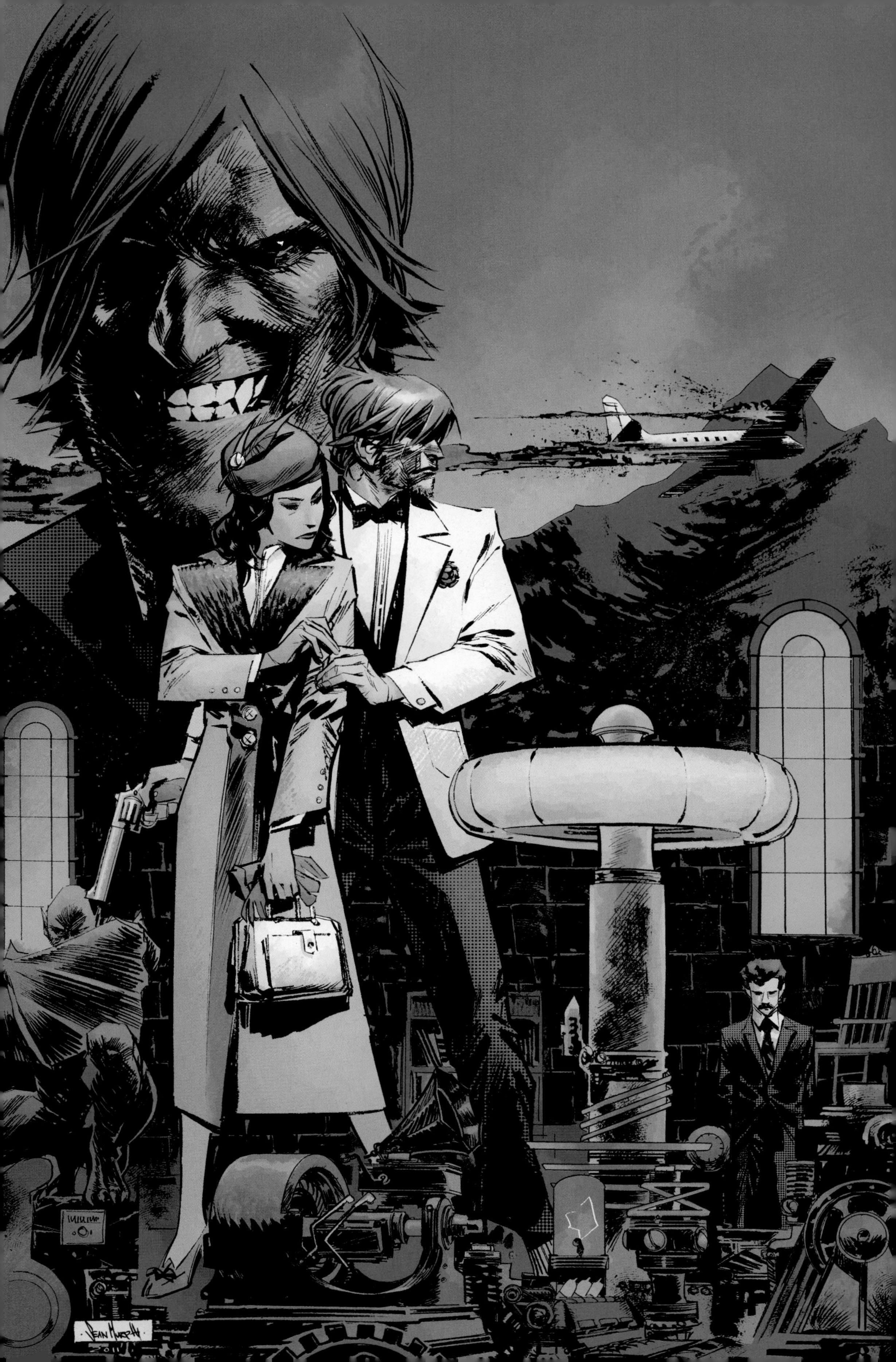

Survival
of the Fittest
Part Two

Sean Murphy
Artist and cover

Dave Stewart
cover color

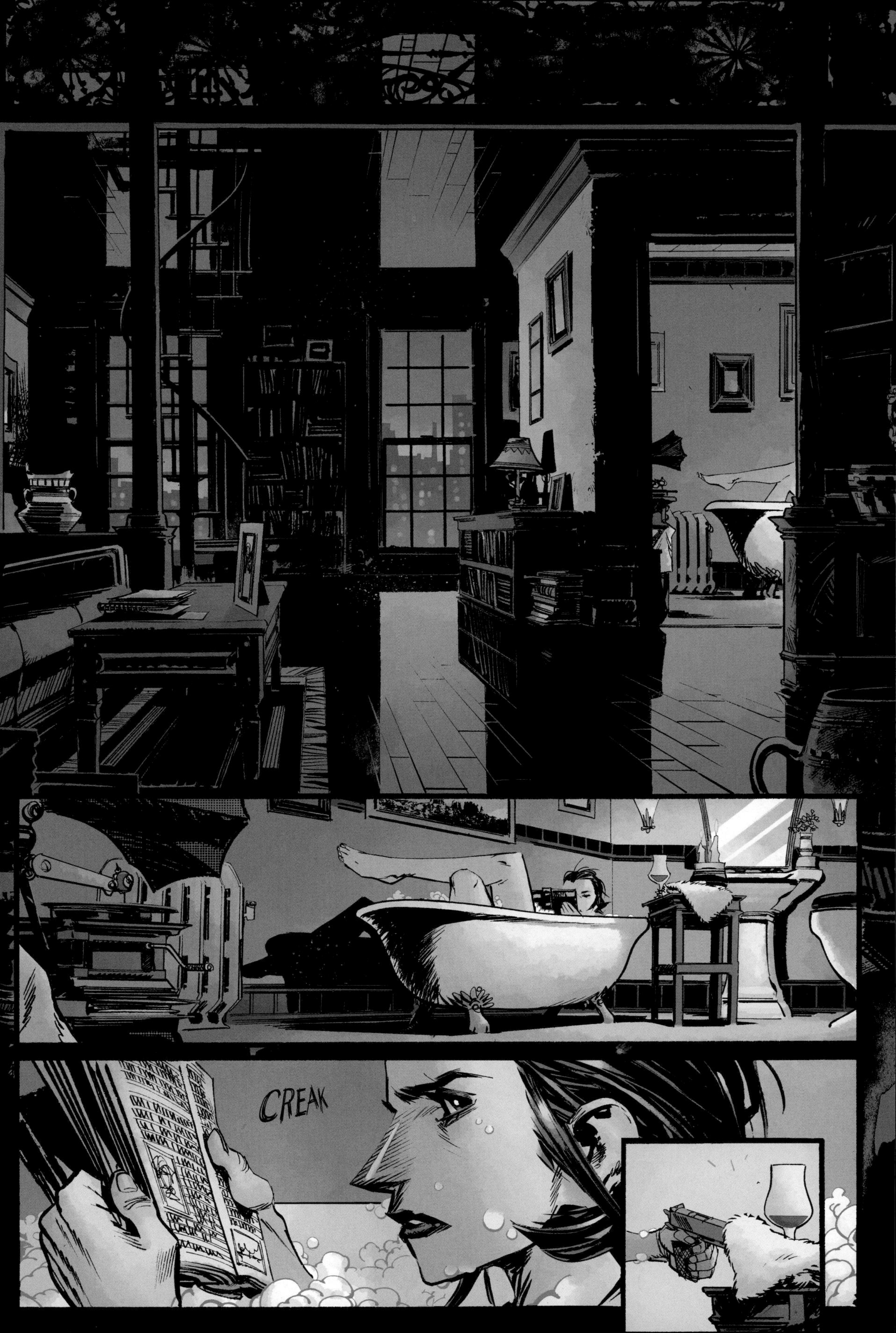
CREAK

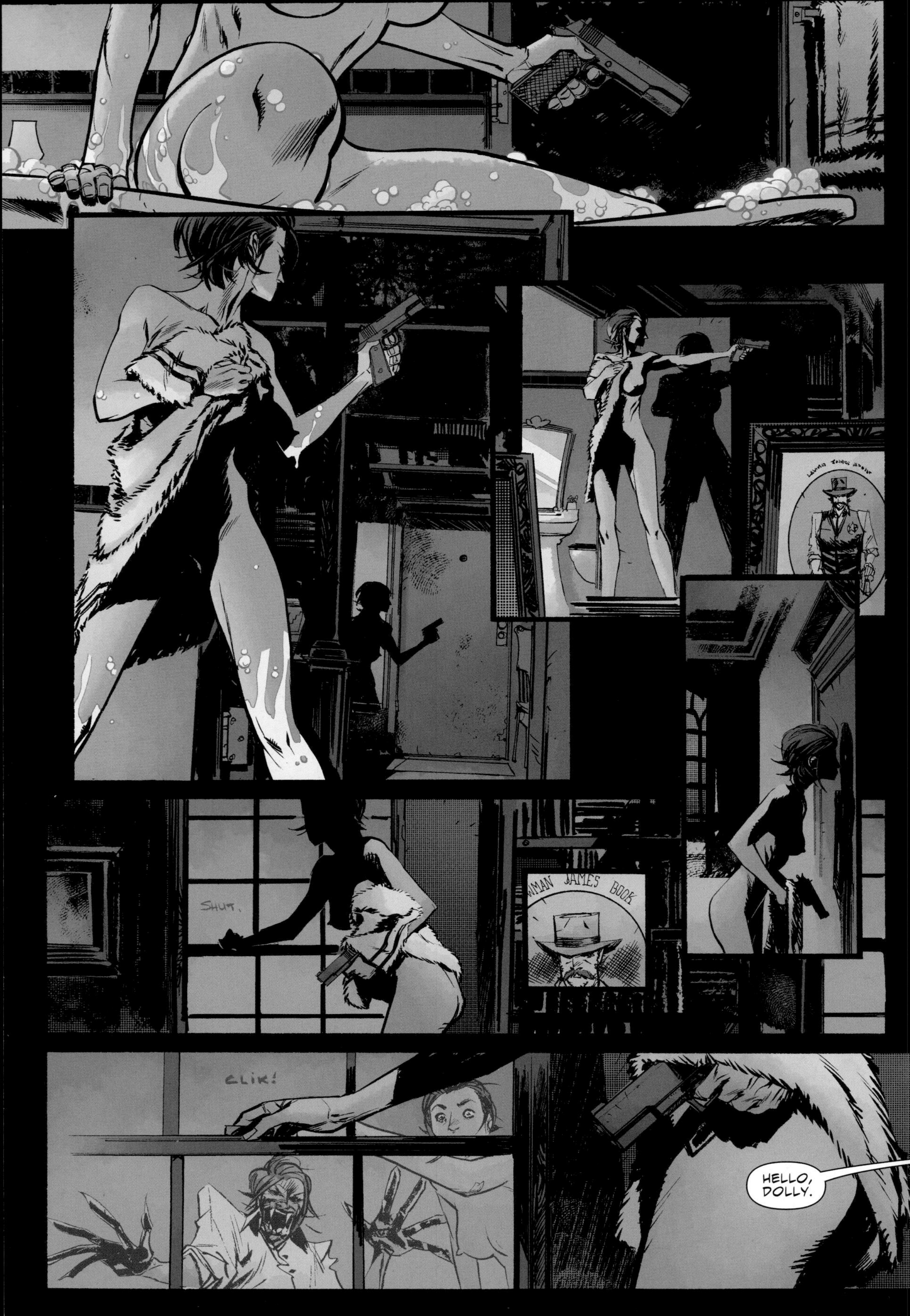
SHUT.
WMAN JAMES BOOK
CLIK!
HELLO, DOLLY.

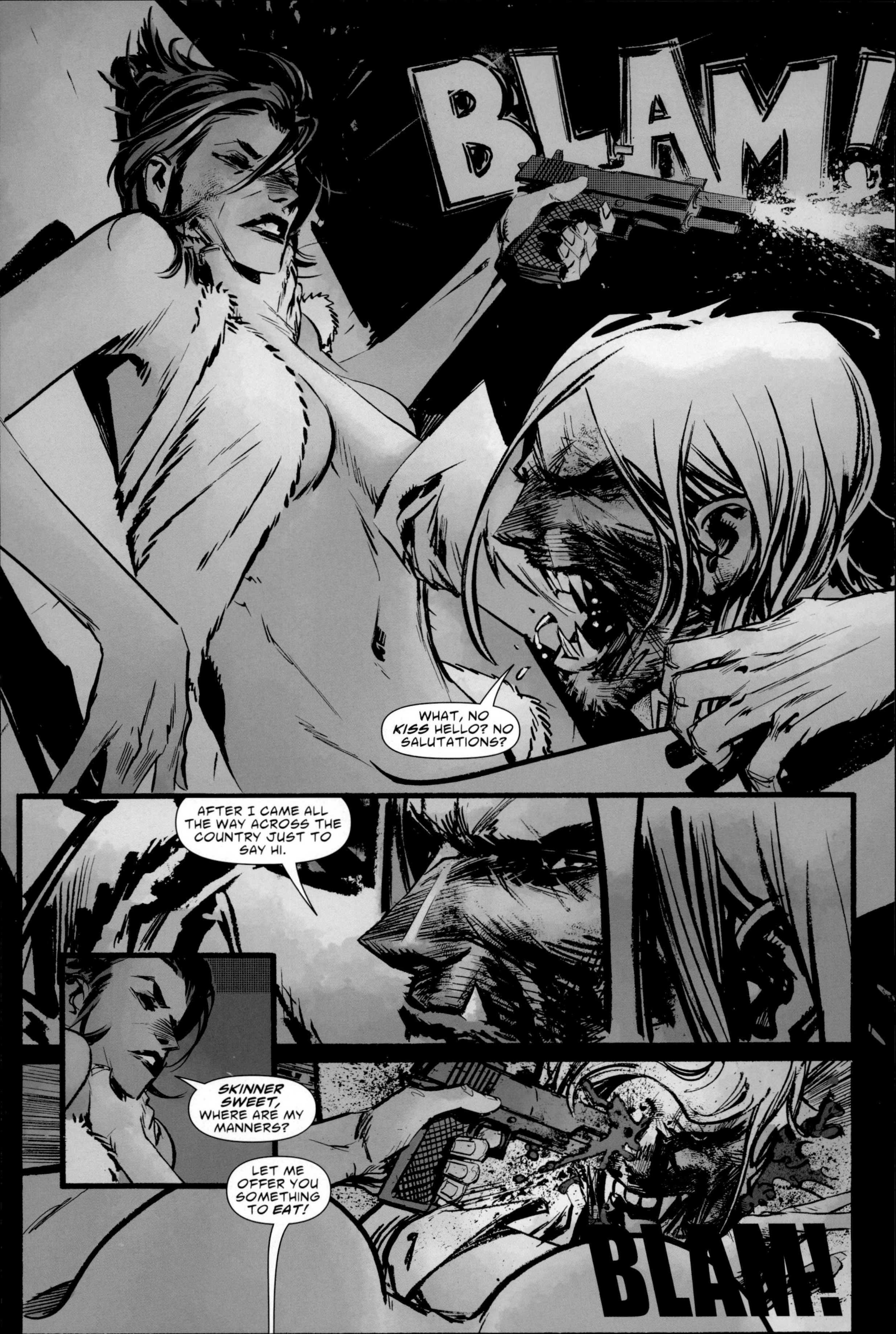
BLAM!
WHAT, NO KISS HELLO? NO SALUTATIONS?
AFTER I CAME ALL THE WAY ACROSS THE COUNTRY JUST TO SAY HI.
SKINNER SWEET, WHERE ARE MY MANNERS?
LET ME OFFER YOU SOMETHING TO EAT!
BLAM!

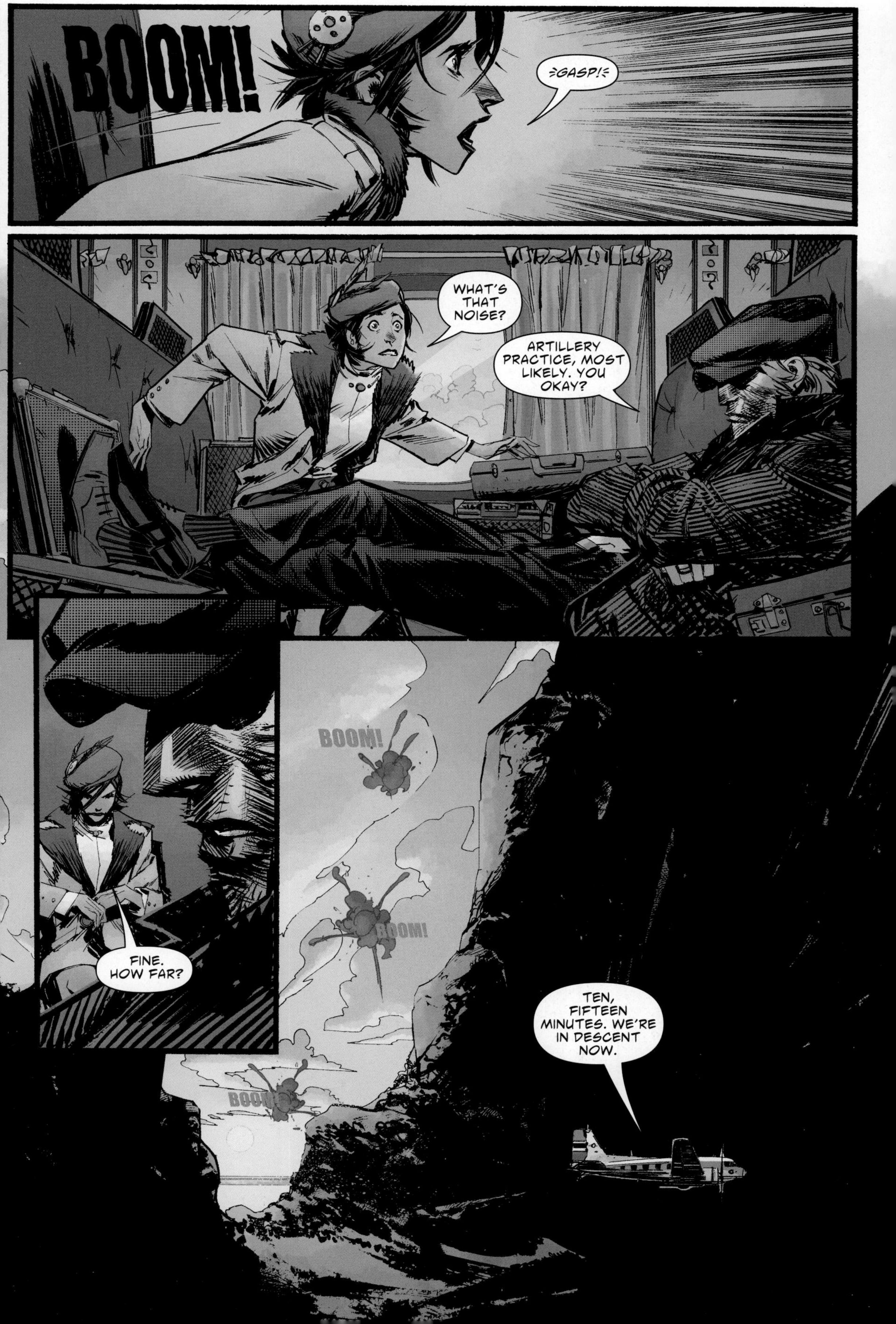
BOOM!
=GASP!=
WHAT'S THAT NOISE?
ARTILLERY PRACTICE, MOST LIKELY. YOU OKAY?
FINE. HOW FAR?
BOOM!
BOOM!
TEN, FIFTEEN MINUTES. WE'RE IN DESCENT NOW.

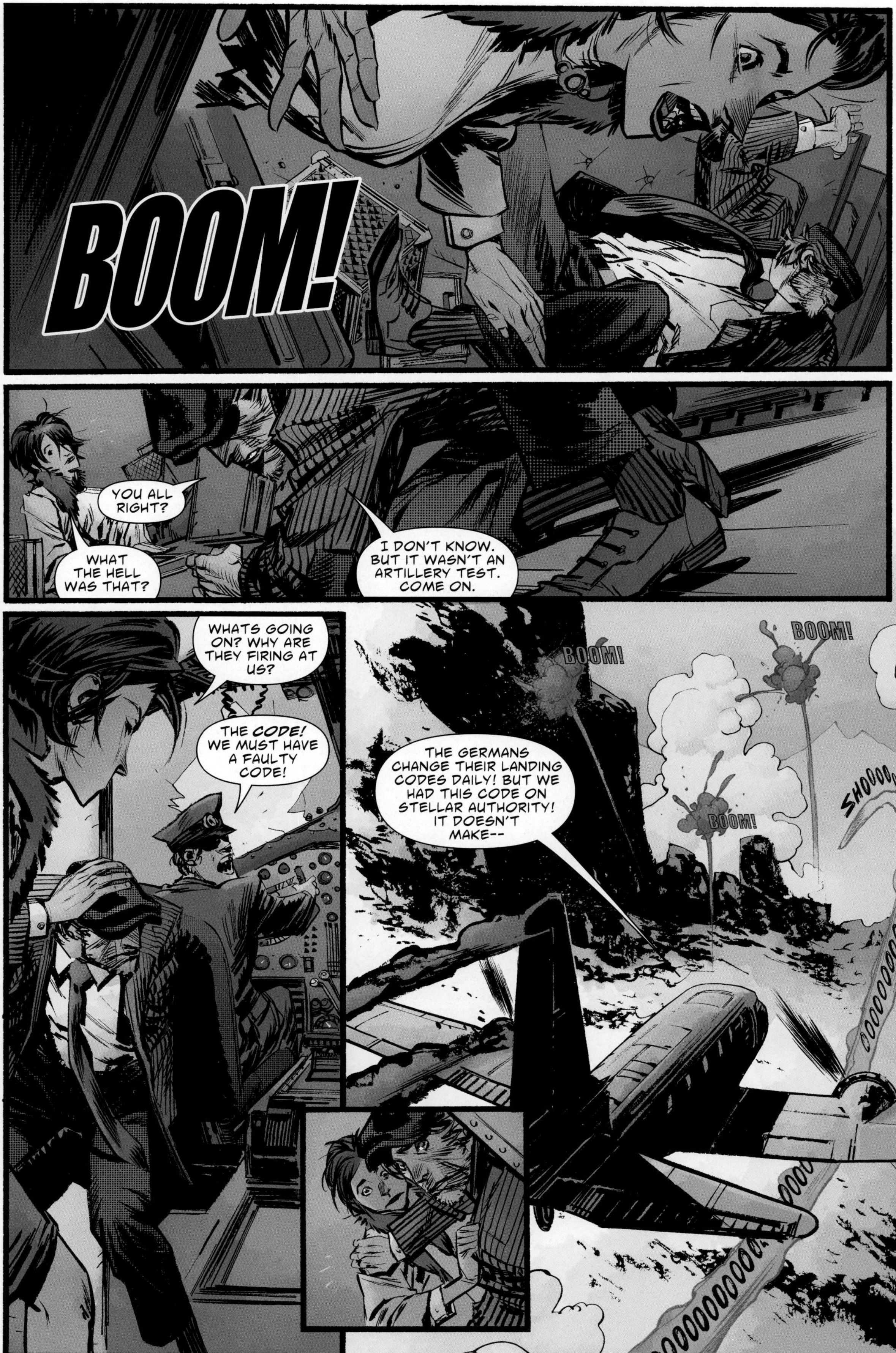
BOOM!
YOU ALL RIGHT?
WHAT THE HELL WAS THAT?
I DON'T KNOW. BUT IT WASN'T AN ARTILLERY TEST. COME ON.
WHATS GOING ON? WHY ARE THEY FIRING AT US?
THE CODE! WE MUST HAVE A FAULTY CODE!
BOOM!
BOOM!
THE GERMANS CHANGE THEIR LANDING CODES DAILY! BUT WE HAD THIS CODE ON STELLAR AUTHORITY! IT DOESN'T MAKE--
BOOM!
SHOOOO

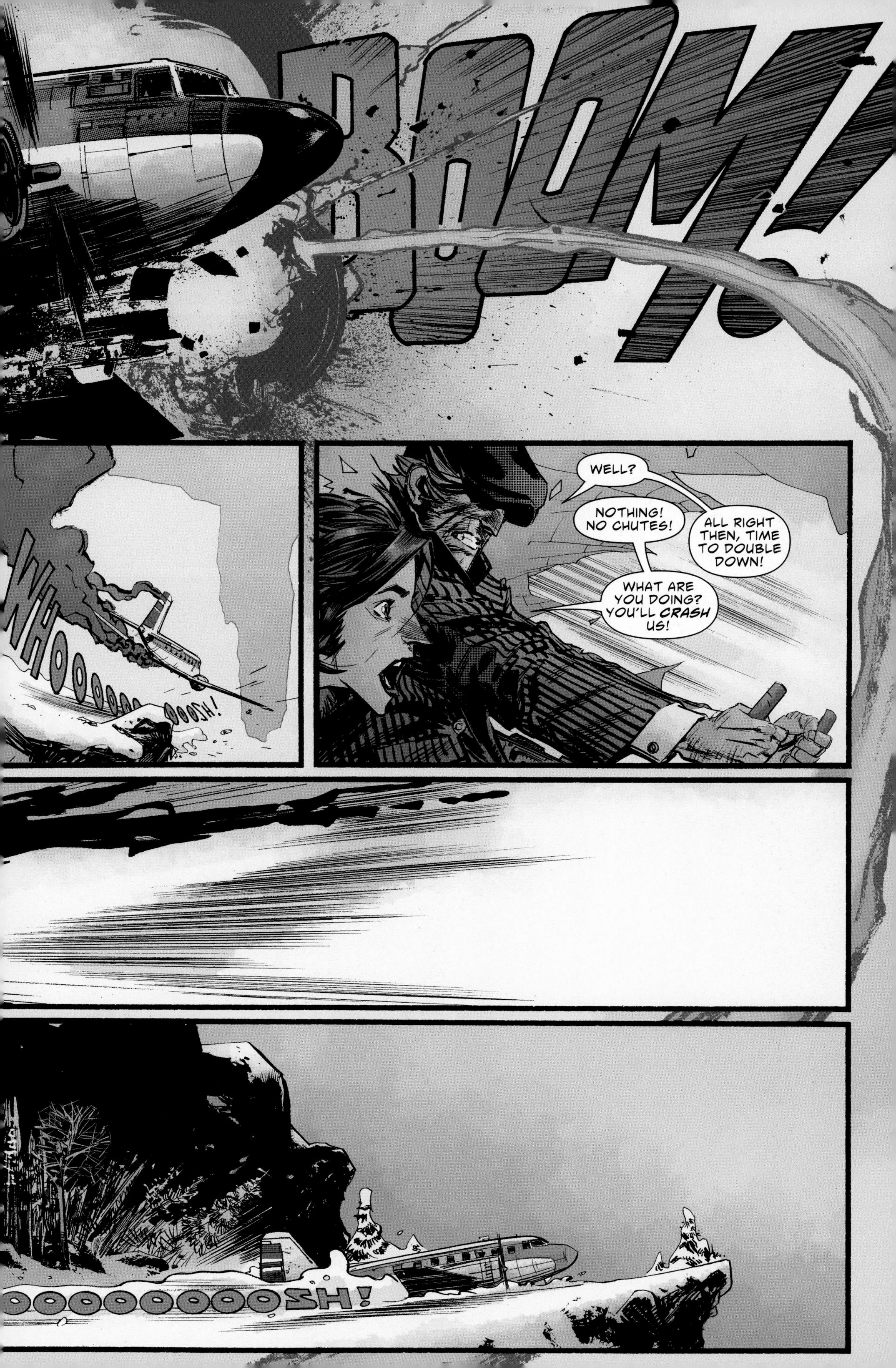

BOOM!
WHOOOOOOOOOOSH!
WELL?
NOTHING! NO CHUTES!
ALL RIGHT THEN, TIME TO DOUBLE DOWN!
WHAT ARE YOU DOING? YOU'LL CRASH US!
OOOOOOOOOOSH!

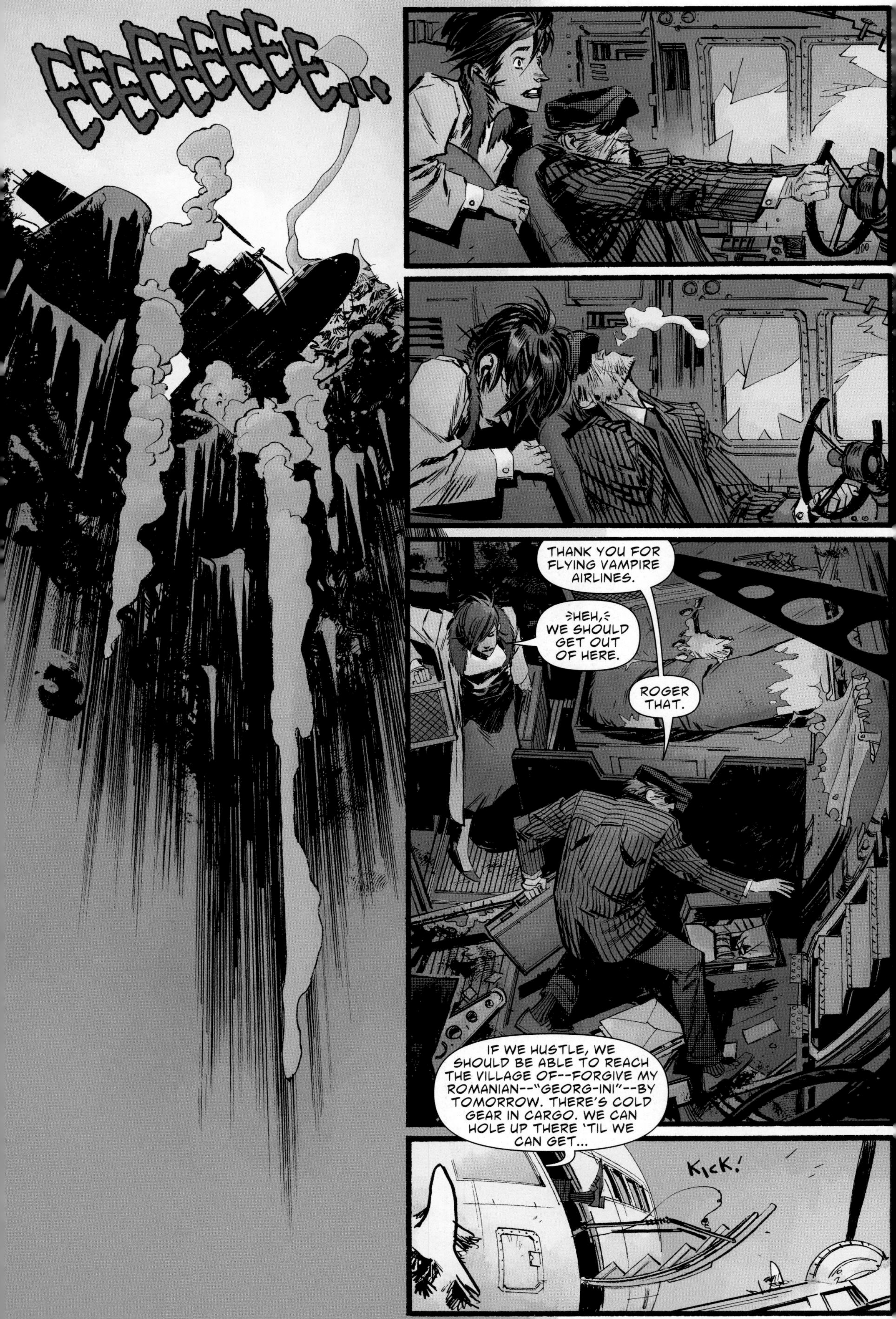
EEEEEEEEEEE...
THANK YOU FOR FLYING VAMPIRE AIRLINES.
HEH, WE SHOULD GET OUT OF HERE.
ROGER THAT.
IF WE HUSTLE, WE SHOULD BE ABLE TO REACH THE VILLAGE OF--FORGIVE MY ROMANIAN--"GEORG-INI"--BY TOMORROW. THERE'S COLD GEAR IN CARGO. WE CAN HOLE UP THERE 'TIL WE CAN GET...
KICK!

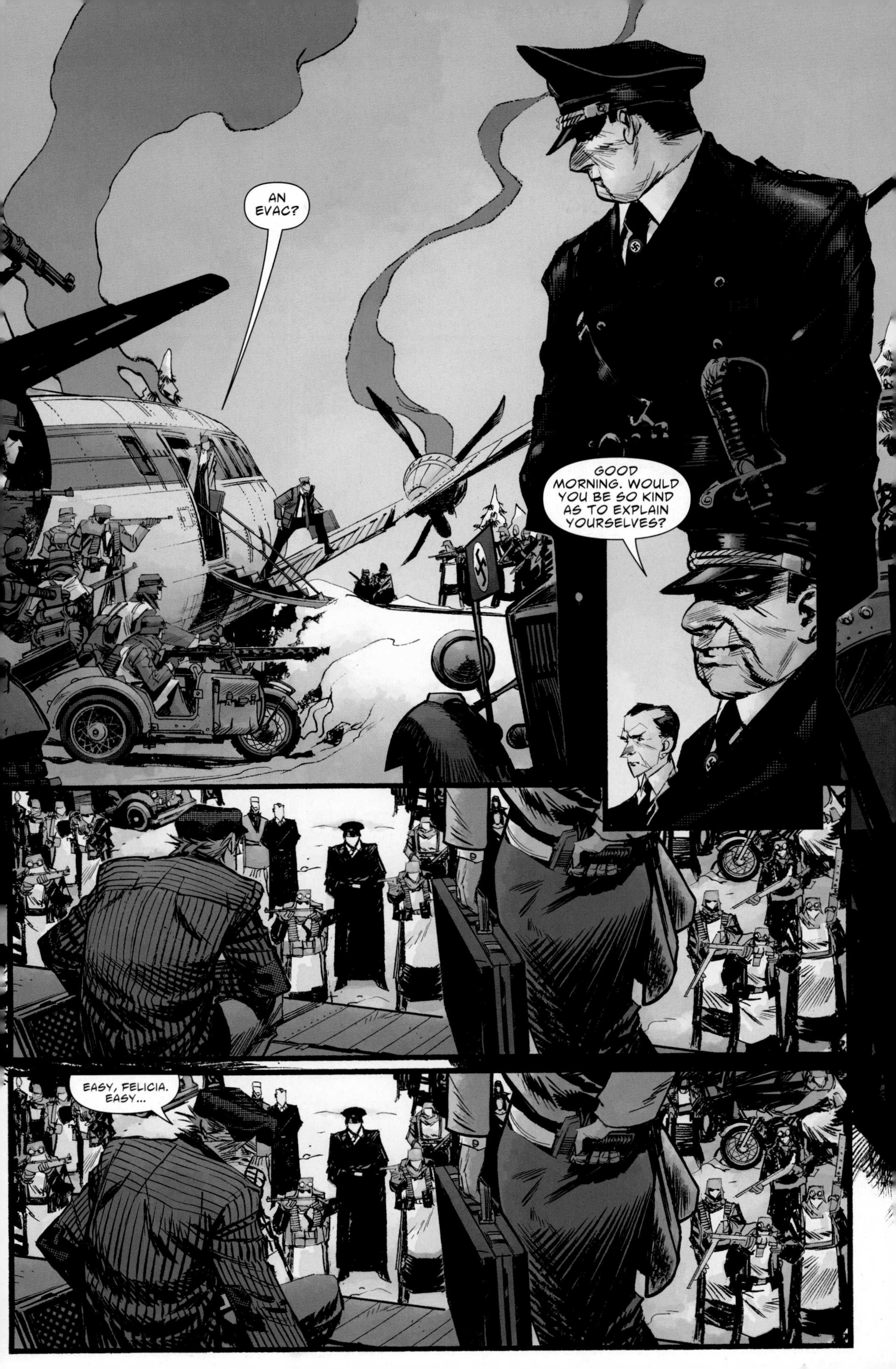
AN EVAC?
GOOD MORNING. WOULD YOU BE SO KIND AS TO EXPLAIN YOURSELVES?
EASY, FELICIA. EASY...

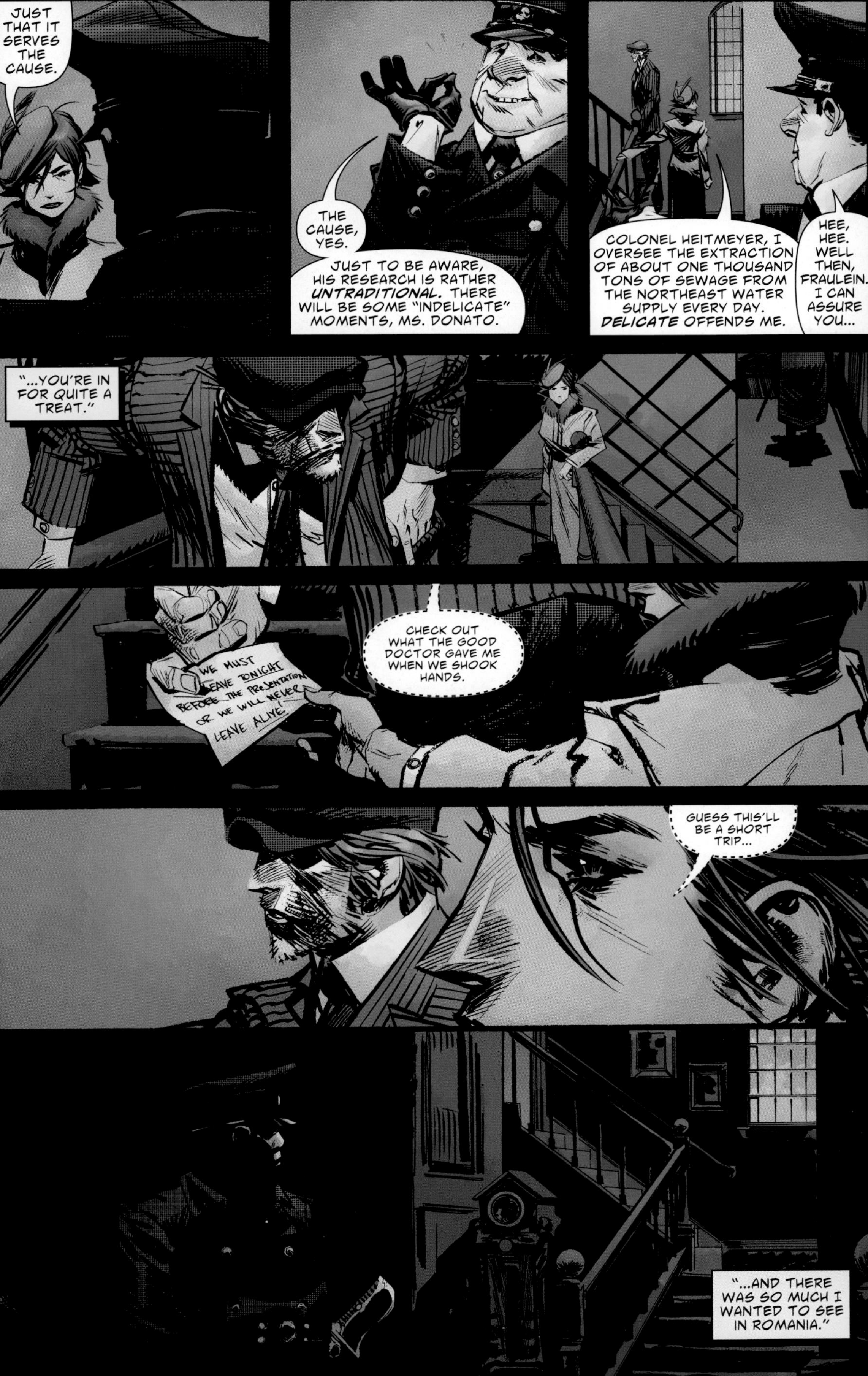
JUST THAT IT SERVES THE CAUSE.
THE CAUSE, YES.
JUST TO BE AWARE, HIS RESEARCH IS RATHER UNTRADITIONAL. THERE WILL BE SOME "INDELICATE" MOMENTS, MS. DONATO.
COLONEL HEITMEYER, I OVERSEE THE EXTRACTION OF ABOUT ONE THOUSAND TONS OF SEWAGE FROM THE NORTHEAST WATER SUPPLY EVERY DAY. DELICATE OFFENDS ME.
HEE, HEE. WELL THEN, FRAULEIN. I CAN ASSURE YOU...
"...YOU'RE IN FOR QUITE A TREAT."
WE MUST LEAVE TONIGHT BEFORE THE PRESENTATION OR WE WILL NEVER LEAVE ALIVE!
CHECK OUT WHAT THE GOOD DOCTOR GAVE ME WHEN WE SHOOK HANDS.
GUESS THIS'LL BE A SHORT TRIP...
"...AND THERE WAS SO MUCH I WANTED TO SEE IN ROMANIA."

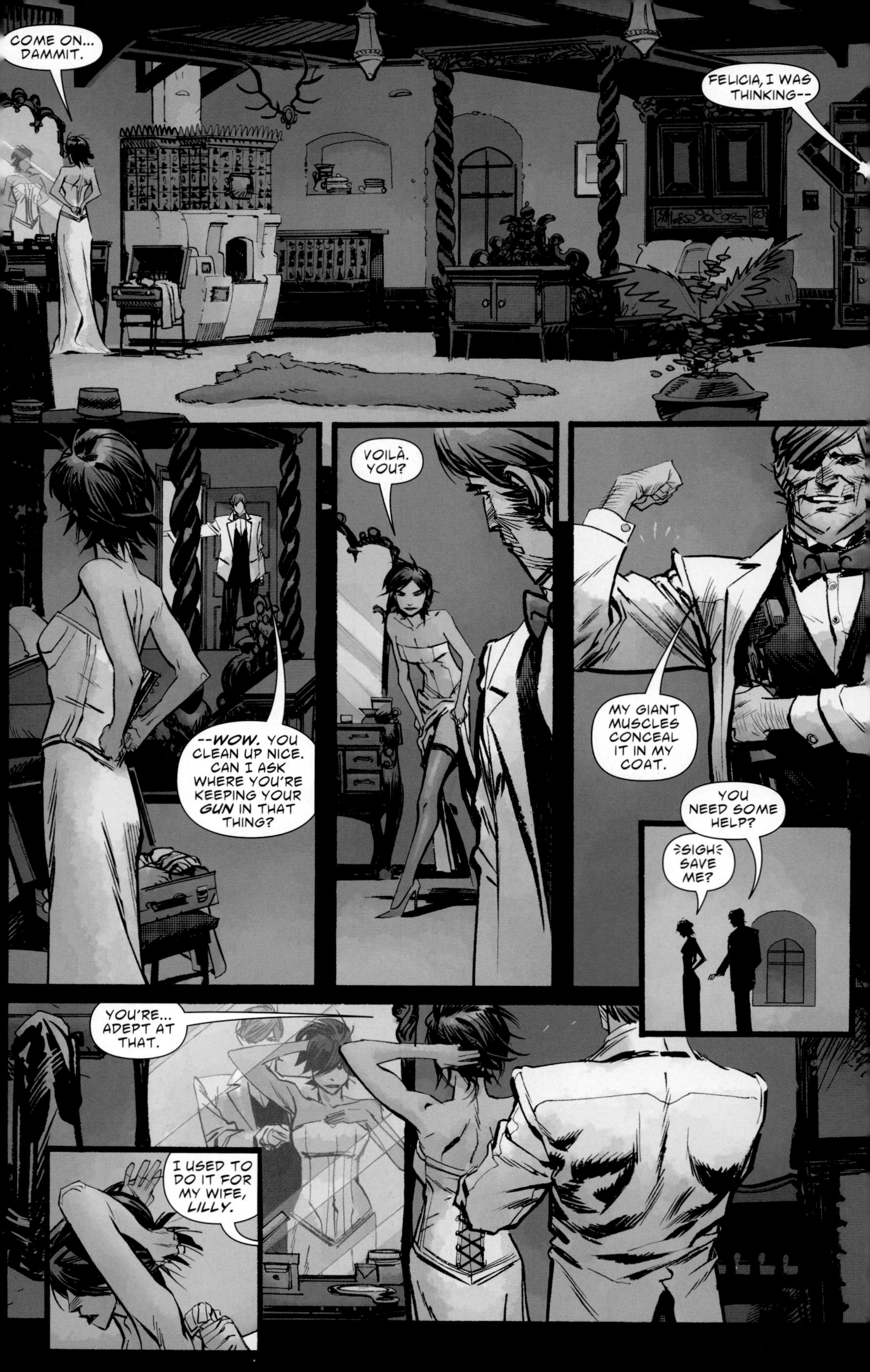
COME ON... DAMMIT.
FELICIA, I WAS THINKING--
--WOW. YOU CLEAN UP NICE. CAN I ASK WHERE YOU'RE KEEPING YOUR GUN IN THAT THING?
VOILÀ. YOU?
MY GIANT MUSCLES CONCEAL IT IN MY COAT.
YOU NEED SOME HELP?
SIGH SAVE ME?
YOU'RE... ADEPT AT THAT.
I USED TO DO IT FOR MY WIFE, LILLY.

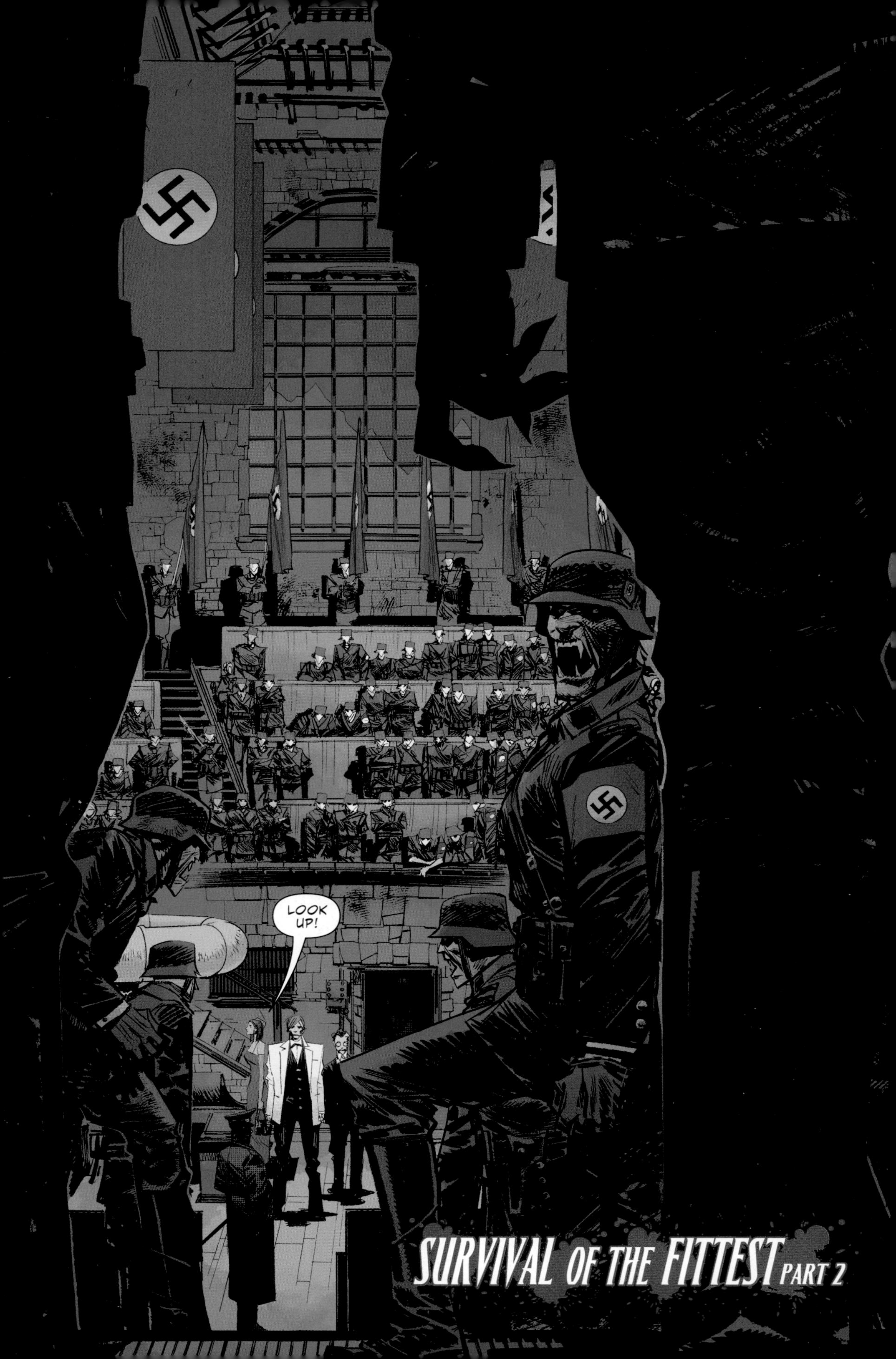
LOOK UP!
SURVIVAL OF THE FITTEST PART 2

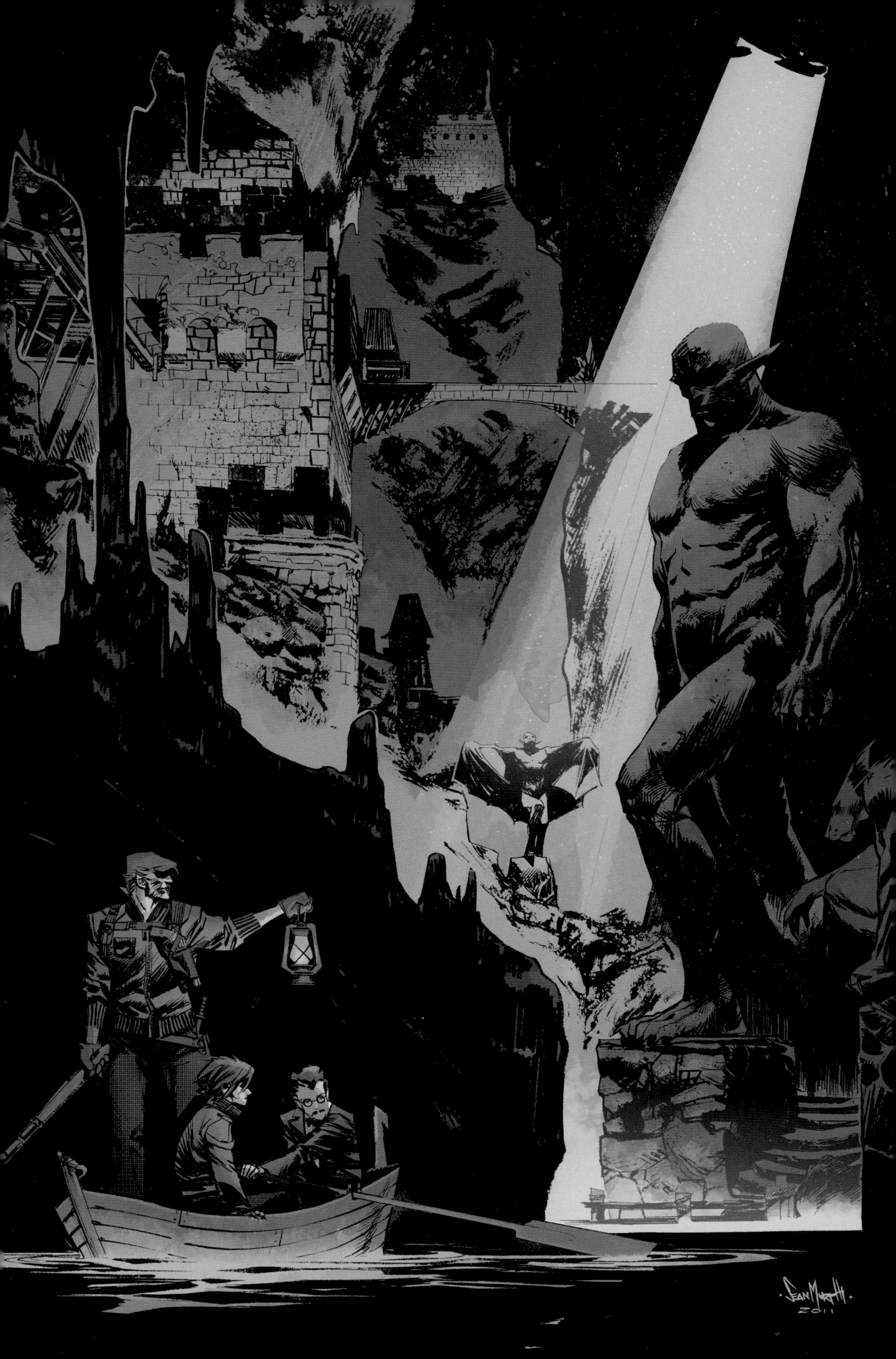
SEAN MURPHY
2011

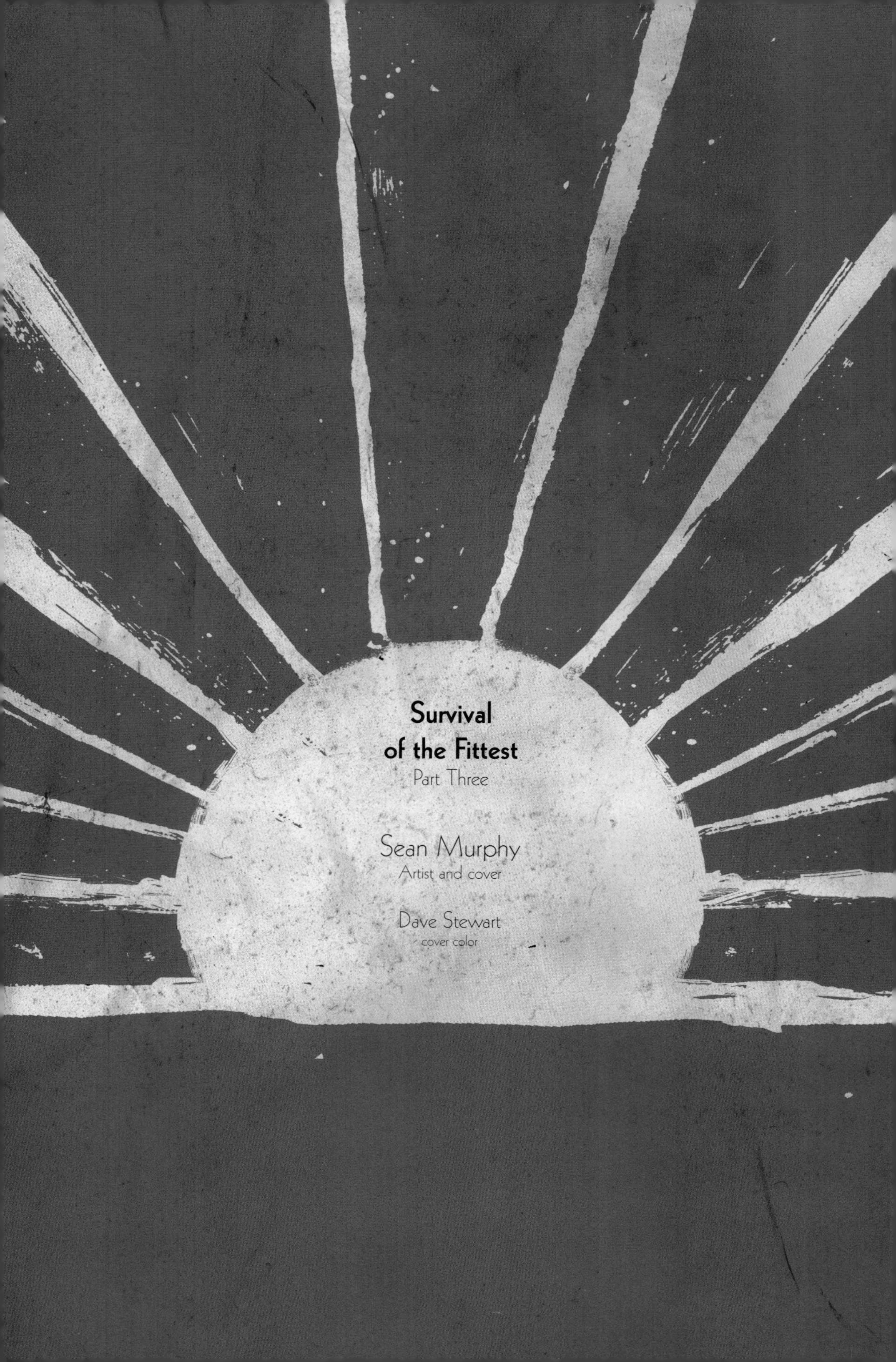

Survival of the Fittest

Part Three

Sean Murphy
Artist and cover

Dave Stewart
cover color

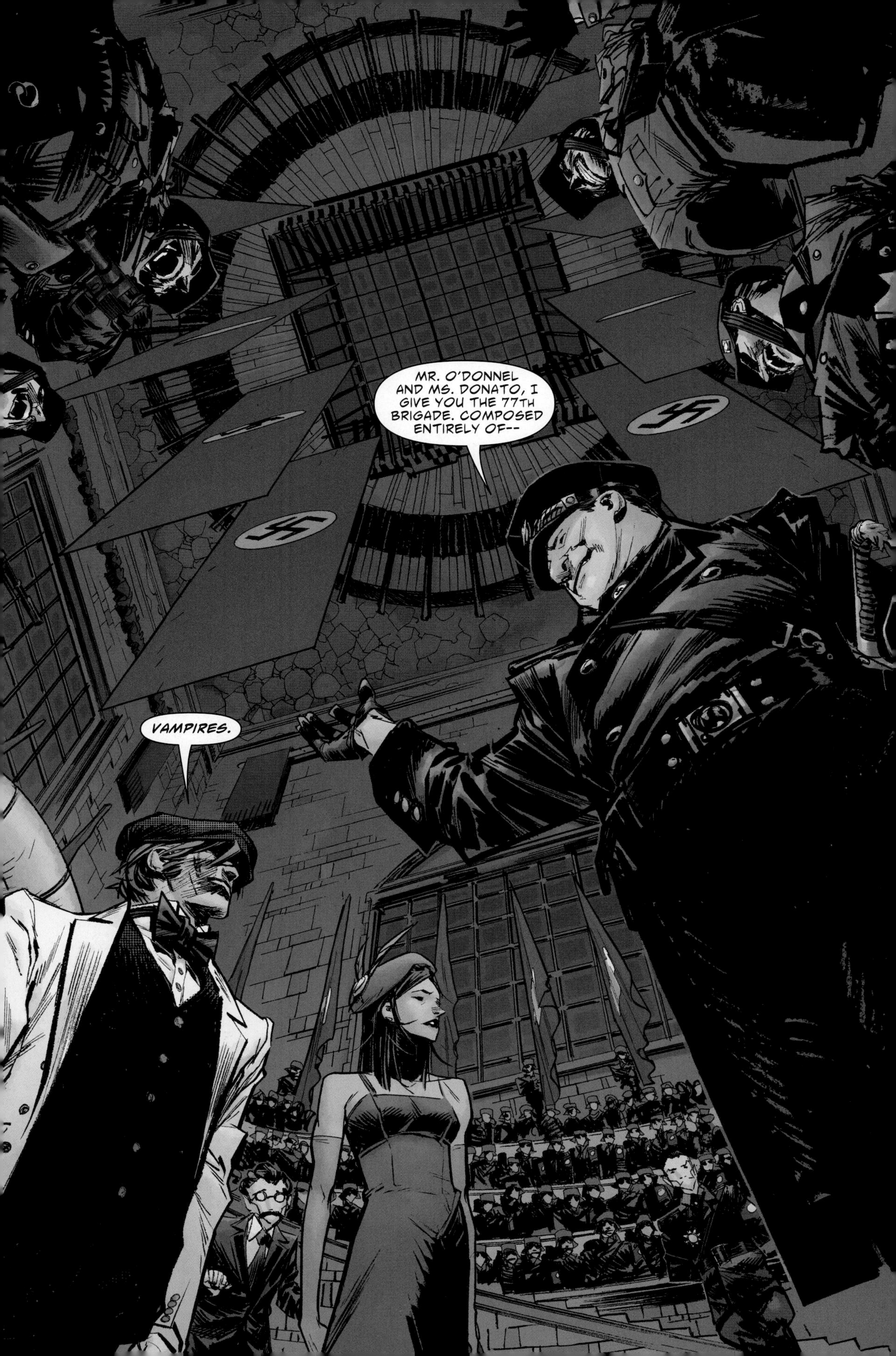
MR. O'DONNEL AND MS. DONATO, I GIVE YOU THE 77TH BRIGADE. COMPOSED ENTIRELY OF--
VAMPIRES.

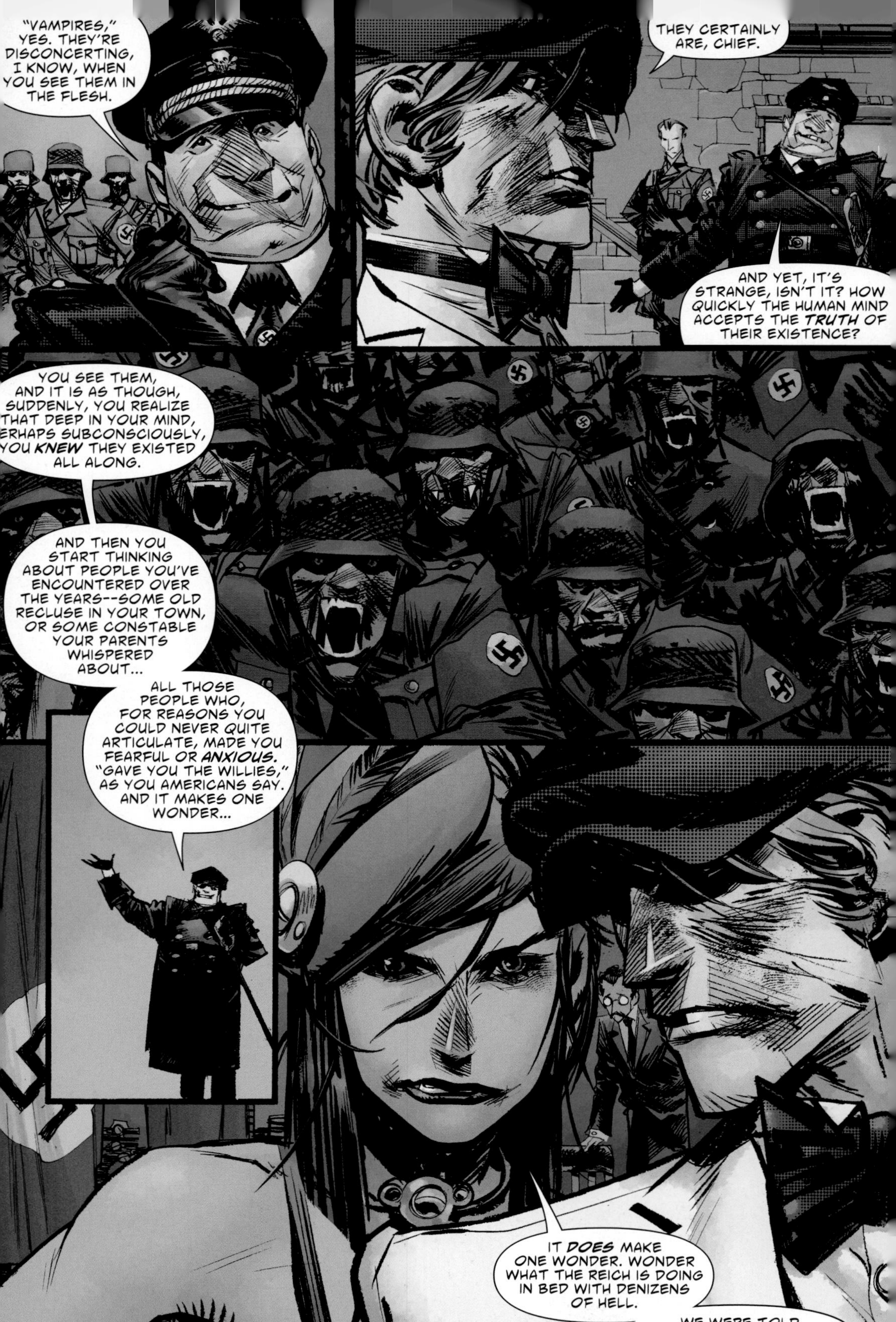
"VAMPIRES," YES. THEY'RE DISCONCERTING, I KNOW, WHEN YOU SEE THEM IN THE FLESH.
THEY CERTAINLY ARE, CHIEF.
AND YET, IT'S STRANGE, ISN'T IT? HOW QUICKLY THE HUMAN MIND ACCEPTS THE *TRUTH* OF THEIR EXISTENCE?
YOU SEE THEM, AND IT IS AS THOUGH, SUDDENLY, YOU REALIZE THAT DEEP IN YOUR MIND, ERHAPS SUBCONSCIOUSLY, YOU *KNEW* THEY EXISTED ALL ALONG.
AND THEN YOU START THINKING ABOUT PEOPLE YOU'VE ENCOUNTERED OVER THE YEARS--SOME OLD RECLUSE IN YOUR TOWN, OR SOME CONSTABLE YOUR PARENTS WHISPERED ABOUT...
ALL THOSE PEOPLE WHO, FOR REASONS YOU COULD NEVER QUITE ARTICULATE, MADE YOU FEARFUL OR *ANXIOUS.* "GAVE YOU THE WILLIES," AS YOU AMERICANS SAY. AND IT MAKES ONE WONDER...
IT *DOES* MAKE ONE WONDER. WONDER WHAT THE REICH IS DOING IN BED WITH DENIZENS OF HELL.
WE WERE TOLD DR. PAVEL'S RESEARCH WAS DEDICATED TO FURTHERING THE CAUSE.

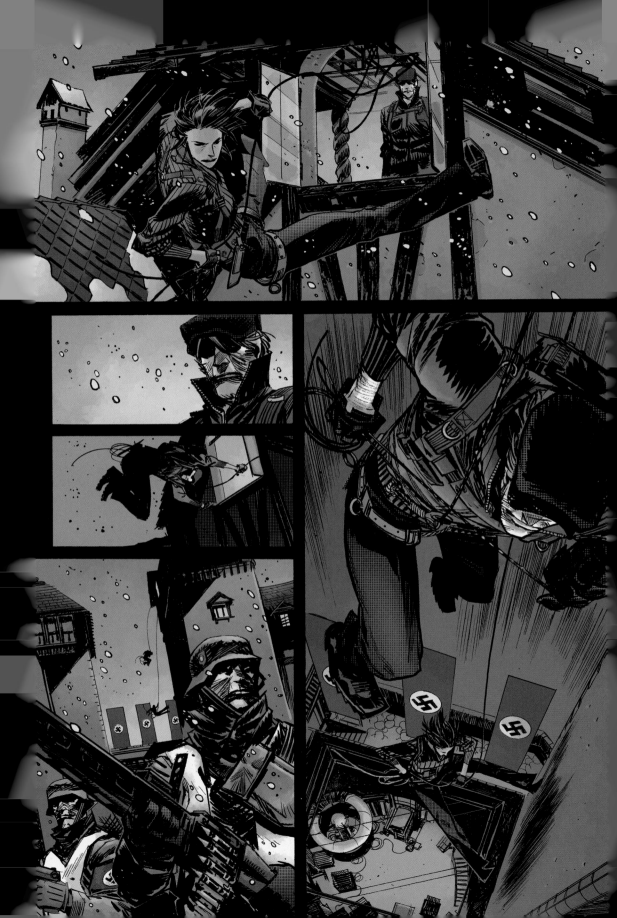

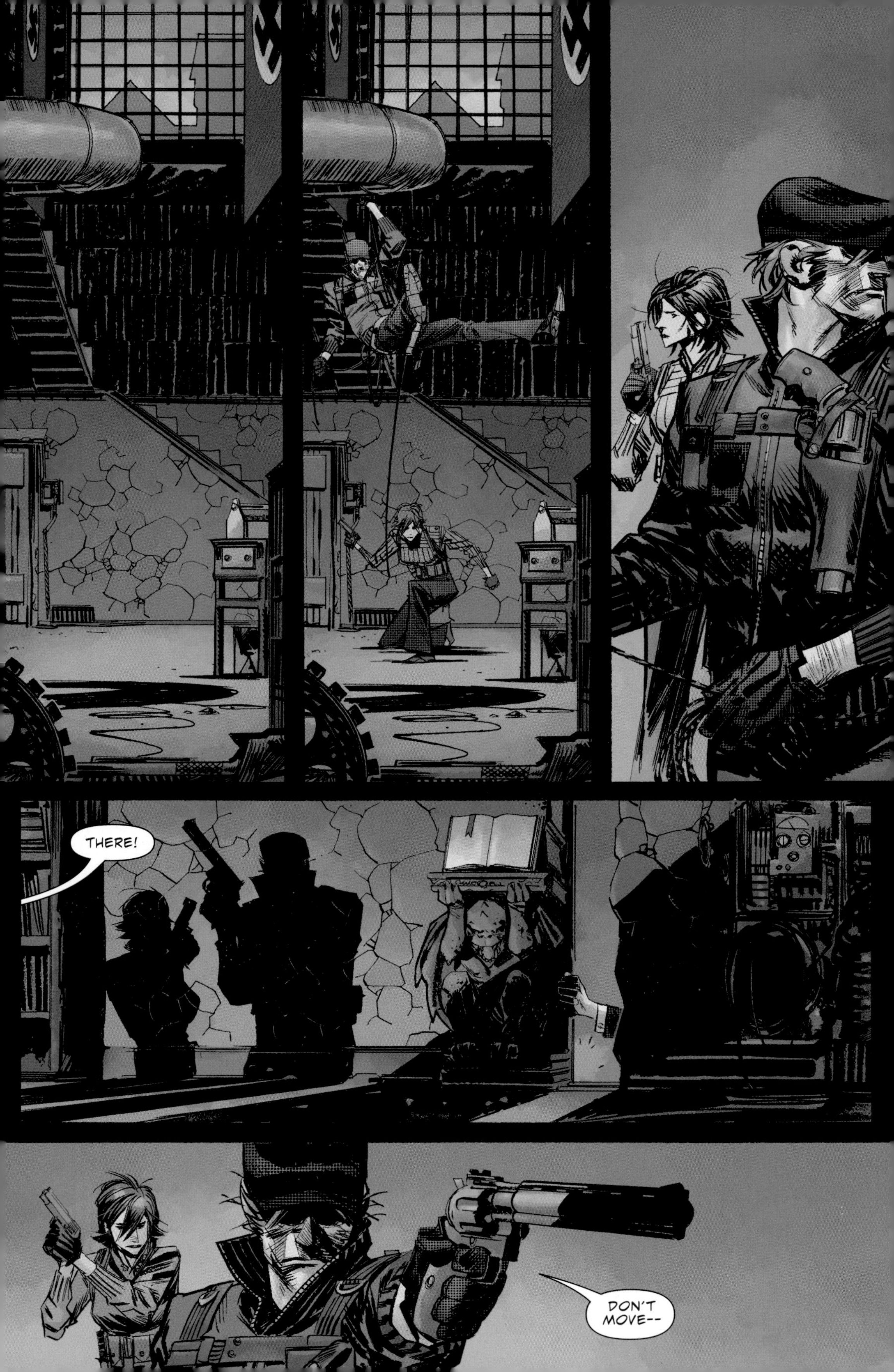
THERE!
DON'T MOVE--

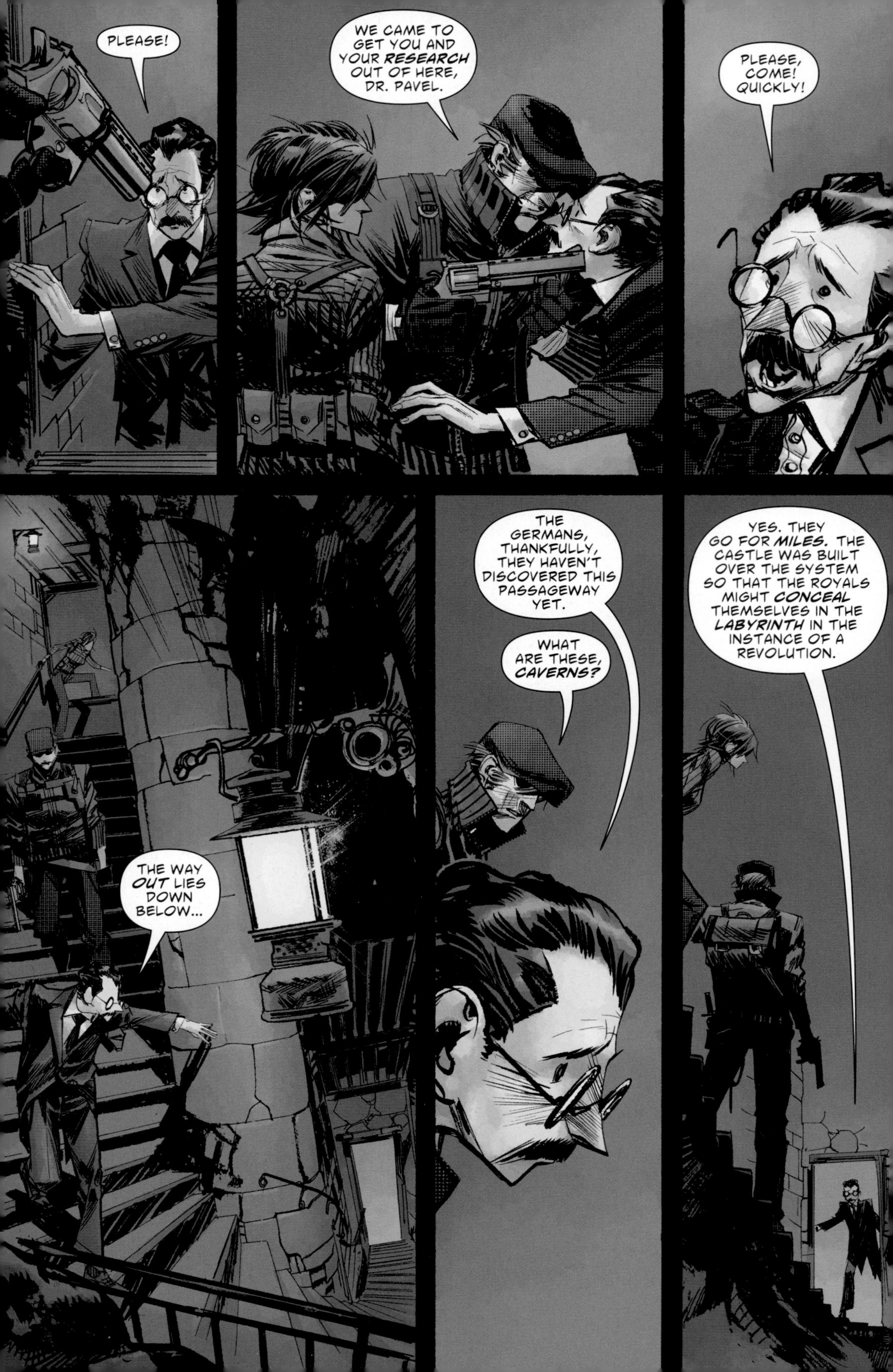
PLEASE!
WE CAME TO GET YOU AND YOUR RESEARCH OUT OF HERE, DR. PAVEL.
PLEASE, COME! QUICKLY!
THE WAY OUT LIES DOWN BELOW...
THE GERMANS, THANKFULLY, THEY HAVEN'T DISCOVERED THIS PASSAGEWAY YET.
WHAT ARE THESE, CAVERNS?
YES. THEY GO FOR MILES. THE CASTLE WAS BUILT OVER THE SYSTEM SO THAT THE ROYALS MIGHT CONCEAL THEMSELVES IN THE LABYRINTH IN THE INSTANCE OF A REVOLUTION.

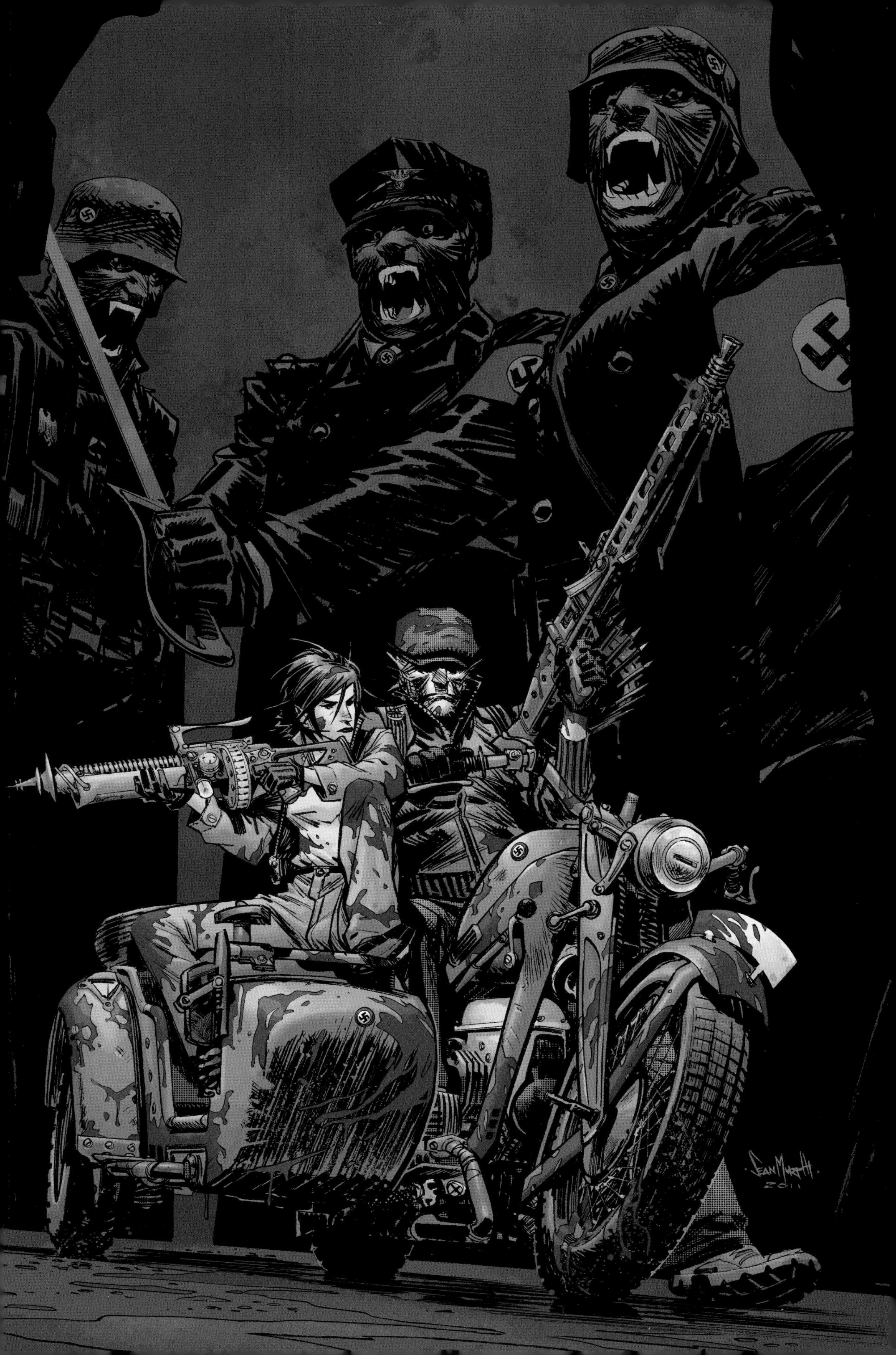

Survival
of the Fittest
Part Four

Sean Murphy
Artist and cover

Dave Stewart
cover color

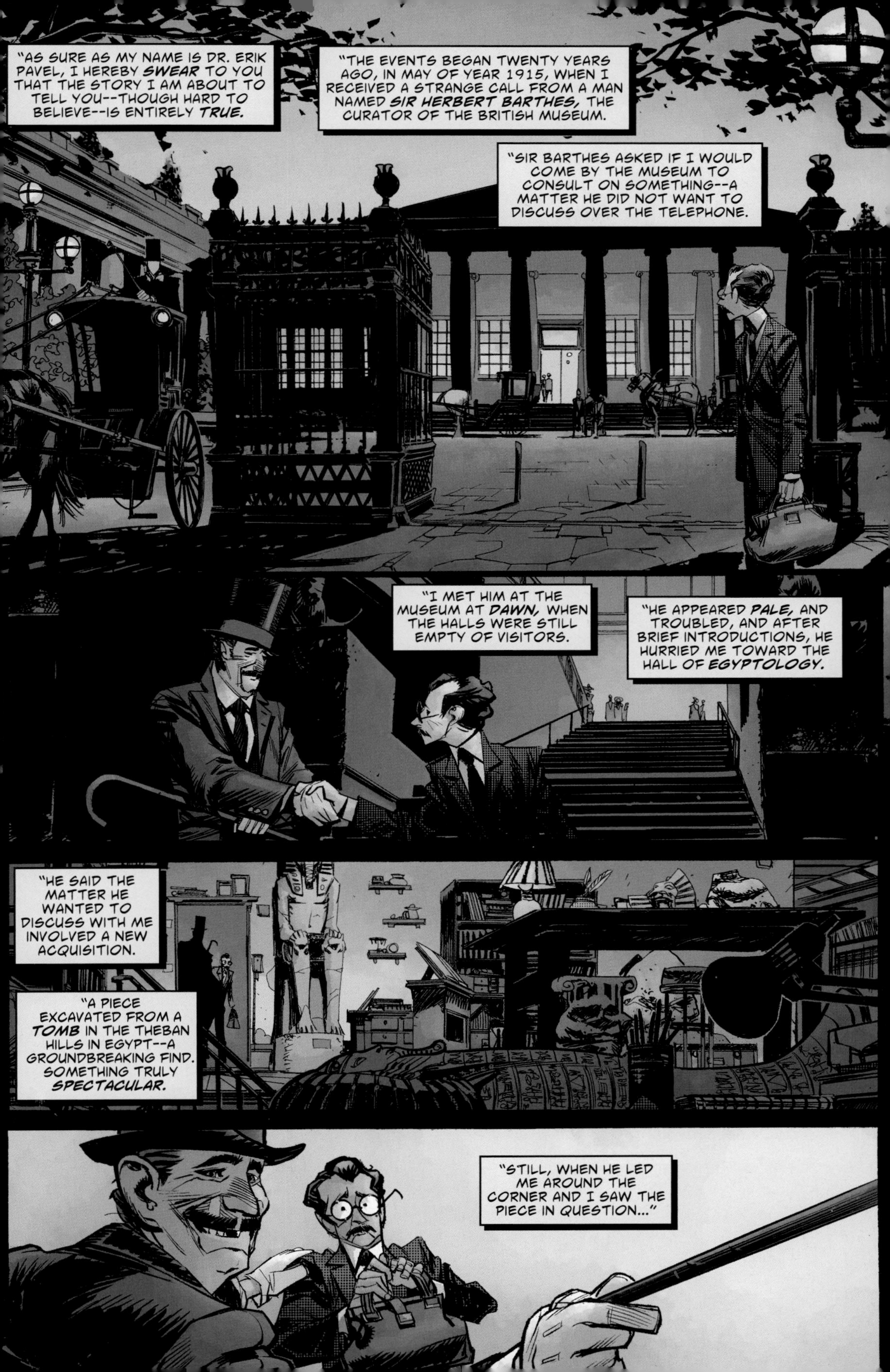

"AS SURE AS MY NAME IS DR. ERIK PAVEL, I HEREBY SWEAR TO YOU THAT THE STORY I AM ABOUT TO TELL YOU--THOUGH HARD TO BELIEVE--IS ENTIRELY TRUE.
"THE EVENTS BEGAN TWENTY YEARS AGO, IN MAY OF YEAR 1915, WHEN I RECEIVED A STRANGE CALL FROM A MAN NAMED SIR HERBERT BARTHES, THE CURATOR OF THE BRITISH MUSEUM.
"SIR BARTHES ASKED IF I WOULD COME BY THE MUSEUM TO CONSULT ON SOMETHING--A MATTER HE DID NOT WANT TO DISCUSS OVER THE TELEPHONE.
"I MET HIM AT THE MUSEUM AT DAWN, WHEN THE HALLS WERE STILL EMPTY OF VISITORS.
"HE APPEARED PALE, AND TROUBLED, AND AFTER BRIEF INTRODUCTIONS, HE HURRIED ME TOWARD THE HALL OF EGYPTOLOGY.
"HE SAID THE MATTER HE WANTED TO DISCUSS WITH ME INVOLVED A NEW ACQUISITION.
"A PIECE EXCAVATED FROM A TOMB IN THE THEBAN HILLS IN EGYPT--A GROUNDBREAKING FIND. SOMETHING TRULY SPECTACULAR.
"STILL, WHEN HE LED ME AROUND THE CORNER AND I SAW THE PIECE IN QUESTION..."

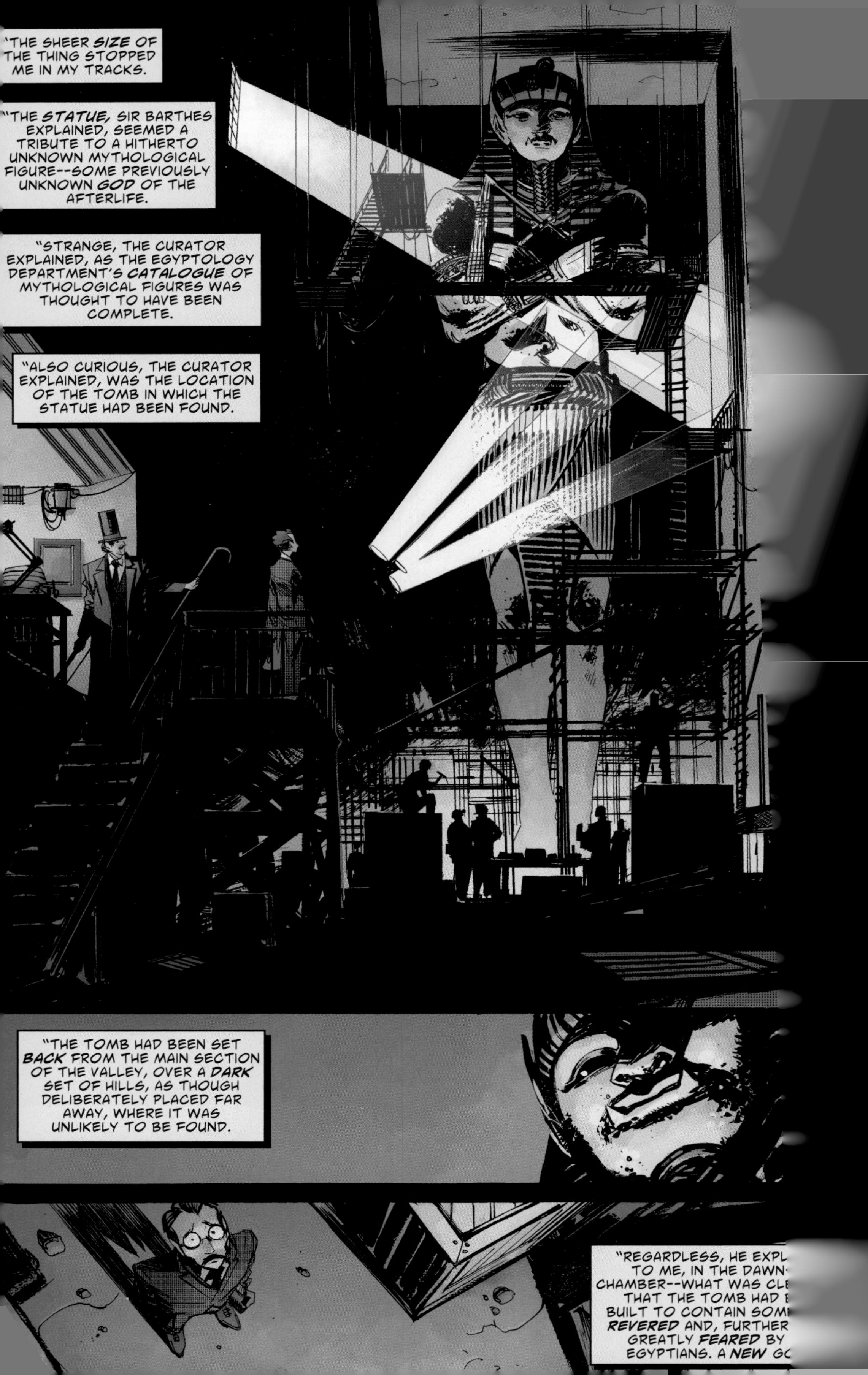
"THE SHEER SIZE OF THE THING STOPPED ME IN MY TRACKS.
"THE STATUE, SIR BARTHES EXPLAINED, SEEMED A TRIBUTE TO A HITHERTO UNKNOWN MYTHOLOGICAL FIGURE--SOME PREVIOUSLY UNKNOWN GOD OF THE AFTERLIFE.
"STRANGE, THE CURATOR EXPLAINED, AS THE EGYPTOLOGY DEPARTMENT'S CATALOGUE OF MYTHOLOGICAL FIGURES WAS THOUGHT TO HAVE BEEN COMPLETE.
"ALSO CURIOUS, THE CURATOR EXPLAINED, WAS THE LOCATION OF THE TOMB IN WHICH THE STATUE HAD BEEN FOUND.
"THE TOMB HAD BEEN SET BACK FROM THE MAIN SECTION OF THE VALLEY, OVER A DARK SET OF HILLS, AS THOUGH DELIBERATELY PLACED FAR AWAY, WHERE IT WAS UNLIKELY TO BE FOUND.
"REGARDLESS, HE EXPL TO ME, IN THE DAWN- CHAMBER--WHAT WAS CLE THAT THE TOMB HAD B BUILT TO CONTAIN SOM REVERED AND, FURTHER GREATLY FEARED BY EGYPTIANS. A NEW GO

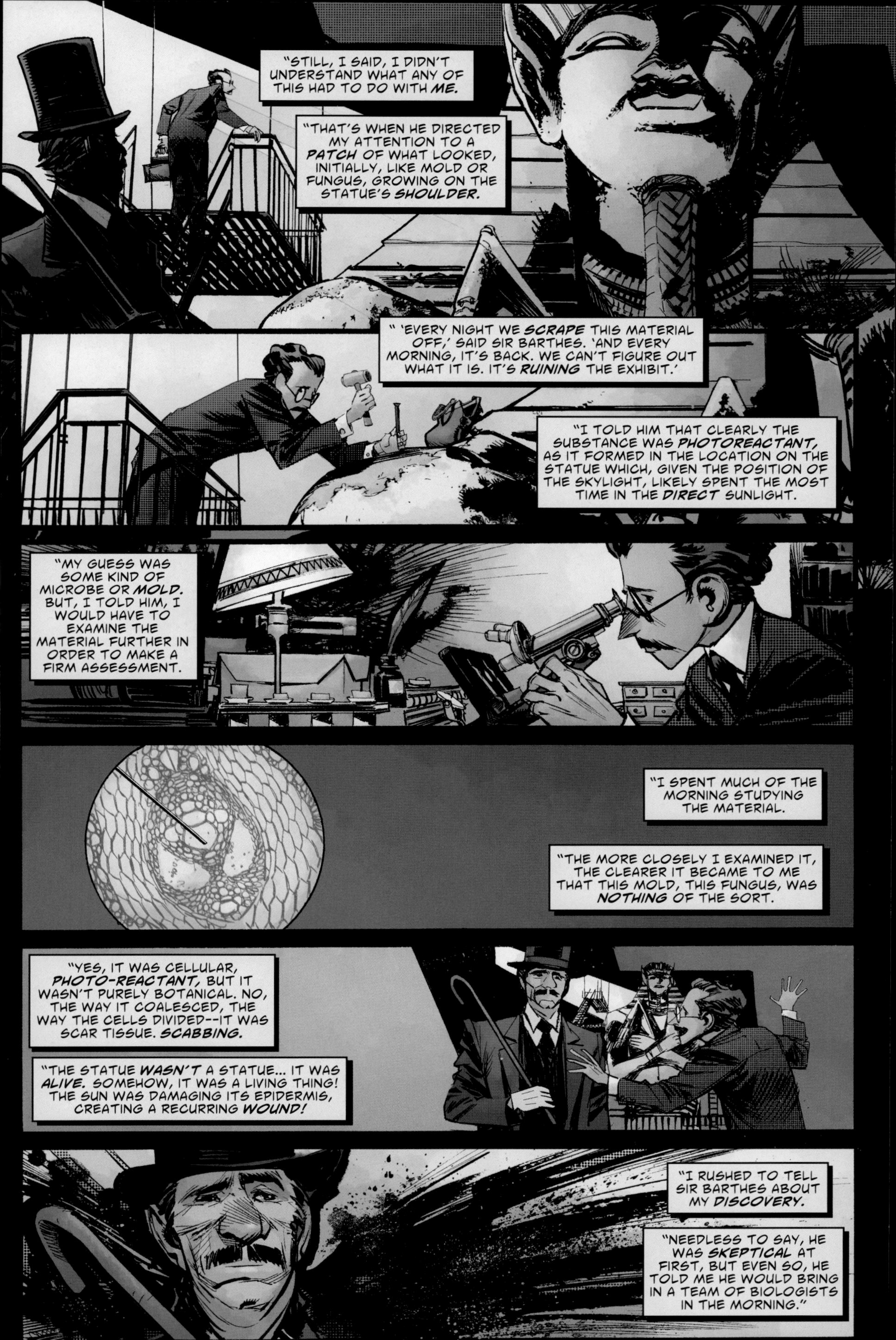
"STILL, I SAID, I DIDN'T UNDERSTAND WHAT ANY OF THIS HAD TO DO WITH ME.
"THAT'S WHEN HE DIRECTED MY ATTENTION TO A PATCH OF WHAT LOOKED, INITIALLY, LIKE MOLD OR FUNGUS, GROWING ON THE STATUE'S SHOULDER.
" 'EVERY NIGHT WE SCRAPE THIS MATERIAL OFF,' SAID SIR BARTHES. 'AND EVERY MORNING, IT'S BACK. WE CAN'T FIGURE OUT WHAT IT IS. IT'S RUINING THE EXHIBIT.'
"I TOLD HIM THAT CLEARLY THE SUBSTANCE WAS PHOTOREACTANT, AS IT FORMED IN THE LOCATION ON THE STATUE WHICH, GIVEN THE POSITION OF THE SKYLIGHT, LIKELY SPENT THE MOST TIME IN THE DIRECT SUNLIGHT.
"MY GUESS WAS SOME KIND OF MICROBE OR MOLD. BUT, I TOLD HIM, I WOULD HAVE TO EXAMINE THE MATERIAL FURTHER IN ORDER TO MAKE A FIRM ASSESSMENT.
"I SPENT MUCH OF THE MORNING STUDYING THE MATERIAL.
"THE MORE CLOSELY I EXAMINED IT, THE CLEARER IT BECAME TO ME THAT THIS MOLD, THIS FUNGUS, WAS NOTHING OF THE SORT.
"YES, IT WAS CELLULAR, PHOTO-REACTANT, BUT IT WASN'T PURELY BOTANICAL. NO, THE WAY IT COALESCED, THE WAY THE CELLS DIVIDED--IT WAS SCAR TISSUE. SCABBING.
"THE STATUE WASN'T A STATUE... IT WAS ALIVE. SOMEHOW, IT WAS A LIVING THING! THE SUN WAS DAMAGING ITS EPIDERMIS, CREATING A RECURRING WOUND!
"I RUSHED TO TELL SIR BARTHES ABOUT MY DISCOVERY.
"NEEDLESS TO SAY, HE WAS SKEPTICAL AT FIRST, BUT EVEN SO, HE TOLD ME HE WOULD BRING IN A TEAM OF BIOLOGISTS IN THE MORNING."

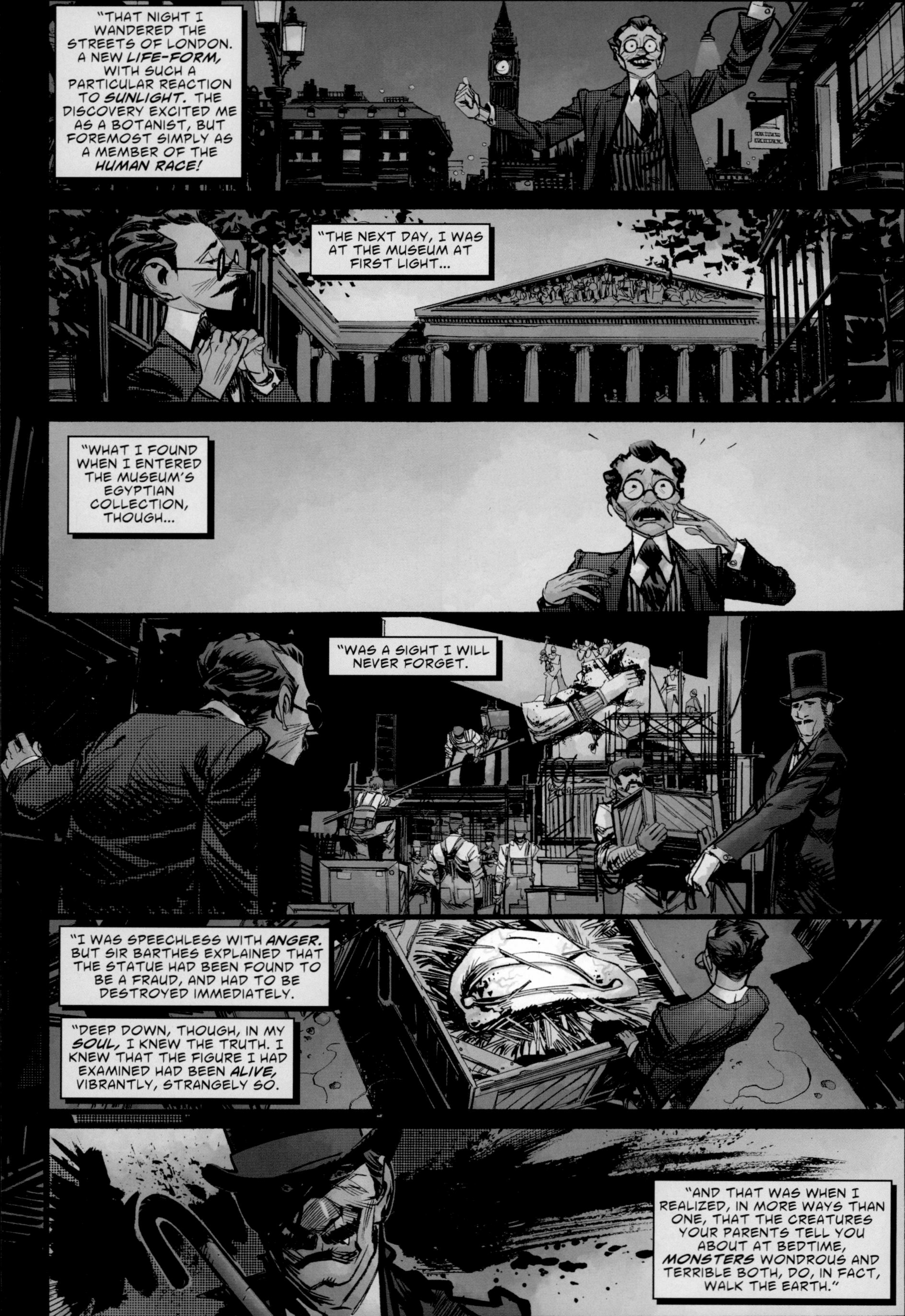
"THAT NIGHT I WANDERED THE STREETS OF LONDON. A NEW LIFE-FORM, WITH SUCH A PARTICULAR REACTION TO SUNLIGHT. THE DISCOVERY EXCITED ME AS A BOTANIST, BUT FOREMOST SIMPLY AS A MEMBER OF THE HUMAN RACE!
"THE NEXT DAY, I WAS AT THE MUSEUM AT FIRST LIGHT...
"WHAT I FOUND WHEN I ENTERED THE MUSEUM'S EGYPTIAN COLLECTION, THOUGH...
"WAS A SIGHT I WILL NEVER FORGET.
"I WAS SPEECHLESS WITH ANGER. BUT SIR BARTHES EXPLAINED THAT THE STATUE HAD BEEN FOUND TO BE A FRAUD, AND HAD TO BE DESTROYED IMMEDIATELY.
"DEEP DOWN, THOUGH, IN MY SOUL, I KNEW THE TRUTH. I KNEW THAT THE FIGURE I HAD EXAMINED HAD BEEN ALIVE, VIBRANTLY, STRANGELY SO.
"AND THAT WAS WHEN I REALIZED, IN MORE WAYS THAN ONE, THAT THE CREATURES YOUR PARENTS TELL YOU ABOUT AT BEDTIME, MONSTERS WONDROUS AND TERRIBLE BOTH, DO, IN FACT, WALK THE EARTH."

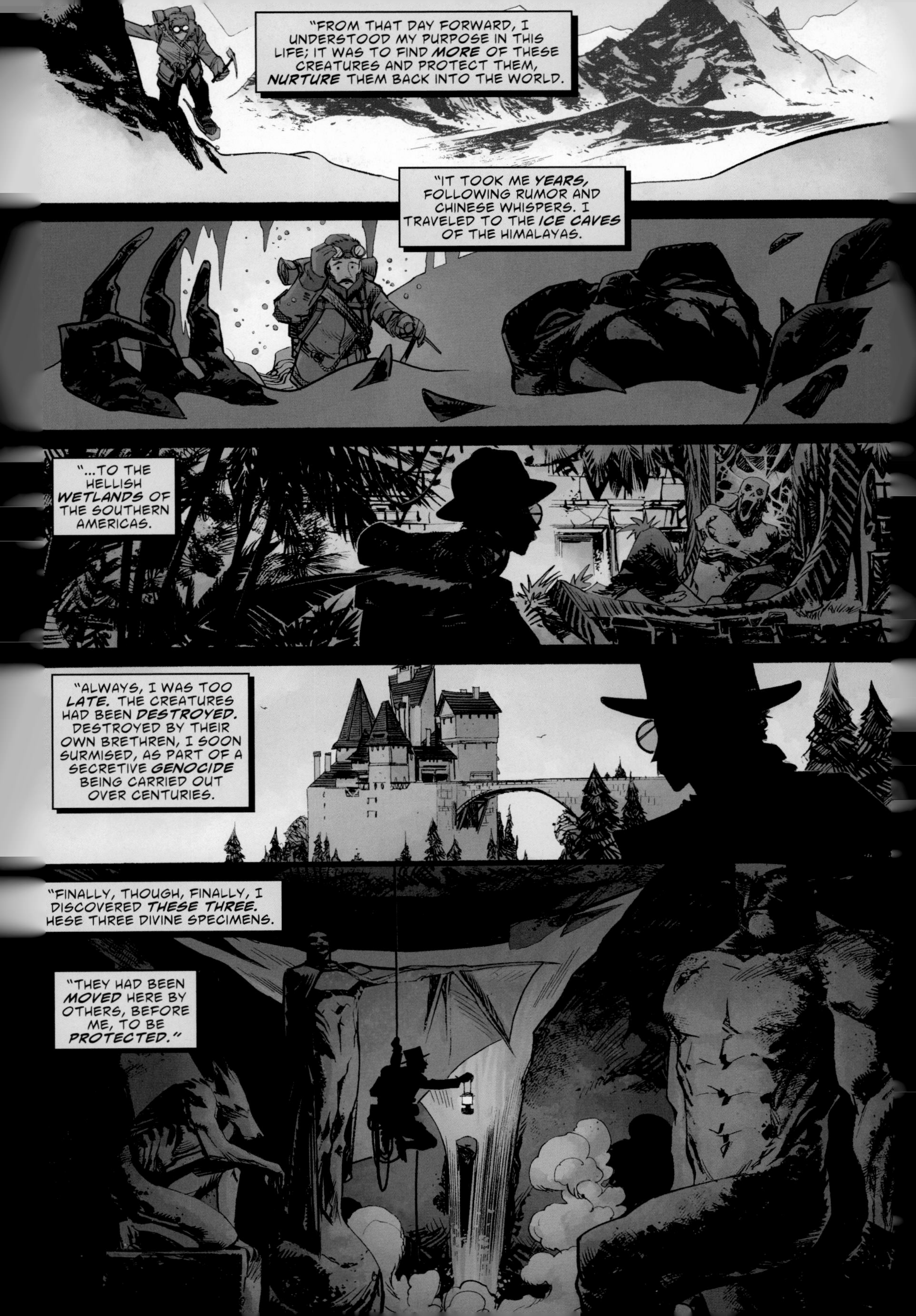
"FROM THAT DAY FORWARD, I UNDERSTOOD MY PURPOSE IN THIS LIFE; IT WAS TO FIND MORE OF THESE CREATURES AND PROTECT THEM, NURTURE THEM BACK INTO THE WORLD.
"IT TOOK ME YEARS, FOLLOWING RUMOR AND CHINESE WHISPERS. I TRAVELED TO THE ICE CAVES OF THE HIMALAYAS.
"...TO THE HELLISH WETLANDS OF THE SOUTHERN AMERICAS.
"ALWAYS, I WAS TOO LATE. THE CREATURES HAD BEEN DESTROYED. DESTROYED BY THEIR OWN BRETHREN, I SOON SURMISED, AS PART OF A SECRETIVE GENOCIDE BEING CARRIED OUT OVER CENTURIES.
"FINALLY, THOUGH, FINALLY, I DISCOVERED THESE THREE. HESE THREE DIVINE SPECIMENS.
"THEY HAD BEEN MOVED HERE BY OTHERS, BEFORE ME, TO BE PROTECTED."

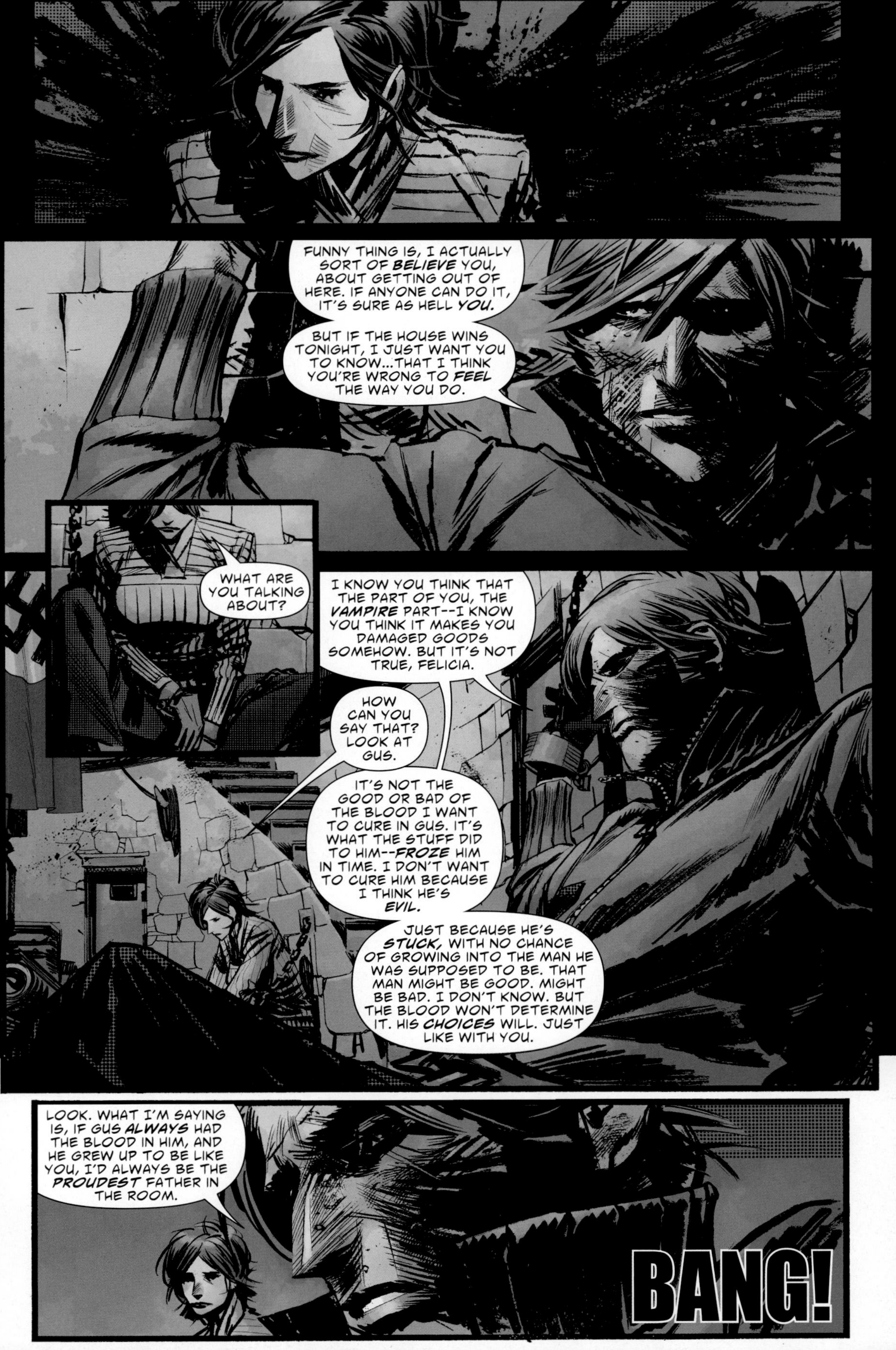
FUNNY THING IS, I ACTUALLY SORT OF BELIEVE YOU, ABOUT GETTING OUT OF HERE. IF ANYONE CAN DO IT, IT'S SURE AS HELL YOU.
BUT IF THE HOUSE WINS TONIGHT, I JUST WANT YOU TO KNOW...THAT I THINK YOU'RE WRONG TO FEEL THE WAY YOU DO.
WHAT ARE YOU TALKING ABOUT?
I KNOW YOU THINK THAT THE PART OF YOU, THE VAMPIRE PART--I KNOW YOU THINK IT MAKES YOU DAMAGED GOODS SOMEHOW. BUT IT'S NOT TRUE, FELICIA.
HOW CAN YOU SAY THAT? LOOK AT GUS.
IT'S NOT THE GOOD OR BAD OF THE BLOOD I WANT TO CURE IN GUS. IT'S WHAT THE STUFF DID TO HIM--FROZE HIM IN TIME. I DON'T WANT TO CURE HIM BECAUSE I THINK HE'S EVIL.
JUST BECAUSE HE'S STUCK, WITH NO CHANCE OF GROWING INTO THE MAN HE WAS SUPPOSED TO BE. THAT MAN MIGHT BE GOOD. MIGHT BE BAD. I DON'T KNOW. BUT THE BLOOD WON'T DETERMINE IT. HIS CHOICES WILL. JUST LIKE WITH YOU.
LOOK. WHAT I'M SAYING IS, IF GUS ALWAYS HAD THE BLOOD IN HIM, AND HE GREW UP TO BE LIKE YOU, I'D ALWAYS BE THE PROUDEST FATHER IN THE ROOM.
BANG!

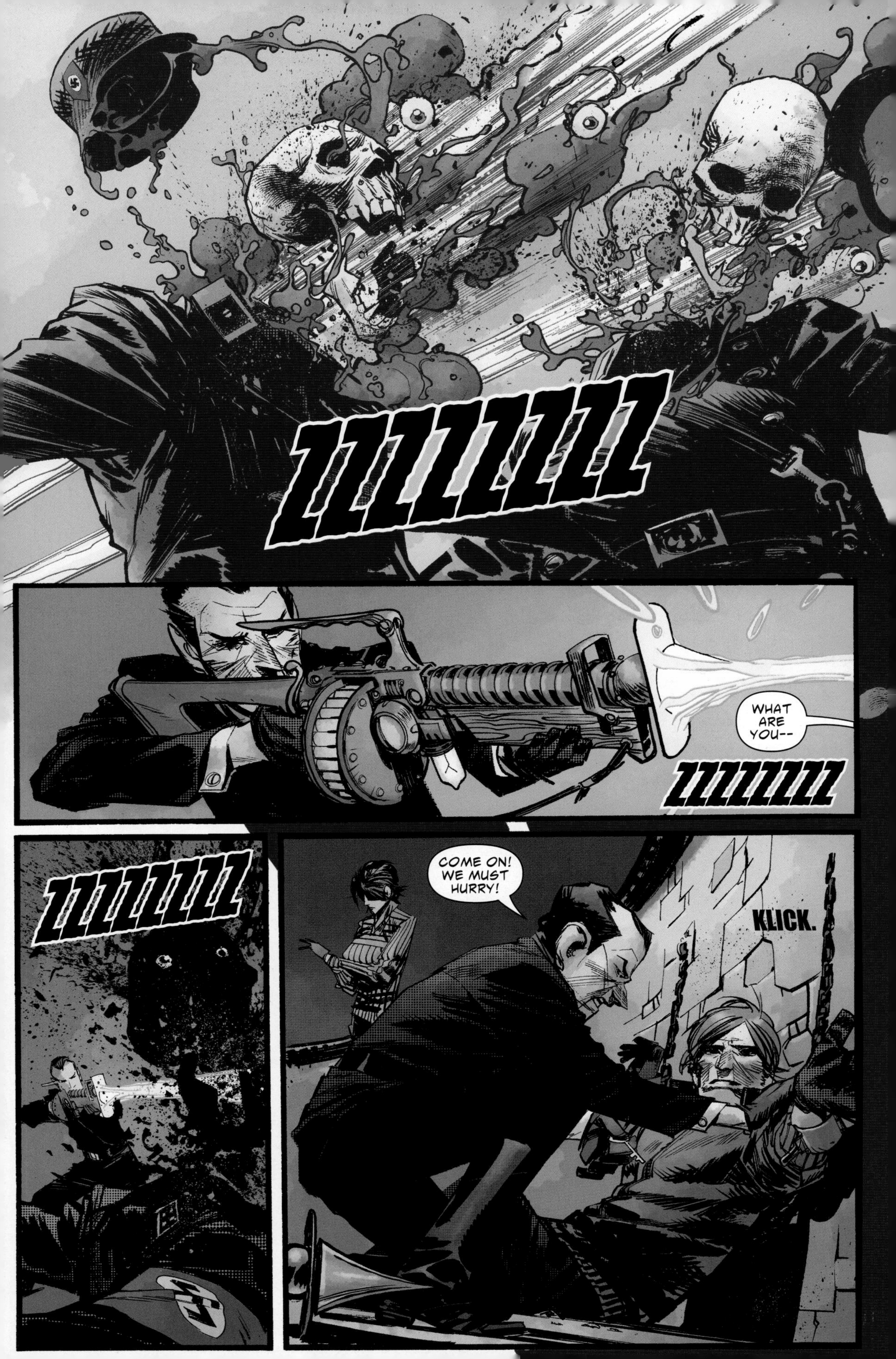
ZZZZZZZZ
WHAT ARE YOU--
ZZZZZZZZ
ZZZZZZZZ
COME ON! WE MUST HURRY!
KLICK.

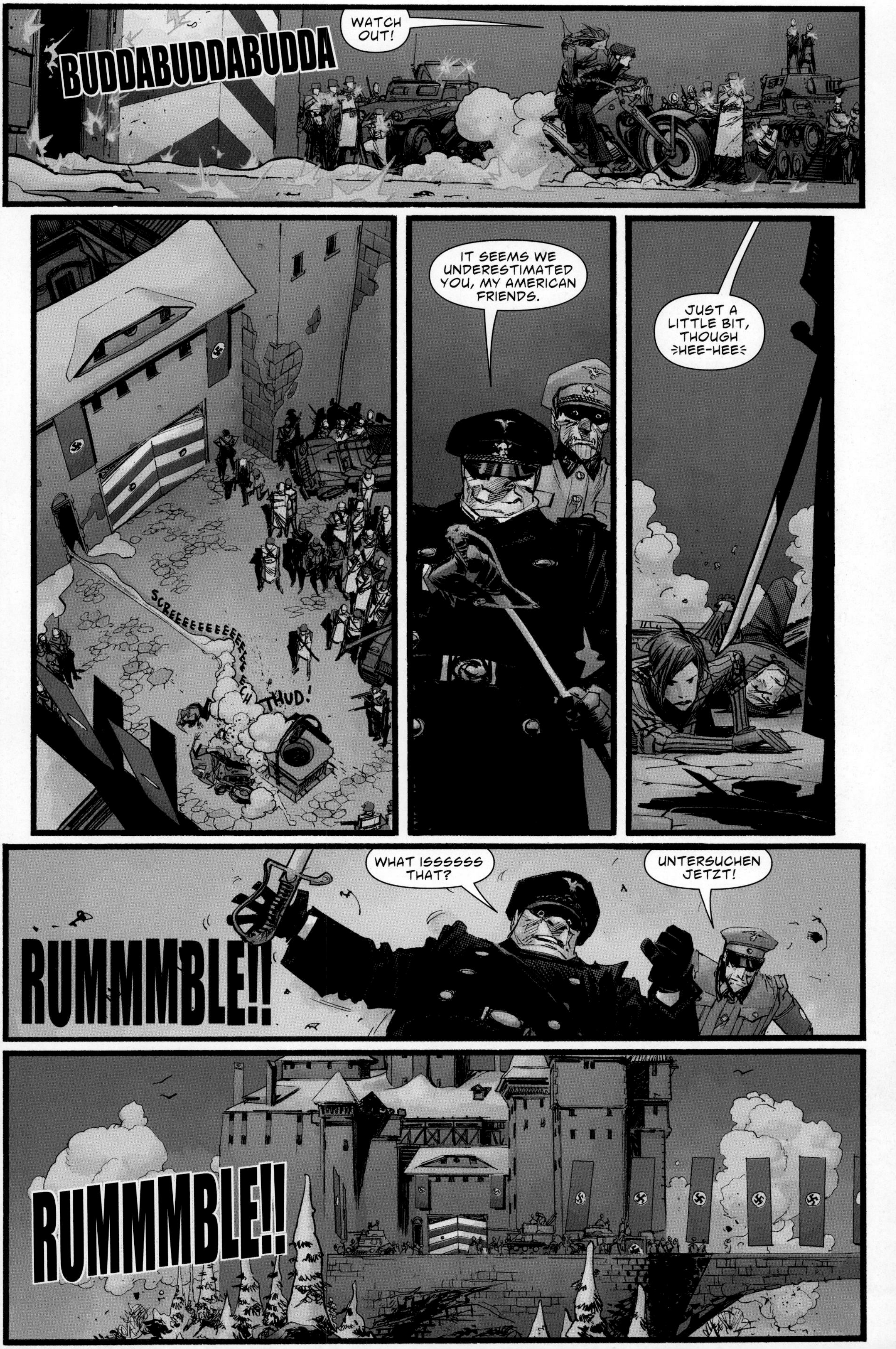
WATCH OUT!
BUDDABUDDABUDDA
SCREEEEEEEEEEEEEEECH
THUD!
IT SEEMS WE UNDERESTIMATED YOU, MY AMERICAN FRIENDS.
JUST A LITTLE BIT, THOUGH
HEE-HEE
WHAT ISSSSSS THAT?
UNTERSUCHEN JETZT!
RUMMMBLE!!
RUMMMBLE!!

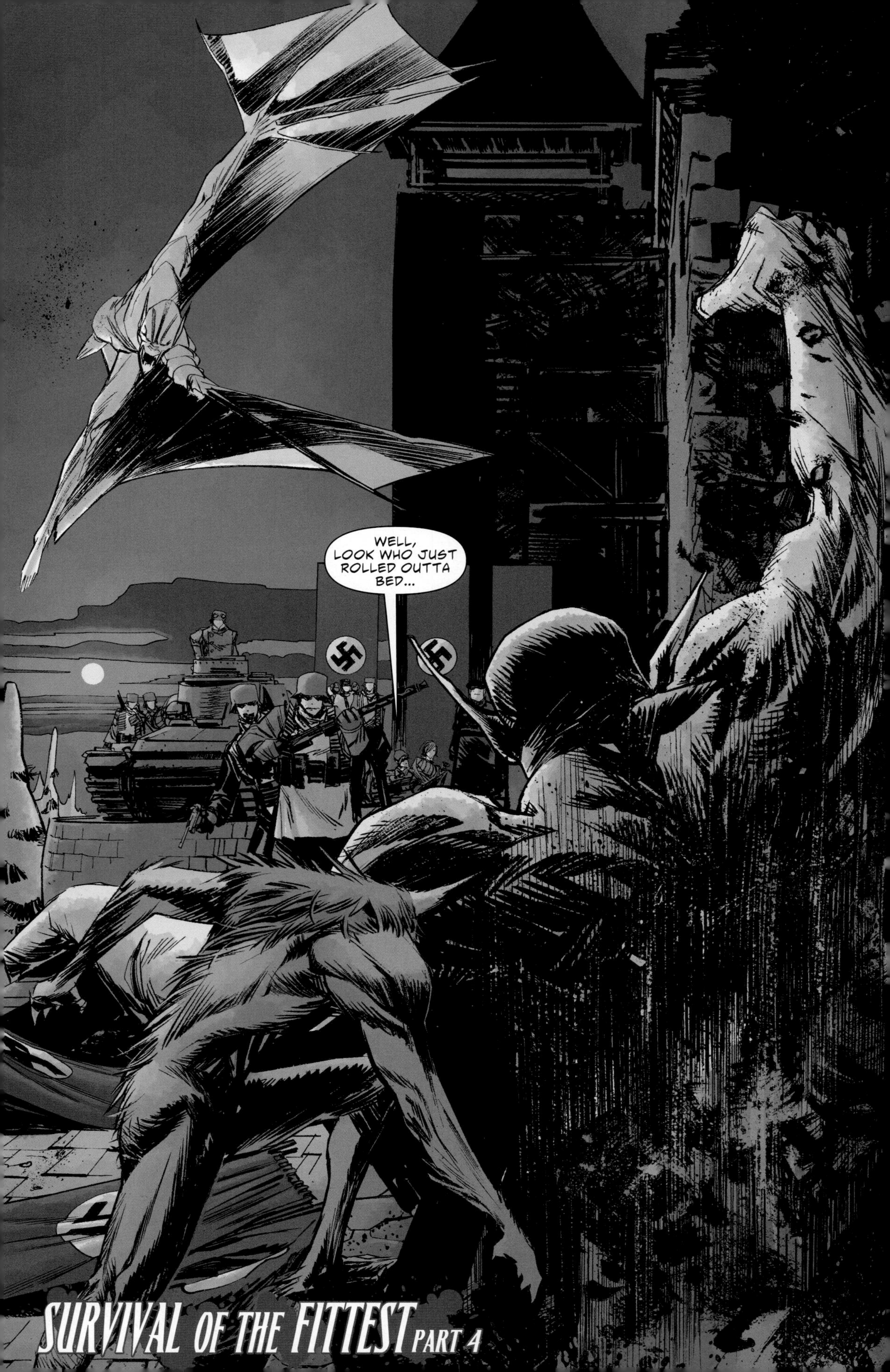
WELL, LOOK WHO JUST ROLLED OUTTA BED...
SURVIVAL OF THE FITTEST PART 4

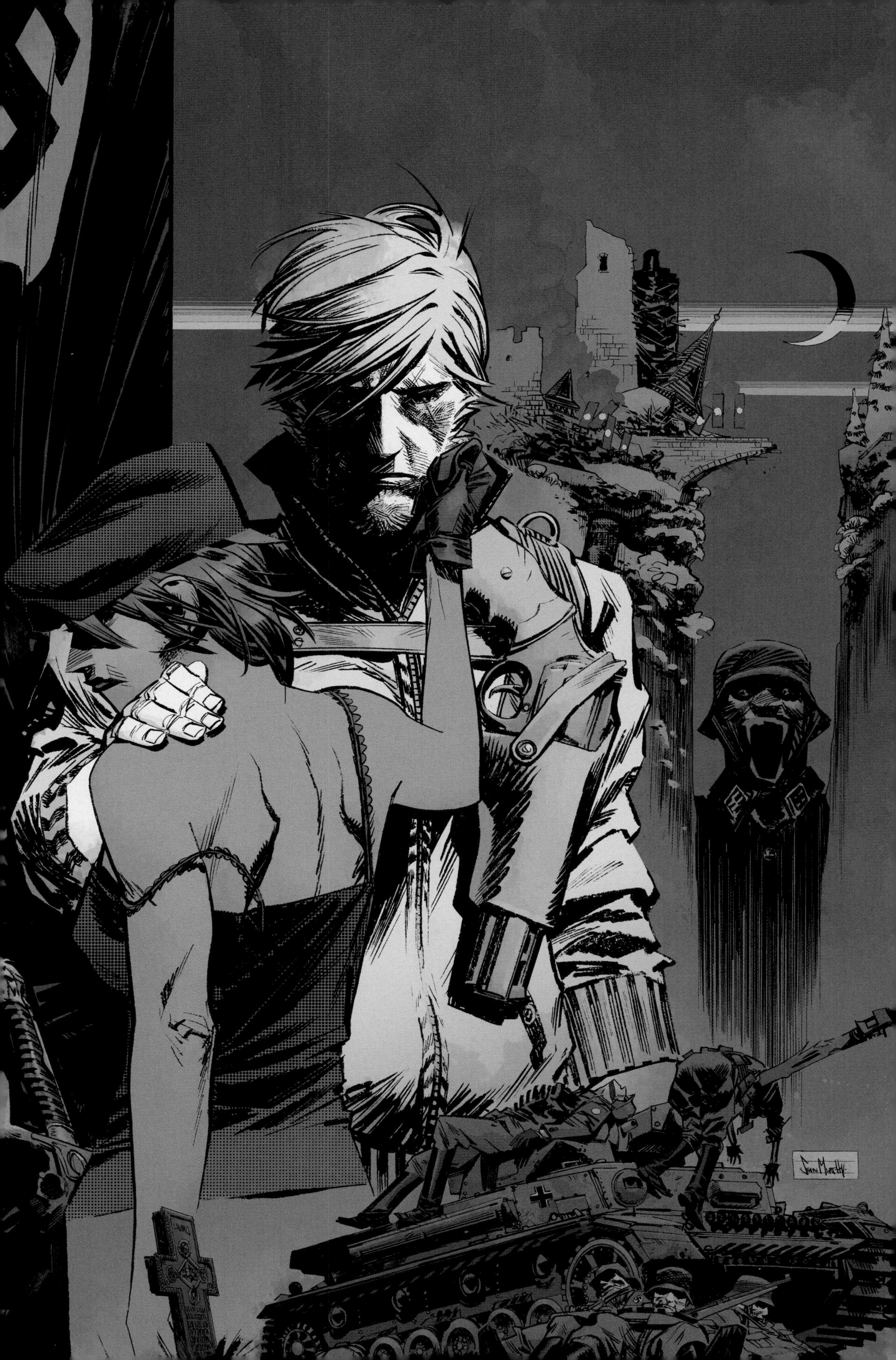

Survival
of the Fittest
Conclusion

Sean Murphy
Artist and cover

Dave Stewart
cover color

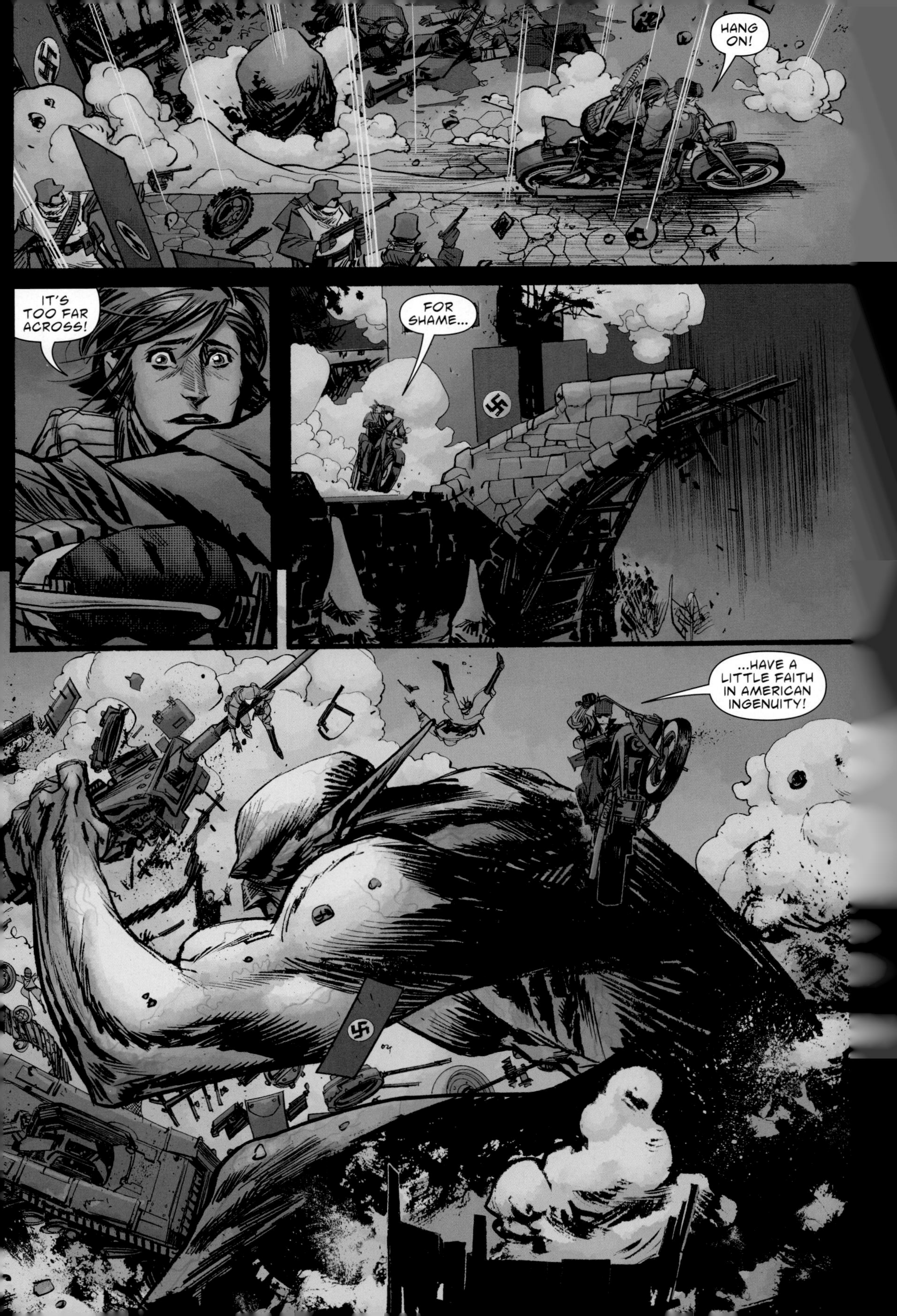
HANG ON!
IT'S TOO FAR ACROSS!
FOR SHAME...
...HAVE A LITTLE FAITH IN AMERICAN INGENUITY!

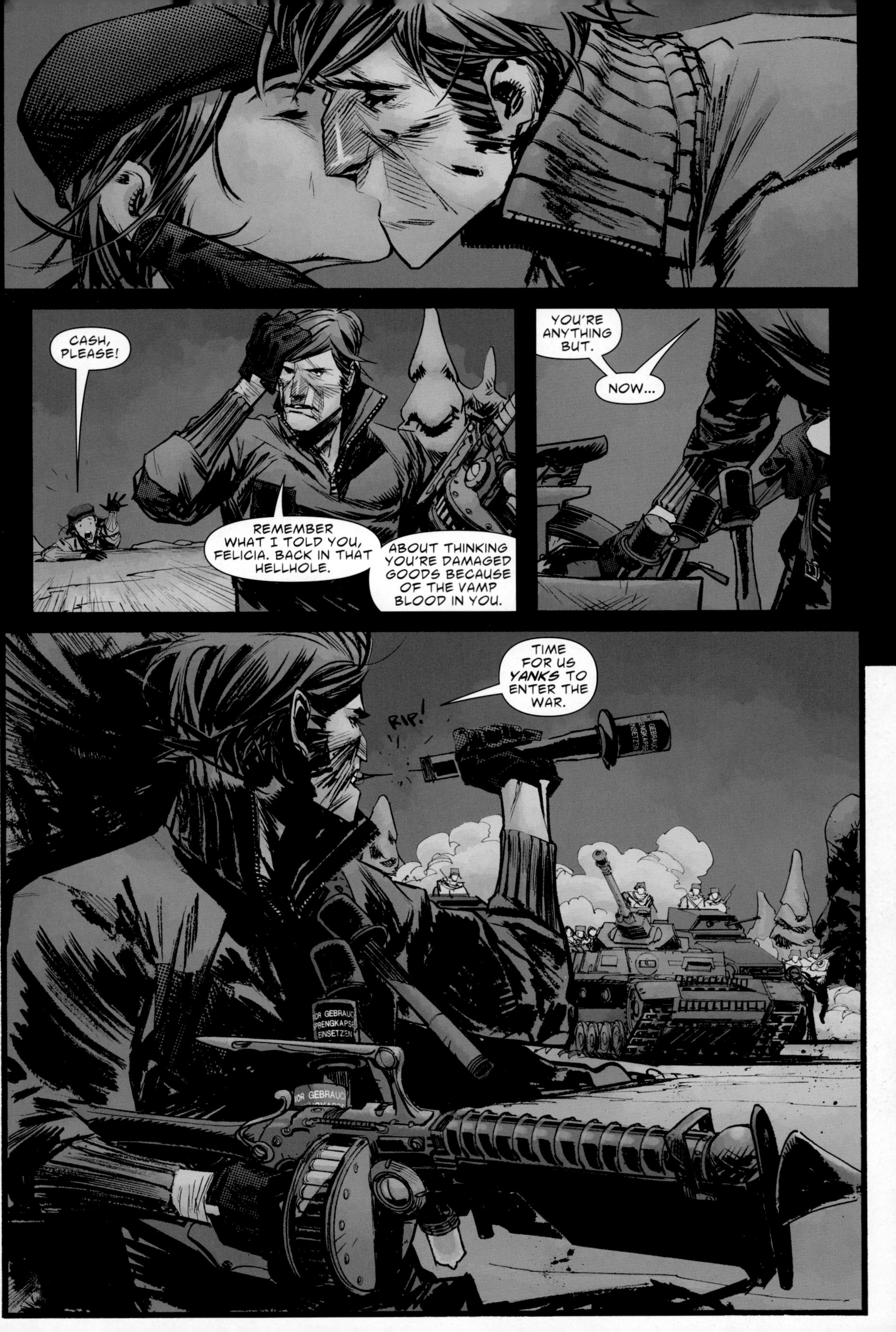
CASH, PLEASE!
REMEMBER WHAT I TOLD YOU, FELICIA. BACK IN THAT HELLHOLE.
ABOUT THINKING YOU'RE DAMAGED GOODS BECAUSE OF THE VAMP BLOOD IN YOU.
YOU'RE ANYTHING BUT.
NOW...
TIME FOR US YANKS TO ENTER THE WAR.
RIP!
VOR GEBRAUCH SPRENGKAPSEL EINSETZEN

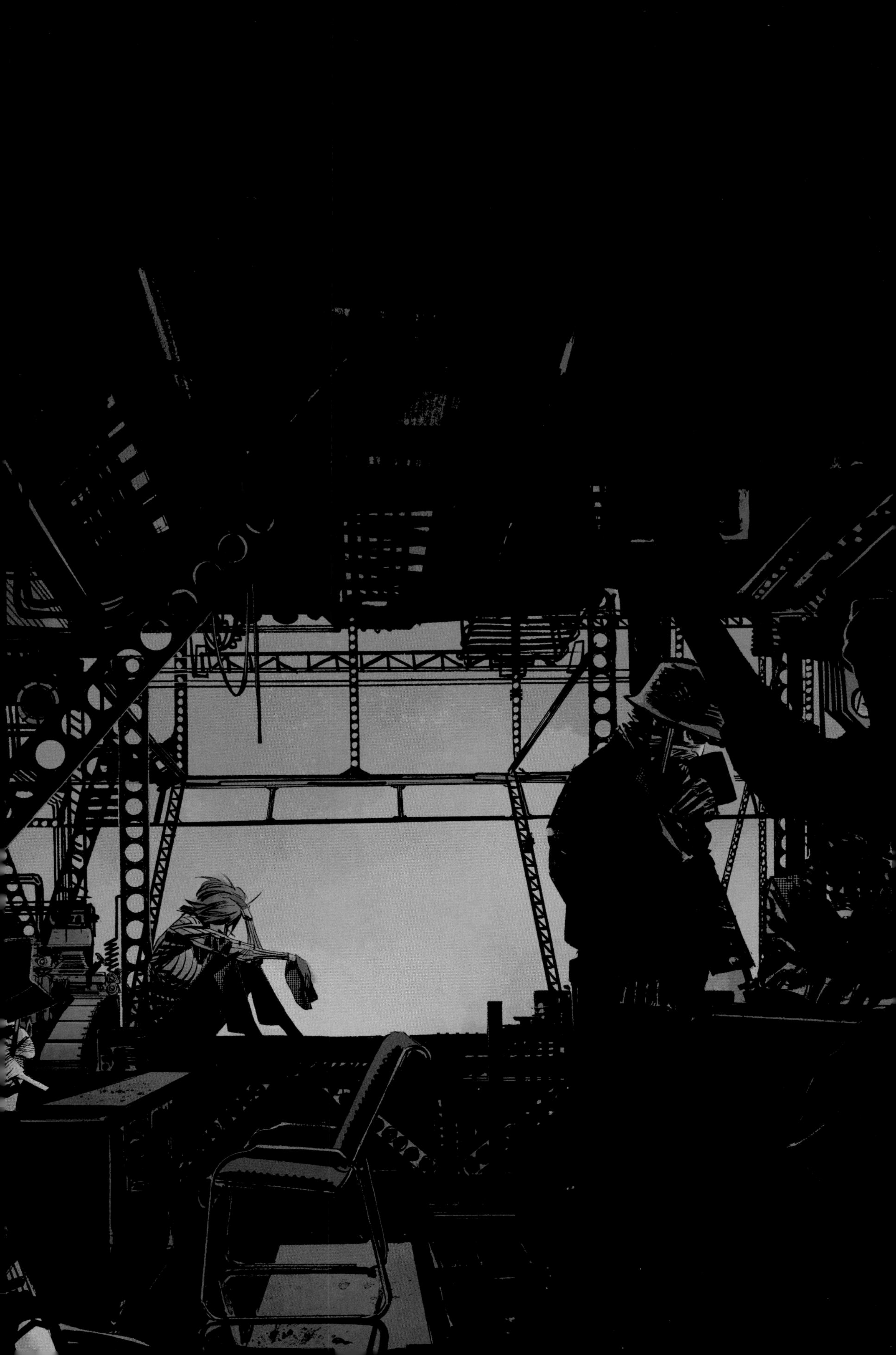

IT'S A WORLD WHERE MONSTERS LIVE, LURKING IN THE DARK...

THE DARK CORNERS OF YOUR HOME...

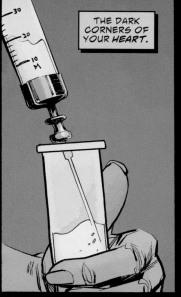

THE DARK CORNERS OF YOUR *HEART*.

FOR MOST PEOPLE, THIS WORLD, IT IS A SHADOW REALM.

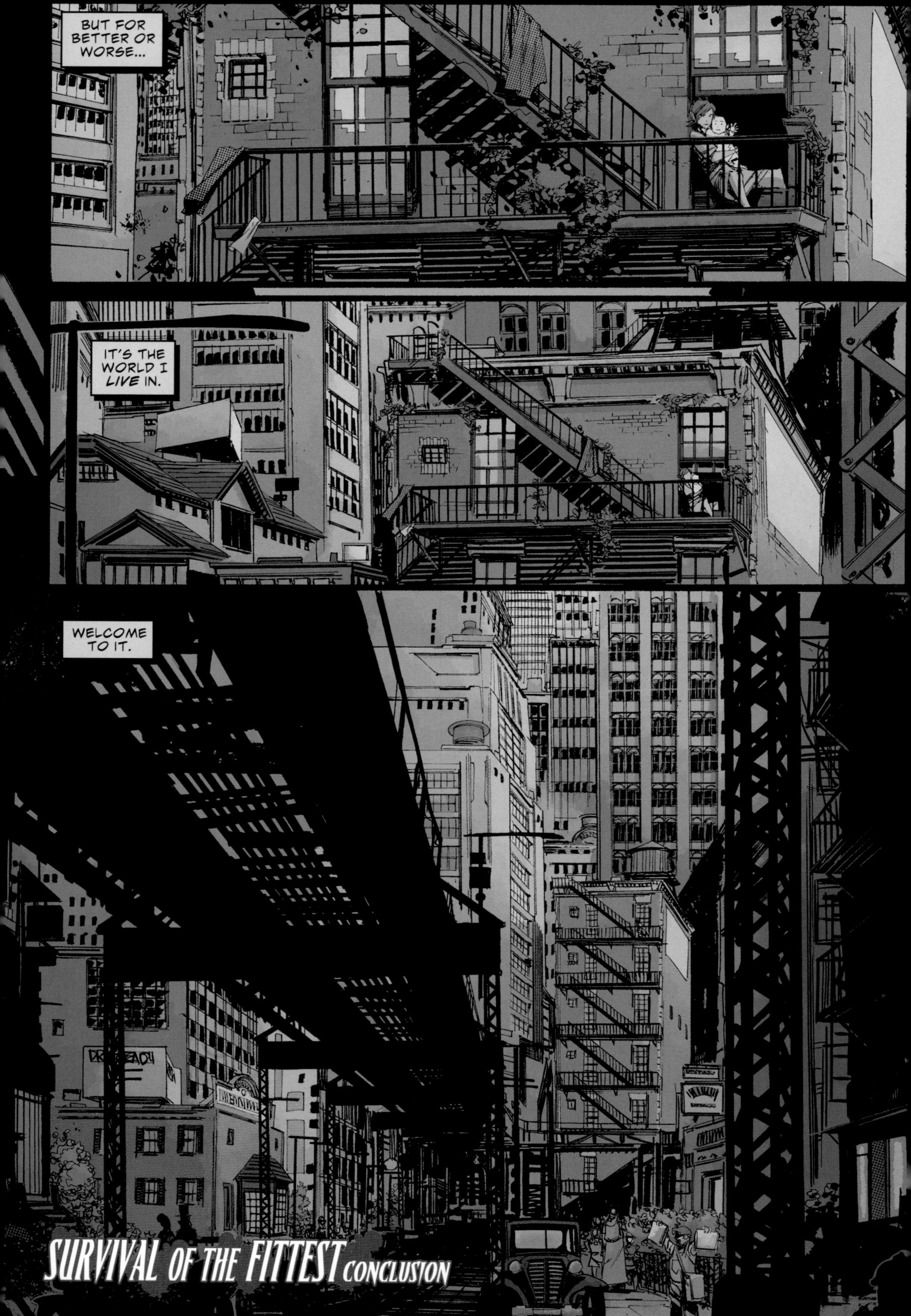
BUT FOR BETTER OR WORSE...
IT'S THE WORLD I *LIVE* IN.
WELCOME TO IT.
SURVIVAL OF THE FITTEST CONCLUSION

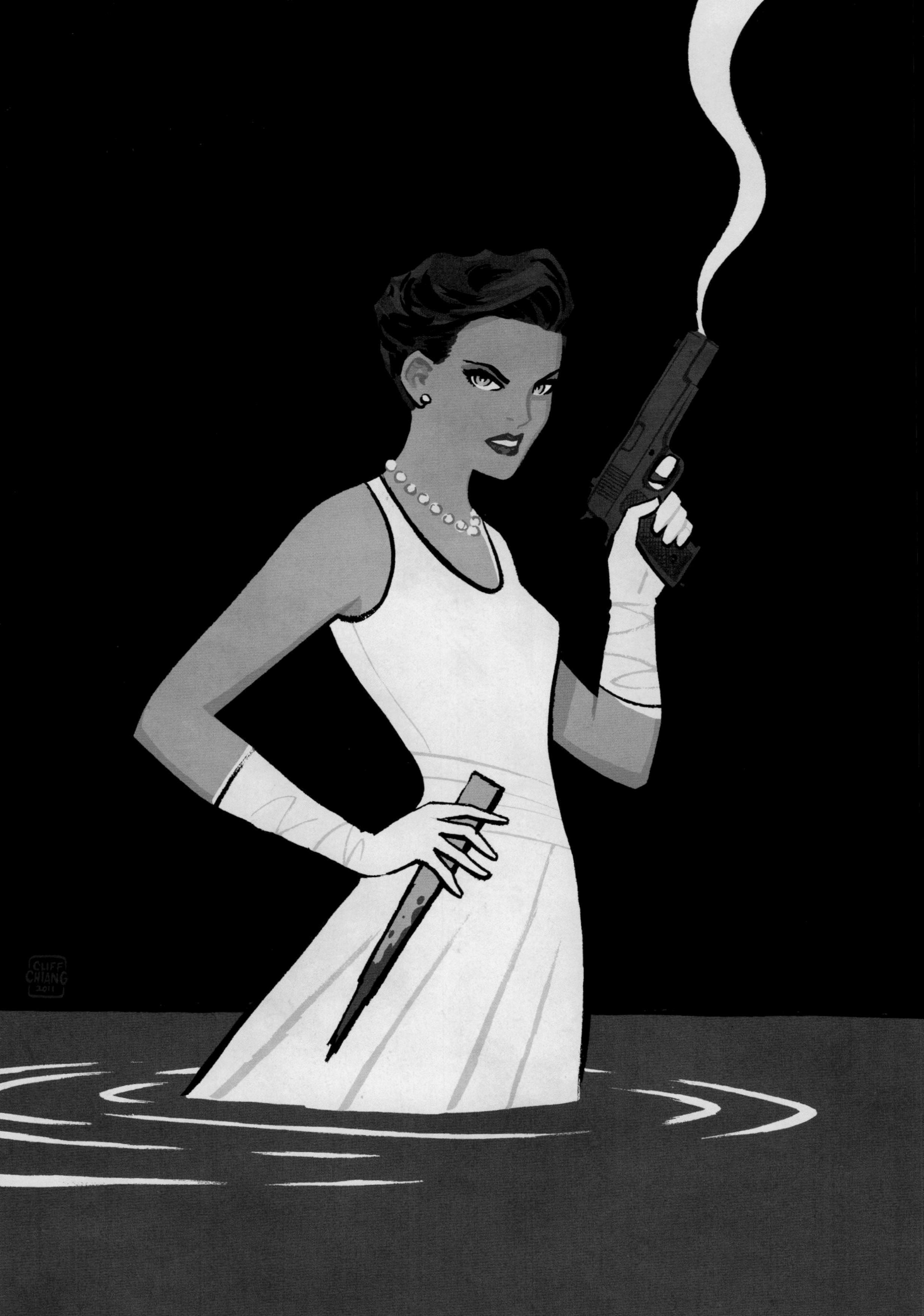
CLIFF
CHIANG
2011

Variant to AMERICAN VAMPIRE: SURVIVAL OF THE FITTEST #1 by Cliff Chiang

SKETCHES AND DESIGNS BY RAFAEL ALBURQUERQE AND SEAN MURPHY

CALVIN POOLE

SKINNER SWEET

LONGER HAIR
↳ (I like it more)

Character sketches and development by Rafael Alburquerqe

Henry is older.
45/50 y/old

White Hair

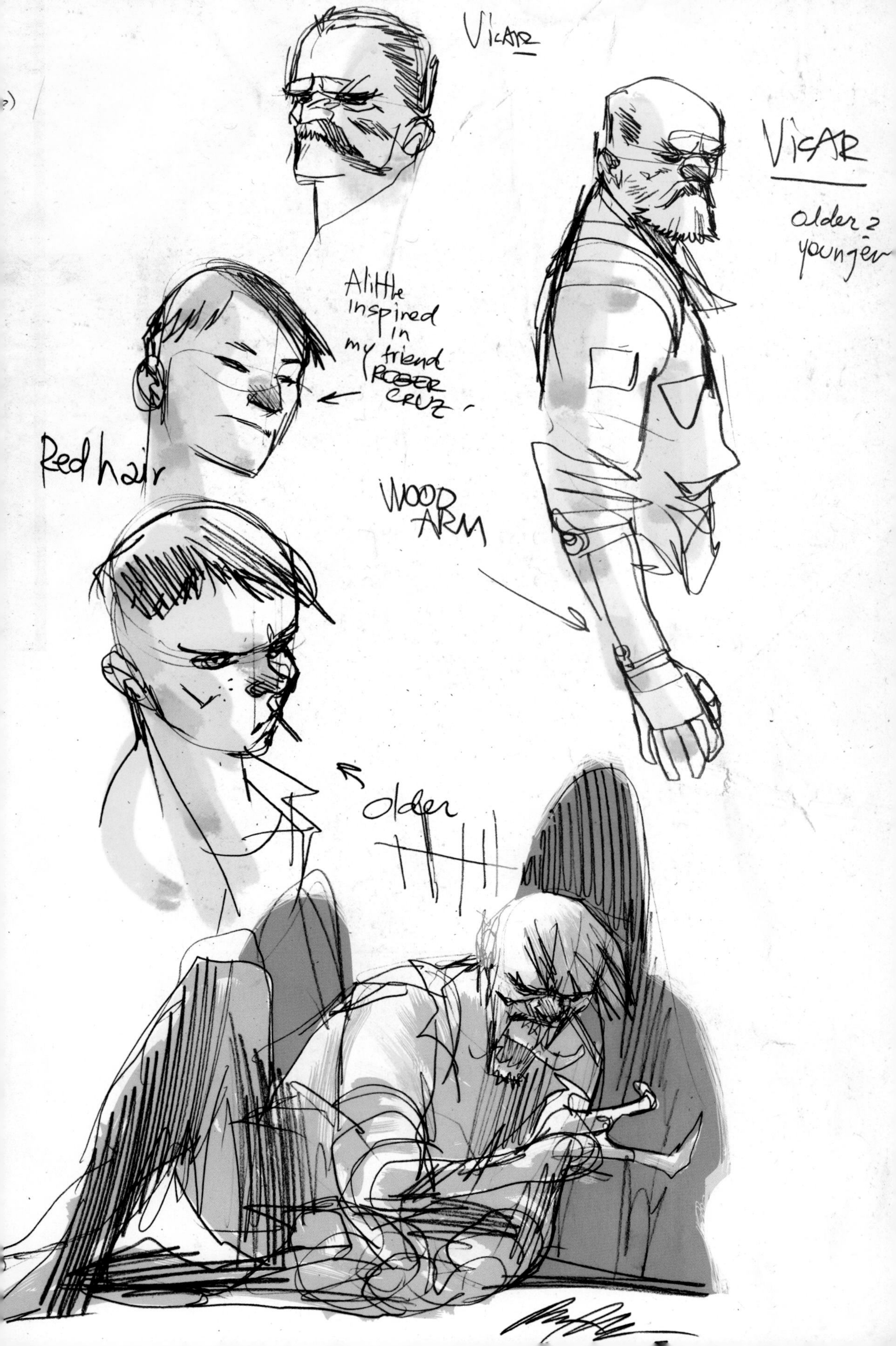

Vicar
Vicar
older ≥ younger
A little inspired in my friend ROBER CRUZ.
Red hair
WOOD ARM
older

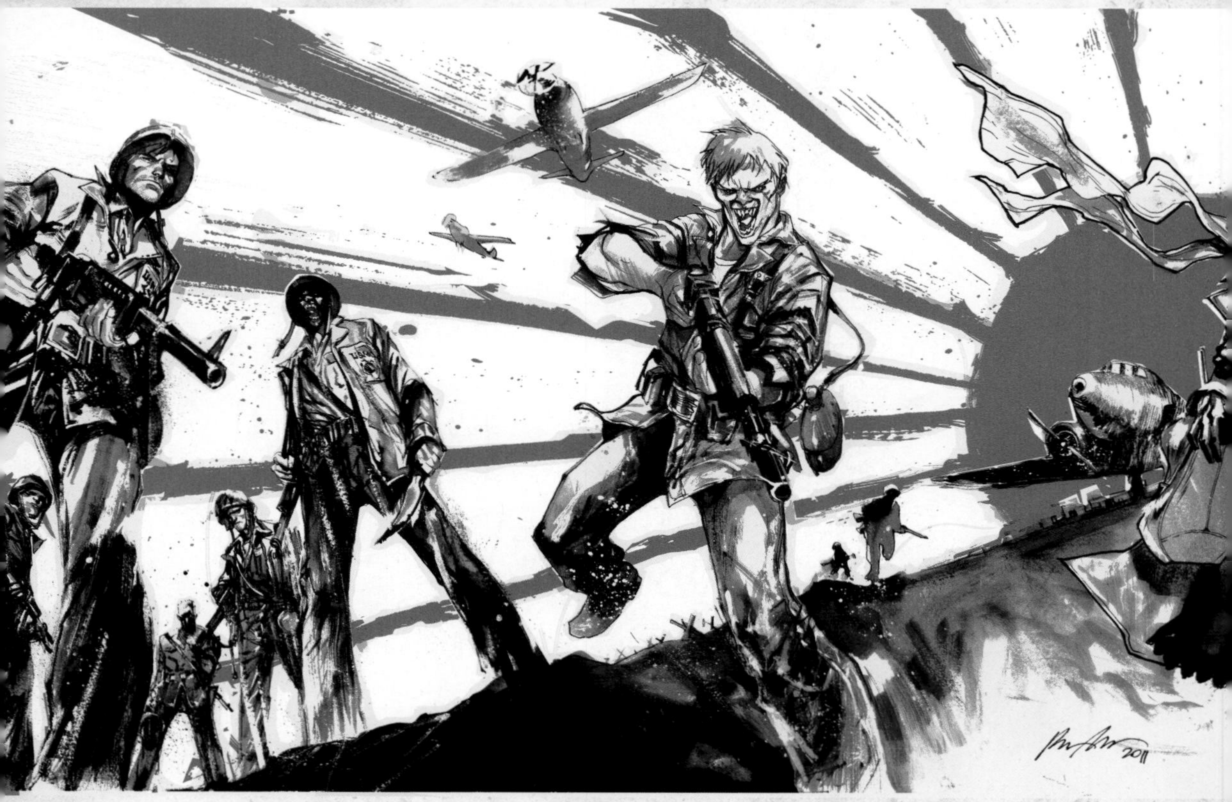
2011

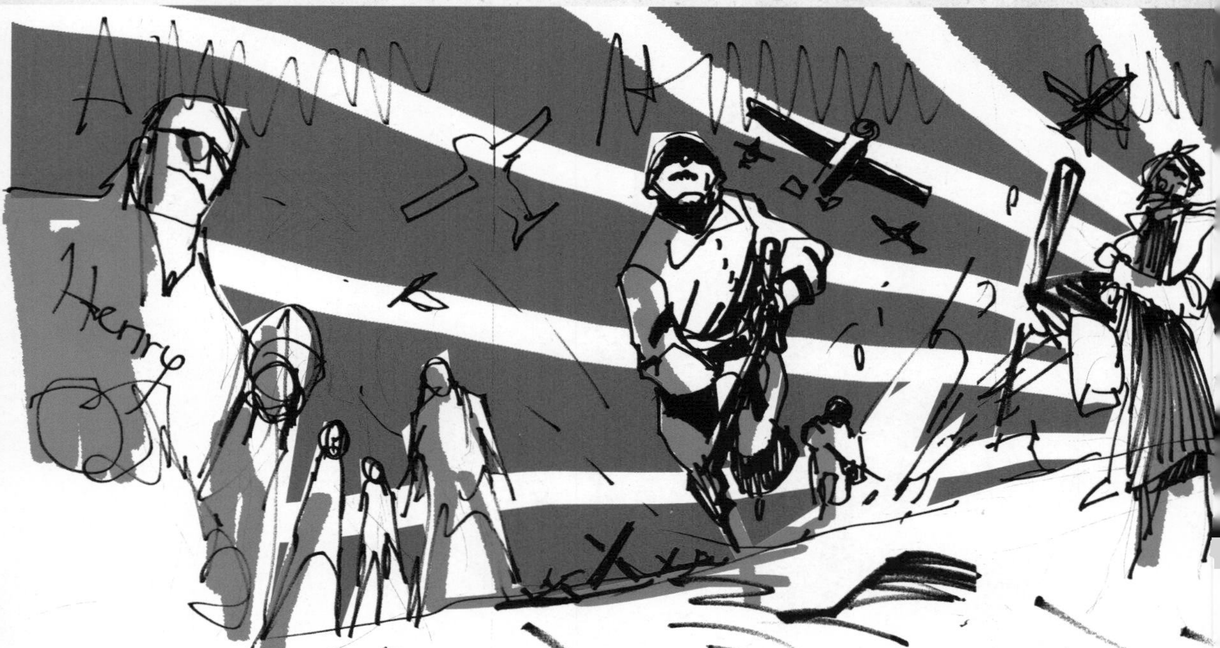
Henry

The covers to AMERICAN VAMPIRE #13-17 connect to create one larger image. Here are the sketches and refined layout for the piece by Rafael Alburquerge. You can see the final images earlier in this collection.

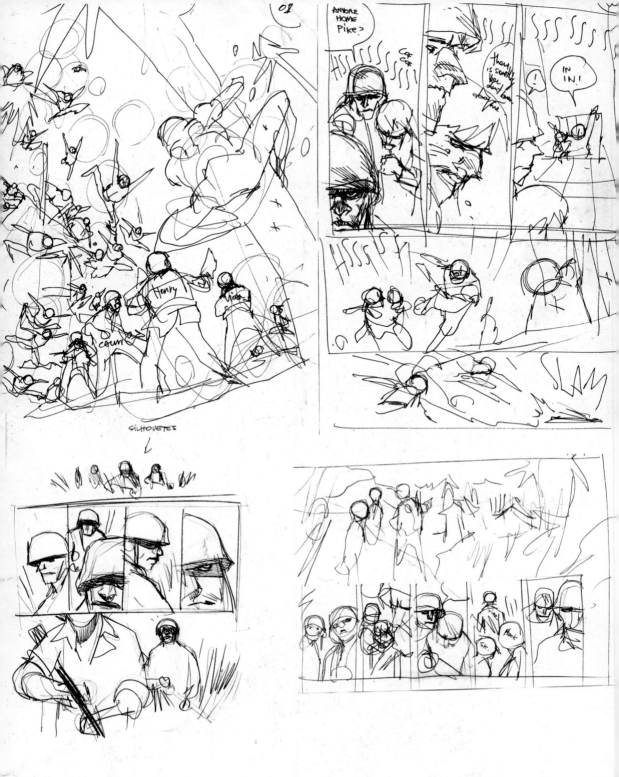

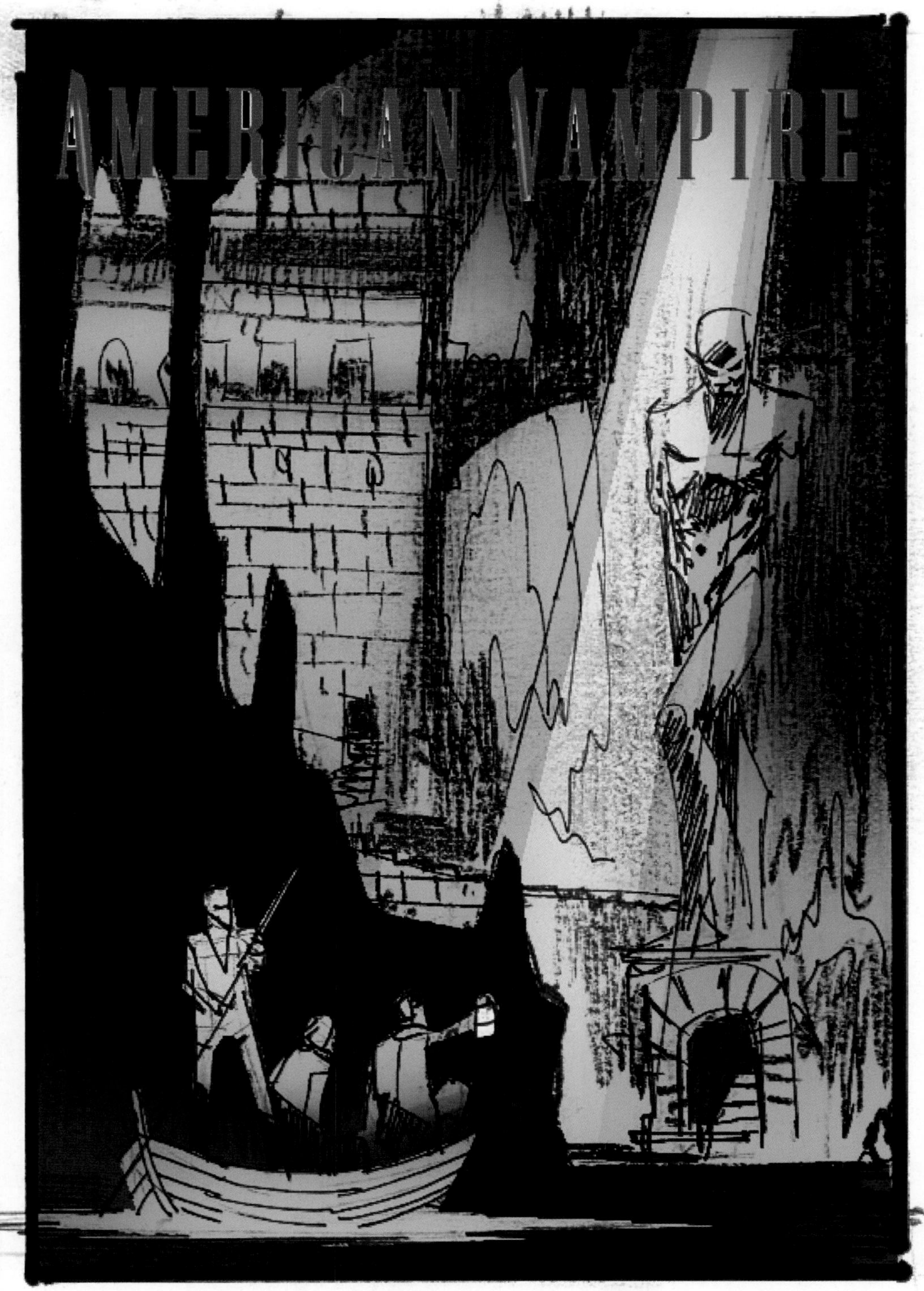
AMERICAN VAMPIRE

Cover 3: Cash, Book and the scientist approach the underground caves beneath the castle. Huge statues of hybernating vampires rest around the stairwell toward the surface.

Original cover sketch to AMERICAN VAMPIRE: SURVIVAL OF THE FITTEST #3 by Sean Murphy.

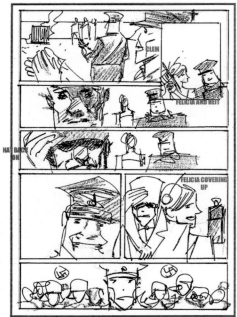

Page development by Sean Murphy — thumbnails, pencils and inks.

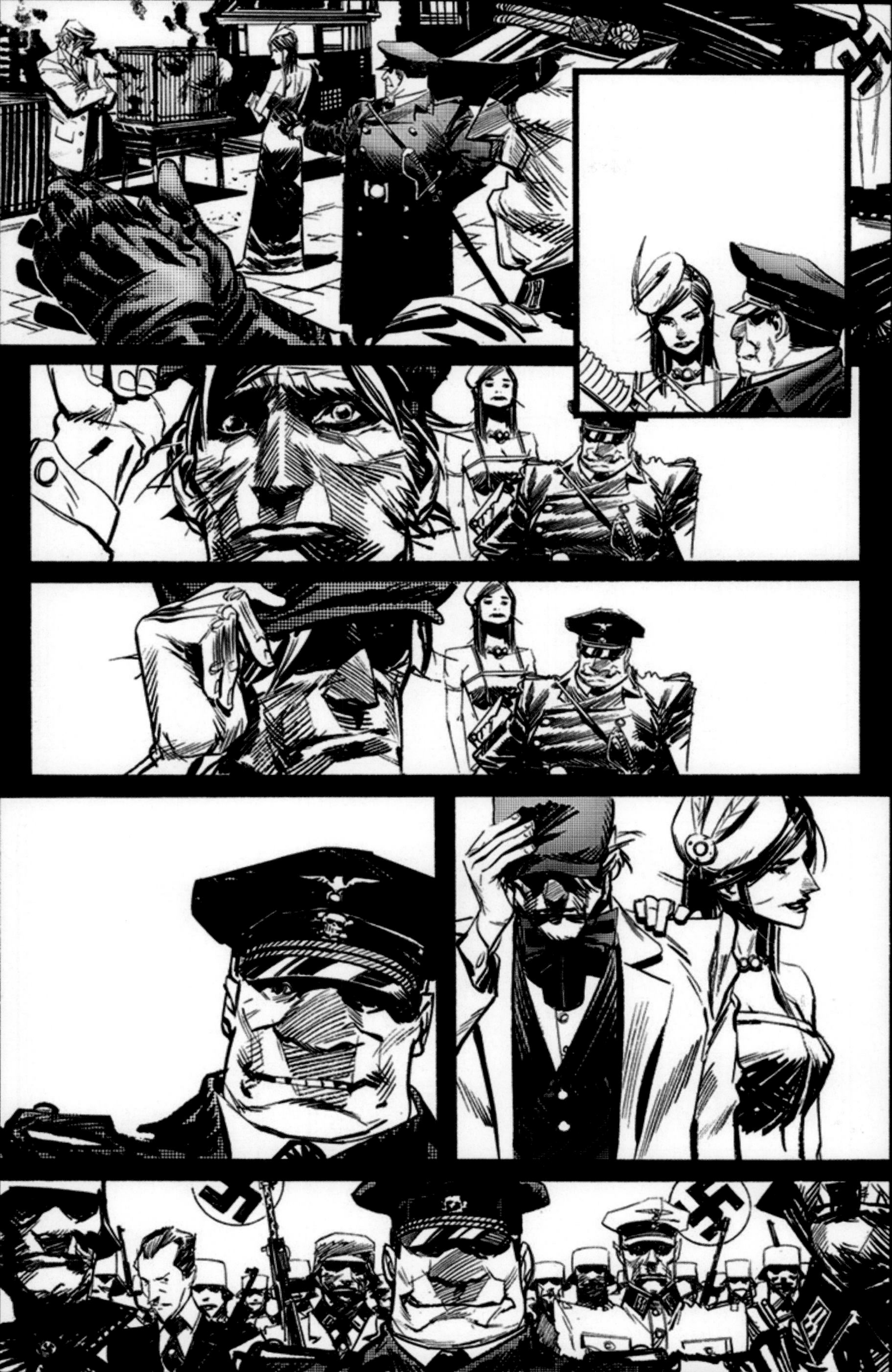

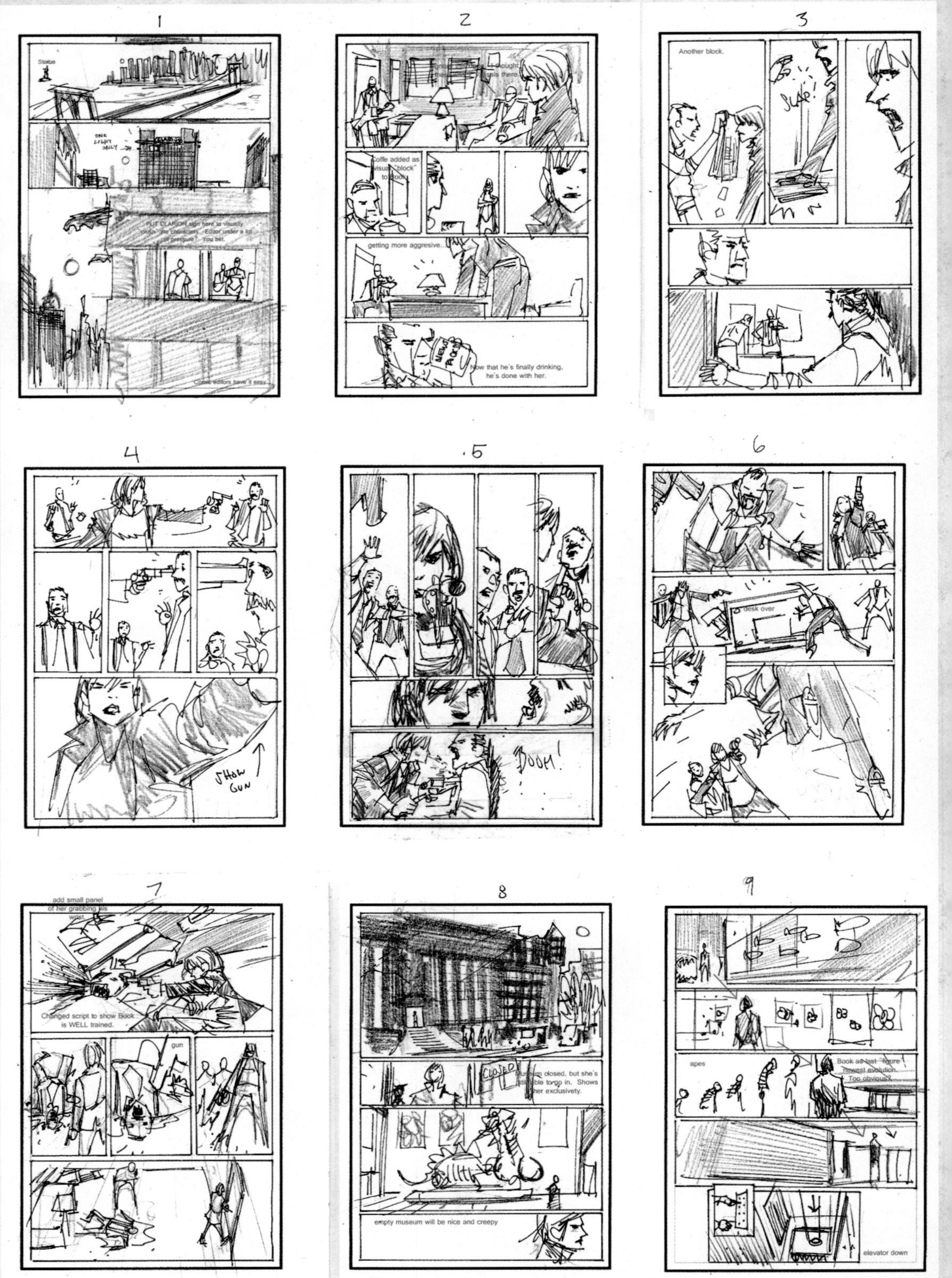

1
2
3
Statue
ONE LIGHT ONLY
Comic editors have it easy.
getting more aggresive...
he's done with her.
Another block.
SLAP!
4
5
6
SHOW GUN
DOOM!
desk over
7
8
9
add small panel
Changed script to show Book is WELL trained.
gun
CLOSED
her exclusivety.
empty museum will be nice and creepy
apes
Too obvious?
elevator down

Thumbnail layouts for AMERICAN VAMPIRE: SURVIVAL OF THE FITTEST #1 by Sean Murphy.

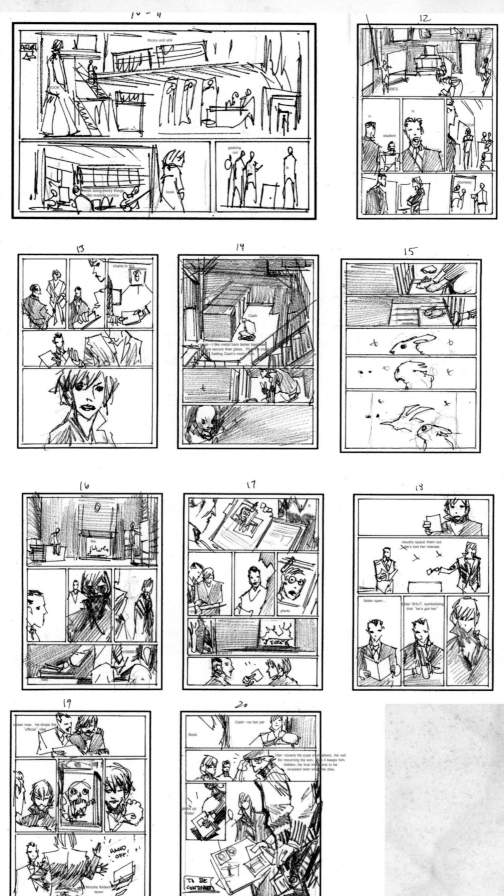

Scott Snyder is the best-selling and award-winning writer of Batman and Swamp Thing as well as the short story collection Voodoo Heart (The Dial Press). He teaches writing at Sarah Lawrence College, NYU and Columbia University. He lives on Long Island with his wife, Jeanie, and his sons Jack and Emmett. He is a dedicated and un-ironic fan of Elvis Presley.

Rafael Albuquerque was born in Porto Alegre, Brazil, Rafael Albuquerque has been working in the American comic book industry since 2005. Best known from his work on the *Savage Brothers*, Blue Beetle and Superman/Batman, he has also published the creator-owned graphic novels *Crimeland* (2007) and *Mondo Urbano*, published in 2010.

After breaking into the industry at a young age, **Sean Murphy** made a name for himself in the world of indie comics before joining up with DC for such titles as BATMAN/SCARECROW: YEAR ONE, TEEN TITANS, HELLBLAZER and the miniseries JOE THE BARBARIAN. He also wrote and illustrated the original graphic novel *Off Road*.

Danijel Zezelj is a comic book artist, painter and illustrator of eighteen graphic novels. His comics and illustrations have been published by DC Comics/Vertigo, Marvel Comics, The New York Times Book Review, Harper's Magazine, San Francisco Guardian, Editori del Grifo and Edizioni Charta among others. In 2001 in Zagred, Croatia, he founded the publishing house and graphic workshop Petikat. He currently lives and works in Brooklyn.